Raise the Debt

Raise the Debt

How Developing Countries Choose Their Creditors

JONAS B. BUNTE

OXFORD
UNIVERSITY PRESS

Oxford University Press is a department of the University of Oxford. It furthers
the University's objective of excellence in research, scholarship, and education
by publishing worldwide. Oxford is a registered trade mark of Oxford University
Press in the UK and certain other countries.

Published in the United States of America by Oxford University Press
198 Madison Avenue, New York, NY 10016, United States of America.

© Oxford University Press 2019

All rights reserved. No part of this publication may be reproduced, stored in
a retrieval system, or transmitted, in any form or by any means, without the
prior permission in writing of Oxford University Press, or as expressly permitted
by law, by license, or under terms agreed with the appropriate reproduction
rights organization. Inquiries concerning reproduction outside the scope of the
above should be sent to the Rights Department, Oxford University Press, at the
address above.

You must not circulate this work in any other form
and you must impose this same condition on any acquirer.

Library of Congress Cataloging-in-Publication Data
Names: Bunte, Jonas B., author.
Title: Raise the debt : how developing countries choose their creditors /
Jonas B. Bunte.
Description: New York, NY : Oxford University Press, [2019] |
Includes bibliographical references.
Identifiers: LCCN 2018030804 | ISBN 9780190866167 (hbk) |
ISBN 9780190866174 (pbk : alk. paper)
Subjects: LCSH: Debts, Public—Developing countries. |
Debts, External—Developing countries.
Classification: LCC HJ8899 .B86 2019 | DDC 336.3/435091724—dc23
LC record available at https://lccn.loc.gov/2018030804

1 3 5 7 9 8 6 4 2

Paperback printed by Sheridan Books, Inc., United States of America
Hardback printed by Bridgeport National Bindery, Inc., United States of America

For Genelle.
Thank you for making everything possible and better.

CONTENTS

List of Illustrations ix
Acknowledgments xi

1. Explaining Variation in Borrowing Portfolios 1
2. How Governments Choose Their Creditors 30

PART I QUALITATIVE EVIDENCE

3. Tracing the Process of Borrowing with Fieldwork 69
4. Ecuador: A Corporatist Coalition Chooses BRIC Loans 82
5. Colombia: A Capital Coalition Prefers Private Creditors 108
6. Peru: A Consumer Coalition Wants Western Creditors 129

PART II QUANTITATIVE EVIDENCE

7. Generalizing the Findings with Statistical Analyses 151
8. Measuring Borrowing Portfolios and Group Strength 156
9. Governments' Borrowing Decisions across the Developing World 180
10. Evaluating Alternative Explanations 208
11. Why Greater Choice Matters for Developing Countries 230

References 245
Index 269

ILLUSTRATIONS

Tables

2.1 Distributional consequences by actor 37
2.2 Local employment by Chinese companies 45
2.3 Distributional consequences by coalition 58

Figures

1.1 The rise in lending volume by BRICs 2
1.2 Variation in creditor sets 7
1.3 Variation of borrowing portfolios across regime type 10
1.4 Variation of borrowing portfolios across credit ratings 11
1.5 Variation of borrowing portfolios across income categories 12
1.6 Variation of borrowing portfolios across humanitarian need 15
3.1 Borrowing portfolios of Ecuador, Colombia, and Peru 75
8.1 Political strength of Labor 168
8.2 Political strength of Industry 172
8.3 Political strength of Finance 177
9.1 Average borrowing portfolio 188
9.2 Borrowing portfolios by coalition 189
9.3 Borrowing portfolios across levels of external debt 191
9.4 Borrowing portfolios and debtor GDP 193
9.5 Borrowing portfolios and debtor current account 194
9.6 Borrowing portfolios and trade with DACs 195
9.7 Borrowing portfolios and trade with BRICs 196
9.8 Borrowing portfolios and natural resources 197

9.9	Borrowing portfolios of autocracies and democracies	200
9.10	Borrowing portfolios across electoral systems	202
9.11	Borrowing portfolios and government ideology	203
9.12	Comparing China to Brazil, Russia, and India	205
9.13	Comparing all Western to non-Western creditors	206
10.1	Borrowing portfolios by income classification	211
10.2	Borrowing portfolios by credit rating	212
10.3	LIBOR and private loans	214
10.4	Borrowing portfolios and political recognition of Taiwan	218
10.5	Borrowing portfolios and loan prices	220
10.6	Comparing concessional loans to all loans	221
10.7	World Bank versus BRICs	222
10.8	World Bank versus BRICs by infrastructure needs	223
10.9	DAC loans and recipient need	225
10.10	IFI loans and debt crises	226
10.11	UN voting and borrowing portfolios	228
11.1	Change in Polity score after first major BRIC loan	242

ACKNOWLEDGMENTS

A very long list of friends, critics, and colleagues have helped shape my thinking as I was working on this book. At the University of Minnesota, I was lucky enough to be guided by a helpful, wise, and engaged committee of advisers: John Freeman, Ben Ansell, David Samuels, and Jane Gingrich. After I completed an initial draft of the book manuscript, I was fortunate that Ken Scheve, Jim Vreeland, and Mark Copelovitch joined me for a book workshop. They played an incredibly important role in the preparation of this book. Their feedback and comments profoundly shaped my thinking and improved the manuscript tremendously. Indeed, at times, they sent me back to the drawing board, and I am incredibly grateful for their constructive feedback. I cannot express how much their enthusiasm meant to me and deeply appreciate their support and encouragement. Many thanks also go to the anonymous reviewers of the manuscript, whose comments were enormously helpful in improving the argument and quality of the book.

In addition, I have also benefited tremendously from a number of valued colleagues, critics, and collaborators. At the University of Minnesota, I want to thank (listed in alphabetical order) Michael Barnett, Arie Beitman, Paul Ching, Geoff Dancy, Bud Duvall, Songying Fang, James Hollyer, Ronald Krebs, Giovanni Mantilla, Erica Owen, Imke Reimers, Libby Sharrow, Geoff Sheagley, Eric Sheppard, Laura Thaut, Shawn Treier, and Paul Vaaler for their feedback and suggestions. To all, I owe a deep debt.

This book was completed at the University of Texas at Dallas, which I joined in 2013. My colleagues in the School of Economic, Policy, and Political Sciences have been congenial and supportive, and I am deeply privileged to work with them. I want to highlight the guidance I received from Clint Peinhardt, Jennifer Holmes, and Todd Sandler. Moreover, I owe thanks to Brian Berry, Patrick Brandt, Tom Brunell, Nadine Connell, Anthony Cummings, Vito D'Orazio, Paul Diehl, Jeff Dumas, Bernhard Ganglmair, Thomas Gray, Beth Keithly, Robert

Kieschnick, Asli Leblebicioglu, Dong Li, Robert Lowry, Banks Miller, Idean Salehyan, Lauren Ratliff Santoro, Richard Scotch, and Andrea Warner-Czyz.

In addition, I have benefited enormously from conversations with, and suggestions from, scholars, colleagues, and friends at other universities. With apologies to those I may have forgotten, I want to thank Eric Arias, Cameron Ballard-Rosa, Patrick Bayer, David Bearce, Bill Bernhard, Glen Biglaiser, Deborah Brautigam, Sarah Brooks, Terry Chapman, Bill Clark, Giselle Datz, Raphael de Cunha, Axel Dreher, Jeff Frieden, Andreas Fuchs, Kevin Gallagher, Anna Gelpern, Geoff Gertz, Lucy Goodhart, Julia Gray, Tobias Heinrich, Nate Jensen, Jürgen Kaiser, Stephen Kaplan, Mark Kayser, Brandon Kinne, David Leblang, Dan McDowell, Layna Mosley, Bumba Mukherjee, Eric Neumayer, Thomas Oatley, Sonal Pandya, Brad Parks, Tom Pepinsky, Jon Pevehouse, Pablo Pinto, Amy Pond, Annalisa Prizzon, Dennis Quinn, Stephanie Rickard, Nita Rudra, Dan Runfola, Christina Schneider, Herman Schwarz, Patrick Shea, David Singer, Stephanie Walter, Rachel Wellhausen, and Alexa Zeitz. Each of them contributed significantly in improving the manuscript and saving me from embarrassing errors.

I am grateful for many opportunities to gain feedback on various elements of this project. These include talks at Yale University, the University of British Colombia, University of North Carolina Chapel Hill, Lewis & Clark College, Elon University, Elizabethtown College, the University of Heidelberg, and Universidad San Francisco de Quito. The participants at meetings of the American, European and Midwest Political Science Associations, International Studies Association, and the International Political Economy Society generously provided feedback and suggestions.

Conducting fieldwork is a significant undertaking. I want to thank each and every one of my interview partners for sharing their views with me. I thank Kathryn Sikkink, Lisa Hilbink, and Erika Busse for their advice prior to my departure. I would particularly like to acknowledge the hospitality and research facilitation offered by the Universidad de los Andes in Colombia, the Centro de Investigacíon at the Universidad del Pacífico in Peru, and the Universidad San Francisco de Quito in Ecuador. I would not have been able to conduct many interviews without the help of others. In Colombia, I am indebted to Maria Berger, Sandra Borda, Carlos Castillo, Ricardo Duarte, Isabela Echeverry, Casey Ehrlich, Ralf Leiteritz, José Antonio Ocampo, Guillermo Perry, Angelika Rettberg, Hernan Rincón, Roberto Steiner, and Miguel Urrutia. In Peru, I thank Mercedes Aráoz, Marcos Felix, Jorge Gonzalez, Ruben Gonzalez-Vicente, Pedro Pablo Kuczynski, Steve Levitsky, Eduardo Morón, Cynthia Sanborn, Martin Tanaka, and Milton Von Hesse. In Ecuador, I owe thanks to Alberto Acosta, Vicente Albornoz, Carlos Espinosa, Hugo Jacome, Simón Pachano, Pablo Paredes, Wilson Perez, and Wilma Salgado. Also, I am indebted to Ibrahim

Levent, Rasiel Vellos, Vivien Foster, and Maryna Taran at the World Bank for their invaluable cooperation.

I have been fortunate to receive financial support for my project from a variety of sources.

I am grateful for the David and Janis Larson Fellowship in Political Economy, the Edward W. and Jean B. Weidner Research Fellowship, and the Andrew Dickinson Fellowship. I thank the Harry S. Truman Presidential Library as well as the Gerald R. Ford Presidential Foundation for their research grants. The University of Texas at Dallas enabled my work with generous research funding. I also gratefully acknowledge the excellent research assistance by Alisha Kim, Les Stanaland, John Taden, Hossein Zahed, and Anh Pham Thi Cam.

I thank LeAnn Harnist and Joan Mortensen for suggesting ways to improve my prose. I am also extremely grateful to my editor at Oxford University Press, David McBride, for seeing the value in this study and his support throughout the review process. Moreover, the careful editorial eye and sharp editorial knife of David, assistant editor Emily MacKenzie, copy editor Richard Isomaki, and production editor Felshiya Samuel helped to improve the manuscript immeasurably.

I also have many friends to thank for their support, including Nicola Bunte, Ben French, Oliver Gloede, Ulrike Hahn, Gautam Patel, Christoph Trautfetter, and Cora Walsh. My deepest gratitude goes to my family. Without their love and support, this book would not have been possible. I thank my parents, Sabine Bethke-Bunte and Bartholomäus Bunte, and my sister Thimna Bunte with her husband Stefan Wagler. I am also grateful for the support of my in-laws, in particular LeAnn Harnist and her husband Kevin Harnist. Finally, I want to thank my wife Genelle Bunte for her love, support, and patience, and our sons Emrys and Timon, who are too young to have a firm opinion on this book but love me nonetheless. I love you all.

Raise the Debt

1

Explaining Variation in Borrowing Portfolios

Developing countries frequently borrow money. Their governments have obtained loans from different types of creditors. For example, governments can borrow from private creditors by issuing bonds or obtaining loans from commercial banks. Between 1970 and 2015, private creditors provided 6,915 loans to developing countries, on average about 150 loans a year. Governments can also borrow from international financial institutions (IFIs), such as the International Monetary Fund (IMF) or the World Bank. In the same time period, developing countries signed 5,317 multilateral loan agreements, or about 115 a year. Lastly, governments can also borrow from other governments. Such government-to-government loans are even more frequent: between 1970 and 2015, developing countries obtained 14,150 bilateral loans, which translates to about 300 bilateral loan agreements signed each year. Loans are extremely important to developing countries: They help recipients overcome financial crises, fund critical infrastructure, and facilitate economic development. Without credit, governments' capacity to function would be severely limited.

In this context, the emergence of new sources of credit has fundamentally transformed the availability of credit. Brazil, Russia, India, and China—also called the BRICs—have become key lenders to developing countries. To clarify, the BRICs are not new lenders, as they have made government-to-government loans since the 1970s. Yet, prior to 2000, the lending volume by BRICs was almost comically small. For example, the loan commitment of China to the Maldives in 1995 totaled $1,560. Comparably small loans were given by Russia ($1,100 to Zambia in 1987), India ($14,160 to Bangladesh in 1993), and Brazil ($12,100 to Bolivia in 1982).[1]

---

[1] These data are obtained from the World Bank's DRS database, which collects the volume and source of monetary inflows into government budgets in developing countries. More information about the data are available in section 8.1 in chapter 8.

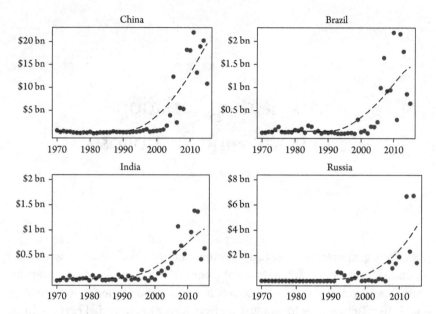

Figure 1.1 The rise in lending volume by BRICs. Note: Annual loan commitments by China, Brazil, Russia, and India. The curve represents a moving average to illustrate the trend that BRICs have expanded their lending activities each year since 2000. Note that the graph depicting Russia's lending excludes an outlier of two $10 billion loans in 2011. All loan data reported in this book come from the World Bank. More information is available in section 8.1.

However, BRICs have dramatically scaled up their global loan book over the past decade.

China has increased its lending most dramatically, but figure 1.1 illustrates that the trend applies to Russia, Brazil, and India as well. Instead of lending tiny amounts, BRICs are now literally lending billions of dollars. The largest individual loans given by BRICs include a $9.8 billion Chinese loan to Angola, a $10 billion Russian loan to Vietnam, a $2 billion Brazilian loan to Angola, and a $1.74 billion Indian loan to Bhutan.[2]

The rise of BRIC loans has affected the market share of Western governments. While the relative share of bilateral, multilateral, and private lending has

---

[2] Notably, these data include only loans, that is, monetary transfers with the expectation of repayment. These loans carry an interest rate, grace period, and maturity. Loans are not the same as foreign aid, also known as official development assistance (ODA). ODA includes grants, in-kind transfers, food aid, and technological assistance, as well as expenses occurred in creditor countries, such as administrative costs and refugee assistance. Extremely cheap loans—for example, with low interest rates and long repayment schedules—may qualify as ODA, while more expensive loans do not. Because the overall share of loans in total ODA has declined over time, there is little empirical overlap between foreign aid and bilateral loans. See section 8.1 in chapter 8 for more information.

remained fairly constant over time, the composition within bilateral creditors has changed markedly. The importance of Western governments as creditors to developing countries has declined as the significance of BRIC loans increased. There appears to be a trade-off between Western and emerging creditors. This has three significant implications.

First, the rise of BRIC loans may imply a decline in Western influence over developing countries. Some analysts suggest, "[China's] loans are empowering anti-American regimes in Latin America" (Dyer, Anderlini, and Sender 2011). Furthermore, "the fear is that . . . China will start to provide pariah states with a means to evade western financial sanctions, thus subverting the diplomatic order as well as the financial one" (*The Economist* 2015). Russia's president, Vladimir Putin, emphasized that BRIC loans can provide developing countries with the means to avoid the "harassment" by the United States or Europe over foreign policy (*The Economist* 2014).

Second, the rise of BRIC lending might allow developing countries to pursue alternatives to the neoliberal Washington consensus. Loans from multilateral organizations and Western governments have attached conditions requiring recipient countries to liberalize and privatize their economies. In contrast, BRICs offer large loans without macroeconomic conditions asking recipients to implement domestic political reforms. Instead, they fund large infrastructure projects that may resolve growth bottlenecks. BRICs thus may allow developing countries to pursue a different model of economic development and thus shape the likelihood of lifting millions out of poverty.

A third implication concerns the prospects for democracy in developing countries. Chinese loans, in particular, might undermine movements toward democratization in poor countries. Critics have argued that Chinese loans undermine democracy in recipient countries, as they lack "good governance" conditions. However, the jury is still out on these questions (Bader 2014). Importantly, we know little about the motivation of governments to choose Chinese loans over other creditors. We need to understand why governments accept Chinese loan offers before we can understand the likely consequences for power, economic development, and democracy.

This book answers a question that has not been asked before: why do countries borrow money from some creditors and not others? Specifically, why do some governments borrow from BRIC creditors, while others continue to use traditional lenders? Until recently, this would not have been an important question to ask in international political economy. However, over the last two decades Brazil, Russia, India, and especially China have become important lenders to the developing world. It is a striking change in the global economy with potential consequences for political and economic development, international economic cooperation, and security relations around the world. To understand this new phenomenon, we need to know what accounts for the variation that we observe in the creditors that developing countries choose. This book is the first systematic treatment of this question.

1.1. The Puzzle: Significant Variation in Borrowing Patterns

Importantly, not all developing countries obtain BRIC loans even if they have been offered to their governments. In fact, there is a remarkable diversity in the responses of developing countries to loan offers. Ecuador and Colombia illustrate two very different reactions to loan offers from China.

1.1.1. Ecuador

On October 15, 2006, no candidate in the first round of the Ecuadorian presidential elections obtained an absolute majority. In the second round, on November 26, voters were asked to decide between Álvaro Noboa of the right-wing party Partido Renovador Institucional de Acción Nacional, and Rafael Correa, representing the social movement Alianza PAIS. Correa won the presidential election with 57% of the vote. After his election—on December 15, 2006, a full month before being sworn into office—Correa announced that his administration would renegotiate Ecuador's external debt, stating, "La vida antes que la deuda"—life should take priority over debt. Correa's words were followed by action, as Ecuador paid off all loans from the IMF at once and in full on April 20, 2007, thereby fulfilling one of his campaign promises.

A month later, in July 2007, Correa issued a decree instituting the Comisión para la Auditoria Integral del Credito Publico (Commission to Audit the Entirety of Public Debt), abbreviated as CAIC. Its task was to examine the legitimacy of different types of debt (multilateral, bilateral, private, and domestic debt) that Ecuador had accumulated over the years and determine whether these debts should be repaid. While these investigations were ongoing, interest payments for the remaining government bonds held by private creditors came due on November 14, 2008. Correa declared that he would not pay the interest payments until the CAIC released its findings. CAIC's final report was presented on November 20, 2008, in Quito, in front of a large crowd of Ecuadorians in a televised ceremony. The commission recommended suspending the debt repayment on many of the remaining bonds. Following this recommendation, the government suspended payments on the principal of the Global 12 Bonds as well as the Global 15 and Global 30 Bonds, making Ecuador's default official.

On April 24, 2009, after it was clear that Ecuador had no intention of repaying this debt, creditors were willing to accept the conditions of a debt swap. The existing bonds were exchanged for new bonds worth only 30% of the original face value. Two days after this announcement, Ecuadorians were again called to the ballots to vote in the first round of a presidential election. Correa won an absolute majority with 51.9% of all votes in the first round. This result was unexpected. For the first time since 1979, a second round of voting was unnecessary.

Notably, Ecuador's behavior toward traditional Western creditors differed markedly from its behavior toward emerging creditors, particularly the BRICs. While Correa effectively stopped servicing existing debt from traditional Western creditors, he continued to pay interest and principal on debt owed to BRICs. For instance, in January 2007, the installments due on loans to Brazil for the San Francisco hydropower project were paid on time. During this time, when Ecuador needed to take out new loans, credit offers by traditional creditors were explicitly rejected. Instead, the government obtained several loans from China, Brazil, and Russia. For example, Ecuador announced on February 20, 2009, that it would borrow $1.7 billion from China. This was only the first of several major loans from China, which through 2015 totaled $7.65 billion. In addition, Ecuador obtained a total of $319 million from Russia and $495 million from Brazil. In contrast, Ecuador obtained only $458.91 million from all 23 Western governments combined. The key insight is that Ecuador's turn toward BRIC creditors occurred *simultaneously* with its decision to not use Western creditors anymore.

1.1.2. Colombia

While Ecuador turned away from traditional Western creditors and toward BRIC loans, neighboring Colombia did the opposite, even though China made several loan offers to Colombia. Interviews with Colombian public officials revealed that the China Export-Import Bank had proposed loans to Colombia on several occasions, but each time, the Colombian government rejected them (Interview 18). Interviews with representatives of the Chinese government corroborate this information. The economic adviser to the Chinese ambassador confirmed loan offers were made, but also that the Colombian government was hesitant to accept these offers (Interview 25). In addition, China offered to finance several public works projects. In 2005, the Colombian government wanted to build an alternative to the Panama Canal, the Canal Seco (Dry Canal). The government inquired whether foreign creditors—the Chinese among them—would be interested in financing this project. The Chinese were initially thought of highly, but they were not selected for the project (Interviews 1, 11). Furthermore,

Colombian officials confirmed that the Chinese offered a loan to the state-owned enterprise ColPetrol. Yet again, this loan offer was rejected (Interview 38). Finally, Colombia rejected a Chinese loan offer for financing a hydropower project, the Acueducto Metropolitano de Bucaramanga. Instead, it favored borrowing from a regional multilateral organization, the Andean Development Cooperation. Even though these negotiations fell through, Colombia still did not use Chinese money, but rather borrowed from a private market actor, Bancolombia.

Colombia received both Chinese and Western loan proposals simultaneously. Yet, instead of borrowing from the Chinese, Colombia continued to borrow from traditional creditors.

Since 2004, the Colombian government has borrowed a total of $5.6 billion from Western bilateral creditors, but not a single dollar from BRICs. The Colombian government's decision to use Western creditors was *simultaneously* a decision against BRIC lenders.

1.1.3. Variation across Countries

Ecuador and Colombia are part of a larger pattern. Developing countries differ significantly in which creditors they use. Figure 1.2 illustrates the frequency with which a particular set of creditors was used. Among governments utilizing a single creditor in a given year, 13.7% of borrowers obtained only BRIC loans, while 11% received only loans from Western governments (DACs, as all Western governments are members of the Development Assistance Committee). Among governments that borrowed from two creditors, 9.1% used both BRIC and DAC creditors. Only 1.8% of borrowers obtained loans from all four types of creditors.

The figure illustrates the heterogeneity across developing countries regarding which creditors they use. Yet we have little understanding of why there is variation in borrowing from various creditors. The key research question of this book is straightforward: what explains this variation in which creditors governments use?

1.2. Active Creditors and Passive Recipients?

The prevailing explanation for this variation focuses on the role of creditors. According to this view, creditors, and creditors alone, decide whether to supply a loan to a particular developing country. If a country has not borrowed from a particular creditor, this does not necessarily mean that it rejected a loan offer. Rather the creditor may have been unwilling to extend a loan in the first place. This reasoning is often applied to private creditors. Conventional wisdom

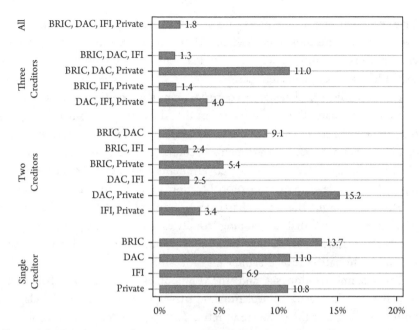

Figure 1.2 Variation in creditor sets. Note: The graph displays the frequency with which a particular set of creditors was used between 2004 and 2015. For instance, among governments utilizing a single creditor in a given year, 13.7% of borrowers obtained only BRIC loans, while 11% received loans from Western governments (DACs). Among governments that borrowed from two creditors, 9.1% used both BRIC and DAC creditors. The graph illustrates the remarkable heterogeneity in the set of creditors that developing countries use.

suggests that governments prefer to deal with private creditors, and only if a country does not have access to the private capital market will it turn to alternative creditors. For example, governments may want to avoid IMF loans unless economic crises force them to approach the Fund. Furthermore, governments might only turn to Chinese loans if they have no access to any other source of credit. Using the terminology of economics, these approaches are supply-side explanations.

Indeed, scholars have studied the motivations of creditors to provide loans. Some supply-side explanations have focused on creditors' search for profit. Thus, scholars have analyzed how creditors can identify debtors likely to repay loans (Schultz and Weingast 2003; Beaulieu, Cox, and Saiegh 2012; Tomz 2007). Others have explained sovereign lending with creditors' search for geopolitical influence (Kinne and Bunte 2018; Bunte and Kinne 2018; Sanderson and Forsythe 2012; Brautigam 2009; Gallagher and Porzecanski 2010; Alden 2007).

Further, creditors might lend to gain access to foreign markets or natural resources (Sanderson and Forsythe 2012; Carmody 2013; Economy and Levi 2014; Caceres and Ear 2013; Andrews-Speed and Dannreuther 2011). Scholars have examined whether creditors lend to prevent economic crises and their spillover effects (Stone 2004; Copelovitch 2010). Given these creditor motivations, creditors may be more likely to offer loans to some countries than others, depending on their characteristics.

I do not dispute that some countries may have better access to particular creditors than others. The theory of the "democratic advantage" suggests that democratic developing countries are more likely to have access to private creditors than autocratic governments (Schultz and Weingast 2003; Beaulieu, Cox, and Saiegh 2012). Similarly, governments with better credit ratings or higher levels of development are probably more attractive to potential creditors.

However, I argue that such characteristics do not predetermine borrowing portfolios. I argue that developing countries have choices. Even if some governments have better choices than others, comparing countries with access to similar alternatives reveals significant variation.

For example, Indonesia and the Philippines share many characteristics: Besides their geographical proximity (neighboring island archipelagos), both countries have the same credit rating (BBB−), similar levels of economic development (GDP per capita of $2,048 and $2,574, respectively), as well as the same level of democracy.[3] Given these similarities, both countries should have access to the same set of creditors. However, in 2013 their borrowing decisions differed sharply: that year, Indonesia sold $1.5 billion of dollar-denominated bonds at an interest rate of 6.125% and a maturity of 5.5 years. In contrast, the Philippines explicitly decided against borrowing from private creditors. Initially, the national treasurer, Rosalia de Leon, noted that the borrowing program could include issuing bonds, but that fact "does not mean we will proceed. Just like this year, we also had it in the financing plan but eventually we decided not to issue offshore. . . . [Issuing bonds] is always one of our funding options" (*Malaysian Insider* 2013). Eventually, however, the Philippine government announced that it had decided not to borrow from foreign private creditors that year (Remo, 2013) and instead obtained two bilateral loans from Japan and South Korea.

Another example is the comparison between Uganda and Rwanda. In 2013, these neighboring countries in East Africa had similar credit ratings (B+ and B, respectively), comparable levels of economic development (GDP per capita of $424 and $473), as well as similarly unfavorable democracy scores (−1 and −3, respectively). Again, given these resemblances, both countries were expected to have access to the same set of creditors. Yet their borrowing decisions differed: While Rwanda attracted more than $3 billion of orders for its $400 million 10-year bond sale at an interest rate of 6.875%, the Ugandan

---

[3] Both countries had a Polity IV score of 8 (on a scale from −10 to 10).

government announced that it had decided not to issue bonds in international financial markets. In communicating this decision, the Ugandan Ministry of Finance, Planning and Economic Development noted "sovereign bonds are expensive, and [the government] is concerned that public debt could rise to unsustainable levels during currency depreciation, increasing bond yields" (Prizzon, Greenhill, and Mustapha, 2017). Instead, Uganda borrowed from France and Germany.

These examples are part of a larger pattern: Countries with access to similar alternatives nevertheless make different choices. Consider the argument about the "democratic advantage" introduced previously. According to this theory, creditors view democracies as less risky, as their institutional characteristics make repayment more likely. Thus, if the borrowing portfolios of countries are a function of creditors' willingness to lend, we would expect that democracies have similar borrowing portfolios. Figure 1.3 displays the borrowing portfolios of a select group of countries. I use a Polity score to classify countries by their degree of democracy, with −10 to −6 corresponding to autocracies, −5 to 5 corresponding to anocracies, and 6 to 10 to democracies. The figure reveals significant variation among democracies: while Costa Rica relies primarily on private creditors, Cape Verde borrows primarily from Western governments, yet Lesotho has obtained mainly BRIC loans. Similarly, countries classified as nondemocracies should have access to the same set of creditors. Yet their borrowing portfolios differ as well: Vietnam relies on DAC loans, while Eritrea uses BRIC creditors.

Countries can also be classified by their credit rating. Rating agencies such as Standard & Poor's, Moody's, and Fitch Group classify countries by their creditworthiness, which effectively captures countries' probability of default based on current economic data and past default history. Presumably, creditors view countries with the same ratings as having the same level of risk. Thus, if borrowing portfolios are determined only by the willingness of creditors to extend loans, we would expect the borrowing portfolios of countries in each group to resemble each other. However, figure 1.4 shows that this is not necessarily the case. Presumably, countries rated "investment grade" (that is, BBB or higher) have similar access to private creditors. Yet not all countries with this rating use private creditors: while Tunisia relies on both DAC and private creditors, Mauritius uses both DAC and BRIC loans. Similar variation exists within groups of countries with lower credit ratings.

While Benin, Ghana, and Mongolia share the same credit rating, their borrowing portfolios differ: Benin relies on BRICs, Ghana on private creditors, and Mongolia on DACs and IFIs.

The level of development might also determine access to creditors. If borrowing portfolios are shaped only by creditors' decisions, we would expect that

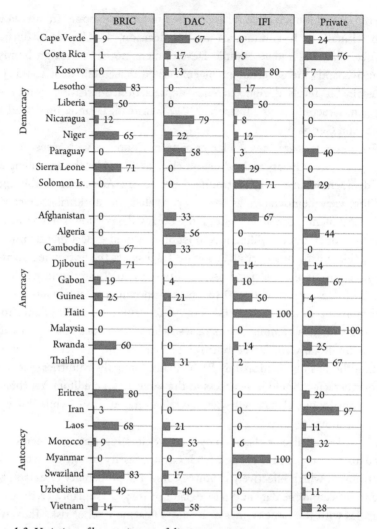

Figure 1.3 Variation of borrowing portfolios across regime type. Note: The figure displays average percentage of loan volume obtained from different creditors. Recipients are classified by regime type. The data show that significant variation in borrowing portfolios exists within democracies as well as anocracies and democracies.

upper-middle-income countries have similar borrowing portfolios. However, figure 1.5 shows that this is not the case.

Belize and Jamaica are both classified as upper-middle-income countries, yet the former borrows primarily from BRICs, while the latter uses private creditors. Conversely, borrowing portfolios also differ among low-income countries: while Djibouti heavily depends on BRIC loans, Tanzania's borrowing portfolio is equally balanced between BRICs, DACs, and private creditors.

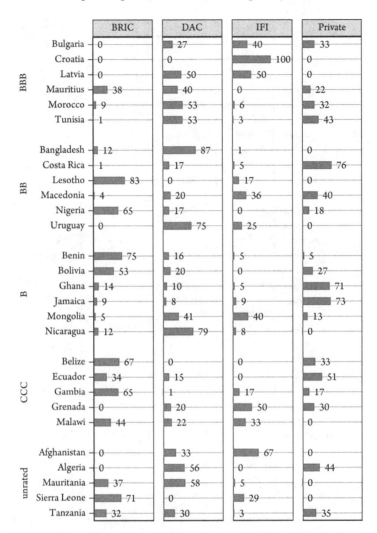

Figure 1.4 Variation of borrowing portfolios across credit ratings. Note: The figure displays average borrowing portfolios for a select group of countries classified by credit ratings. The share of loans obtained from different creditors varies across countries with the same credit rating.

While these graphs show only a subset of countries, they illustrate the key insight: even if some countries have better choices than others, countries with similar alternatives still exhibit significant variation in their borrowing portfolios. Borrowing decisions differ, even among countries with the same income levels, credit rating, or degree of democracy. Comparisons of the Philippines to Indonesia and Uganda to Rwanda suggest that borrowing portfolios of developing countries are not merely a function of creditor decisions.

I *do not* argue that supply-side approaches are unimportant. My work does not negate the significance of supply-side considerations. In fact, my empirical

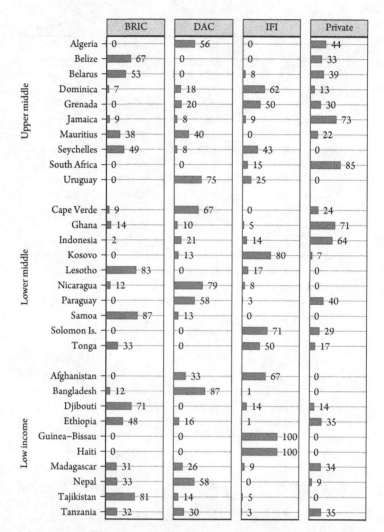

Figure 1.5 Variation of borrowing portfolios across income categories. Note: The figure displays the share of loan volume obtained from various creditor types. Recipient countries are categorized by income classification. The graph indicates that countries' borrowing portfolio differs significantly, even if they have the same income classification.

analyses confirm that supply-side factors are at play. However, I argue that supply-side approaches must be complemented with a demand-side perspective. After all, the outcome of any voluntary transaction—such as a loan agreement—should reflect the intersection of supply- and demand-side considerations. We know that developing countries are not passive recipients. I take issue with the assumption that recipients are merely passive actors happily gobbling up whichever loan happens to be offered. Rather, their governments have preferences, and they have the political will to act upon them (Vreeland 2003a; Nooruddin and Simmons 2006; Caraway, Rickard, and Anner 2012; Mukherjee and Singer 2010). For this reason, I complement existing supply-side theories about lending with a demand-side theory about borrowing. Why do some governments rely primarily on loans from Western governments, while others prefer borrowing from BRICs? How do governments choose their creditors? This book develops such a theory explaining how developing countries choose their creditors.

1.3. Specific Creditors for Specific Tasks?

The variation in borrowing portfolios across developing countries indicates that governments have some say in which type of creditor they use. However, how do loan recipients decide which creditor to use? Using the terminology of economics again, what determines the demand for a particular creditor?

One possible explanation suggests a needs-based theory. It might be the case that debtors use specific creditors for specific purposes. After all, the expertise of creditors varies. For example, an IMF loan might be a natural choice for a developing country facing an economic crisis because IMF specializes in helping countries with balance-of-payment difficulties. In contrast, countries might borrow from Western governments if they intend to fund social projects such as schools and hospitals, as DACs' expertise focuses on human development projects. In cases where governments want to finance large infrastructure projects, such as hydroelectric power dams or road networks, they might borrow from BRICs or the World Bank. If creditors' relative expertise differs, then recipient countries might not truly have a choice: their borrowing portfolios would merely reflect the types of projects that need to be undertaken.

While the relative expertise of creditors may vary, there are good reasons to believe that the borrowing portfolios of developing countries are *not* merely a function of their financing gaps. Consider IMF loans. The logic outlined above suggests that only countries in crises should turn to this lender for an emergency loan. However, existing research suggests that IMF loans are not necessarily directed at countries that need them most, that is, those with balance-of-payment crises. For example, Vreeland (2003b) compares Uruguay and Tanzania. According to the level of foreign reserves in 1983, Tanzania would have been a prime candidate for an IMF loan. However, its government decided against this loan, despite negative consequences for foreign direct investment. In contrast, Uruguay ostensibly did not need an IMF loan in the early 1990s: its balance of payments was in surplus, as was the current account balance, and it held a strong foreign-reserves position. Yet it signed an IMF agreement in 1990 and 1992.

Vreeland argues that Tanzania rejected an IMF loan because of the macroeconomic conditions attached to these loans, while Uruguay sought these loans precisely because these conditions would allow it to pursue unpopular reforms against the resistance of some domestic interest groups. Drazen (2005) and Ramcharan (2003) make similar arguments. Presbitero and Zazzaro (2012) expand on these insights and show that the severity of crises does not make a difference in the likelihood of obtaining an IMF loan, though it does increase the loan volume should a loan be granted. Apparently, then, recipient governments have preferences for or against IMF loans, and they do pursue these preferences. While accepting or rejecting an IMF loan comes with distinct costs and benefits, it appears that the willingness of countries to incur these costs or enjoy these benefits differs.

In contrast to the IMF's expertise in financial crises, Western governments tend to focus on humanitarian needs. For instance, DACs are especially generous in financing social expenditure in areas such as health or education. Should recipient humanitarian need predetermine the type of creditor used, we would expect countries with high child mortality rates to primarily borrow from DACs. However, figure 1.6 shows that this is not the case. I use the infant mortality rate per 1,000 live births provided by the World Bank to classify recipient countries: less than 20 deaths represents low need, between 20 and 40 deaths stands for intermediate need, between 40 and 60 describes high need, and more than 60 deaths per 1,000 births represents very high need. The data show that the utilization of DAC loans differs considerably among countries even if they have comparable humanitarian needs. As a result, there does not appear to be a strong connection between social needs and the use of DAC creditors.

I fully acknowledge that differences across creditors exist and that the needs of recipient countries differ. Yet countries' needs apparently do not predetermine the choice of creditor. Why is this the case? A large part of the answer lies in the fact that transferred resources are fungible. Fungibility occurs when a recipient receives a loan earmarked for a specific sector but subsequently reduces its own resources in that sector (Jones 2005, 168). If the borrowed resources replace spending that would have otherwise been included in the budget, the replaced funds can be used in whichever way the loan recipient deems necessary—irrespective of the originally intended use of the loan.

A hypothetical example illustrates how fungibility explains the apparent disconnect between a creditor's expertise and the final use of resources by the recipient country. The budget of a developing country might initially include $100 million for large infrastructure projects and $50 million for small microprojects in the education sector. However, the country now obtains a DAC loan of $20 million under the condition that the resources are spent in the education sector. This makes sense, as DAC creditors' expertise includes social

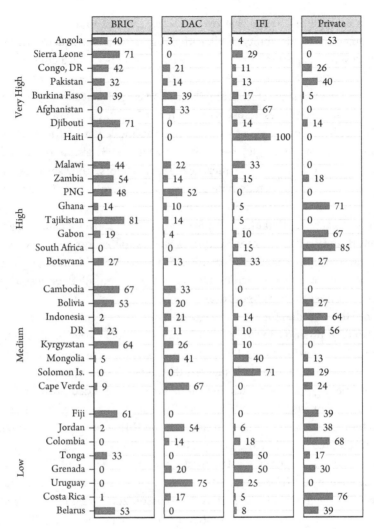

Figure 1.6 Variation of borrowing portfolios across humanitarian need. Note: The figure shows the percentage of loan volume obtained from different types of creditors, while recipients are classified by the extent of child mortality. The graph indicates that countries with similar humanitarian needs do not all borrow from DAC creditors.

projects aimed at increasing human capital. However, even if the DAC loan is tied to the education sector, this does not mean that the country's education budget rises to $70 million. Knowing the loan will be arriving shortly, the government can reduce the budget for education to $30 million and reallocate the "saved" resource to the infrastructure budget. The infrastructure budget would then amount to $120 million, while the education budget, supplemented with the external loan, would stand at $50 million. Ultimately, the DAC loan intended for education has allowed the government to increase its spending on infrastructure.

This example illustrates that even if loans are tied to a particular project, governments have flexibility in allocating funds. As a consequence, we would not necessarily expect to observe a close correlation between a country's needs and the creditors' expertise.

Much evidence suggests that fungibility is an empirical reality and leads to the reallocation of resources across sectors (Jones 2005). For example, Pettersson (2007) finds that over 65% of aid given to a specific sector is ultimately used in a different sector. Feyzioglu, Swaroop, and Zhu (1998) also find sectoral fungibility, though they identify differences across sectors. They show that aid to the agricultural sector is fully fungible, aid to the energy sector is partially fungible, while aid to the transport and communication sectors is nonfungible. In contrast, Devarajan, Rajkumar, and Swaroop (2007) show that aid going to the transport and communication sectors as well as the energy sector is also fungible. Swaroop, Jha, and Rajkumar (2000) report that aid in India is financing projects that would have been undertaken anyway, and the freed resources are spent on nondevelopment purposes.

Since these studies focus on foreign aid, it might be argued that loans and aid differ in their potential for fungibility. However, scholars have produced similar findings for loans. Even with IMF loans, whose conditions are among the most stringent and specific, research suggests that the IMF cannot adequately ensure that recipient governments use the funds for their intended purpose (Dreher 2009, 246). For example, Rodrik (1996, 26) shows that governments use IMF loans for repaying private creditors and that the IMF cannot veto such reallocation of resources. Epstein and Gang (2009, 17) remark that "for many years, at least since the introduction of structural adjustment aid in the 1980s, aid policy has assumed near 100% fungibility." In sum, "Targeting assistance to specific projects is essentially a futile exercise" (Svensson 2000, 72). Instead, creditors and donors "should take it for granted that their financing is fungible because that is reality" (Dollar and Pritchett 1998, 91).

Without doubt, the expertise of creditors varies. I do not argue that all creditors are the same—clearly, their loans and conditions differ—but fungibility obscures the functional differences of lending sources. For this reason, governments may view different creditors as functionally equivalent, irrespective of differences in creditor expertise, loan characteristics, and country need.[4]

An anecdote from Pakistan illustrates this phenomenon (Stacey, Bokhari, and Sender 2017). In the spring of 2017, Pakistan's financial position deteriorated

---

[4] See section 10.4 in chapter 10, which offers an empirical analysis of this claim. I show that the use of World Bank and BRIC loans differs across countries, even if infrastructure needs are similar. I illustrate that the use of DAC loans differs, even if health and education concerns are similar. I show that the use of IMF loans differs across coalitions, even if default histories are similar.

dramatically: In a short period of time, its net reserves dwindled to only $17.1 billion. This forced the government to seek emergency loans from external creditors. One option might have been to borrow from the IMF. However, Pakistan instead obtained $1.2 billion in loans from China to stave off a potential currency crisis. The government-run China Development Bank provided $600 million and another $600 million came from the state-owned Industrial and Commercial Bank of China, the only mainland bank to have a branch in Pakistan. When asked about the reasons for the decision to borrow from China rather than the IMF, Vaqar Ahmed, deputy executive director of the Islamabad-based Sustainable Development Policy Institute, noted, "Technically speaking, we should have gone back to the IMF in January, but ministers are likely to try and wait until after the election [for parliament planned for 2018]" (*CNBC* 2017). One member of the ruling Pakistan Muslim League (Nawaz) party confirmed to the *Financial Times* that ministers were reluctant to return to the IMF until after the election in an effort to limit the political fallout: "The IMF is a politically volatile issue in our country. If we go to the IMF to deal with our needs, that will send a very negative political signal and the opposition [parties] will use that against the government" (*Financial Times* 2017). This anecdote clearly illustrates that Pakistani decision-makers view Chinese and IMF loans as functionally equivalent despite providing vastly different types of loans. It also illustrates that politicians have the reactions of their electorate in mind as they make borrowing decisions.

1.4. The Argument: Distributional Consequences and Societal Coalitions

The Pakistani example illustrates the need for a demand-side explanation, but a theory that is not based on recipient need. Clearly, financing gaps do not explain why Pakistan chose one creditor over another. Rather, the example highlights political factors: citizens have preferences across creditors, and politicians are concerned about electoral effects of their choice of creditor. The example of Tanzania and Uruguay offered by Vreeland (2003b) points to a similar dynamic: Tanzania desperately needed an IMF loan but decided against it because its government was concerned about electoral backlash due to the macroeconomic conditions attached to these loans. In contrast, Uruguay did not need an IMF loan but obtained an IMF loan because some segments in society wanted to use the macroeconomic conditions to implement reforms, against the resistance of other interest groups. Clearly, citizens have preferences with respect to loan characteristics and governments respond to these interests. What explains these preferences?

I argue that a government's choice among competing creditors can be explained by the distributional consequences of loans and social coalitions in the recipient country. The term "distributional consequences" refers to the way in which economic decisions create winners and losers. For example, the IMF and China might offer a government exactly the same loan volume—but with different strings attached. Because of the differences in conditions, one societal group would benefit from the IMF loan but not from the Chinese loan, while the opposite would be the case for another group. For example, the domestic financial sector in the recipient country has an interest in a stable banking sector and low inflation. IMF loans typically come with conditions that require the recipient government to balance the budget, liberalize the economy, and avoid inflation. In contrast, Chinese loans are often attached to particular investment projects. This implies increased competition for the domestic financial sector, as an external actor now finances investment projects that it previously funded. The differences in conditions attached to these loans imply that the IMF loan would have positive distributional consequences for the domestic financial sector, while the distributional consequences of the Chinese loan for that sector would be negative. Even though the IMF and the Chinese offer the exact same amount of money, domestic Finance prefers the IMF loan to the Chinese loan.

In contrast, domestic workers might prefer the Chinese loan to the IMF loan. As already mentioned, the conditions attached to IMF loans require the recipient government to balance its budget; in many cases this is accomplished by cutting social expenditure. Similarly, the requirement to liberalize the economy does not always have positive consequences for workers. For these reasons, the distributional consequences of an IMF loan for Labor are negative. The opposite might be the case with loans from China. If Chinese loans are associated with additional investment projects that would not materialize otherwise, these loans might provide new employment opportunities for workers. For these reasons, Labor would prefer a loan from China to an IMF loan.

While this example refers only to two specific creditors—the IMF and the Chinese government—my explanation is based on the conflicting preferences of economic groups over the following four types of creditors: (*a*) Western governments, (*b*) multilateral institutions such as the IMF or World Bank, (*c*) private foreign banks or the bond market, and (*d*) the BRICs.[5] I begin

---

[5] I group Brazil, Russia, India, and China together. Clearly, China is the largest of these new creditors. However, their lending conditions are exceptionally similar since they require the money lent to be used for specific investment projects. The distributional consequences of their loans for the social groups in recipient countries are therefore very much alike. However, I later test whether my argument applies to Brazil, Russia, and India if analyzed separately from China. The results, shown in chapter 9, suggest that these four countries have similar effects and thus can be grouped together.

building my theory by analyzing the kind of conditions attached to loans from each of these creditor types. Because these conditions differ, each tends to create a different set of relative winners and losers.

In a second step, I examine the characteristics of three domestic interest groups: the domestic financial sector, the domestic industrial sector, and Labor. Each of these groups relies on different types of resources to make a living: mobile assets, fixed assets, and wages, respectively. Each group has distinct interests because their livelihood depends on different types of assets. Finance wants a stable banking sector and low inflation to preserve the value of its assets. Industry is interested in a market for its goods and continued investment. Labor requires employment opportunities and reasonable wages, since workers do not own assets.

I then combine the information on what interest groups want with the distributional consequences of creditors to derive which type of loan is preferred by what societal group. As illustrated by the previous example, it is likely that Finance favors IMF loans, seeing that conditions attached to these loans are designed to prevent banking crises and ensure an efficient market system. In contrast to Finance, Labor is interested in higher wages and employment opportunities. IMF loans are unlikely to serve these interests. However, BRIC loans are typically tied to specific investment projects that result in employment opportunities. By comparing the interests of the three actors to the characteristics of the four borrowing options, I identify distributional consequences that allow me to derive a preference profile for each actor across the different types of creditors.

Do these preferences determine which loan the government will obtain? I argue that a government will choose its creditors by analyzing which social coalition is politically powerful. If politicians want to get re-elected, they have every incentive to cater to the interests of powerful social groups. In fact, if their borrowing decision can satisfy two (instead of just one) interest groups, even better. In this case, the government will want to borrow from the type of creditor that two interest groups jointly prefer, that is, the creditor with the most favorable distributional consequences for the politically powerful coalition. By analyzing which coalition dominates politically, I can explain why some governments turn to BRICs and others turn to the IMF or private foreign creditors.

I show that there are three types of social coalitions that politicians respond to when deciding between competing loan offers. First, a *Corporatist Coalition* exists if Labor and Industry dominate the political landscape and Finance is comparatively weak. In this case, the government will tend to borrow from BRIC creditors, as this is the jointly preferred creditor of these two interest groups. Second, if Finance and Industry are dominant, a *Capital Coalition* prevails. The preferences of this coalition provide the government with the incentive to borrow from multilateral institutions and private creditors. Lastly, a *Consumer*

Coalition exists when Finance and Labor are strong and Industry is relatively unimportant. Here the government will tend to obtain bilateral loans from Western governments. In sum, the differences in the distributional consequences across societal coalitions combined with information on the political strength of these coalitions allow me to predict the government's choice among competing loan offers.

1.5. The Empirical Strategy: Combining Qualitative with Quantitative Evidence

I pursued a mixed-methods approach to test my theory. Specifically, this book offers both qualitative evidence from months of fieldwork and quantitative evidence based on statistical analyses.

1.5.1. Fieldwork and Elite Interviews

The motivation for conducting fieldwork was twofold: First, my theory makes several critical assumptions about actors' preferences. Interviews with representatives of societal interest groups, politicians, and creditors allow me to verify whether these assumptions are accurate. The interviews generally confirmed my expectations.

For example, a high-level executive of an Ecuadorian investment bank made quite clear the preferences of financial actors concerning BRIC loans: "[The Chinese] grab you by the [expletive deleted] and take advantage of you." In contrast, I learned that domestic firms do not fear Chinese companies because "subcontractors are actually paid quite generously by the Chinese" (Interview 87) due to the lack of a competitive bidding process for projects funded with Chinese loans.

Second, my theory proposes that these preferences translate into borrowing decisions. I assume that politicians listen to societal actors and have the incentive to act upon their preferences. Furthermore, I expect that politicians affect borrowing decisions. Conducting fieldwork allowed me to trace the process by which preferences are translated into borrowing decisions, thereby verifying these assumptions. For each country, the qualitative insights allowed me to analyze what type of societal coalition dominates the political landscape.

Interviews also illuminated how politicians respond to the interests of the dominant social groups, which ultimately shape their borrowing decisions.

I conducted several months of fieldwork in Ecuador, Peru, and Colombia. These countries offered an almost ideal setting for this fieldwork, as they share a number of characteristics: They are located in the same geographical area, share the same language, have a similar culture, were subject to the same colonial history, have comparable political systems, and so on. As several characteristics were constant across these countries, these ceteris paribus conditions allow eliminating some possible alternative explanations. Significantly, the three countries differed in the relative strength of societal interest groups. Prior research suggested that Ecuador might approximate a Corporatist Coalition in which Labor and Industry are strong, Colombia might be a Capital Coalition in which Finance and Industry are powerful, and Peru might represent a Consumer Coalition in which Finance and Labor are politically influential. This variation on the independent variable makes it possible to test whether or not societal interest groups have a causal effect on borrowing decisions.

Once on the ground, I conducted 112 interviews with a wide range of actors. First, I spoke with representatives of Labor, Industry, and Finance. For example, I conducted interviews with bankers, factory owners, and union representatives. Through these conversations, I verified the theoretical expectation regarding which type of actor—Finance, Industry or Labor—hopes to benefit from which type of loan. Second, I interviewed politicians and bureaucrats. Among elected officials, I spoke with prime ministers, finance ministers, and senators; among bureaucrats, I had conversations with officials in public debt departments, finance ministries, and planning departments. These interviews shed light on how politics shape borrowing decisions. Lastly, I spoke with creditors. I interviewed representatives of multilateral institutions (IMF, International Bank for Reconstruction and Development, and International Development Association) as well as German, American, and French lending organizations. I also interviewed Chinese officials, both from the public sector (Chinese Development Bank, Chinese embassies) and from the private sector (Chinese commercial banks, Chinese mining companies).[6]

1.5.2. Statistical Analysis of Borrowing Portfolios

I complement the qualitative insights gained in the field with a statistical analysis of quantitative data. The motivation for this analysis is straightforward: it is important to test whether my argument applies beyond Ecuador, Colombia, and Peru. While qualitative evidence allows tracing the causal process in a handful of

---

[6] More information about sample, interview technique, and interview partners is available in chapter 3. Chapter 4 presents the findings from Ecuador, chapter 5 from Colombia, and chapter 6 from Peru.

cases, quantitative tests can determine whether borrowing decisions of a larger set of countries follow theoretical predictions.

However, conducting statistical analyses requires quantitative information on both the dependent and independent variables. In this process, I faced two challenges. First, loan data are available for most, but not all creditors. For example, Chinese lending data are state secrets and not available from the Chinese government. Researchers have pursued various strategies to estimate capital *outflows* from emerging lenders, with limited success. In contrast, I analyze all capital *inflows* to recipient countries. Once I collected all inflows to developing countries originating from China, I was able to reverse-engineer Chinese lending data. The resulting data set covers the borrowing activities of 127 developing countries from DACs, BRICs, IFIs, and private creditors for the years 2004–2015. Note that these data capture only loans obtained by the recipient government, not private actors in the recipient country.

The second challenge concerns the need for a quantitative measure capturing which societal coalition dominates a particular developing country. Such data are not easily available, as these coalitions are not directly observable. For instance, there are no formal arrangements between Finance and Industry to lobby the government regarding their preferred choice of creditor. Yet interviews with politicians clearly indicated that they understood whose interests were aligned, and that they aimed their political choices at satisfying two interest groups at once. In response, I create three novel measures to capture the relative political power of Finance, Industry, and Labor. Using these measures as independent variables in the statistical analysis allows capturing which type of coalition is present in each country at a specific time.

I also faced a methodological hurdle, as the outcome to be explained, recipient countries' borrowing portfolio, is a compositional variable. It measures the share of lending volume obtained from four types of creditors. This implies that all shares must add up to 100%, and, importantly, an increase in one creditor's share must be offset by a relative decrease in the shares of the remaining creditors. It is difficult to account for these characteristics of compositional data with an appropriate estimation method, especially if individual shares are allowed to equal zero. I address this challenge by extending a fractional logit model to multiple fractions.[7]

---

[7] Chapter 8 provides details on the data used for quantitative analysis. It discusses in detail the source and definition of borrowing data and how borrowing portfolios—the dependent variable—are constructed. In addition, it offers details on how I empirically measure the strength of societal groups across developing countries, which is the key independent variable. Chapter 9 introduces the methodological approach in detail. It also presents the findings of the main analysis. Chapter 10 subsequently examines the validity of rival explanations.

1.5.3. Findings

Both qualitative and quantitative analyses provide strong support for my theory. Interviews with societal interest groups revealed that they have strong and defined preferences across different types of creditors. Furthermore, conversations with politicians showed that they cater to the dominant interest groups and have the ability to shape borrowing decisions. In sum, the fieldwork in Ecuador, Colombia, and Peru confirmed that domestic considerations of recipient countries are an overlooked driver of lending patterns.

The statistical analysis shows that societal coalitions strongly shape borrowing portfolios across the developing world. Countries dominated by a Corporatist Coalition between Labor and Industry borrow more from BRIC creditors than governments responding to other coalitions; nations in which a Capital Coalition is the strongest societal force borrow more from private creditors than other countries; governments responding to a Consumer Coalition borrow more from DAC creditors than countries accountable to other types of coalitions. The effect of societal coalitions is robust to the inclusion of control variables such as existing debt and other economic variables. Furthermore, the findings are robust to a wide range of robustness tests:

- Differences in borrowing patterns persist even after accounting for variation in access to creditors. Here I consider borrowing portfolios conditional on income levels, credit rating, and default history. The findings suggest that borrowing portfolios are the result of *both* supply- and demand-side considerations.
- The analysis provides strong support for the claim that developing countries do not use specific creditors for specific tasks. For example, countries with similar infrastructure needs use either BRIC or World Bank loans, depending on the societal coalition. Similarly, borrowers with similar social needs, as measured by infant mortality or literacy rates, use different creditors. Furthermore, countries with similar default histories differ in their preferred source of credit depending on their societal coalition.
- Societal coalitions shape borrowing portfolios in a variety of institutional environments. For example, the influence of societal interest groups exists in both democracies and autocracies, across different types of electoral systems, and under left- and right-wing governments.
- The effect exists both when all BRICs are grouped together and when Brazil, Russia, India are analyzed separately from China. Thus, the results are not driven by China alone. Instead, the findings point to significant differences in loan conditions attached by Western versus emerging creditors.

- I show that societal coalitions exert significant influence on borrowing decisions even after accounting for differences in loan prices. This indicates that the financial terms of loan offers are less important than the political conditionalities attached to these loans.
- The findings are robust to alternative demand-side explanations, such as using specific creditors for specific purposes, or borrowing from lenders that share similar ideology.

1.6. What Is the Contribution of This Book?

The rise of BRICs has fundamentally transformed sovereign lending and borrowing. This development has significant implications for international relations, economic development, and democracy. We need to know what accounts for the variation in the creditors that developing countries choose. Why do countries decide to borrow money from some creditors and not others? This book is the first systematic treatment of this question.

The variation in borrowing portfolios across developing countries can, in part, be explained by supply-side factors. However, supply-side approaches that focus on decisions by creditors are only part of the answer. First, as shown previously, we observe significant variation in borrowing decisions even among countries with similar access to creditors. Second, existing work has characterized developing countries as passive recipients. However, much evidence suggests that developing countries are active agents with agendas, incentives, and preferences. My contribution lies in developing a demand-side theory that can complement (not replace!) existing supply-side explanations.

Furthermore, supply-side approaches to sovereign debt focus on countries' decisions to borrow from a *single* creditor in isolation. For example, scholars have analyzed whether or not a country receives a loan from the IMF (Copelovitch 2010; Vreeland 2003b, 2007; Thacker 1999). Others have analyzed whether or not governments borrow from private creditors (Eichengreen, Hausmann, and Panizza 2004; Tomz 2007). However, governments cannot borrow unlimited amounts. This debt ceiling introduces interdependency among creditors: A government's choice *for* one creditor is simultaneously a choice *against* other creditors. This insight is significant. Analyzing a government's decision for or against a single creditor in isolation would be methodologically flawed, as it would misrepresent a crucial characteristic of the situation in which the government makes its decision. Instead of focusing only on the determinants of the *choice for or against a single creditor*, it is necessary to analyze the *choice among competing creditors*. The experience of a former US Department of State adviser illustrates the importance of studying the choice among multiple creditors: "Cambodia was considering a $600 million loan from the World Bank that had conditions about transparency, anti-corruption, and accountability. The Cambodians basically told the World Bank to go to hell and the next day they received a $601 million loan from the Chinese with no conditions" (Duke 2011). If we were to analyze Cambodia's decision against the World Bank loan without taking into consideration the alternative loan offers its government received from the Chinese, we would likely misjudge why Cambodia decided against the loan from the World Bank. Cambodia's decision cannot be understood without reference to the full set of options that Cambodia had at the time it made the decision. This book accounts for this interdependency by analyzing the choice among multiple creditors simultaneously.

Lastly, I challenge the assumption that borrowing countries are unitary actors. We know that trade (Rogowski 1989) and capital inflows (Frieden 1991) generate winners and losers within countries. I build on these insights and pursue a disaggregated analysis. I first identify the distributional consequences of loans by four creditors (BRICs, DACs, IFIs, and private creditors) and the interests of three domestic interest groups (Labor, Industry, and Finance). By connecting distributional consequences to actors' interests, I can derive preferences of specific groups with respect to specific creditors. Incorporating the preferences of domestic interest groups makes possible an analysis of the political dynamics that lead governments to accept loan proposals from one creditor but reject loan offers by others.

With respect to empirics, I present novel qualitative evidence on the borrowing decisions of developing countries drawn from a large number of elite interviews. I also create new quantitative data for statistical analyses. For example, I create a measure capturing which societal interest groups are politically dominant in developing countries. Social scientists, at times, claim that institutions explain certain economic or political outcomes, and one wonders whether the reason they emphasize institutions is that institutions are easier to measure. I provide a reasonable proxy for interest group strength that is comparable across countries. Furthermore, given the difficulties in obtaining accurate data on Chinese loans from the Chinese government, I focus on reverse-engineering such data by analyzing capital *inflows* into developing countries. This approach allows me to construct credible data on countries' borrowing portfolios.

Finally, my theoretical and empirical work has normative significance. In the domestic context, observers worry about the effect of Chinese or Russian loans on democracy in recipient countries. Furthermore, how will BRIC loans affect economic growth, corruption, and institutional quality, considering the lack of good-governance criteria attached to their loans? If debtors have a choice in whether or not they obtain BRIC loans, we face a selection problem: to understand the consequences of new lending from the BRICs, we first need to understand why countries choose to borrow from them. My work sheds light on the motivation of borrowers.

Furthermore, increased lending by BRICs has implications in the international arena.

For instance, the rise of emerging creditors probably reduces the influence of traditional, Western lenders. As China becomes a rival to the United States, sovereign loans may become an even more important tool of international diplomacy. In addition, the increase in financial competition between creditors may offer opportunities for recipient countries: The emergence of an "outside option" in the form of BRIC loans might increase the bargaining power of recipient countries vis-à-vis Western creditors.

1.7. Plan of the Study

The book is structured as follows. This introduction has illustrated that borrowing patterns differ significantly across developing countries, even if they have the same credit rating, income level, and degree of democracy. These empirical patterns suggest that it is not only creditors who determine loan allocations, but that recipient governments have preferences and act upon them.

Chapter 2 introduces a demand-side theory to explain how governments choose their creditors. Labor, Industry, and Finance are important interest groups in recipient countries. Their government can borrow from four types of creditors: Western governments, BRICs' governments, multilateral institutions, and private creditors. These creditors may offer the same loan amount, but the strings attached to their loans differ. Therefore, the expected distributional consequences of a particular loan differ across domestic interest groups.

Policymakers have the incentive to satisfy the demands of the two most influential groups simultaneously by borrowing from the creditor that is jointly preferred by both groups.

The theory predicts that a government will rely on loans from BRICs if a Corporatist Coalition between Labor and Industry dominates the political landscape. In contrast, governments will tend to borrow from private creditors if a Capital Coalition between Finance and Industry predominates, but will obtain loans by Western governments if faced with a Consumer Coalition between Labor and Finance.

My theory makes several assumptions about actors' preferences and the process by which borrowing decisions are made. Qualitative evidence is needed to assess the accuracy of these assumptions. Chapter 3 introduces the rationale for the case selection. I identify three countries that are as similar as possible in many dimensions (history, geography, culture, economic and political system, etc.) but represent variation in the key independent variable proposed by the theory: the type of societal coalition. The chapter also offers details on the qualitative methodology, including recruitment process and interview method.

Chapter 4 analyzes Ecuador and argues that it is characterized by a Corporatist Coalition between Labor and Industry that marginalizes Finance. Interviews with representatives of these groups demonstrate that they have a strong preference against loans from multilateral organizations such as the World Bank and the IMF. Instead, both groups expect to gain material benefits with loans from the Chinese government. The qualitative evidence shows that Ecuadorian politicians know of these preferences. They are responsive to the demands of the Corporatist Coalition to increase the chances of their electoral success. Furthermore, interviews show that borrowing decisions are not a technocratic exercise, but rather the result of an explicitly political process that allows politicians to influence which creditor is used. As a result, the Ecuadorian government has rejected loan offers by multilateral organizations and Western governments, and instead has borrowed from China and Brazil.

Chapter 5 shows that Colombia's borrowing choices match the preferences of the Capital Coalition between Finance and Industry. Both groups are alarmed by the prospect of increased Chinese competition. Moreover, both prefer the government to borrow from the capital market even if cheaper loans from public sources are available. Interviews suggest that Colombian politicians are well aware of the dominant groups' preferences. Consequently, politicians are ready to act upon the interests of the Capital Coalition when making borrowing decisions. The qualitative evidence suggests that Colombia's process of contracting loans significantly disadvantages Chinese loan offers. As a result, Colombia has rejected several Chinese loan offers and instead relies on private creditors for its financing needs.

Chapter 6 demonstrates that Peru is characterized by a Consumer Coalition. Labor and domestic Finance dominate the political landscape, while domestic Industry is relatively weak as a result of the economic crisis in the 1990s. Interviews reveal that both Labor and Finance prefer bilateral loans from Western governments. While Labor is less enthusiastic about private creditors than Finance, recent experiences with hyperinflation resulted in congruent preferences regarding this creditor as well. Qualitative evidence shows that Peruvian politicians are acutely aware of the need to satisfy the demands by local banks, as well as the population. Interviews suggest that politicians have much influence over the process of making borrowing decisions, allowing them to significantly shape borrowing strategy. As a result, Peru relies more on bilateral loans from Western governments than its neighboring countries. It also uses private creditors, while loan offers by the Chinese government have been rejected.

Qualitative evidence is useful to trace the process by which borrowing decisions are made. However, the question is how generalizable the findings from Ecuador, Colombia, and Peru are to other developing countries. Statistical analyses of a large set of countries can provide insights into whether domestic political dynamics within recipient countries affect borrowing portfolios. Chapter 7 describes three challenges that need to be resolved before such analyses are possible: First, data on incoming loans must be obtained, which is particularly difficult for Chinese loans. Second, estimating the political strength of societal interest groups is challenging, as it cannot be observed directly. Third, analyzing a compositional variable presents several methodological challenges.

Chapter 8 describes how data for the statistical analysis were obtained. First, the dependent variable captures countries' borrowing portfolios, that is, the share of loans obtained from a particular type of creditor. The main difficulty lies in obtaining reliable data on loan inflows from emerging creditors, such as China. In contrast to existing approaches focused on loan outflows from China, this book instead collects information on the loan inflows as recorded in the budgets of recipient countries. Second, the key independent variable is societal coalitions. The relative political strength of Labor, Industry, and Finance determines which type of coalition is present. However, their relative political influence cannot be observed directly. The chapter describes how proxies were derived by combining information about the groups' ability to overcome collective action problems with their importance to the domestic economy.

I then use the newly created variables capturing the coalition type to test whether societal coalitions shape borrowing portfolios. The results presented in chapter 9 indicate that borrowing portfolios differ significantly across coalitions: Corporatist Coalitions rely primarily on BRIC loans, Capital Coalitions on private creditors, while Consumer Coalitions mainly use bilateral loans from Western governments. These differences remain significant after controlling for economic factors (recipient GDP, current account, existing debt levels, trade, and natural resources) and political considerations (democracies versus autocracies, type of electoral system, and government ideology). Furthermore, the results are robust to analyzing China separately from Brazil, India, and Russia, as well as when combining Western bilateral with multilateral loans. The evidence strongly supports the argument that developing countries actively make choices among competing loan offers.

Chapter 10 examines the validity of several alternative explanations and how they compare with my theory. First, the analysis suggests that the final borrowing portfolio results from the interaction of supply- and demand-side factors: both are important predictors of borrowing portfolios, through their relative importance differs across creditors. Loans from private creditors are more heavily shaped by creditors' preferences, while recipient preferences strongly affect borrowing from public creditors. Second, the analysis finds no evidence that recognizing Taiwan might negatively affect the loan volume obtained from China. Third, recipient governments do not appear to decide among creditors based on the interest rate of loans offered. Fourth, borrowing portfolios do not depend on the use to which the loan is put; differences in borrowing portfolios across coalitions remain irrespective of infrastructure needs, humanitarian emergencies, or debt crises. This suggests that recipients do not use particular creditors for specific projects. Lastly, domestic political considerations appear to be more important in determining governments' borrowing decisions than their ideological alignment with creditor governments, as measured by UN voting.

Finally, chapter 11 reviews the implications of the findings. What does the emergence of BRICs as creditors imply for the power of developing countries in an increasingly globalized world? Are BRIC loans "good" for economic development? What are the implications of Chinese loans for the prospects of democracy in the recipient country?

2

How Governments Choose Their Creditors

The borrowing portfolios of developing countries starkly differ. Supply-side factors are likely at play: governments have different access to various creditors depending on their level of income, credit rating, and degree of democracy. However, as demonstrated in the introduction, we see variation in which type of creditor is chosen even among countries with similar access to creditors. This points to demand-side factors. In this chapter, I propose a theory describing how governments of developing countries choose among the loan offers available to them.

I argue that societal coalitions and distributional consequences explain the borrowing decisions of governments. The characteristics of loans differ across creditors: some loans attach conditionalities requiring loan recipients to balance the budget and lower inflation; others are granted only if the borrowed resources are used for a particular investment project, and so on. I argue that differences in the strings attached to loans translate into different distributional consequences across societal groups: some loans benefit workers, others are advantageous to bankers, while yet others are beneficial to industrialists, all depending on the loan characteristics. My argument suggests that politicians will respond to the politically powerful societal groups and borrow from these groups' preferred creditor.

I begin by identifying the societal actors within each country—Finance, Industry, and Labor—and their overall objectives. I then derive the specific preferences of these actors across different types of creditors by connecting the overall objectives of these groups to the characteristics of loans offered by different creditors. In turn, I model the process by which these preferences are translated into borrowing choices by examining the coalitions these groups can form to advance their goals. I show that there are three possible coalitions: a Capital Coalition between Finance and Industry, a Corporatist Coalition consisting of Labor and Industry, and a Consumer Coalition between Labor and

Finance. I then formulate hypotheses regarding which type of creditor the government will choose depending on what kind of coalition is politically dominant.

2.1. The Actors: Industry, Finance, and Labor

Loans from different creditors have distinct distributional consequences. Which societal groups in the recipient country benefit from what type of loan? In a first step, I define three domestic groups that stand to benefit or lose: the domestic financial sector (Finance), domestic producers (Industry), and workers (Labor). In doing so, I draw on Gourevitch and Shinn (2005, 23), Rogowski (1989, 6), and Pepinsky (2008, 439), who also distinguish between mobile capital, fixed capital, and Labor to explain government decisions.

2.1.1. Finance: Owners of Intangible Assets

Finance comprises actors that own intangible assets, such as money, stocks, or bonds. This includes banks, insurance companies, and investors—in short, actors offering financial services. Their income is consequently generated from returns on their investments as well as from fees charged for these services. Significantly, their income depends on the continued existence of their capital stock.

The type of assets that Finance owns directly determines their objectives. Finance owns financial capital, and consequently has an interest in political decisions that preserve its capital stock. Thus, Finance is primarily interested in a stable macroeconomic environment and political decisions that prevent inflation, as inflation would undermine the value of financial assets. Similarly, these assets are useful only insofar as a domestic financial infrastructure exists, which explains the preference for a profitable and stable banking system. In addition, a stable banking system, crucial for attracting potential clients of financial services, is essential to the interests of Finance.

2.1.2. Industry: Holder of Tangible Assets

In contrast to Finance, Industry consists of actors who own tangible, fixed assets. Examples include manufacturing factories, infrastructure, and other production equipment necessary to produce tangible products. Hence, Industry comprises factory owners or infrastructure firms. I also conceptualize landowners as members of Industry because they, too, own a fixed asset used for production of tangible products. Similarly, Industry includes both productive and extractive industries, as both depend on fixed, tangible assets. In all cases, their income depends on the continued existence of the physical capital stock as well as the presence of a market for inputs and outputs.

All fixed assets are potentially liquid, as the owner of a production plant can sell that plant, converting physical assets into liquid assets. However, such conversions are challenging in developing countries because the number of potential buyers is small. For this reason, I assume that fixed assets are immobile: The difference between Finance (intangible/mobile capital) and Industry (tangible/fixed capital) follows the distinction made between "financial capital" and "industrial capital" (Maxfield 1990; Winters 2007, 1996).[1]

The characteristics of assets owned by Industry strongly shape its political objectives. Unlike Finance, Industry is not immediately concerned with inflation as the value of fixed assets is comparatively insulated from inflation. Instead, Industry is dependent on sufficient supply of production inputs as well as adequate demand for their outputs. They are also concerned with the level of investment as this is their main source of maintaining their sources of income.

2.1.3. Labor: Workers without Assets

Labor encompasses all actors who do not own any assets. Workers consequently do not obtain significant income from either intangible assets or fixed capital. As a result, they are forced to sell their labor. The income of this group thus consists entirely of wages. In the interest of parsimony, I assume that Labor is anyone with wage income, and I therefore do not differentiate between formal and informal work, or between skilled and unskilled labor. Note that workers in developing countries typically do not own shares and thus are unlikely to be members of Finance.

Importantly, I also consider government employees as members of Labor. As salaried employees, their main source of income is wages (Tomz 2004). They typically do not own assets and thus do not derive a large share of their income from capital investments. Government employees have thus been shown to oppose cuts to wages and benefits as they are their main source of income. If government expenditures are reduced, "The brunt . . . is borne by public sector employees. Wage and salary earners in the public sector as a whole generally

---

[1] The military can be an important actor in the economies of developing countries. Besides a security force, it is often also an industrial actor. For example, the Ecuadorian military is the owner and operator of a large construction firm whose contracts include building bridges for civilian use (Interviews 36, 79). Similarly, the military in countries like Egypt (Morsy 2014), Pakistan (Siddiqa 2007), and Malaysia (Balakrishnan 2008) are engaged in construction business and industrial production of nonmilitary goods. For this reason, I abstract from the military as its own actor in the domestic economy and consider it part of domestic industry.

experience some decline in their real rate of remuneration, so that their relative income position tends to deteriorate" (Johnson and Salop 1980, 12). Precisely because they depend on wages, government employees opposed reduced public employment and cuts to wages and benefits imposed by the IMF in the aftermath of debt crises (Frieden 1989; Haggard and Kaufman 1992; Kaufman 1988; Nelson 1990), just as ordinary workers oppose cuts to government spending (Pastor 1987; Vreeland 2002). In light of these considerations, employees in the public sector share the defining characteristic of most workers: they do not obtain income from capital, but from wages.

This defining characteristic of Labor—its dependence on wage income—strongly shapes its objectives. For one, workers are concerned with sufficient employment opportunities: Without work this societal group does not have any other source of income. As a result, they are interested in continued public and private investment to generate jobs. Labor is also interested in maintaining or increasing real wages, just as social transfers and antipoverty programs by external actors would also be in their interest. As is the case with Finance and Industry, the type of assets (or the lack thereof) defines the overall objectives of this societal group.

2.2. Actors' Preferences across Creditor Types

The previous section analyzes the general interests of Finance, Industry, and Labor. Next, I connect the interests of these groups to the characteristics of loans available from four different creditors. These loans come with conditions. Depending on the types of strings attached to loans, one societal group might benefit from a loan, while another group might be negatively affected.

However, which group will benefit from what type of loan? To answer this question, I examine whether the strings attached to a particular loan will help or hinder a group to utilize its assets. For example, IMF loans require the government to lower inflation by cutting public expenditure and balancing the budget. Finance will benefit from the conditions attached to an IMF loan, as its assets are vulnerable to high inflation. In contrast, Industry's fixed assets are not affected by inflation. Industry consequently does not have strong preferences. Labor, however, will not benefit from the conditions attached to IMF loans, as reduced public expenditures are likely to have a negative effect on employment and wages. After identifying these diverging distributional consequences, I assume that Finance prefers IMF loans, while Labor does not. In short, by comparing the characteristics of societal actors to the conditions attached to different loans it is possible to derive the groups' preferences across creditors.

I derive the preferences of three societal groups (Finance, Industry, and Labor) across loans from four types of creditors: loans from multilateral institutions, bilateral loans from Western governments, government-to-government loans from emerging creditors, and loans obtained from private creditors. Who stands to win from a particular loan and who loses?

2.2.1. Preferences with Respect to Multilateral Loans

Loans by international financial institutions (IFIs) are granted by institutions such as the IMF and the World Bank. These institutions pool the money from multiple member governments, which is why the loans from these institutions are also known as multilateral loans. To obtain these loans, recipient governments are required to fulfill certain macroeconomic conditions. These conditions typically follow the prescriptions of the Washington Consensus (Williamson 2000), intended to remove obstacles to an efficient market system in the recipient country (Chwieroth 2010, 2015). While the rhetoric of IFIs might change over time (Clegg 2014), Kentikelenis, Stubbs, and King (2016) find no evidence of a fundamental transformation of IMF conditionality over time.

Conditions are imposed to improve the business environment for both domestic and foreign companies. For example, IFIs can require governments to reduce inflation to preserve the purchasing power of capital by implementing tight monetary policies as well as austerity measures (Stone 2008). The requirements for a balanced budget are often met by implementing spending cuts in government welfare, pension, or social programs (Cho 2013; Nooruddin and Simmons 2006). IFIs have also required borrowers to undertake deeper structural reforms. For example, to stimulate economic growth,

> The IMF called for privatization and deregulation. Privatization involves transferring the ownership of national assets to the private sector, where free markets would bring about greater efficiency. Deregulation involves removing restrictions on businesses and prices. allowing the forces of markets to operate, which is desirable if the decentralized decisions of individuals bring about greater efficiency than the actions of the central authority. Other structural changes might involve fundamental changes to taxation policies, labor market policies, or national pension programs. Structural conditions sometimes even involve reducing barriers to trade, such as tariffs on imports or subsidies to exports. (Vreeland 2007, 24)

In return for such drastic measures, IFIs offer exceptionally generous financial terms. Interest rates on IMF and World Bank loans are low by comparison to loans from other lenders. Similarly, they feature long grace periods, which implies that borrowing governments have several years until the first repayment is due. Loans also have long maturities, so that repayment rates are spread over several years or even decades, which—in theory—should make repayment of these loans less burdensome.

2.2.1.1. Finance

Finance has positive preferences with regard to multilateral loans, for three reasons. First, financial sector actors have a favorable view of the macroeconomic conditions attached to IFI loans. Reforms pertaining to the removal of capital controls and restrictions on exchange rates, as well as curbing inflation are in the interest of Finance, as these would preserve the value of the type of assets it holds. Furthermore, existing literature suggests that the IMF may help implement such reforms against domestic resistance (Drazen 2005; Vreeland 2003a; Ramcharan 2003), while other creditors do not offer such assistance. Second, Finance prefers IFI loans because they are often significantly cheaper than alternative sources of credit. Anecdotal insights support this notion. In the late 2000s, Ecuador announced it would use available resources to repay World Bank and IMF loans early instead of repaying other creditors. The financial sector groaned, noting that if a government wants to reduce its debt burden, it should use available resources to repay the most expensive loans first and hold on to low-interest loans (Interviews 92, 93). Third, IFIs might positively affect Finance by preventing financial crises such as banking crises (Papi, Presbitero, and Zazzaro 2015) or sovereign default (Copelovitch 2010). By preventing crises, IMF loans benefit the domestic financial sector, as such crises seriously limit its ability to operate. In addition, the prospect of potential IMF loans might allow domestic banks to engage in profit-seeking activities that otherwise would not be available.

2.2.1.2. Industry

In contrast to Finance, Industry is likely to hold ambivalent preferences regarding multilateral loans. On the one hand, austerity measures imposed by the IMF are likely to lower public investment and consequently reduce business for domestic companies (Conway 1994). In addition, output and growth tend to contract after signing IMF agreements (Przeworski and Vreeland 2000; Vreeland 2003a; Barro and Lee 2005; Dreher 2006).

Lower overall economic activity would negatively affect Industry. On the other hand, IMF conditions might improve the business climate, particularly when governments intend to pursue questionable economic policies (Cho 2013). For instance, the risk of expropriation might decline (Biglaiser, Lee, and Staats 2015). In sum, Industry is unlikely to have strong preferences either for or against IFI loans.

2.2.1.3. Labor

In contrast to Finance and Industry, Labor has negative preferences regarding IFI loans. Existing research documents that the material position of workers typically deteriorates. For instance, Pastor (1987, 258) argues that "the single most consistent effect the IMF seems to have is the redistribution of income away from workers." Vreeland (2002) finds that the labor share of income from manufacturing activities decreases due to IMF programs, while it improves the economic position of capital owners. With respect to Ecuador he writes:

> This country participated in its first IMF agreement in 1973. In 1974, the labor share of income from manufacturing was 24.8%. Labor share grew until 1982 when it reached 52.8%. In 1983, the government entered into another IMF program. Labor share plummeted to 34.8%. Ecuador experienced a drastic contraction that year with economic growth of −5.76%. But the owners of capital experienced an increase in income in 1983. Earnings from manufacturing in 1982 were 3,413 million, of which 1,611 million went to capital. The following year, earnings from manufacturing dropped to 3,366 million, but 2,195 million of this went to capital. The income of capital grew by 36%! (Vreeland 2002, 132)

In addition to lower income, IFI loans also reduce social expenditures. According to Nooruddin and Simmons (2006), the IMF may demand that a country reduce its budget deficit by a particular amount, but not specify which spending programs to cut. Rather, the government can often decide which parts of the budget to reduce. In making this decision, governments tend to cut spending on social programs that benefit the poor rather than on particular goods targeted at specific interest groups (Nooruddin and Simmons 2006). Nooruddin and Simmons suggest that this is because smaller groups of richer individuals are easier to organize and thus can lobby their government more effectively than the poor. As a result, IMF programs have particularly negative consequences for health and education expenditures. Similarly, Tomz argues that the budget cuts required by the IMF for debt repayment also hurt unemployed

Table 2.1 **Distributional consequences by actor**

	IFI creditors	DAC creditors	BRIC creditors	Private creditors
Finance	+	+	−	+
Industry	o	−	+	+
Labor	−	+	+	−

Note: The table summarizes the predicted preferences of three societal interest groups across the four types of creditors. For instance, Finance has positive preferences regarding IFI creditors, as the conditions attached to their loans aim to reduce inflation and balance budgets. In contrast, Labor exhibits negative preferences toward IFI loans, as budget cuts are likely to hurt workers. Conversely, Finance does not like BRIC loans, as these creditors represent competition for funding infrastructure projects. Labor, however, views BRIC loans tied to specific loans favorably, as they are likely to create new job opportunities.

and poor citizens. "Programs for these groups usually make up a large component of current spending and are, therefore, targets for governments that need to impose austerity quickly" (Tomz 2004, 5).

As a result of both lower income and lower social spending, IMF programs are associated with an increase in inequality (Pastor 1987; Garuda 2000; Oberdabernig 2013). It is therefore not surprising that Labor has negative preferences with respect to IFI loans.

In sum, I expect Finance to have positive preference with respect to IFI loans, while Industry is ambivalent. In contrast, Labor opposes IFI loans. Table 2.1 summarizes these preferences.

2.2.2. Preferences in Regards to Western Bilateral Creditors

Governments can also obtain loans directly from other governments. The characteristics of these bilateral loans depend on the identity of the creditor government. I distinguish between bilateral loans from Western countries (DACs) and bilateral loans from emerging creditors Brazil, Russia, India, and China (BRICs). DAC loans and BRIC loans have different characteristics. I define Western governments as the members of the Organization for Economic Cooperation and Development (OECD), a club of advanced, industrialized, and democratic countries. These creditor governments coordinate their activities in the Development Assistance Committee (DAC) within the OECD. The Western governments include Australia, Austria, Belgium, Canada, the Czech Republic, Denmark, Finland, France, Germany, Greece, Iceland, Ireland, Italy, Japan, the Republic of Korea, Luxembourg, Netherlands, New Zealand, Norway, Poland, Portugal, the Slovak Republic, Slovenia, Spain, Sweden, Switzerland, the United Kingdom, and the United States. DAC loans can be given by a variety of governmental institutions within creditor governments, such as a specific aid agency like USAID or the US government directly. Western creditor governments have agreed to harmonize their lending procedures. "Periodic peer reviews among DAC members are the primary mechanism used to secure common ground. In short, traditional donors have been accumulating a set of institutions for concerted self-restraint that include ex-ante restrictions on aid behaviors and ex-post vigilance for ensuring compliance with certain norms and principles by each member" (Sato et al. 2011, 2092). For this reason, the basic characteristics of the loans by DACs are sufficiently similar to group them together.

Bilateral loans differ from multilateral loans in several ways. Most importantly, multilateral loans are considered more efficient and less politicized (Rodrik 1996). While not free of political influence by major shareholders (Stone 2008, 2004; Copelovitch 2010), multilateral loans are considered less tied to the foreign policy agendas of creditor governments than bilateral loans. There are two reasons for this assessment: First, creditor governments do not have as much control over the process of allocating multilateral loans as with their own bilateral lending institutions (Milner and Tingley 2013; Milner 2006). Second, multilateral institutions coordinate the resources of multiple creditor governments whose interests may not always align (Copelovitch 2010). Multilateral agencies thus can moderate pressures for politically biased lending by noting any contradictory interests of different shareholders (Neumayer 2003). As result of both factors, multilateral institutions may be somewhat shielded from direct political pressure from their member states (Martens et al. 2002). For these reasons, recipients' need is relatively more important for multilateral institutions, whereas political, economic, and military strategic interests dominate the allocation of bilateral assistance (Tsoutsoplides 2008; Martens et al. 2002; Rodrik 1996; Maizels and Nissanke 1984).

Due to the multilateral character of IFIs, their conditionalities primarily include economic requirements aimed at improving the functioning of the recipient's economy. These conditions limit the role of the state in the economy to facilitate the efficient functioning of markets. Examples of such policies include privatizing state-owned enterprises, floating exchange rates, and abolishing capital controls. Conversely, bilateral loans allow creditor governments greater control (Milner and Tingley 2013; Milner 2006). DACs appear to skew the allocation process in favor of their strategic and political considerations, as opposed to recipient need (Nunnenkamp and Thiele 2006; Sippel and Neuhoff 2009). Bilateral loans are often provided with the benefit of the creditor country in mind (Berthélemy 2006; Bermeo 2011).

DACs' loan conditions reflect their political and economic interests. With respect to political interests, bilateral loans are used to purchase influence (Bunte and Kinne 2018; Bueno de Mesquita and Smith 2007; Findley et al. 2017). For example, governments use bilateral loan conditions to elicit military cooperation from loan recipients (Kinne and Bunte 2018), and loans are used to gain political influence in recipient countries (Bunte and Kinne 2018). With respect to economic interests, DAC loan conditions differ from those attached to multilateral loans. While economic conditions required by IFIs are comparatively apolitical, DAC creditor governments impose "good governance" conditions. This seemingly innocent heading disguises the political nature of loan conditions. For example, DAC loans have required governments to increase anticorruption efforts, improve their transparency, and require equal treatment of domestic vis-à-vis foreign firms (Dollar and Levin 2006; Collier and Dollar 2002). While these conditions were well intended, they have prevented governments of recipient countries from implementing industrialization policies akin to those that helped East Asian tigers rapidly develop their economies in the second half of the twentieth century (Wade 1990; Chang 2002; Woo-Cumings 1999; Rodrik 2004; Amsden 1992). In addition, evidence suggests that DAC loans are "door-openers" that allow Western firms from the creditor country to enter new markets in debtor nations, which is not necessarily the case with multilateral loans (Bunte 2018a; Rodrik 1996).

A further characteristic of DAC loans is that they are typically untied. The resources provided by DAC loans are not attached to a particular project. Instead, the funds are paid directly into the recipient government's budget. Nevertheless, loans are often earmarked for social expenditures such as schools and health facilities (Brautigam 2011).

2.2.2.1. Finance

Finance has positive preferences regarding DAC loans. There are several reasons for this expectation. First, bilateral loans from both DACs and BRICs are likely to purchase influence in the recipient country. However, since financial sectors in developing countries are likely more connected to Western money centers than those in China or India, Finance prefers influence from DACs to BRICs. In fact, anecdotal evidence suggests that they might welcome it: In an interview, a Colombian businessman stated, "With the US, Colombia isn't quite sure what their political agenda is. However, whatever it is, we can live with it." Similarly, in Peru, an investment manager noted, "The Chinese are not a good business to have.... We are going to miss the Americans. Their values of how to do business are not shared by the Chinese" (Interview 61). Even an Ecuadorian business representative agreed, noting, "It is scary if you are in the hands of China. If I would have to choose hands, I would probably choose the US because I know them" (Interview 103).

Second, industrial policy of the type conducted in South Korea, Taiwan, and other East Asian Tigers involved significant government interference in the financial sector. Industrial policy involves directing credit at specific sectors to allow Industry to upgrade its technological capacities (Chang 1993). In most cases, credit was allocated to sectors that a free market would not have provided with resources (Wade 1990; Amsden 1992). Finance favors DAC loans, as good-governance conditions prevent government from placing severe restrictions on domestic financial institutions, such as directing the flow of credit.

2.2.2.2. Industry

In contrast to Finance, Industry has negative preferences with respect to DAC loans. First and foremost, if bilateral loans are given primarily for reasons benefiting the creditor country, such loans are unlikely to have positive growth effects in the recipient country. Furthermore, the emphasis on social development, such as health and education, might very well have positive effects on the economy in the long run. However, the effects of human capital investment on economic growth can take years, if not decades, to materialize (Mayer 2001). As a result, domestic firms do not immediately benefit from higher growth rates.

Instead, domestic firms are the primary beneficiaries of industrial policies. Governments in developing countries often do attempt to boost and diversify domestic production. For example, Colombian president Uribe instigated the Productive Transformation Program, which his successor, President Santos, has continued, albeit under a different name (Locomotivas). The program is aimed at boosting productivity of the Colombian manufacturing sector.

DAC loans would make such programs significantly more difficult to implement. Furthermore, bilateral loans and aid are strongly correlated with bilateral investment treaties (Neumayer 2006), preventing governments from treating domestic and Western companies differently.

In this context, it is understandable why industry associations welcomed Ecuador's decision to renounce investment protection treaties with Western governments. After all, such treaties allow Western companies to sue in foreign courts, which put Ecuadorian companies at a disadvantage because they lack the resources to adequately represent their interests.

2.2.2.3. Labor

In contrast, Labor's preferences for DAC loans are favorable. After all, workers welcome the increased resources for education and social expenditure, particularly since domestic politicians have incentives to limit the provision of intangible public goods (Harding and Stasavage 2013). Labor effectively perceives the effect of DAC loans as similar to that of Western aid programs. Evidence suggests that such programs improve how the recipient population perceives the Western donors. For example, Goldsmith, Horiuchi, and Wood (2014) analyze the effect of a US aid program specifically targeted to address HIV and AIDS. They find that this program improved the opinion of the United States among citizens of the recipient countries.

In addition to increased social expenditure, Labor is likely to be in favor of the good-governance requirements attached to DAC loans because they should result in increased transparency and reduced corruption. Attempts to battle corruption are extremely popular among citizens in developing countries (Ferraz and Finan 2011; Olken and Pande 2012).

Industrial policies also often do not benefit workers. For example, industrialization in South Korea squeezed wages of workers in order to extract capital for investment in key industries (Kay 2002). Labor will thus approve of DAC loans if they hinder the pursuit of policies prioritizing industrialists over workers.

In sum, Finance and Labor will exhibit positive preferences with respect to DAC loans, while Industry will oppose loans from this creditor (see table 2.1).

2.2.3. Preferences regarding Bilateral Loans from BRICs

Besides loans from Western creditors, developing countries can also obtain bilateral loans from emerging economies. Brazil, Russia, India, and China (the BRICs) have significantly increased their lending volume since the early 2000s and have become a significant source of funding for developing countries. Government-to-government loans from BRICs thus represent the third type of creditor that governments could approach for loans.

Admittedly, of the four BRIC countries, China has by far the largest lending volume. Furthermore, BRICs are a somewhat heterogeneous grouping. For these reasons, one might wonder if these four emerging creditor governments should be grouped together or if the analysis should focus on China only. I maintain that there are good reasons to jointly analyze their lending. Note that the group of DAC creditors consists of 29 Western creditor governments, notwithstanding some heterogeneity across lenders such as the United States, South Korea, Portugal, and Lichtenstein. However, I analyze these Western creditors jointly because of the similarity of their lending conditions. Similarly, I argue that BRIC creditor governments should be also grouped together, as their lending conditions are extremely similar. The characteristics of loans by China, India, Brazil, and Russia are homogenous, but differ from the set of conditions imposed by DAC creditors. For this reason, the distributional consequences of loans by BRIC countries are likely to be comparable, thus facilitating a joint analysis.[2]

The characteristics of BRIC loans differ significantly from conditions attached to DAC loans. First, while most DAC loans are paid directly into the government's budget, BRIC loans are typically attached to a specific project. In addition, BRIC loans focus on funding infrastructure. Representatives of several BRICs noted an overemphasis on "social projects" at the expense of building productive capacity (Mwase and Yang 2012). While DAC loans, though untied, have been earmarked for spending in education and health, BRIC loans fund primarily bridges, roads, dams, and ports (Brautigam 2011).

In contrast to DAC loans, BRIC loans typically require that borrowed funds be spent on materials or services obtained from the lending country. Mattlin and Nojonen (2014, 9) note that "the recipient country needs to adhere to a number of project-related demands regarding, for example, the use of Chinese contractors and sub-contractors, as well as China-sourced technology, equipment suppliers, management and training. . . . The China Exim Bank, for example, normally requires in its concessional loans that at least 50% of the goods and services be sourced from Chinese contractors." This is illustrated by a $2.8 billion loan provided by the Chinese Development Bank (CDB) to the Ecuadorian government for the construction of the Coca Codo Sinclair hydroelectric power dam. As part of the agreement, Ecuador was required to use a Chinese firm to construct the dam (Interview 98). A survey of Chinese companies in Sudan provides additional insights. Three-quarters of respondents indicated that conditions attached to Chinese loans are the reason why a Chinese company is implementing their current project. Moreover, 88% of managers called the loan conditions responsible for the purchase of machines, equipment, and raw materials from China (Nour 2011, 13).

2.2.3.1. *Finance*

In light of these characteristics, Finance does not like BRIC loans. Recall that loans from BRIC creditors are often tied to specific investment projects and require the debtor to use companies from the creditor country to execute the

---

[2] However, I will directly address possible differences between China and the remaining three emerging creditors in the quantitative analysis. Section 9.5 disaggregates the analysis and distinguished the estimated effect of societal coalitions for Chinese loans versus loans from Brazil, India, and Russia. The analysis produces identical results across all BRIC creditors. This finding suggests that the differences in lending volume across China, Brazil, Russia, and India are not driving the observed borrowing patterns, but that the similar loan characteristics are the defining factor.

project. Chinese loans are viewed as a "door-opener" allowing Chinese firms to secure investment concessions and contracts for public works projects (Bunte 2018a). Finance might worry about being crowded out: in the absence of BRIC loans to developing countries, the domestic financial sector is the primary source of funding for investment projects, particularly in the infrastructure sector. With the arrival of BRICs, however, Finance is no longer the only player in this market. Rather, domestic financial firms now face strong competition from an external creditor who is also interested in funding investment projects. It is reasonable to assume that the domestic financial sector will not like such competition.

In addition, BRIC loans explicitly refrain from prescribing specific economic policies to governments of recipient countries. In contrast to IFI and DAC loans, Finance cannot expect the government to move toward its preferred economic policy emphasizing liberal markets and capital mobility. Rather, BRIC loans will likely enable recipient governments to pursue some form of industrial policy.

2.2.3.2. Industry

In contrast, Industry favors BRIC loans precisely because such loans allow governments to implement some sort of industrial policy. Without good-governance requirements or other external interference in domestic affairs, recipient governments are free to implement policies promoting domestic manufacturing and exports. As I have noted, programs such as Colombia's Productive Transformation Program aimed at diversifying and strengthening domestic industry benefit Industry directly.

More importantly, BRIC loans may have a direct positive effect on domestic industry. Initially, observers worried that loans requiring the use of Chinese companies could crowd out domestic construction firms. However, anecdotal evidence suggests that these concerns are unfounded. For example, Ecuador borrowed $1.7 billion from China to construct Coca Codo Sinclair hydropower dam. The loan required that a Chinese company construct the dam. The contract was subsequently awarded to Sinohydro, a Chinese state-owned company. However, Ecuadorian businesses noted that no crowding out took place, for two reasons: first, no Ecuadorian firm had the capacity for such a massive project. Instead, projects funded by BRIC loans are typically viewed as additional in the sense that the Chinese are tackling projects that Western companies have been unwilling to take on. Second, while some specialist firms are likely to guide the implementation of projects funded by BRIC loans, domestic firms can expect increased business via subcontracting. These subcontracting opportunities would not have been available otherwise (Interviews 79, 86, 89, 92). Moreover, since BRIC loans are typically not market-based, expected payments to domestic companies for their services may be larger than under the transparent bidding rules that would otherwise prevail. For this reason, BRIC loans are welcomed, as they represent a true increase of subcontracting opportunities, not just a mere replacement of Western companies by Chinese firms.

2.2.3.3. Labor

Labor also has favorable preferences with respect to BRIC loans. If loans from BRICs indeed increase public investment in infrastructure, positive effects on employment are likely. Yet some observers have raised the concern that the Chinese bring their own labor to build infrastructure projects. For example, Chinese firms are accused of bringing Chinese workers to employ instead of hiring local labor (Alden 2005). Brautigam and Xiaoyang (2011) analyze special economic cooperation zones set up by African countries for Chinese companies. They write that "inadequate local learning and local participation could affect the ability of the zones to catalyze African industrialization." This practice reduces positive spillover effects into the local economy.

However, available evidence suggests that these perceptions do not correspond to reality (Mwase and Yang 2012). Table 2.2 summarizes the available information on the use of local labor by Chinese companies. The World Bank conducted a survey in Ethiopia in 2011. It noted that

> Chinese companies employed 18,368 permanent, full-time employees from both China and Ethiopia. The employment size has increased by 19 percent since the end of 2008. Among the full-time permanent employees, 15,910 are Ethiopians. In addition, Chinese firms also hired 7,813 seasonal or temporary workers in 2011. (World Bank 2012, 22)

A survey of 42 Chinese enterprises in Uganda revealed that "Chinese companies employed a total of 9,845 workers, including 1,004 Chinese employees. For all Chinese companies in Uganda, it can be estimated that they created in total some 30,000 jobs" (Warmerdam and van Dijk 2013, 292). They further provide disaggregated information noting that

> 45% of the Chinese companies are composed of less than 75% Ugandans. 55% of companies employ more than 75% Ugandans. In 17% of the cases less than half the number of workers is from the host country. The role of Ugandan labor depends very much on the type of companies and their ownership. The State-Owned Enterprises have a higher percentage of Ugandans in the workforce, with 67% employing more than 75%, and 22% employing between 51–75% Ugandans. Only 33% of mixed ownership companies employed more than 75%

Table 2.2 Local employment by Chinese companies

Sample			Employment					Source
	Location	Companies	Year	Total	Local	Chinese	% local	
Country studies	Ethiopia	24 Chinese companies	2011	18,368	15,910	2,458	87%	World Bank (2012)
	Namibia	36 Chinese state-owned companies	2013	4,900	4,000	900	82%	The Namibian (2013)
	Kenya	75 Chinese companies	2014				78%	Xinhua (2015)
	Uganda	42 Chinese companies	2012	9,845	8,841	1,004	90%	Warmerdam and van Dijk (2013)
	Angola	30 joint Chinese-Angolan projects	2007				62%	Tang (2010)
	Africa	Sinohydro	2012	31,250	25,000	6,250	80%	Sinohydro (2012)
Company studies	Africa	China National Petroleum Co.	2014	25,400	17,600	7,800	69%	Ntambara (2014)
	Nigeria	China Civil Engineering Construction Corporation	2013	20,000	19,000	1,000	95%	Mohan (2013)
	Nigeria	Li Group	2013		20,000			Agabi (2013)

Note: Summary of data on employment of Chinese companies in developing countries. The data show that the workforce of Chinese companies primarily consists of local workers, not imported Chinese labor.

Ugandans. This figure is higher again for privately owned enterprises with 56% employing more than 75% Ugandans. (Warmerdam and van Dijk 2013, 293)

Similar data are available from other countries. Tang (2010) surveyed 30 joint Chinese-Angolan projects in 2007. He finds that an average of 61.8% of workers are Angolans, but this figure varies significantly depending on the sector. In high-tech industries such as telecommunication, the average localization rate is only 37.8%, in contrast to 81.0% in agriculture. A survey of 36 Chinese state-owned companies in Namibia noted that they employ 4,000 Namibians and about 900 Chinese, which is an 82% localization rate (*The Namibian* 2013). A survey of 75 Chinese companies in Kenya puts the localization rate at 78% of full time employees (*Xinhua* 2015).

In addition to these country-level studies summarizing the employment by multiple Chinese firms in Ethiopia, Uganda, Angola, and Namibia, analyses of individual Chinese companies suggest significant employment of local workers. A study by Mohan (2013) reports employment data of the Li Group operating in Nigeria:

> There are ways in which Chinese bosses are seen by Nigerians to have promoted local welfare and progress. At the most basic level, there is gratitude for the jobs that Chinese companies have created in a country blighted by unemployment. In Kano, for example, local trade union and industry figures highlighted the Hong Kong Chinese-owned Li Group of factories, which ... is the second biggest employer in the city after the government, employing some 7,000 locals and over 20,000 Nigerians across the country. (Mohan 2013, 1264)

A meta-analysis of available data by Sautman and Hairong (2015) concludes that "locals are more than four-fifths of employees at 400 Chinese enterprises and projects in 40 African countries" (Sautman and Hairong 2015, 1). In addition, a McKinsey report concludes that

> at the more than 1,000 companies we surveyed, 89 percent of employees were African, adding up to more than 300,000 jobs for African workers. Scaled up across the more than 10,000 Chinese firms in Africa, these numbers suggest that Chinese-owned businesses employ several million Africans.... In trade, for example, the workforce is 82 percent African; in manufacturing, it's 95 percent African. Comparing public and private enterprises, SOEs employ an 81 percent African workforce, and private companies employ a 92 percent African workforce. (Sun, Jayaram, and Kassiri 2017, 42)

To be sure, working conditions are not rosy (Sun, Jayaram, and Kassiri 2017; Shen 2015).³ However, workers "are quick to point out that local workers have few other employment options and that 'hard bread is better than none.' An official of the Kano branch of the Manufacturers Association of Nigeria stressed that the Chinese-owned factories have been the most resilient, being largely responsible for maintaining the last vestiges of the city's, and Nigeria's, manufacturing sector" (Mohan 2013, 1264). In addition to providing jobs, infrastructure projects funded by BRIC loans are likely to have positive effects on workers' income. Yang and An (2017, 1) quote a Kenyan's woman: "I have a friend who works in a Chinese company, and I want to work at a Chinese company in the future because the company offers high wages." More systematic evidence collected by Bunte et al. (2018) suggests that incomes of Liberian workers working in the vicinity of Chinese concessions increased significantly relative to those living further away from the project sites. Such developments would be in line with the expectation that workers benefit from foreign direct investment, primarily through increased wages (Pandya 2010, 2014; Pinto 2013; Pinto and Pinto 2008; Pinto and Weymouth 2016; Quinn and Inclan 1997). In sum, the benefits of new employment opportunities and increased wages likely outweigh the drawbacks. For these reasons, Labor is expected to have positive preferences regarding BRIC loans.

Table 2.1 summarizes the preferences of societal actors with respect to BRIC loans. Labor and Industry are expected to favor BRIC loans, while Finance opposes this source of credit.

2.2.4. Preferences concerning Private Creditors

Governments of developing countries can also obtain resources from a fourth type of lender: private creditors. There are two ways governments borrow from private creditors (Kaplan 2013; Tomz 2007). First, governments can obtain loans from commercial banks. Second, governments can issue bonds and sell them to private investors. These securities pay investors interest for the duration of the bond, and the government will repay the principal once the maturity date has arrived. Investors purchasing such bonds range from individuals and private companies to institutional investors. Importantly, bondholders can include

---

³ However, by some accounts, labor conditions are improving. For example, Rounds and Huang (2017) suggest that employment conditions in Chinese and US firms operating in Kenya are not very different. Furthermore, the US Embassy in Lesotho reports that "labor conditions in Chinese-owned textile plants are a widely-quoted grievance, though labor union leaders told Park and Sautman that conditions had improved substantially since 2005." See "Chinese Engagement in Lesotho and Potential Areas for Cooperation," US Embassy in Lesotho, February 12, 2010.

both foreign investors and domestic individuals and institutions located in the issuing country; for this reason, private creditors are not necessarily "external" creditors. While bank loans are still common, their importance has declined relative to that of bond issuances. Ballard-Rosa, Mosley, and Wellhausen (2016) show that between 1990 and 2015, 56 developing countries have issued bonds. In 2013 alone, Gabon ($1.5 billion at an interest rate of 6.375%), Ghana ($1.0 billion, 7.940%), Laos ($49.2 million, 4.5%), Mozambique ($500 million, 8.5%), Nigeria ($500 million, 5.375% and $500 million, 6.625%), Rwanda ($400 million, 6.875%), South Africa ($2.0 billion, 6.060%), and Tanzania ($600 million, 6.285%) issued bonds. In 2014, the Côte d'Ivoire ($750 million, 5.625%), Ethiopia ($1.0 billion, 6.625%), Kenya ($2.0 billion, 6.875%), Senegal ($500 million, 6.250%), Vietnam ($1.0 billion, 4.8%), and Zambia ($1.0 billion, 8.500%), among others, followed suit.

The characteristics of loans obtained from private creditors differ significantly from bilateral and multilateral lenders' loans. In particular, these loans do not have conditions in the traditional sense. Private investors can voice their discontent over certain policies in the recipient country, and they can threaten to withhold funds in the future, but they technically cannot demand particular policy reforms. In return, private creditors receive a risk premium (Kaplan 2013). For this reason, loans from private creditors are typically more expensive than those from public lenders, such as IFIs or other governments.

Furthermore, loans from private creditors are paid directly into the budget of recipient governments and are typically not tied to a specific purpose. A bond prospectus may state that the proceeds will be allocated to infrastructure development or debt rescheduling, but any mention of a use of funds is nonbinding. A Ghanaian debt specialist noted that "once [a government] issued a bond, and the money rolls in, they can spend it how they like" (*Africa News* 2015). Therefore, loans from private creditors are extremely fungible.

2.2.4.1. *Finance*

Finance has positive preferences concerning private creditors. One reason relates to the incentives governments have to assist the domestic financial sector in times of crises. If governments issue bonds, domestic banks may want to purchase them to economize on equity. Should government bond prices fall, local banks take a large hit. In these situations, the perception of vulnerable banks may have the potential to drag sovereigns down. Thus, by purchasing government bonds, banks give the government a stake in the survival of the banking sector, increasing the likelihood of bailouts during crises. Such a safety net is in the interest of the domestic financial sector, but not necessarily of the workers, who are taxpayers footing the bill of such bailouts.

In addition, sovereign private loans from foreign sources increase the supply of credit. This can both harm and benefit domestic Finance. For example, faced with increased supply of credit, domestic financial actors may need to reduce the price of their services as well as offer commercial loans at lower interest rates. Without doubt, this reduces the profits of domestic banks because it lowers the returns to lending. However, increased money supply also has positive distributional consequences for Finance. Specifically, lower interest rates tend to increase asset prices and thereby benefit the wealthier segments of society, given that asset holdings are mainly concentrated among richest households. Consider evidence from a related phenomenon, quantitative easing, which also increases the money supply. Bernanke (2015) notes, "The claim that Fed policy has worsened inequality usually begins with the (correct) observation that monetary easing works in part by raising asset prices, like stock prices. As the rich own more assets than the poor and the middle class, the reasoning goes, the Fed's policies are increasing the already large disparities of wealth in the United States." Montecino and Epstein (2015) as well as Claeys et al. (2015) find that asset price increases due to increased money supply have significant distributional consequences, precisely because asset holdings are very much concentrated among the richest households. Moreover, they argue that these effects far outweigh any possible negative effects on the household income of wealthy individuals.

2.2.4.2. Industry

Industry also favors government borrowing from private creditors. The successful placement of government bonds is a signal to investors that the business climate and outlook are favorable. In turn, this allows Industry itself to benefit from easier access to foreign loans to finance its own operations. After all, credit ratings and instances of successful bond placements can serve as shortcuts to investors (Brooks, Cunha, and Mosley 2014).

2.2.4.3. Labor

Determining the preferences of Labor with respect to private creditors is challenging. Initially, one might compare private creditors investing in a developing country to foreign direct investment (FDI) since both involve foreign capital inflows. If this analogy were accurate, we would expect Labor to prefer these inflows. Pandya (2010, 2014), Pinto (2013), Pinto and Pinto (2008), Pinto and Weymouth (2016), as well as Quinn and Inclan (1997), among others, have established that Labor benefits from incoming investment.

However, this analogy does not hold, as FDI and government bonds are fundamentally different types of capital inflows. FDI directly connects two private actors, the investor and the worker. Here workers immediately benefit from an outward shift in labor demand and the potential for higher levels of productivity. In contrast, borrowing from the capital market connects private investors with the government, not workers. Thus, there is no direct employment effect of government borrowing. It is possible for governments to use these funds in ways that benefit Labor, but that is not guaranteed.[4] For instance, governments borrowing from private capital markets often increase spending on military purposes (Shea 2016).[5]

Instead of comparing the distributional effects of FDI to those of government borrowing, I derive Labor's preferences by drawing on the literature on government default. Government default on loans from private creditors is inversely related to government borrowing from private creditors. A substantial literature examines the distributional consequences of default and suggests that default does not affect all segments of society equally.

Stasavage (2003) shows that a government's decision to default on bonds negatively affects those who own public debt, while nondefault increases the burden of taxation for others. In later work, Stasavage (2011) extends this argument and suggests that elites with ties to the financial market have incentives to pressure leaders to honor their debt obligations. Credit downgrades and default hurt Finance, while the consequences of repayment are borne by the entire society. Thus, decisions to repay debt reward constituencies that own either government debt or some other type of asset sensitive to domestic interest rates. At the same time, the government must find new sources of revenue or divert government expenditures to repay debt. Along these lines, DiGiuseppe and Shea (2015) show that if the government decides to repay debt, it must find new sources of revenue (usually in the form of taxes) or divert government expenditures (usually away from social spending).

Having derived the distributional consequences of default on financial elites versus other taxpayers, scholars have used these insights to explain government behavior. Stasavage (2011) argues that the presence of an influential financial elite reduces the likelihood of government default on its debt. Kohlscheen (2010) finds that a larger share of stakeholders (i.e., owners of debt) in the population relative to peasants (i.e., rely on selling labor) decreases the likelihood of

---

[4] For example, left-wing governments might use funds in ways benefiting Labor, while right-wing governments do not. I examine this possibility in section 9.4. I find that Labor's preferences regarding private creditors do not depend on the government's partisanship.

[5] See also Wellhausen (2015), who shows that bondholders and FDI investors have diverging preferences after expropriations.

default. Dixit and Londregan (2000, 81) show that in cases where debt-holders are more powerful than other taxpayers (i.e., workers), the government is less likely to default. Kim (2013) suggests that poorer voters are less affected by the negative consequences of default, and thus societies with poorer median voters are more likely to default (Kim 2013, 7). Lastly, Shea and DiGiuseppe (2015) study the size of the "haircut" private creditors suffer in negotiations to reschedule debt following debt crises. They find that left-wing governments, representing constituents most likely to be hurt from higher debt repayment, extract greater concessions from creditors, resulting in terms more favorable to debtor states. In contrast, as right-wing governments represent those with a greater interest in repayment, these governments secure fewer concessions from creditors during negotiations.

These insights from cross-national empirical studies are complemented by survey evidence supporting the notion that workers disapprove of private creditors. In Argentina, a survey revealed that unemployed citizens or those at risk of losing a job are less likely to support repayment than those with more secure employment. Furthermore, richer citizens and individuals who value capital mobility are more likely to oppose default (Tomz 2004).

In Iceland, citizens with investment assets worried about the inflationary effects of a currency devaluation that would follow default. In contrast, the unemployed and those in weaker economic positions tended to favor default (Curtis, Jupille, and Leblang 2015).

Lastly, historical evidence also suggests that government decisions regarding debt respond to the preferences of workers if they are politically powerful. For instance, Britain defaulted on its debt to the United States in 1933. Britain's main negotiator, Frederick Leith-Ross, admitted that Britain's "objections were fundamentally political" and that $60 million was "within our capacity to pay" (Leith-Ross 1968, 174). However, the "overwhelming majority" of British supported suspension of payments (Self 2006, 192).

This body of work establishes that Finance abhors default, while workers are not necessarily opposed to it. To the degree that defaulting on private loans is inversely related to borrowing from private creditors, we can derive actors' preferences: just as financial elites want their government to avoid defaulting on bonds, they are presumably in favor of their government issuing bonds. Conversely, just as workers disapprove of continued debt service and consequently prefer default, workers object to issuing bonds and borrowing from private creditors. For these reasons, Labor has negative preferences with respect to its government borrowing from private creditors.

In sum, I expect both Finance and Industry to have positive preferences with respect to private creditors, while Labor does not. Again, table 2.1 provides a summary of actors' preferences across the four types of creditors.

2.3. Translating Societal Demands into Borrowing Decisions

Having defined the relevant actors and described their preferences across the four types of creditors, we may ask how these interests affect government policy. I start with the assumption that leaders—in both democracies and autocracies—want to remain in office. Because leaders wish to stay in power and rely on the support of domestic actors to maintain their leadership position, leaders want to pursue policies favored by their core societal support groups (Mattes, Leeds, and Carroll 2014; Leeds, Mattes, and Vogel 2009). This allows domestic interest groups to influence government decisions (Moravcsik 1997). Specifically, politicians respond to the demands of the most dominant political groups (Skocpol, Rueschemeyer, and Evans 1985; Schmidt 2009; Bunte and Kim 2017). The approach taken in this book follows Frieden (1991) in assuming that the role of the government is to aggregate the preferences of domestic actors weighted by their relative power and subsequently implement the dominant policy demands. In short, I argue that politicians will listen to the preferences of the dominant societal groups when deciding among competing loan offers.

This approach, however, assumes that ideological beliefs of policymakers are not important causal factors in and of themselves. I recognize that this may be a questionable assumption given that a significant body of work points to the importance of ideas (McNamara 1999; Morrison 2016; Bell 2012; Jacobs 2008). In response, I point to three observations.

First, much empirical evidence suggests that lobbying by societal groups based on their economic interests does exert strong influence over the decision-making process of politicians. For example, the interests and relative strength of interest groups have been found to shape the behavior of politicians with respect to trade policy (Busch and Reinhardt 1999, 2000; Rickard 2014), foreign aid (Milner and Tingley 2010, 2011), and military cooperation (Fordham 1998; Narizny 2003, 2007; Solingen 2009). With respect to the IMF, scholars have shown that domestic interest groups are influential in both creditor (Broz 2008, 2011; Copelovitch 2010) and recipient countries (Nooruddin and Simmons 2006; Caraway, Rickard, and Anner 2012).

Second, besides pointing to existing literature making similar conjectures, I verified these assumptions while undertaking fieldwork in Ecuador, Peru, and Colombia. As will be shown in chapters 4, 5, and 6, interviewees noted examples of leaders who did not have strong preferences themselves and subsequently solicited public opinion surveys on debt repayment prior to making decisions. Furthermore, I encountered situations where foreign and finance ministries had opposing preferences regarding which creditor to use. In such situations, it is not obvious how to evaluate the effect of ideological beliefs. Lastly, the statistical analyses in chapter 9 examines how left-wing and right-wing governments respond to societal interest groups. I find that accounting for government ideology does not significantly affect the results.

Third, and most importantly, even if politicians have their own ideological preferences, my argument still stands. Politicians may be elected precisely because their ideological beliefs represent those of the most powerful interest groups. In such cases, politicians would exhibit strong preferences. However, the selection process—in both democracies and autocracies (Bueno de Mesquita and Smith 2012, 2010; Weeks 2008, 2012)—by which politicians obtain their leadership positions would ensure that these preferences corresponded to those of the most powerful interest groups. In contrast, politicians are likely to be replaced if their preferences differ from those of the politically powerful. In fact, strong evidence points to a close correlation between the ideological positions of politicians and those of their constituencies. For example, Findley, Milner, and Nielson (2017) report only minimal differences between core constituencies and members of parliament in Uganda with respect to preferences across different donor of foreign aid. According to Jameson, Ecuador is another example for the close connection between constituencies and political representatives. Lucio Gutiérrez became president of Ecuador in 2003 after running on a populist, antiglobalization platform. As a consequence, he had the active support of the indigenous movement. Shortly after taking office he went to Washington, DC, and declared himself the United States' "best ally and friend" in the hemisphere. The indigenous broke with him, exited his government within the year, and Gutiérrez was removed from office shortly thereafter (Jameson 2008, 70).

I build on these insights as I develop a theory explaining sovereign borrowing. If societal interest groups lobby politicians for their preferred type of creditor, which interest group will politicians listen to? I follow Johnson and Salop by suggesting that "the choice of policy instruments will be influenced by the political power of various... groups" (1980, 12). In other words, politicians will implement the borrowing preferences of the politically dominant interest groups (Moravcsik 1997; Skocpol, Rueschemeyer, and Evans 1985; Frieden 1991). Importantly, these authors refer to *groups*, that is, to multiple groups. Specifically, considering Finance, Industry, and Labor, I argue that politicians will attempt to satisfy the preferences of two of these groups while ignoring the interests of the third.

There are both supply- and demand-side reasons for expecting that borrowing decisions will address the interests of multiple groups simultaneously. On the supply side, politicians have the incentive to concurrently satisfy the demands of multiple groups. Mahoney and Baumgartner (2015) show empirically that government policymakers respond to the overall structure of conflict, not the resources of individual lobbying groups. "Government actors, thinking about where to invest their resources, may well want to help an individual group. But before leading the charge, they take a careful look at the full range of who is involved" (Mahoney and Baumgartner 2015, 214). Holyoke (2009) and Hula (1999) argue that pressures from politicians require interest groups set aside their differences and support joint positions. The reason is simple: if politicians are seeking office, they have the incentive to implement policies satisfying two groups to maximize support. Drawing on Shepsle (1979), I argue that politicians carefully craft policies that satisfy the demands of multiple societal groups simultaneously. In other words, politicians have incentives to borrow from the type of creditor that satisfies the preferences of two actors at once, allowing them to kill two birds with one stone, so to speak. In this process, politicians aggregate the preferences of various actors. As a result, they think in terms of informal coalitions between the most influential societal groups and subsequently identify a policy that resonates with the interests of both groups. In the case of sovereign borrowing, politicians have an incentive to choose the creditor jointly preferred by the two most important societal groups.

On the demand side, individual groups have incentives to collaborate. As Box-Steffensmeier and Christenson note, "That interest groups coordinate to pursue shared political objectives—thereby forming coalitional networks—is hardly surprising" (2015, 78). Working together in coalition is one of the most common tactics that groups use in attempting to influence policy (Heaney and Lorenz 2013; Schlozman and Tierney 1986; Hojnacki et al. 2012). The reason for coordination among interest groups is fairly obvious. Interest groups turn to coalitions as a mechanism to pool resources (Hula 1999), to demonstrate to policymakers that they have resolved their internal differences and achieved a consensus on a position (Mahoney 2008; Nelson and Yackee 2012), and to aggregate political intelligence (Heaney 2006; Box-Steffensmeier and Christenson 2015; Whitford 2003). Importantly, coalition formation among diverse interests is not unusual (Hojnacki 1997, 61), and coalitions are not limited to ideologically similar groups (Browne 1990). Similarly, coalitions stretching across traditional ideological divides frequently occur (McFarland 1993). For example, Pagliari and Young (2013) show that coalitions between the financial and nonfinancial sectors are common.

Which two groups will shape borrowing decisions? My argument is straightforward: If two groups are more influential than a third, then leaders have the incentive to disregard the weakest actor. As previously noted, leaders think in terms of informal coalitions between the most important societal groups. By identifying creditors that are jointly preferred by both groups, politicians can gain the political support of the most important groups simultaneously.

Before moving on, I want to clarify the terminology used throughout this book: when using the term "coalition," I do not mean a formal coalition. For example, representatives of business and unions will not sign a formal document asking the government to borrow from a particular creditor. Rather, I use the term to describe an informal alignment between interest groups. In this, I follow Whitford (2003), Lowery (2007), and Box-Steffensmeier and Christenson (2015), who argue that scholars should study communities of interest groups that form tacit coalitions. Similarly, Gourevitch and Shinn (2005) focus on informal coalitions between owners, managers, and workers to explain variation in corporate governance of industrialized countries.

In addition, I want to clarify the role of preferences and institutions. Political institutions reflect the impact of preferences on policy outcomes. Yet "political science has for many years been split into two camps, those emphasizing preferences and those emphasizing institutions. Each school holds constant the variance of the other to explore the impact of what they study: Holding preferences constant reveals the power of institutions; holding institutions constant reveals the power of preferences" (Gourevitch and Shinn 2005, 58). I acknowledge that each approach has virtue. Ideally, I would want to explore the interactions of the two variables over time. However, lending by BRICs in significant volumes is a comparatively new phenomenon; in fact, the first BRIC loan larger than US$1 billion occurred only in 2004. Furthermore, borrowing data are only available until 2015. These start and end points show that the time period under investigation is comparatively short. As institutional change is slow, my analysis holds institutions constant to reveal the influence of preferences. However, I address the effect of institutions empirically later on. For example, section 9.4 examines the effect of preferences in different institutional environments. To preview the findings, the effect of societal interest groups persists across regime types (democracy versus autocracies) as well as electoral institutions (proportional representation versus majoritarian systems).

2.4. Capital, Corporatist, and Consumer Coalitions

Politicians have the incentive to implement policies satisfying two groups simultaneously to maximize their prospects of maintaining incumbency. Following Shepsle (1979), I argue that politicians craft policies that satisfy the demands of multiple societal groups simultaneously. In short, I argue that politicians will implement policies that are jointly preferred by two of the three groups. With three actors—Finance, Industry, and Labor—this implies that there are three coalitional possibilities: between Finance and Industry, between Industry and Labor, or between Labor and Finance. This section introduces the three possible coalitions and analyzes which type of creditor the two coalition partners in each coalition jointly prefer.

2.4.1. Capital Coalition: Finance and Industry

2.4.1.1. Characteristics

The coalition between Finance and Industry combines the interests of the owners of capital. Thus, I call this the Capital Coalition. Such a coalition exists when the owners of capital—whether it is mobile or fixed, tangible or intangible—have similar interests contrary to those of noncapital owners. In these countries, Finance and Industry view Labor as just another commodity that is a required input in their production process, ideally at the lowest possible wage, with maximum flexibility in hiring and firing. In contrast, workers seek higher wages, access to healthcare, and unemployment benefits, all of which reduce the profits of Industry and Finance. In short, this coalition is characterized by the class conflict between capital owners and workers.

The theoretical underpinnings of this coalition can be found in the works of Karl Marx. In his view, the interests of individuals are determined by their position in the structure of production. Accordingly, capital owners share interests, which contrast sharply with the objectives of those without access to the means of production. The reason is that the only source of profits for capital owners, surplus value, is the exploitation of workers. Consequently, wages and profits are inversely related. Society is thus divided into classes whose interests are fundamentally opposed. Similar class-based conflict is present in modern economic theories as well. For example, the Stolper-Samuelson theorem suggests a cleavage between capital-intensive goods and labor-intensive goods. The theorem describes the relationship between real wages and real returns to capital as such that if the prices for capital-intensive goods increase, the real returns to capital will increase at the expense of real wages. Consequently, the owners of capital—Finance and Industry—are pitted against the interests of Labor.

2.4.1.2. Examples

Applications of this approach are common. For example, political scientists have used the division between owners and nonowners of capital to analyze the power of societal groups in democracies. Przeworski and Wallerstein (1988) pit workers against capital owners as they analyze whether democracy allows workers to tax capital owners to produce an egalitarian society. Other examples include Rogowski and Kayser (2002), who assume that producers and consumers are mutually exclusive groups. Furthermore, because of the differences in capital ownership, owners and nonowners of capital have unequal access to policymakers. Consumers can contribute only votes while producers can offer both votes and money. The power resource theory by Korpi and Esping-Andersen (1984) focuses on the power of wage earners relative to capital owners in explaining the type of welfare state a country develops. In the area of trade policy, Rogowski (1989) identifies a rural-urban divide as well as a class divide, the latter of which pits the interests of capital owners (either financial capital or landowners) against those of Labor.

This approach has also been used to classify countries. For example, the varieties-of-capitalism literature identifies liberal market economies in which market relations dominate (Hall and Soskice 2001; Pontusson 2005), leading to a weak position of Labor relative to that of capital owners. A different example is Indonesia, which Pepinsky (2008, 447) suggests is dominated by an alliance of mobile and fixed capital. Particularly, under General Suharto's rule, the capital assets owned by the military and indigenous Indonesians were primarily fixed, while Indonesians who were ethnically Chinese provided financing. In many cases, the two groups participated in joint ventures, with the latter providing investment capital and business expertise and the former ownership of physical stock and physical protection. South Korea's industrial development is a different example of a country in which Finance and Industry are allied, while Labor is marginalized. Scholars such as Wade (1990), Amsden (1992), Kay (2002), and Gourevitch and Shinn (2005, 123) identify different ways in which the consumption, wages, and rights of workers were subordinated to the interests of capital owners.

2.4.1.3. Joint Preferences

I derive the preferences of a Capital Coalition across the four types of creditors by aggregating individual actors' preferences. If Finance and Industry agree in their assessment of whether the government should or should not borrow from a particular source, the joint preference will reflect this concurrence. However, if the preferences of Finance and Industry are contradictory, the joint preference of the coalition will be undecided with respect to that borrowing option. The resulting joint preferences of the Capital Coalition are shown in table 2.3.

A Capital Coalition approves of IFI loans. Industry is undecided with respect to the distributional consequences it can expect from the macroeconomic conditions attached to these loans. Finance, in contrast, stands to benefit from reduced inflation and increased efforts toward capital account liberalizations.

Table 2.3 **Distributional consequences by coalition**

		IFI loan	DAC loan	BRIC loan	Private loan
Capital coalition					
	Finance &	+	+	−	+
	Industry	0	−	+	+
	⇒	+	0	0	++
Corporatist coalition					
	Industry &	0	−	+	+
	Labor	−	+	+	−
	⇒	−	0	++	0
Consumer coalition					
	Finance &	+	+	−	+
	Labor	−	+	+	−
	⇒	0	++	0	0

Note: The table illustrates how the preferences of individual interest groups are aggregated to arrive at the joint preferences of a coalition between two interest groups. For example, a Corporatist Coalition exists when Industry and Labor are the strongest interest groups, dominating Finance. If both Industry and Labor agree in their assessment of whether the government should borrow from a particular source, the joint preference will reflect this. However, if their preferences are contradictory, the joint preference of the coalition will be undecided with respect to this borrowing option. For this reason, a Corporatist Coalition prefers BRICs.

Taken together, the preferences of Industry and Finance indicate that Capital Coalitions welcome IFI loans. However, this coalition exhibits an even stronger preference for private loans. In this case, both Industry and Finance can expect to benefit. Private loans tie the survival of the domestic financial sector to the well-being of the government, increasing the likelihood of a bailout should it be needed. In addition, Industry's ability to raise capital increases if the government successfully places bonds. In contrast, Capital Coalitions do not have a strong preference for or against BRIC loans. Industry is positively inclined toward the additional investment projects attached to BRIC loans because they offer subcontracting opportunities. In contrast, Finance dislikes the external competition, which may crowd out the domestic financial sector as a source of investment finance for domestic projects. Considering the contrasting individual-level preferences of Industry and Finance, the joint preference of the Capital Coalition is ambivalent about BRIC loans. This is also the case for DAC loans, albeit with reversed signs. Industry dislikes the good-governance conditions attached to DAC loans, as they hinder industrial policies. In contrast, Finance is interested in an increase of transparency and accountability. Their joint preference with respect to DAC loans is also undecided. I show in chapter 5 that Colombia can be characterized as a Capital Coalition.

2.4.2. Corporatist Coalition: Industry and Labor

2.4.2.1. Characteristics

It is intuitive to position the capital owners, Industry and Finance, in opposition to Labor. Yet we do not always observe a conflict between capital owners and workers, as Industry and Labor have friendly relationships in some countries. In cases where workers and manufacturers are dependent on mutual cooperation for common goals, such as advancing technological innovations or productivity, the interests of Labor and Industry are quite complementary. Under certain circumstances, the two actors exchange courtesies: Labor restricts the use of strikes or slowdowns in return for guaranteed participation in Industry's decision-making process. In return for labor peace, Industry vows job security and reasonable wages. In these instances of mutual cooperation, Industry and Finance form a Corporatist Coalition.

The theoretical foundations for these cross-class alignments between Industry and Labor are found in both economics and political science. In economics, the main challenge to the Stolper-Samuelson theorem arises from the Ricardo-Viner theorem. The latter questions the assumption of perfect factor mobility between sectors, which Stolper-Samuelson assumes. Instead, the approach by Ricardo-Viner emphasizes the possibility of so-called specific assets that cannot easily be reallocated in response to market conditions. In these instances, workers and owners of these specific assets have compatible interests in the face of economic uncertainty. Industry wants to protect its investment in physical capital, while Labor wants to ensure that asset-specific human capital continues to be valuable. In the words of Gourevitch and Shinn (2005, 152), in these countries "Workers may join their bosses and owners in political efforts to shelter 'their' sector and 'their' firm." Confronted with these contradictory explanations, scholars such as Hiscox (2002) have explained under which conditions class-based conflicts or cross-class alignments dominate.

The concept of skill complementarity also features prominently in the analysis of different types of economies. From the perspective of workers, individuals who have invested in industry-specific skills want protection from an eventuality in which these skills are no longer useful (Iversen and Soskice 2001). This line of argument has been used to explain the historic compromise that emerged in several countries after World War II, which combined a mixed economy, a welfare state, and government regulation of labor markets. This approach can also explain instances in which firms did not perceive workers as a threat but rather as partners. Mares (2003) argues that large firms supported the introduction of employment insurance in France and Germany. Similarly, Swenson (2002) shows that the economic development of Denmark and Sweden was not characterized by clashes between classes, but by a cross-class alliance in the sectors that were most exposed to trade and competition.

2.4.2.2. Examples

Applications of approaches that allow for cooperation between Industry and Labor are common. For example, trade protections are explained by the common interests of Labor as voters and Industry as employers. Busch and Reinhardt (1999) argue that firms employing workers in many districts are more likely to get trade protection, as workers vote according to their (and their firms) interest. The varieties-of-capitalism approach also emphasizes that a subset of countries is characterized by an informal coalition between Industry and Labor. Hall and Soskice (2001) and Pontusson (2005) show that coordinated market economies are characterized by strong complementarities between Industry and Labor as evidenced by vocational training systems, specific skills, and mutual veto possibilities in the production process.

There are many examples where scholars have used the cross-class alignments between Industry and Labor to classify countries. Gourevitch and Shinn (2005) classify Japan as a Corporatist Coalition, as workers and managers are united in joint efforts against shareholders.

A different example of a Corporatist Coalition is Uruguay, which has a mixed economy and a pluralistic democracy that incorporates a broad range of business and labor groups (Buchanan 2008; Klimovich and Thomas 2014). Uruguayan unions have traditionally cooperated with domestic capital in coalitions supporting import substitution and rejecting neoliberal policy proposals (Grassi 2014). Another example is Malaysia, which in Pepinsky (2008) has been characterized by a coalition between fixed capital and workers. Since independence, the democracy has been governed by a coalition of three ethnic parties. As a consequence, successive governments have implemented policies aimed at ethnic Malays, irrespective of class. One example of the cross-class economic policies is the New Economic Policy implemented in the 1970s and 1980s and the New Development Program in the 1990s. These programs were developed to consolidate the societal support for the ruling parties, which included constituencies as diverse as teachers and public servants as well as the Malay business class. At the same time, they aimed to marginalize ethnic Chinese Malaysians, who primarily owned mobile capital. The economic policies included heavy industrialization and state-led development, resulting in a range of Malay businesses with fixed assets and workers in support of these new industries. In contrast to Indonesia's alliance between fixed and mobile capital, Malaysia's political system therefore rests on a cross-class coalition of Industry and Labor defined through Malay ethnicity. Later in this book, I argue that Ecuador represents such a Corporatist Coalition (see chapter 4).

2.4.2.3. Joint Preferences

I derive the preferences of a Corporatist Coalition by combining the individual preferences of Labor and Industry. If both Labor and Industry prefer or reject a particular creditor, the joint preference will reflect this consensus. However, if their preferences are contradictory, the joint preference of the Corporatist Coalition will be undecided. Table 2.3 illustrates that the combination of Industry and Labor into the Corporatist Coalition results in different joint preferences than exhibited by the Capital Coalition in section 2.4.1.

Corporatist Coalitions dislike IFI loans. As Industry is ambivalent toward this creditor, Labor determines the joint preference because of its strong opposition to the macroeconomic conditions attached to these loans, which typically hurt workers and the poor. In contrast, the coalition prefers BRIC loans. Industry benefits from subcontracting opportunities that arise from the investment projects attached to these loans, while Labor embraces the employment opportunities that come with these projects. The Corporatist Coalition does not have strong preferences for or against the use of private creditors. Industry welcomes the signal of an improved business climate, but Labor does not prefer private creditors, as workers typically do not benefit from these securities. Similarly, DAC loans are neither preferred nor rejected by the Corporatist Coalition. Labor welcomes the emphasis on social expenditure, while Industry detests the transparency and good-governance criteria that might open the markets to Western competition.

2.4.3. Consumer Coalition: Labor and Finance

2.4.3.1. Characteristics

Of the three possible combinations, the coalition between Finance and Labor appears the least probable. Intuition suggests that more often than not, the interests of Finance and Labor are contradictory. After all, shareholders often seem to benefit from firms firing workers in the name of efficiency. In contrast, strikes can send stock prices plummeting. Yet there are instances where the interests of Labor and Finance are aligned.

For example, both Finance and Labor dislike inflation, though for different reasons. Inflation devalues the financial assets of Finance, as it decreases the purchasing power of monetary resources. The money Finance owns and works with will be worth less over time if inflation is rampant. Similarly, Labor dislikes inflation, as it lowers workers' real wage. Even if the dollar amount on their paycheck remains stable, inflation increases prices and consequently reduces the purchasing power of nominal wages. In contrast, the primary type of asset owned by Industry is unaffected by inflation. In situations of high inflation, the overall objectives of Finance and Labor overlap.

In addition, the interests of Finance and Labor can align in countries where they are each other's best customers. This reasoning applies in countries where banks' financial services are primarily aimed at domestic citizens. For example, when citizens are dependent on remittances or the use of microcredits is widespread, Finance is a natural ally for Labor and vice versa. Because of these characteristics, I call the informal coalition between Labor and Finance a Consumer Coalition.

The theoretical underpinnings for this alignment can be found in the literature examining the behavior of banks. The main distinction is that between countries with concentrated banking sectors dominated by a few large banks, and other countries characterized by a multitude of small banks, resulting in a decentralized banking sector. Kroszner and Strahan (1999) and Pagano and Volpin (2001) argue that small banks behave differently than large banks. In a decentralized banking sector, small banks have every incentive to resist deregulation since it increases the likelihood of takeover by larger banks. Instead, they want to lobby for existing regulations to protect their local markets. In short, where banks depend on individuals and small customers, Finance favors cooperation with Labor; in contrast, large banks in countries with concentrated banking sectors prefer collaboration with Industry.

The research on corporate governance, in turn, indicates that the motivations of Finance and Labor are sometimes complementary. For example, if controlling shareholders exist, they want low investor protection to extract larger private benefits of control. These shareholders need electoral support to obtain the legislation providing such benefits. Pagano and Volpin (2005b) show that in these situations, Finance is willing to make concessions to Labor, such as limits on the right to fire workers. Finance and Labor therefore strike a political agreement whereby workers trade low shareholder protection for high job security, which enables both social groups to preserve their rents. In additional work, Pagano and Volpin (2005a) show that workers can be natural allies of Finance in hostile takeovers. If the threat of a hostile takeover exists, Finance can offer workers long-term labor contracts. As the potential new owner of a firm will be unable to renegotiate these contracts, the higher wage level reduces the firm's attractiveness to competitors. In these situations, Labor will also align itself with Finance.

After all, workers have an incentive to protect their high wages and will lobby policymakers against approving the takeover. In short, there are instances in which the interests of Finance and Labor are aligned.

2.4.3.2. Examples

The coalition between Finance and Labor may not be as intuitive as the alliance between capital owners against workers or alignments between Labor and Industry.

Nevertheless, scholars have used this coalition to characterize countries. For example, Gourevitch and Shinn (2005, 228) show that the interests of Finance and Labor are aligned in Chile. On the one hand, shareholders were excluded from the decision-making process of the industrial conglomerates that dominated the Chilean economy. They were eager to support corporate governance reforms that demanded more accountability and transparency from Industry, which would allow them to better protect their investments. At the same time, prior pension reforms under Pinochet resulted in the unusual case of workers holding a significant portion of shares. The multitude of individual owners and the resulting collective action problems made direct supervision of companies difficult. Workers therefore also had an incentive to restrain Industry. Gourevitch and Shinn (2005) show that the informal coalition between Finance and Industry was the driving force behind the corporate governance reforms in Chile. I argue that Peru is characterized by a Consumer Coalition between Finance and Labor (see chapter 6).

2.4.3.3. Joint Preferences

The joint preferences of a Consumer Coalition are marked by a strong preference for DAC loans from Western bilateral creditors. Labor prefers DAC loans because of their emphasis on social expenditure such as education and health. Finance is attracted to DAC loans thanks to their good-governance requirements for increased transparency and accountability. In contrast to the strong joint preference for DAC loans, a Consumer Coalition does not exhibit strong partiality for or against either of the other creditors.

Labor welcomes BRIC loans, as additional investment projects promise jobs, but Finance disapproves of this creditor, as it represents external competition in the field of investment finance. Given these contradictory preferences, the joint preferences of the Consumer Coalition are undetermined with respect to BRIC creditors. The same is the case for IFI loans. Finance would be pleased by the imposition of macroeconomic conditions requiring low inflation and a balanced budget, while Labor is wary of these conditions, as they typically hurt workers. Lastly, the Consumer Coalition is internally divided on private creditors as well. Interest payments on bonds represent a resource transfer of tax revenues to bondholders. Since these payments flow to bondholders, while Labor represents the taxpayers paying for these transfers, the former favor this redistribution, while Labor opposes it. Consequently, a Consumer Coalition does not exhibit a strong preference for or against private creditors.

2.4.4. Resulting Hypotheses

Table 2.3 summarizes how the preferences of each coalition partner relates to the joint preferences of each coalition. The Capital Coalition between Finance and Industry has a strong joint preference for loans from the private market, as both actors individually prefer this option. IFI loans are preferred over bilateral loans from DAC or BRIC countries, but not as strongly favored as private creditors. In contrast, the Corporatist Coalition exhibits a strong joint preference for BRIC loans, as both Labor and Industry favor this creditor. At the same time, this coalition has a strong aversion to IFI loans. DAC loans and private loans are jointly neither liked nor disliked, as the coalition partners have contradicting individual preferences. Lastly, the Consumer Coalition shows a strong joint preference for DAC loans, while being indifferent to IFI, BRIC, and private creditors.

It is important to stress that these joint preferences indicate which coalition *on average* tends to prefer what type of creditor. I do not suggest that a particular coalition will never borrow from a specific creditor. However, I do argue that—on average—countries characterized by a particular coalition will tend to favor the jointly preferred creditor over other lenders.

The resulting composition of total new borrowing should therefore reflect the tendency to utilize one creditor to the detriment of the others. I argue that the type of social coalition present in a country can explain the composition of new loans acquired in a particular year. As a result, I hypothesize the following:

Hypothesis 1: Corporatist Coalition
Governments in countries characterized by a Corporatist Coalition between Labor and Industry prefer borrowing from BRICs more than do governments in countries characterized by other coalitions. At the same time, when making borrowing decisions, these governments are more likely to dismiss loan offers by traditional creditors, in particular IFIs.

Hypothesis 2: Capital Coalition
Governments in countries characterized by a Capital Coalition between Finance and Industry prefer borrowing from traditional creditors and

exhibit an aversion to BRIC creditors. In particular, such countries favor private creditors and IFIs.

Hypothesis 3: Consumer Coalition
Governments in countries characterized by a Consumer Coalition between Finance and Labor prefer borrowing from traditional creditors. In particular, these countries favor DAC loans.

2.5. Synopsis and Next Steps

My theory suggests that borrowing decisions by governments can be explained by analyzing the distributional consequences of different loans across societal actors. I identified Finance, Industry, and Labor as the relevant societal groups and defined their overall objectives. I then analyzed the preferences of these actors across different types of creditors by connecting the overall objectives of these groups to the characteristics of the loans by different creditors. I subsequently examined the coalitions these groups can form to advance their goals. Lastly, I identified the joint preferences of these coalitions to hypothesize under which conditions the government has the incentive to use which type of creditor.

The following chapters provide evidence for the argument that borrowing decisions are political decisions. I present both qualitative and quantitative evidence. Chapters 3, 4, 5, and 6 present insights drawn from several months of fieldwork in Ecuador, Colombia, and Peru. In these chapters, I trace the political process by which governments arrive at borrowing decisions and show how societal interest groups exert strong influence over the choices of politicians. Chapters 7, 8, 9, and 10 present quantitative evidence suggesting that the effect of societal groups on borrowing decisions can be generalized to all developing countries.

PART I

QUALITATIVE EVIDENCE

3

Tracing the Process of Borrowing with Fieldwork

My theory follows the open economy politics (OEP) approach (Lake 2009). This paradigm uses economic reasoning to deduce what types of individuals can be reasonably assumed to share identical interests. Having defined the relevant unit of analysis, OEP then derives preferences over alternative policies from the distributional implications of different economic choices (Lake 2009, 225). Subsequently, actors are assumed to lobby policymakers to ensure politicians make decisions in their favor (Grossman and Helpman 1994).

In following this approach, I make a number of assumptions. For example, I assume that the distributional effects of different loans are sufficiently large and "knowable" to allow Finance, Industry, and Labor to coalesce along interest-based lines. This appears to be a perfectly reasonable assumption—and, in fact, a large literature takes it as a given. However, I acknowledge that this approach is not uncontroversial. Specifically, critics have raised two objections.

First, scholars have questioned the existence of exogenous preferences. OEP assumes that actors derive their preferences from their position in the market. Consequently, actors in the same position hold the same preferences. However, this may not be the case. For example, experimental evidence reveals that individuals may not have a good understanding of how trade policies affect them; instead, their preferences depend on how issues are framed (Rho and Tomz 2017; Naoi and Kume 2011; Hiscox 2006). Concerning debt, experimental evidence indicates that partisan cue-taking shaped individual-level preferences over settling Argentina's sovereign debt dispute (Nelson and Steinberg 2018). These findings suggest that the connection between actors' positions in the economy and their preferences may be shaped by factors other than economic theory (Crystal 2003). Specifically, preference formation might rely on a logic of social embeddedness (Woll 2015, 2008) by which sets of causal beliefs shape the process of preference formation (Laffey and Weldes 1997; Sikkink 1991; Goldstein 1988; Goldstein and Keohane 1993).

As these beliefs differ across individuals, their preferences depend on factors that influence these beliefs (Hafner-Burton et al. 2017; McNamara 1999). As a result, the translation of economic position into preferences can be shaped by dispositions rooted in emotion (Lu, Scheve, and Slaughter 2012; Mansfield and Mutz 2009), social psychology (Sabet 2016), and even genetic differences (Guisinger 2016; Burgoon and Hiscox 2004; Goldstein, Margalit, and Rivers 2008).

Second, scholars have pointed out that individuals' preferences are, at times, inconsistent with their "objective" material interests. For example, Sikkink (1991) shows that Argentine industrialists opposed developmentalist politics that would have meant significant material benefits for them. She explains that industrialists interpreted their interests with reference to the government's accommodating policy toward Peronism. As a result, they saw the state's industrial policies as part of an overall package that threatened, rather than helped, business. With respect to trade policy, Vogel (1999, 187) shows that Japanese consumer groups have repeatedly advocated policy positions that result in higher prices and fewer choices. One explanation is that in the prevalent narrative, citizens see themselves primarily as income-earners concerned with jobs rather than consumers concerned with prices (see also Naoi and Kume 2011, 2015). Similarly, Ahlquist, Clayton, and Levi (2014) show that US workers socialized in a particular labor union exhibited trade preferences that were inconsistent with their "objective" material interests. Concerning FDI, Li and Zeng (2017) find that skill level does not always predict preferences for or against foreign investment, even though economic theory suggests that highly skilled workers benefit from such investment.

These insights raise potential difficulties for my theory. After all, I assume that societal actors are able to translate their material position into preferences in a straightforward manner: For instance, I assume that workers do not care for loans from the IMF because Labor owns no assets and thus does not benefit from conditionalities limiting inflation.

Furthermore, I assume that societal groups' preferences are consistent with their material interests: Labor prefers loans from emerging creditors like the BRICs because workers materially benefit from job opportunities at new investment sites. How does my theory relate to these critiques?

Importantly, the critical works summarized above acknowledge that the degree to which individuals have clear, exogenous, and articulate preferences may differ across issue areas. For example, McNamara (1999, 462) suggests that individuals find it especially difficult to form clear preferences with respect to monetary policy, which is fairly abstract, but find it easier to discern their preferences regarding other areas of economic activity. I argue that government debt is one issue area in which individuals can relatively easily derive their interests. Empirical evidence supports this assertion. For instance, survey evidence from Iceland suggests that individuals do have a good understanding of how government debt affects their material interests (Curtis, Jupille, and Leblang 2015). Experimental evidence suggests that Argentinean citizens evaluate their government's borrowing activities in ways that are consistent with the economic consequences (Tomz 2004). In both cases, individuals have clear preferences that are consistent with their material interests.[1]

In addition, some work suggests that citizens do not need complete information to form preferences consistent with their material interests. For example, Jensen and Lindstädt (2013) show that individuals use cognitive shortcuts if they find it difficult to assess the personal costs and benefits of globalization. These appear to be remarkably accurate. For instance, US citizens correctly identify the expected benefit from incoming FDI—for example, in terms of domestic job creation—when considering the country of origin as a cognitive shortcut. Lupia (1994, 65) shows that in the context of referenda on insurance reform in California, voters were able to use the identity of information providers to choose a position on the issue consistent with their own interests even in the absence of much information. In addition to cognitive shortcuts, recommendations from trusted political parties, interest groups, the media, colleagues, and friends allow badly informed individuals to emulate the behavior of better-informed citizens (Fordham and Kleinberg 2012, 321). This line of argument about the indirect influence of economic interests is similar to what Popkin (1994, 7) calls "low-information rationality." For example, Scheve and Slaughter (2001, 43) argue that voters combine rudimentary political knowledge acquired in the course of daily life with information gathered from publicity during a campaign to select candidates who reflect their preferences.

In sum, this discussion reveals two factions, each with reasonable arguments: OEP critics rightly point out that the translation of material conditions into preferences may not be straightforward. OEP defendants often acknowledge the difficulties in this translation, but suggest that they are not as great as commonly assumed since individuals use cognitive shortcuts and informational cues. Furthermore, because most people understand the material consequences of government debt, debt policy may be an area where these criticisms do not apply. Where to go from here?

---

[1] With respect to foreign aid—an issue area related to sovereign borrowing—citizens also seem to have little difficulty translating expected material consequences into preferences. Findley et al. (2017) and Milner, Nielson, and Findley (2016) show that citizens do have an understanding of how aid will affect them vis-à-vis government spending. Scholars have produced similar findings with respect to a range of public goods (Kim and Bunte 2018).

3.1. Why Fieldwork?

In my view, this debate is ultimately an empirical question. Lake (2009, 232) suggests that "the question is not whether OEP or any other theory accurately captures all aspects of the real world, but what empirical regularities are missed or perhaps incorrectly estimated by the particular theoretical simplifications employed." In this spirit, Vogel asks,

> Should political scientists abandon all models that define group interests in strictly economic terms? I am not suggesting such abandonment. As noted at the outset these models can be parsimonious and powerful. And, in any case, defining interests in terms of economic theory can be a useful first step in political analysis. But to establish a causal link from group interests to policy outcomes we need to determine that groups actually bore the assumed preferences, that they acted upon these preferences, and that their actions influenced outcomes. Establishing a causal link requires empirical verification. (1999, 202)

To the issue of whether a theory's assumptions are accurate, Crystal (2003, 419) notes, "The problem is not insuperable. One could gather more detailed information about the actor, which might lead to a more precise delineation of its policy preference." This is precisely why I undertook fieldwork. Instead of simply making assumptions about societal interests, I sought to verify these assumptions empirically. I spent several months in Ecuador, Peru, and Colombia to speak with business men and women, labor representatives, members of parliament, bankers, industrialists, union members, senators, factory workers, even former prime ministers. With these interviews, I intended to accomplish three objectives.

First, I wanted to verify the assumptions my theory makes with respect to actors' preferences. Do individuals hold preferences across different creditors? If so, are these preferences consistent with their material interests? Interviews provided answers to these questions.

For example, when a high-level executive of an Ecuadorian investment bank stated that the Chinese "take advantage of you," it is reasonable to assume that this actor has negative preferences with respect to this creditor. Conducting fieldwork in multiple countries (rather than a single nation) also allowed me to verify whether groups' preferences were identical across countries. For example, interviews would reveal whether the preferences of Labor in Ecuador are the same as the preferences of Labor in Peru or Colombia, and so on. In short, fieldwork would provide "causal process observations" confirming that representatives from each group espouse the preferences regarding creditors that are deduced in the theory.

The second objective was to verify the hypothesized process by which preferences are translated into borrowing decisions. Do politicians listen to societal actors? Do they have an incentive to act upon these preferences? Do they have the ability to affect borrowing decisions? Conducting fieldwork allowed me to trace the process by which preferences are translated into borrowing decisions. For each country, I first analyzed what type of societal coalition dominates the political landscape. Interviews then illuminated how politicians respond to the interests of the dominant social groups. Analyzing the process of borrowing decisions revealed whether politics can shape borrowing decisions or if these decisions are merely technocratic choices. Again, conducting fieldwork in multiple countries allowed me to verify whether the process of translating preferences into political decisions is similar across countries.

The third objective of fieldwork was to establish a plausible explanation for the variation in outcomes across countries. If my theory is correct, the case studies would demonstrate a correlation between coalition type and the composition of debt portfolios. While the statistical analysis in later chapters will verify that this relationship also exists in a larger sample of cases, these quantitative models use blunt proxies for coalitional strength. Qualitative analysis would allow a more nuanced analysis of how countries' borrowing decisions relate to societal interests.

3.2. Rationale for Case Selection

I pursued these objectives with several months of fieldwork. The case selection was guided by methodological concerns. First, the cases would need to be similar in as many ways as possible. Such similarities constitute ceteris paribus conditions and thus allow the elimination of some alternative explanations. After all, the quality of the causal inference would be compromised if I were to compare an autocracy characterized by a Corporatist Coalition to a democracy dominated by a Capital Coalition. If the former country borrows more heavily from China than the latter, we would not know whether this difference is explained by the type of coalition or the type of government—after all, autocratic governments might be more likely to borrow from a similarly autocratic China than democracies, just as Corporatist Coalitions might be more likely than Capital Coalitions to use Chinese loans. I need to compare two democracies—one characterized by a Capital Coalition and another by a Corporatist Coalition—to show that the type of coalition is associated with distinct borrowing behavior. If the creditors these two democracies use do not differ, then the type of coalition does not explain the outcome. However, if these two democracies do use different creditors, then it is possible to confidently conclude that the type of coalition matters while holding regime type constant.

Ecuador, Peru, and Colombia offer an almost ideal setting for fieldwork, as they share a number of characteristics. In terms of *politics*, these three countries are established democracies, not autocracies. Moreover, these countries all have presidential democracies. With respect to *economics*, all three countries are characterized by a capitalistic system allowing free enterprise. In addition, Ecuador, Colombia, and Peru all have significant natural resources. In terms of *geography*, these neighboring countries are the same distance from China and other potential creditors. They also all have direct or indirect access to the Pacific,[2] and all have mountainous terrain. In regards to *history*, three countries were Spanish colonies. They also share many *cultural* traditions. Ecuador, Colombia, and Peru share Spanish as the official language, and are all primarily Roman Catholic. I recognize that differences exist between Ecuador, Colombia, and Peru; however, they are minor in comparison to the differences between, say, Bangladesh and Bulgaria. For the purposes of this study, these three countries do not vary significantly. Any differences in observed borrowing behavior therefore cannot be explained by differences in their political systems, economic endowments, geographic position, historical legacy, or cultural values.[3]

In contrast, these countries *do* differ with respect to the type of dominant coalition. Importantly, the relative strength of the relevant interest groups differs in ways that mirror the hypothesized variation in the independent variable. The popular sector in Ecuador is strong in comparison to capital owners. Since the mid-1990s, social movements, such as the indigenous movement, environmentalist groups, and labor groups, have become a visible presence in Ecuadorian domestic politics. They have demanded a stronger voice in the political process

---

[2] In the case of Colombia, the port Buenoventura may not be viable, but ships have easy access via the Panama Canal, which is only a short distance away.

[3] While geographical similarity has the advantage of creating ceteris paribus conditions, it also has a disadvantage: Given that Ecuador, Colombia, and Peru are all located in South America, one may wonder whether the argument travels to other regions. I have two responses. First, the policymaking process in these countries is not significantly different from that in other countries. The key components of my theory—the presence of interest groups and their desire to influence government policies—is similar across developing countries. Similarly, the available evidence suggests that the loan conditions attached to loans offered to Ecuador, Colombia, and Peru do not differ from the loan conditions creditors attach to offers to African or Asian countries. Second, I conduct an extensive statistical analysis in later chapters to analyze whether my argument applies to a larger set of countries. Moreover, I conduct several robustness tests examining whether the influence of societal coalitions differs across democracies and autocracies, left-wing versus right-wing governments, countries in economic crisis versus not, and so forth. I find that the influence of societal coalitions on borrowing portfolios exists across many different settings.

ever since. In contrast, Colombia is characterized by an absence of civil society representation, particularly labor or social movements. This is partly because of the civil war, during which left-leaning societal groups were labeled terrorist factions, preventing an institutionalized movement of labor and civil society. In addition, two strong political parties, both representing the domestic elite, dominate the political landscape.

Lastly, the situation in Peru falls somewhere between these two extremes. While Labor and other groups were repressed during the Fujimori regime, the liberal policies implemented were consistent with the existing strong interests of Finance. Yet, despite its prominence in domestic politics, Labor has not necessarily resisted this neoliberal agenda since Fujimori's demise. Given these backgrounds, Ecuador, Colombia, and Peru represent the three types of coalitions that I argue are the drivers behind borrowing decisions: Ecuador approximates a Corporatist Coalition in which Labor and Industry are strong, Colombia a Capital Coalition in which Finance and Industry are powerful, and Peru a Consumer Coalition in which Finance and Labor are politically powerful.

As a result of the ceteris paribus conditions and the variation in the key independent variable, these cases allow me to test, while controlling for several potential alternative explanations, whether societal interest groups have a causal effect on borrowing decisions. The borrowing portfolio of these countries differs significantly. As shown in figure 3.1, Ecuador borrows more from BRICs than does either Colombia or Peru. In contrast, Colombia obtains more loans from

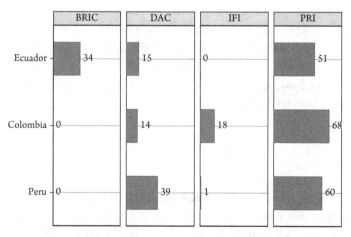

Figure 3.1 Borrowing portfolios of Ecuador, Colombia, and Peru. Note: The figure shows that of these three countries, Ecuador borrows more from BRICs than either Colombia or Peru. In contrast, Colombia obtains more loans from private creditors than the other countries. Lastly, Peru borrows more from Western creditors than either of its neighbors. Data come from the World Bank's internal DRS database. More information on the source is available in section 8.1.

private creditors than the other countries. Lastly, Peru borrows more from Western creditors than does either Ecuador or Colombia. If my theory is correct, we would expect the differences in societal coalitions—should they exist—to be correlated with the variation in borrowing decisions.

My qualitative study focuses on the years from 2005 through 2011. BRIC loans of considerable size are a relatively recent phenomenon, as the first BRIC loan larger than $1 billion was made by China in 2004. Hence, I begin my analysis at the time when Ecuador, Colombia, and Peru could first have received large BRIC loans. The end point is determined by the fact that I undertook fieldwork in 2011.

3.3. The Interview Process

3.3.1. Interview Partners

I conducted 112 interviews with a wide range of elite actors. First, I spoke with representatives of Labor, Industry, and Finance. I conducted interviews with bankers, factory owners, and union representatives. Through these conversations, I verified the theoretical expectation regarding which type of actor—Finance, Industry, or Labor—hopes to benefit from which type of loan. Second, I interviewed politicians and bureaucrats. Among elected officials, I spoke with prime ministers, finance ministers, and senators; among bureaucrats, I had conversations with bureaucrats working in public debt departments, planning departments, and finance ministries. These interviews shed light on how politics shapes borrowing decisions in these countries. Lastly, I spoke with creditors. I interviewed representatives of multilateral institutions (IMF, IBRD, and IDA) as well as German, American, French, and Chinese lending organizations. I also interviewed Chinese officials, both from the public sector (Chinese Development Bank, Chinese embassies) and from the private sector (Chinese commercial banks, Chinese mining companies).

3.3.2. Recruitment Process

Gaining access to elites presents a particular challenge. Traditionally, obtaining interviews with nonelites is understood to require a sympathetic understanding of the subject. For instance, Taylor and Bogdan (1998) suggest that interviewers should be attentive to their "superior" position in society relative to that of the typical subject. Accordingly, interviewers should avoid being perceived as patronizing.

Elite interviews present a different challenge: "The issue is rather a matter of proving one's professional credentials and standing. Researchers must demonstrate they are worthy of the time and support of busy and often powerful individuals" (Welch et al. 2002, 612). In other words, researchers only "get in and get useful data from them if [the researchers] know others that [elites] know and respect" (Ostrander 1993, 12).

I followed the advice of Peabody et al. (1990) and Richards (1996) to present myself as a credible interviewer by obtaining institutional affiliations in each country. I was affiliated with the Universidad de los Andes in Bogotá, Colombia. In Peru, I worked with the Centro de Investigación at the Universidad del Pacífico in Lima, and in Ecuador with the Universidad de San Francisco in Quito. These affiliations gave me initial contacts with public and private actors. In addition, several former high-level officials were on staff at these institutions, providing a starting point for subsequent "snowballing," allowing me to expand the set of interviewees beyond my initial contacts. Lastly, I cold-contacted potential interviewees whose contact information I obtained from United Nations and IMF conference attendance lists or the websites of respective institutions.

3.3.3. Interview Setting

The vast majority of interviews were conducted face-to-face at the workplace of the interviewee. Meeting elites at their offices introduces a particular sensitivity with respect to the power dynamics between interviewee and interviewer. In nonelite settings, the interviewer is assumed to have higher social status (Taylor and Bogdan 1998, 111). The issue may be different when interviewing elites. In addition, since elites are typically accustomed to public speaking, whether on behalf of their organizations or themselves, elite interviewees often dominate the interview. They are "used to addressing a wide range of audiences and developing elaborate and persuasive arguments; they are used to taking command and being deferred to; and they are confident that their opinions are deserving of attention and respect" (Welch et al. 2002, 612). Because of this imbalance, scholars suggest that researchers risk "overestimating the importance of what elites have to say, assuming, for example, that they necessarily know more and better what is going on in an organization" (Ostrander 1993, 19). Researchers may therefore attribute causality to elites where none in fact exists (Welch et al. 2002).

This is a serious issue. To address it, I opted for the following approach. If I conceptualized the relationship between the elite subject and myself as competitive, I might have been forced to "fight back" in order to seize control. However, rather than understanding interviews as an aggressive battle for control, I treated them as an opportunity for learning. Delaney describes this approach:

> I accept the fact that the interviewee will act as a spokesperson, may treat me as status subordinate, and may try to control the interview. Given these tendencies, how can I best gain what I need from the interview?... I have no problem assuming the role of someone who needs to learn something (after all, that is the essence of interviewing). In fact, being a "status subordinate" can be turned to an advantage in that it allows you to say in a very non-threatening way, "I don't really understand that, can you explain..." (Delaney 2007, 215)

In addition, I interviewed a variety of elites in different positions—Finance, Industry, Labor, domestic government, and foreign creditors. This multitude of sources allowed me to triangulate information obtained from a single elite subject, as recommended by Berry (2002). In addition, some scholars have cautioned that the responses by elites may leave the researcher disappointed, as subjects may assume the role of a "spokesperson" (Ostrander 1993) for the organization or institution. However, this would only be a problem if I were interested in the feelings and interpretations of the interviewee. In this case, my theory suggests that the leaders of societal interest groups should act on behalf of their constituencies, so the "spokesperson" concern did not resonate with my experiences in the field. In fact, I was surprised at how frank many of the responses were. This corresponds to the pattern noted by Sinclair and Brady (1987), who observed that the level of frankness was directly related to the interviewee's seniority: The higher in the hierarchy, the more candid the statements.

3.3.4. Interview Method

The interviews were semistructured and open-ended. Structured interviews ask the list of questions in exactly the same order with most questions only allowing a closed response. Semi-structured interviews give the subject the opportunity to expand on questions in whichever way they see fit, while keeping the set of questions consistent across interviewees (Huit and Peabody 1969, 28). While this approach makes it more difficult to directly compare the interviews as the order of questions may differ, I agree with Aberbach and Rockman (2002) that the advantages of the conversational depth of the responses outweigh the disadvantages of inconsistent ordering. After all, an open-ended approach gives interviewees the opportunity to organize their answers within their own frameworks and thus increases response validity. In addition, as alluded to previously, elites are typically confident speakers, accustomed to dominating discourse. As such, they "do not like being put in the straight-jacket of closed-ended questions" (Aberbach and Rockman 2002, 674).

The process by which I arrived at the set of questions was also shaped by the particularities of elite interviews. Since the time available in interviews with elites was generally short, I had to limit the number of questions I asked. I generally proceeded by asking the most important questions first. In addition, I started with the factual questions and moved to more judgmental-oriented queries later on. I also ran pilot interviews with Colombian academics to test the time it took to administer the interview, and to experiment with the wording and ordering of different questions (see Peabody et al. 1990). By the end of this process I arrived at three sets of interview questions for each subject type: Government officials of the recipient country, representatives of the domestic interest groups (i.e., Finance, Industry, and Labor), and representatives of external creditors.

I also chose to focus my questions on China rather than all BRICs, for several reasons. First, Chinese lending volume is significantly larger than that of Brazil, Russia and India. It is therefore most reasonable to assume that the Chinese would have offered loans of substantial size to Ecuador, Colombia, or Peru. As larger loans are easier to track down, interview partners are more likely to remember them. This facilitates fieldwork by increasing the chances of learning about instances of accepted or rejected loan offers. Second, research prior to entering the field provided additional evidence suggesting that China was an active presence in these countries. For example, at the time of my fieldwork, the Chinese Development Bank maintained offices in Ecuador, Colombia, and Peru. In contrast, the lending institutions of Russia, India, and Brazil did not have a physical presence in every country. For this reason, my focus on China addressed the possible confounding factor of unequal loan supply.

Lastly, the lending conditions of Brazil, Russia, and India are extremely similar to those of China. They prefer providing loans attached to specific investment projects but do not require political reforms or macroeconomic conditions. This allowed me to focus on Chinese loans rather than BRIC loans without loss of generality.

In terms of formalities, I asked each interviewee at the beginning of our conversation if he or she wanted to conduct the interview in English or Spanish. Most of the time, English was preferred, as it is the professional language of elites. I then asked whether I had permission to quote the interviewee by name. Lastly, I asked whether I had permission to record the audio of the interview. Before asking the first substantive questions, to alleviate any trust issues I stressed that the interview was for academic purposes only. In addition, I shared my background as an academic, a German citizen, who was educated in the United Kingdom, worked in the United States, and was interviewing in Latin America about China. This signaled that I did not have any business interests but was genuinely interested in the topic as an academic pursuit.

3.4. Preview of the Qualitative Evidence

Chapter 4 presents the findings from Ecuador, chapter 5 from Colombia, and chapter 6 from Peru. The structure within each chapter is largely similar. I first analyze what type of coalition dominates the political landscape in the respective country. I then analyze the preferences of the dominant societal actors across the different loan options. Next I investigate whether politicians are responsive to societal demands. I subsequently scrutinize the formal process of contracting loans to examine whether politicians can influence borrowing decisions or if they are merely the result of technocratic procedures. Lastly, I discuss the resulting borrowing decisions.

The qualitative evidence strongly supports the argument that differences in societal coalitions explain the variation in borrowing portfolios.

Labor and Industry dominate the political landscape of Ecuador. At the same time, the domestic financial sector is underdeveloped. For these reasons, Ecuador represents a Corporatist Coalition. Labor has strong aversion to multilateral loans as a result of negative experiences of IMF programs in the late 1990s, and to bonds as a result of several corruption scandals. Both Labor and Industry favor Chinese loans, as they offer employment and subcontracting opportunities. Politicians are responsive to the demands by the Corporatist Coalition. Interviews revealed that President Correa uses surveys to capture public opinion and caters to Labor with events such as televised debt audits. Statements by government officials are in line with Industry and Labor demands, as they emphasize the positive effects Chinese loans have on industrialization. The resulting borrowing decisions therefore reflect the desire of politicians to satisfy both Labor and Industry. Ecuador prefers borrowing from BRICs, while Western creditors are disdained.

Colombia, in turn, represents a Capital Coalition. Finance and Industry are the dominant actors, with strong ties to the political establishment. In addition, the civil war with left-wing violence discredited Labor and repressed political expressions by workers. Industry wants to avoid increased competition from Chinese manufacturers and construction companies, while Finance dislikes the competition from external creditors for domestic investment. Politicians can satisfy both groups simultaneously using high political hurdles for budget loans and separate bidding processes for funding and execution of projects. As a consequence of discriminating against tied loans, Colombia does not borrow from China and instead relies heavily on private creditors.

Peru exemplifies a Consumer Coalition. The drastic neoliberal reforms by Fujimori effectively destroyed domestic Industry. Nevertheless, the reforms were successful in creating growth, macroeconomic stability, and physical security. This resulted in Labor being unusually inclined toward market-oriented, proconsumer policies. At the same time, Finance survived the "Fujishock," but increased foreign competition forced the domestic financial sector to withdraw from the business of funding large-scale projects and instead focus on their comparative advantage in local knowledge. For this reason, Finance primarily serves individual savers and entrepreneurs. Politicians satisfy the two groups with actions that appeal to both. This results in proconsumer policies in the areas of procurement and trade, with announcements of (but not necessarily follow-through on) projects. With respect to creditors, Peruvian officials do not disparage Chinese loans but are not partial toward them. Instead, Peruvian borrowing decisions favor bilateral loans from Western governments and private creditors.

4

Ecuador

A Corporatist Coalition Chooses BRIC Loans

The summary of borrowing portfolios presented in figure 3.1 suggests that Ecuador relies on loans from emerging creditors such as Brazil, Russia, India, and China (the BRICs) more heavily than does either Colombia or Peru. In contrast, Ecuador obtains significantly fewer loans from the private sector. Existing work suggests that supply-side considerations might explain these differences. For example, Zettelmeyer and Sturzenegger (2007) and Porzecanski (2010) argue that Ecuador's history of default causes private creditors to be hesitant to offer new loans. However, these supply-side considerations must be complemented by a demand-side perspective. As Mansell and Openshaw (2009, 34) observe with respect to Ecuador, "The harm assumed to have been inflicted on the country's ability to borrow may prove less damaging than at first thought."

I examine politics in Ecuador to gain insights into why the government chose to borrow from BRICs rather than private creditors. Should my theory be correct, we would expect Ecuadorian politicians to prefer borrowing from BRICs to satisfy the demands of a Corporatist Coalition between Labor and Industry. This chapter presents the qualitative evidence examining whether this is the case in Ecuador. I proceed in several steps. First, section 4.1 determines what coalition dominates the political landscape in Ecuador. I argue that the Ecuadorian government faces a Corporatist Coalition of Labor and Industry. Section 4.2 provides insights into the preferences of societal actors in Ecuador. I show that the preferences of these groups closely align with the theoretical predictions summarized in table 2.1. The borrowing decisions of politicians should correspond to the preferences of that coalition. Section 4.3 shows that politicians attempt to garner support by appealing to the interests of Labor and Industry. Section 4.4 outlines the process of contracting loans in Ecuador. It illustrates that politicians strongly influence borrowing decisions. Lastly, I provide details on the resulting borrowing portfolio. In sum, there is strong evidence that politicians respond to societal coalitions when deciding which creditor to use.

4.1. The Coalition: Labor and Industry Dominate

A Corporatist Coalition between Labor and Industry dominates Ecuador's political landscape, while domestic Finance is comparatively marginalized. There are several reasons for this state of affairs. Labor has held a comparatively strong position in the economy ever since the military government carried out social reforms and established the Codigo del Trabajo (Labor Code) in 1925 along with a variety of other social reforms. This code provided Labor with both workers' rights and a political voice (Interview 99).

Roughly at the same time, domestic industry began to organize into institutionalized associations such as chambers of commerce (Interview 105). It is noteworthy that a multitude of small companies rather than a handful of large firms characterize the industrial landscape. Interviewees noted that this is likely a function of geography. While there are two major population hubs—Guayaquil and Quito—they together account for less than 50% of the Ecuadorian population (Interview 101). In addition, the capital, Quito, is located within an area of farmland. Thus, farmers and other fixed-capital owners gained influence within the corporatist structure that developed (Interview 96). Due to their comparatively long tradition and humble beginnings, the resulting industry associations tend to represent a multitude of smaller to medium-sized companies rather than a handful of large firms.

These developments in the early twentieth century suggest that Ecuadorian society has been characterized by a corporatist structure since the 1940s (Interview 96). This structure shaped state-society relations in Ecuador and resulted in a decentralized political arena with a multitude of actors. In contrast, Peru and Colombia have fairly centralized political systems (Interview 79).

This tendency was strengthened in the 1970s. The oil boom during this decade created a comparatively large middle class of well-educated workers (Meléndez 2007; Pachano 2009; Paramio and Hopenhayn 2010). Yet their interests were closely aligned with those of domestic industry. The middle class was created quite rapidly, in contrast to that in Peru and Colombia, where it grew more slowly (Interview 105). The new actors were acutely aware that their class was directly tied to industrial success.

The return to democratic rule in the early 1980s meant political opportunities for many of these actors, and the newly created middle class demanded political representation. New groups, such as the Democratic Left (Izquierda

Democrática) and the Democratic People's Movement (Movimiento Popular Democrático) appeared on the political scene. However, the end of the oil boom translated into increasing fiscal constraints, which severely limited the opportunities for cross-group redistribution, upon which the stability of the corporatist system depended (Interview 96). The resulting competition between different political factions discredited the political parties. One interviewee stated that after democratization, citizens first tried to make their voices heard through available political parties, but citizens became increasingly disappointed with the options available (Interview 101). One observer noted that parties developed into conglomerates, with each party strongly linked to its own media companies and bank. He was not surprised that citizens lost their faith in political parties (Interview 98).

The financial crisis in 1999 further discredited the traditional parties (Interview 101) and revealed them to be instruments of the oligarchy (Interview 99). In addition, a former finance minister noted that the financial crisis was an opportunity for different social groups "to get their act together" (Interview 91). Social movements—in particular, the indigenous movement (Interview 95)—were relatively weak until the end of the 1980s, but they began to openly protest in the 2000s (Interview 101). As social movements gained strength, it became possible that new coalitions among societal elements such as mestizos (i.e., Ecuadorians of mixed African, European, Arabian, and indigenous descent) and the indigenous would also align with Labor and Industry (Interview 91).

For this reason, social movements appeared as a viable alternative to the established political parties (Interview 96). Consequently, the electorate began to vote for people and movements rather than parties. The first example is the 2003 election of Lucio Gutiérrez, the candidate of the January 21 Patriotic Society Party (Partido Sociedad Patriótica 21 de Enero), named for the date of the protest in 2000. He proposed an alliance with the indigenous Pachakutik Plurinational Unity Movement (Movimiento de Unidad Plurinacional Pachakutik—Nuevo País). He was elected on a platform against Finance, promising the reversal of neoliberal reforms and a fight against corruption. However, it appears that Gutiérrez's reasons for catering to the interests of Labor and Industry were opportunistic, as he broke the alliance and continued the neoliberal reforms of his predecessor. His government thus quickly lost legitimacy (Interviews 90, 101).

The election of Rafael Correa and his Proud and Sovereign Fatherland Alliance (Alianza Patria Altiva y Soberana—Alianza PAIS) in 2006 can be seen as a natural progression of these developments. It further contributed to the degeneration of the established parties that catered to traditional constituencies, continuing the tendency to support broader social movements that included diverse stakeholders. While this diversity might have hampered the ability to organize around common goals, interviewees stated that the proposals of the intellectual leadership went beyond demanding goods for their own narrow clientele only (Interview 98). Observers noted that the primary social forces in Ecuadorian politics are social movements, while the dominant social forces in Peru and Colombia are the "big companies" (Interview 90).

Ecuador's political landscape is characterized by a wide range of institutionalized associations, such as chambers of commerce and small unions, as well as a variety of noninstitutionalized movements (Interview 105). Civil society has a comparatively large voice in the political arena because it was able to insert itself into the well-established corporatist structure of state-society relations (Interview 96). There is "more space for a multitude of actors to participate in the political process because of this corporatist structure" (Interview 95).

The degeneration of institutionalized parties and rise of broader movements meant that Ecuadorian "governments were more receptive to popular demands" (Interview 96). The political spectrum on the left includes both producers and workers and is a powerful force in society (Interview 77). These coalitional dynamics, along with a political environment characterized by a multitude of veto points, have been used to explain a variety of economic outcomes. For example, Pachano (2007) argues that the implementation of neoliberal reforms failed because of these veto points.

While Labor and Industry dominate the political landscape in Ecuador, Finance is marginalized. This is a result not only of the political developments already described, but also due to the lack of a developed domestic financial sector. Interviewees noted that competitor stock markets in Bogotá, Lima, and Santiago de Chile are merging their stock exchanges to compete with the established stock markets in São Paulo and Mexico City. In contrast, Ecuador has two small stock markets—Quito and Guayaquil—that are "completely separate and not integrated at all" (Interview 79).

4.2. The Preferences: Labor and Industry Favor Chinese Loans

I have established that Ecuador's political landscape is dominated by a Corporatist Coalition. What creditors does this coalition between Industry and Labor prefer? According to my theory, both Industry and Labor are expected to favor BRIC loans. In contrast, they should dislike loans from international financial institutions (IFIs). However, Labor and Industry have contradictory preferences concerning bilateral loans from Western governments (DACs) and private creditors: while Labor prefers DAC loans and Industry does not, the opposite is true for private lenders. As a result, the coalition should not have strong opinions for or against these creditors. This section examines whether the stated preferences of the groups align with these theoretical expectations.

4.2.1. IFIs

In the interviews, representatives of the Corporatist Coalition expressed strong opinions against multilateral loans from IFIs. Several interviews with Labor officials emphasized that prior IMF programs had undermined the productive capacity of their country, which, in turn, made repayment of debt even more difficult (Interview 100). A former finance minister noted that in the aftermath of the financial crisis in 1999, both Labor and Industry believed that IMF policies undermined Ecuador's productive capacity. The conditions of the IMF program were thought to have contributed to the bankruptcy of three million businesses and the emigration of 20% of the productive population (Interview 91). The interviewee was therefore not surprised that political movements demanded employment and investment instead of IMF-imposed austerity measures. In short, the political establishment that implemented neoliberal reforms was discredited in the aftermath of the crisis (Interview 96). The preferences of Labor and Industry were evident. Labor was interested in increasing the levels of domestic investment to create employment opportunities. Industry was tired of austerity measures that undermined efforts to increase public investment.

4.2.2. BRICs

In contrast to multilateral loans, BRIC loans are viewed favorably. Chinese loans offered necessary funds without mandating neoliberal reforms similar to those implemented after the financial crisis. Moreover, Labor representatives did not seem worried about the employment effects of Chinese companies but rather encouraged the additional investment that comes with these loans but not necessarily with Western bilateral loans.[1] Their views echoed the findings of the studies on the localization of labor by Chinese companies cited in section 2.2.

Industry representatives noted several reasons for their preference for BRIC loans.

---

[1] To be sure, there have been protests by Labor against foreign companies, which included Chinese firms. For example, in 2012 protests erupted in the province of Zamora-Chinchipe and resulted in a march toward Quito. However, protesters were primarily concerned about the environmental impact of open-cast industrial copper-mining concessions granted to both Chinese and Canadian companies, not their employment effects.

First, Industry representatives indicated that they were not concerned about Chinese companies crowding out their business. I asked whether Chinese loans put Ecuadorian companies at a disadvantage if they require that a Chinese company execute the project. For example, Ecuador borrowed $1.7 billion from China to construct the Coca Codo Sinclair hydropower dam. The loan required that a Chinese company construct the dam, resulting in the Ecuadorian government awarding the contract to Sinohydro, a Chinese state-owned company. However, virtually all interviewees denied that Ecuadorian companies are disadvantaged by such requirements, because there are no Ecuadorian firms that have the capacity for such massive projects (Interview 89). For this reason, "There are no losers" among domestic industries (Interview 101).

Instead, several interviewees noted that domestic companies welcome the additional investment funded by Chinese loans because they expect to get "part of the cake" (Interview 89). These projects result in subcontracting opportunities that would not have been available otherwise (Interviews 79, 86, 87, 92, 101). It is important to note the sharp contrast with Industry's opinion of Western companies. While Western companies also create subcontracting opportunities, people affiliated with domestic industries believe that the Chinese are tackling projects that Western companies have been unwilling to take on. For this reason, BRIC loans are welcomed because they mean more actual subcontracting opportunities, not just a replacement of Western companies by Chinese firms.

The third reason Industry has a positive attitude about loans by the BRICs is that such creditors offer loans tied to specific projects. A representative of an Ecuadorian bank that usually finances investment undertakings by domestic industry stated that companies are actually quite happy to work with the Chinese. Because the loans are tied, the prices are not "right" (i.e., set by market standards) due to the lack of a competitive bidding process. Thus, "Ecuadorian subcontractors are actually paid quite generously by the Chinese" (Interview 87). This has positive effects on Industry's profit margins.

4.2.3. DACs

In contrast to the positive preferences for BRICs, an Industry representative notes Industry's antipathy toward DAC loans. One reason is Industry's desire to benefit from government industrial policy. Some interviewees mentioned that good-governance conditions "overprotected foreign investors" (Interview 95). For example, one business representative complained that import taxes do not sufficiently protect certain industries (Interview 103). These are precisely the taxes that Western governments would like developing countries to remove. Thus, several respondents welcomed Ecuador's decision to renounce investment protection treaties with Western governments. After all, allowing these companies to sue the Ecuadorian government or domestic firms in foreign courts puts Ecuadorian companies at a disadvantage, as they lack the resources to adequately represent their interests. In contrast, the Chinese, according to interviewees, do not insist on investor protection clauses that give them a legal advantage over domestic companies.

4.2.4. Private Creditors

Labor has negative preferences concerning private creditors. In Ecuador's recent past, debt rollovers were managed so poorly that observers were certain of corruption (Interview 98). This impression was heightened when videotapes, leaked in February 2007, showed Ecuador's minister of the Treasury Ricardo Patiño and his adviser, Héctor Égüez, meeting with Carlos Abadi and Alan Dayan. The latter two work for Abadi & Company, an American firm that specializes in renegotiating foreign bonds of poorer countries. Armando Rodas, the former Ecuadorian minister of the Treasury, arranged and attended the meeting. At the meeting, the businessmen appeared to suggest that the government should announce its refusal to pay $135 million in interest on private bonds. The resulting panic would allow insurance companies to increase their profit, as the value of their contracts with debt-holders would multiply. While it was claimed that subsequent stock market transactions would save Ecuador about $150 million, public outrage over the leaked videos—the so-called *pativideos*—was immense. Needless to say, these events did not improve Labor's opinion of private creditors. Furthermore, interviewees in Ecuador repeatedly mentioned that private creditors have contributed to the country's economic problems by demanding high interest rates (Interview 91).

4.2.5. Preferences of Finance

The preferences of Labor and Industry align well with the theoretical expectations. Is this also the case for Finance, the actor dominated by the Corporatist Coalition? If my theory is correct, Finance should exhibit negative preferences toward BRIC loans and favor instead IFI, DAC, and private creditors. Did the interviews with representatives of Finance confirm these expectations?

Ecuadorian members of Finance had negative views of BRIC loans. They believed that BRIC loans caused more competition for domestic Finance. Recall that loans from BRIC creditors are often tied to specific investment projects and require the debtor to use companies from the creditor country to execute the project. Chinese loans are viewed as a "door opener" to secure investment concessions and contracts for public works projects. Several interviewees noted that these loans were the reason oil concessions and contracts for hydropower projects were given to Chinese companies (Interviews 86, 92). A former finance minister noted that this is the case because the Chinese "can demand whatever they want" (Interview 91). A high-level executive of an Ecuadorian investment bank added that "they grab you by the [expletive deleted] and take advantage of you." From the perspective of domestic financial firms, there is reason to worry that BRIC loans will crowd out their services. After all, domestic Finance was formerly the primary source of funding for domestic investment projects. Domestic firms now face increased competition by an external and financially potent creditor that might replace them in the long run. A banker voiced his outrage that the general population does not view the Chinese conditions critically: "I am angry because of the kinds of conditions that the Chinese impose, and that the government is willing to accept. I am angry that my people don't realize this" (Interview 102).

In contrast, Finance in Ecuador would have preferred loans from DACs, IFIs, or the private capital market. Financial firms had a favorable attitude toward DACs because of their past experience with Western actors. While good-governance conditions could very well increase competition for domestic financial institutions, Finance nevertheless prefers competition by Western companies over competition from firms of emerging creditors. "I prefer the evil that I know over the unknown" is a saying that I encountered frequently during my interviews with financial actors. An Ecuadorian business representative stated, "I love the Chinese, but I fear them because I saw what they are capable of. It is scary if you are in the hands of China. If I would have to choose hands, I would probably choose the US because I know them" (Interview 103).

Interviews in Ecuador also revealed Finance's strong preference for loans from multilateral institutions. In particular, loans from the IMF were viewed in a positive light. Financial experts noted that the conditions attached to multilateral loans are advantageous, for two reasons. First, conversations with actors in the financial sector revealed their preferences for loan conditions that aim to improve the macroeconomic stability of an economy. Interviewees stressed that the neoliberal conditions attached to IMF loans typically reduce inflation, which in turn preserves the value of their assets. An Ecuadorian business representative stated, "It is better to sign with the IMF, even if you disagree, instead of shouting 'imperialism.' Having more unemployment in your country because of your five minutes of pride is not worth it" (Interview 103). Second, the financial conditions of IFI loans are often unrivaled. In one instance, Ecuadorian financial experts voiced their frustrations with the Ecuadorian government using available resources to pay off its IMF loans early instead of repaying other creditors. Logically, if a government wants to reduce its debt burden, it should use available resources to repay the most expensive loans first and hold on to low-interest rate loans. Ecuador therefore should have held on to IMF loans, since they have relatively low interest rates (Interviews 92, 93).

Lastly, representatives of Finance agreed that the Ecuadorian government had treated private creditors unfairly. Even though Ecuador's global bonds required a higher interest rate than other debt, financial experts condemned the decision to default on these bonds. The interviewees noted that there was no economic necessity for default at that time, as Ecuador's debt stock was relatively moderate. The ratio of external debt to GDP was about 30%, and the annual debt service obligations amounted to about 1.5% of GDP, which is considered acceptable. One representative remarked, "From a financial point of view, there was no reason to default. This was only done to satisfy an ideological dream. They [the government] defaulted because they believe that debt is something evil that keeps developing countries underdeveloped" (Interview 92).

4.3. The Politicians: Responsive to Labor and Industry

Interviews in Ecuador revealed that the preferences of Labor, Industry, and Finance closely resemble their hypothesized interests in table 2.1. In the case of Ecuador, Labor and Industry dominate Finance. As a result, politicians should be particularly sensitive to the demands of a Corporatist Coalition. I interviewed Ecuadorian politicians to examine whether this is the case.

In a first step, it is necessary to clarify whether Labor and Industry have access to politicians. Interviewees agreed that the corporatist structure of the political economy allowed Labor and Industry to insert their voice into the political process. Moreover, interviewees repeatedly noted that societal groups used the opportunities to express their views with respect to which creditor they would prefer (Interview 89).

With respect to workers, interviewees noted that the financial crises of the 1990s provided an opportunity to organize effectively. Different societal groups belonging to the class of Labor "got their act together," such as the coalition between the mestizos and indigenous (Interview 91). United by their negative experience with IMF policies, these groups organized a social movement that resulted in Correa's election and a new constitution. Importantly, Labor used the chance not only to convey general messages but also to express views on specific issues such as foreign debt (Interview 89).

Similarly, Industry has access to politicians. Interviewees commented that the political landscape of Ecuador is characterized by a wide range of industry associations and chambers of commerce with networks (Interview 105). In sum, observers noted the corporatist character of Ecuador's political economy, where the interests of Industry and Labor dominate the political discourse (Interview 96).

Second, even if groups have access to politicians, are they responsive to demands from constituencies? The qualitative evidence collected in Ecuador suggests that this is the case. Politicians in Ecuador, for example, are sensitive to the demands of Labor. A member of the constitutional assembly told me that President Correa strongly relies on surveys among workers to design policy initiatives. For example, prior to officially announcing his candidacy in 2005, Correa used surveys to learn more about the main concerns of the electorate. He consequently built his electoral campaign around issues such as foreign debt to maximize his electoral chances (Interview 101).

In addition to actively gathering information on preferences of citizens, politicians chose targeted communication strategies. For example, interviewees noted that Correa ensured his voters—Labor—understood that he was listening to them. This affected how he communicated with his constituencies. For example, an investigation into the legitimacy of external debt began in 2007, about nine months after Correa's electoral victory, after significant social pressure (Interview 91). The final report was presented live on television. An interviewee noted, "It was more of a circus, and less of an investigation. [Correa] had a big show presenting this report. I have it on tape if you should want to watch it" (Interview 87). In addition, interviews clearly indicate that politicians consciously choose communication strategies directed at Labor. An anecdote about the *pativideos* mentioned in section 4.2 reinforces this point. Recall that this meeting was arranged by Armando Rodas, who invited Ecuador's minister of the Treasury, Ricardo Patiño. The latter secretly filmed this meeting and subsequently used the videos to discredit Western creditors as corrupt. An interviewee with intimate knowledge of this process told me that Armando Rodas and Ricardo Patiño met in a televised talk show after the incident. During a commercial break, Patiño supposedly told Rodas, "I know that you are a good guy, but this is politics" (Interview 103), adding to the notion that Correa's government behaved opportunistically to capitalize on existing sentiments among the population.

In a third step, the qualitative evidence should also establish that Ecuadorian politicians specifically respond to Labor and Industry. After all, demonstrating that societal groups have access and that politicians are responsive to constituencies are necessary, but not sufficient, conditions for my argument to hold in Ecuador. The qualitative evidence suggests that while politicians very much favor Labor and Industry, they alienate Finance.

4.3.1. Politicians Appealing to Labor

The interviews with government officials noted that the political leadership listens to the demands of Labor. A government official in the Department of Public Debt in the Finance Ministry noted that the government needed the political force to implement promised constitutional and legal changes. Yet this was not possible while the IMF was involved in policymaking. While an IMF loan would have provided needed resources, the political costs were far too high for the government to pursue it (Interview 97). A former minister of finance concurred, stating that IMF policies were extremely unpopular among citizens because IMF conditions were perceived to have undermined Ecuador's productive capacity and employment opportunities.

By moving away from the IMF, the government was merely responding to the demands of powerful social movements to reorder priorities (Interview 91). A high-ranking official in the Coordinating Ministry of Economic Policy went a step further and considered the overall implications of creditors' conditions and the functioning of the economy. He stated that Ecuadorians believe that owners of capital should also consider social development. Responding to this sentiment, the interviewee noted that the government advocates for a different way to distribute value. It is not that they do not want to achieve growth, but they want to distribute it more equally. The Ecuadorian government wants to support a broader basis of economic actors, rather than just a handful of large companies as in Colombia (Interview 78).

Ecuadorian academics agreed that government officials are responding to Labor's concerns. One interviewee mentioned that Correa ran an electoral campaign emphasizing nonrepayment of debt in order to prioritize spending on education and health. Consequently, Correa paid off the IMF because he wanted to avoid the macroeconomic audits and thereby "avoid the IMF telling him what to do" (Interview 89). Private bankers also understand that their government is responding to social pressures. One interviewee summarized the government's position on Western loans with the following words: "The government stated that 'our economic model was compromised by these conditions. There are huge social costs'" (Interview 87). Another banker pointed out that it is only the IMF and Western conditions that governments want to avoid. "[They] don't have anything against multilateral institutions as such, as they continue to borrow from the CAF [a regional multilateral institution]" (Interview 82).

As a consequence, Correa has expressed concern for workers even in private conversations with US officials. The US Embassy in Quito noted in a cable, "In just one specific example, the [the previous government] planned significant reductions in personnel in order to reduce budget outlays on salaries. Correa has announced that there will be no personnel reductions as, 'with unemployment at 12%, reducing government employment would be irresponsible'" (US Embassy in Ecuador 2005a).

4.3.2. Politicians Responding to Industry

Interviews with high-ranking government officials also suggest that politicians recognize the preferences of Industry. When interviewing a top-level official of the National Secretariat for Planning and Development (Secretaría Nacional de Planificación y Desarrollo, SENPLADES), it became clear that the government mirrors the statements made by Industry representatives in other interviews. In particular, he agreed with Industry that IMF loans might not be ideal if industrialization of the domestic economy is a policy objective. Sharing Industry's perspective, he emphasized that he did not expect negative distributional consequences from Chinese loans, even if they require the use of Chinese companies (Interview 94). Interviews with other government officials revealed the same logic. A high-ranking executive of the National Institute of Procurement (Instituto Nacional de Contratación Pública, INCOP) stated that Chinese loans were chosen because Ecuadorian companies receive subcontracting opportunities that would otherwise not be available (Interview 104).

Moreover, Chinese loans are understood as assisting Ecuadorian efforts to further industrialization. One government official defended the practice whereby Ecuador does not require a competitive bidding process when procuring goods from the public sector—which includes state-owned enterprises from China. "There is a sense that Ecuador needs to level the playing field: When big [Western] firms come to Ecuador, domestic companies do not stand a chance" (Interview 104). He argued that Ecuador uses this policy to emulate the industrialization strategies of Korea described in Ha-Joon Chang's book *Kicking Away the Ladder* (2002). Korea directed investment by forcing domestic companies to focus on specific sectors using financial incentives.

In contrast, Ecuador picks projects in specific sectors and uses Chinese companies, knowing that domestic companies will want to serve as subcontractors. This results in domestic firms shifting their business portfolios toward sectors favored by the government. The official's department produced a Spanish translation of a paper entitled "Public Procurement as an Industrial Policy Tool—An Option for Developing Countries?" (Kattel and Lember 2010). The interviewee recognized that this practice amounts to a particular type of protectionism. However, "The United States did protect itself as well [when in the process of industrialization]. Thus we do the same. After all, we need time to develop and become strong enough [to compete]" (Interview

104). A former negotiator for the Ecuadorian government confirmed that the government highly valued the ability to pick partners without a competitive bidding process. "There was a lot of fight about this when we negotiated the FTA with the Andean countries and the US" (Interview 103). In particular, Ecuador wanted to retain this policy option, while the United States insisted that procurement processes rely on competitive bidding. In the end, Ecuador was the only Andean country that did not sign the treaty with the United States.

Significantly, Correa did not oppose capitalism. North quotes Correa describing his presidency in clearly nonsocialist terms: "Basically we are doing things better within the same model of accumulation, rather than changing it, because we do not want to harm the rich; but it is our intention to have a more just and equitable society" (cited in North 2013, 113). To be sure, Ecuador's business community is more fragmented, and some industries were initially skeptical of Correa (Bowen 2014). However, according to Wolff (2016, 133), business-government dialogue, which picked up quickly in 2008, has gradually evolved into a stable pattern.

4.3.3. Politicians Alienating Finance

While politicians listen to the demands by Labor and Industry, they also recognize that their rhetoric and policies are alienating Finance. According to an official of the National Secretariat for Planning and Development, "The rich are not happy, as they don't know China. They [would] rather have relations with the US or Europe" (Interview 94). Specifically, the relationship between the Correa government and Ecuador's private banks has been characterized by tensions or outright confrontation (*América Economía* 2012). Wolff (2016, 129) notes that "Correa did not openly confront 'the economic elite' as such, but instead his discourse included attacks targeted against the financial or banking sector (as opposed to the productive sector), against those economic conglomerates that he depicted as concentrating too much economic power and manipulating public opinion (usually involving banks that also owned private media outlets), and against 'speculative' and 'corrupt' practices (again, usually seen as characterizing banks)." As a result, the banking sector has faced both repeated criticism from the government and continuing measures of state regulation (Alvaro 2014; Conaghan 2013; Weisbrot, Johnston, and Lefebvre 2013).

Interviewees in the Ecuadorian financial sector, in turn, recognized that their interests are not represented. Private Ecuadorian bankers lament that the government listens to the interests of social movements—such as the anti-debt movement Jubileo 2000—rather than Finance. After all, "The Jubileo 2000 group are crazy people" (Interview 87). A banker noted that the government thought that "the Chinese were 'Brothers in arms,' but [the government] has not realized that the Chinese are behaving like capitalists like everybody else" (Interview 87). A Peruvian businessman had just returned from a visit to Ecuador, where he had spoken with his partners, most of whom are in the financial sector. He reported that they were "depressed" because "they feel that Correa is somewhat of a nut" (Interview 55).

4.3.4. Is Correa Responding to the Public, or Is the Public Following Correa?

The qualitative evidence so far suggests that societal groups have preferences and that politicians respond to these preferences. In other words, Correa followed the cues of societal groups. However, an alternative interpretation of developments in Ecuador could reverse the direction of causality: It may be that Correa did not merely ride an already existing anti-American wave but instead stirred it up himself in formulating policy. Indeed, a small number of interviews support this interpretation. With respect to the strong sentiments against Western creditors, an investment manager stated that President Correa introduced these ideas to the population (Interview 86). According to the director of marketing for a major wholesaler, it was only after considerable efforts and advertisement that people began to identify these policies as being in their interest (Interview 84). In a more moderate statement, a former congressman noted that the general population was aware of debt as a political issue, but it was not a top priority. Rather, in his opinion, debt was only a major concern for a small circle of academics forming the core of the Jubileo 2000 movement. He believed that debt only became a larger societal issue after Correa made it a top priority (Interview 92).

However, the weight of the evidence suggests that Correa exploited the existing preferences of societal groups instead of creating new interests. Three sets of facts support this interpretation. First, anti-Western sentiments existed in Ecuador long before Correa came to power. In the 1990s, Ecuadorian governments—faced with economic crises and IMF conditions—implemented a series of neoliberal policies in line with the Washington consensus (Hey and Klak 1999; Larrea and North 1997). Among other things, these reforms cut social sector spending (Conaghan 2008; Lucero 2001; Chase 2002). In response, popular movements rose up in protest against neoliberal policies (Jameson 2010; Yashar 2005). Almeida (2007) quantifies the participation in anti-neoliberal protests in Latin America between 1995 and 2001. He ranks Ecuador first in the number of arrests, second in the number of protest campaigns, third in the number of protest events, and fourth in the number of deaths and injuries. Protests continued in the 2000s. Even Ronald

McDonald statues in front of American fast-food restaurants became the target of attacks (Choudhury 2005; Al Shebil, Rasheed, and Al-Shammari 2011).

> In one of the largest protests against structural adjustment measures in August 2003, petroleum workers marched the streets of Quito, joining many other sectors dissatisfied with the neoliberal policies of President Lucio Gutierrez. Representatives of CETAPE depicted privatization by using puppets symbolizing the "marriage" of convenience between the Ecuadorian government and the International Monetary Fund (IMF). As they described, this was "la boda del anõ" ("the wedding of the year"), one that enriched some but kept the majority of Ecuadorians poor. (Valdivia 2008, 467)

As a result, Gamso (2015, 116) notes, "Prior to Correa's election, coalitions of civil society groups representing labor, indigenous people, and other special interests had conducted well-coordinated protests in response to the Washington Consensus reforms of the late 1990s and the 2000s." Importantly, these mobilizations significantly influenced Ecuadorian politics. Protests against neoliberal reforms resulted in the removal of elected presidents—Abdalá Bucaram in 1997 and Jamil Mahuad in 2000 (Gerlach 2003).

Second, Correa was not the first presidential candidate in recent history to appeal to anti-Western sentiments. Correa's predecessor, Lucio Gutiérrez, became president of Ecuador in 2003 after running on a populist, antiglobalization platform (Jameson 2008). As a consequence, he had the active support of the indigenous and other social movements. However, he too was removed from office in 2005. "Shortly after taking office he went to Washington, D.C. and declared himself the U.S.'s 'best ally and friend' in the hemisphere" (Jameson 2008, 70). Given his betrayal of campaign promises, the indigenous broke with him and exited his government within the year. In the words of Gamso (2015, 116), "These protests demonstrated the power of civil society groups to obstruct the political process and prompt political change and pressured Correa to discontinue the neoliberal policy approach." This sequence of events indicates that Correa followed existing sentiments, rather than creating them in the first place.

Furthermore, Correa was not the first Ecuadorian president to consider loans from non-Western creditors. For example, in 2005, protests in the oil-producing regions of Sucumbíos and Orellana causes losses of more than $400 million in government revenues. At the same time, $200 million in debt payments became due in October. As it was not clear how Ecuador could meet all its obligations, President Palacio considered an offer by Venezuela's president Hugo Chávez to purchase $500 million in Ecuadorian bonds (US Embassy in Ecuador 2005b, 2005c). While this particular loan did not materialize, Ecuador has obtained loans from non-Western creditors in the recent past. For example, facing demands by the World Bank to privatize water in exchange for loans, then-president Sixto Durán Ballén—a member of the right-wing Republican Unity Party—obtained loans from China (1993 and 1994), Brazil (1996), and South Korea (1996). Similarly, President Gustavo Novba, a member of the center-right party Popular Democracy, obtained at least one loan from Brazil in 2000.

Third, there is direct evidence that Correa exploited existing preferences rather than creating new ones. Several interviewees noted that the electorate already preferred to reject Western loans and choose BRIC loans and that President Correa capitalized on this. A former minister of finance noted that citizens had a strong sense of what they wanted: "Public opinion definitely came first" (Interview 91). Correa only made debt a top priority of his government because it was already a top priority among the population (Interview 102). For example, a strong societal movement by the name of Grupo Nacional contra la Deuda that included Jubileo 2000 as well as academics, demanded debt cancellation and withdrawal from Western creditors (Interview 89). Others add that the negotiations of the various debt rollovers were done so poorly that the public believed there must have been some corruption (Interview 98).

Interviewees suggest that Correa subsequently capitalized on these existing sentiments (Interview 96). As previously noted, interviewees stated that Correa created his policy platform only after fielding a significant number of public opinion surveys (Interview 101). In fact, interviewees pointed out that the name of Correa's newly founded movement, Alianza PAIS, attempts to capture the sentiments of the population: PAIS stands for "Patria Altiva y Soberana" (Proud and Sovereign Party), indicating that the emphasis on Ecuador's sovereignty with respect to foreign creditors was essential from the inception of the party (Interview 102). The presence of a strong anti-imperialist discourse meant that Correa's rhetoric fell on fertile ground and that he did not have to fear electoral backlash by choosing Chinese loans—which are comparatively expensive—over Western loans (Interview 77).

Scholars agree that Correa reacted to popular wishes. Jameson (2010, 68) notes that "Correa's policies were nationalistic and antagonistic to external international influences such as the World Bank, the IMF, and the major international oil companies. His stance was quite consonant with positions that had been taken by the indigenous movement, especially at the strategic level." Newspaper coverage suggests that "anti-American sentiment is widespread in the Andean nation of Ecuador. And the leading presidential candidate, U.S.-educated economist Raphael Correa, has tapped into this rich vein" (McCarthy 2006).

Even the US government recognized that "Correa's outbursts and the subsequent expulsions were driven by... electoral concerns" (US Embassy in Ecuador

2009). In sum, the evidence suggests that Correa exploited existing preferences rather than created them.

4.4. The Process: Contracting Loans in Ecuador

Even if societal groups have preferences and politicians listen to these preferences, do politicians have the opportunity to act upon these demands? In other words, societal interest groups can affect borrowing decisions only if politicians, not unelected technocrats, decide on which creditor to use. I trace the process of contracting loans in Ecuador to examine whether politicians can shape borrowing decisions.

In Ecuador, the first step in obtaining sovereign loans is identifying the purpose for borrowing.[2] For example, it may be necessary to borrow for the general budget or to finance a particular project. With respect to the latter, SENPLADES creates a national investment plan (*plan nacional de inversión*) that includes all projects the government wants to undertake. SENPLADES decides which projects to include based on the viability of the respective projects. Following this step, the Public Debt Office (Subsecretario de Credito Publico) within the Finance Ministry solicits offers from a variety of creditors, such as multilateral institutions and bilateral and private creditors. The public debt officials I spoke with stated that Ecuador typically receives several competing credit offers, each of which is typically willing to provide 85% of the amount necessary, with domestic resources expected to cover the remainder.

Next, the Finance Ministry evaluates the loan offers received. Interestingly, the financial terms of the offer are not a major factor in this process. Rather, my interviewees noted that it often is not a question of how expensive these loans are, but whether or not Ecuador can use the loans in a way it would like. Officials do not have formal criteria in place by which to judge the relative benefit of each loan offer. When I asked why Ecuador began to accept loan offers by the Chinese rather than Western creditors, the Ecuadorian debt officer responded that "it was a political decision," while pointing his index finger upward. In absence of precise economic criteria, there is room for political considerations influencing the initial choice of creditor.

Once the decision among the loan offers has been made, the Public Debt Office within the Ministry of Finance and the creditor negotiate the actual loan contract. Once the loan contract has been written, the creditor has to approve and sign it. After the creditor signs it, Ecuador has another three months to sign the

---

[2] The information in this section is based on interviews with several government officials (Interviews 10, 83, 84, 94, 100).

contract. Within that time frame, several political offices within the Ecuadorian government evaluate the debt contract. First, the state attorney (*procurador del estado*) must verify that the legal aspects of the contract meet Ecuadorian law. In particular, this office focuses on the arbitration clause (*clausula arbitraje*) of the contract and assesses whether it allows foreign companies to sue the Ecuadorian government in foreign courts, which would be unconstitutional. If approved and the loan proposal is for $35 million or less, the Ministry of Finance is authorized to sign the loan right away. In contrast, if the loan amount is larger than $35 million, the proposal must be presented to the Debt Committee (Comité de la Deuda). This committee has the final say on whether or not the Finance Ministry signs the loan.

The Debt Committee is an explicitly political body. The Ecuadorian president himself chairs it, even though it is said that he usually delegates this power to the minister of the Coordinating Ministry of Economic Policy. In addition to the president, the Debt Committee consists of the minister of finance, a representative from SENPLADES, and a representative of the undersecretary for public credit, as well as a secretary. In other words, it consists of a relatively small number of elected officials or representatives appointed by elected officials. It is no surprise that political considerations play into the committee's final decision. Once the Ecuadorian actors have approved the loan, the Ministry of Finance is authorized to sign the loan on behalf of the government.

To summarize, there are several opportunities for politicians to intervene in the Ecuadorian process of contracting loans. In particular, the Debt Committee is essentially a political body, as its members include Ecuador's president and minister of finance. Consequently, politicians, not technocrats, control the decision of which creditor to use. Moreover, the loan officers executing these borrowing decisions are not isolated from government interests. Instead they directly implement orders of elected officials. For example, when asking Ecuadorian loan officers about the rationale for borrowing from the Chinese, I was told, "It is a political decision. I am just following orders." Considering the process of contracting loans, it is no surprise that several interviewees pointed out that borrowing decisions are shaped by political considerations. For example, an Ecuadorian central banker rhetorically asked, "Why has Ecuador borrowed from China instead of the IMF? It just has political reasons" (Interview 85).

4.5. The Decision: Resulting Borrowing Portfolio Favors BRIC Loans

The qualitative evidence suggests that Labor and Industry dominated the political landscape in Ecuador in the late 2000s, that Labor and Industry both prefer Chinese loans over loans from Western creditors, and that the government listens to the demands of Labor and Industry. What remains to be shown is whether the borrowing decisions by the Ecuadorian government mirror the societal demands of the dominant interest groups.

Note, my argument suggests that societal coalitions shape the borrowing decisions of recipient governments. I have not argued that a Corporatist Coalition never borrows from private creditors, but that *on average* such a government will borrow relatively less from private creditors than governments responding to different societal coalitions.

4.5.1. Multilateral Creditors

In the past, Ecuador has borrowed frequently from multilateral creditors. For example, when faced with economic difficulties in the 1990s and early 2000s, Ecuador obtained several loans from the IMF ($89 million in 1994, $174 million in 2000, and $102 million in 2003).

While Ecuador has not borrowed from IFIs in recent years, government officials did not completely sever ties to multilateral agencies. Informal consultations do occur. However, Ecuadorian politicians are keenly aware that public opinion would not welcome such meetings. For example, in 2007, the minister of economy and finance, Fausto Ortiz, told the US ambassador that he "had met with the IMF's representative in Ecuador, Jorge Guzman. [Ortiz] told Guzman that he'd continue to meet with Guzman, but only after the September 30 Constituent Assembly elections; in the interim, he could not take the risk of being seen as 'the IMF's best friend' in Ecuador" (US Embassy in Ecuador 2007). Clearly, politicians understand the potential electoral consequences of acting against the wishes of a Corporatist Coalition, particularly with respect to the IMF.

4.5.2. Private Creditors

Ecuador also has a long history of borrowing from private creditors. It relied primarily on private loans from banks in the 1970s and early 1980s, but defaulted on these loans in 1987 in the aftermath of collapsing oil prices. To deal with these bad loans Ecuador converted the private loans to Brady bonds in 1994, but defaulted on these bonds again in 1999. According to one interviewee, the reasons for the renewed default are two-fold (Interview 92). On the one hand, social movements such as Jubileo 2000 were beginning to gather steam and exerted some—but not excessively much—influence on the government. On the other hand, debt burden became problem as debt service ranged between 6% and 8% of GDP.

In 2000, then, the government hastily rescheduled existing debt by converting the Brady bonds to global bonds. Two types of global bonds were offered, one with a maturity of 12 years, due in 2012, and another with a maturity of 30 years, due in 2030 (Interview 92). However, in an interview, a government official claimed that these bonds were issued under pressure and not through a transparent and competitive process. Consequently, the bonds were expensive for Ecuador, with an interest rate of 12% for the 12-year bonds and about 10% for the 30-year bonds (Interview 94). Ecuador then issued another global bond in 2005 with a maturity of 10 years and an interest rate of 7%; proceeds were used primarily to repay the global bonds due in 2012 (Interview 92).

In 2006, Rafael Correa was elected and immediately announced that his administration would renegotiate Ecuador's external debt, stating, "La vida antes que la deuda"—life should take priority over debt. In July 2007, Correa established the Comisión para la Auditoria Integral del Credito Publico (Commission to Audit the Entirety of Public Debt, CAIC). This commission was to audit the existing debt and investigate, in particular, whether these loans were contracted in a fair and democratic manner. Correa vowed to refuse to repay loans that were determined to be illegitimate. While these investigations were ongoing, interest payments on the global bonds came due on November 14, 2008. Correa declared that he would not pay the interest payments on these bonds until CAIC's findings were obtained. CAIC's final report was presented on November 20, 2008, in Quito, in front of a large crowd of Ecuadorians, with a televised ceremony. Following the recommendation of the commission, on December 12, the government suspended payments on the principal of the Global 12 Bonds and Global 30 Bonds, worth $3.2 billion, or around a third of Ecuador's debt stock owed to private creditors. By suspending payments, Ecuador violated the legal terms of the debt contract and was in default.

Naturally, the interpretation of these events differed starkly among interviewees. Interviewees from the financial sector noted that there was no economic necessity to default, as economic indicators, such as the ratio between total external debt and national economic strength (ETD/GDP), was only 30%, while debt service was only 1.5% of GDP. Both figures are reasonably low. "From a financial point of view there was no reason to default. This was only done to satisfy an ideological dream. They [the government] defaulted because they believe that debt is something evil that keeps developing countries underdeveloped" (Interview 92).

However, it is also possible to interpret these actions as a smart move by rational politicians to maximize economic benefits while minimizing political fallout. While Ecuador's actions constituted default, Correa did not repudiate the bonds. In other words, while Correa suspended payments, he did not refuse to honor the debt, which would have encouraged bondholders to sue for repayment. Instead, he sought to restructure the debt owed to private creditors.

> In April 2009, an invitation [was issued] to bondholders to take part in an auction to determine the price at which Ecuador would buy back the bonds, starting at a discount of 70%. The offer was eventually improved by 5 per cent, with the majority of bondholders (91 per cent) agreeing in May and June of this year to sell their bonds back to the government at the rate of 35 cents in the dollar. In addition, it seems that in the interval between announcing the decision to default in December 2008 and the conclusion of the formal repurchase six months later, the government bought up a substantial amount of the 2030 and 2012 bonds on the secondary debt market perhaps as much as 50 per cent.... If so, it not only took advantage of lower prices once the default had been announced, but also prevented the 2030 bondholders from reaching the necessary threshold enabling them to call for a repayment of principal. To date, it appears that the government has succeeded in retiring $2.9 billion-worth of debt for $900 million, saving around $300 million per annum on interest payments. (Mansell and Openshaw 2009, 178)

Several interview partners (Interviews 89, 94) and other scholars confirm this interpretation:

> The way the Correa Administration dealt with these undesirable obligations was to buy them back from intimidated investors, indirectly at first and then directly, paying cash for a fraction of their face value (or rather, their pre-default market value), for the purpose of extinguishing them. The government reportedly began to purchase the 2012 bonds in the secondary market after their price collapsed following the mid-November 2008 decision to default on them.... As a result, by the end of 2009, the government had successfully bought back about 95% of the 2012 and 2030 bonds. (Porzecanski 2010, 266)

Correa's treatment of private creditors did not damage his political career. In fact, two days after announcing the debt swap, Ecuadorians were asked to vote in the presidential election: Correa won an absolute majority, with 51.9 % of all votes in the first round. It appears that "the Ecuadorian government was primarily interested in using the illegitimacy of the 2030 and 2012 bonds as a reason not to disclaim responsibility for them altogether, but rather as a means of 'incentivizing' the bondholders to agree to a substantial reduction in the sum owed. In doing so, the government was able to retire a large part of Ecuador's commercial debt quickly; maintain a civilized, if strained, relationship with the bondholders; avoid a protracted court battle; and minimize the damage to the country's economic reputation" (Mansell and Openshaw 2009, 179).

As a result, Ecuador's reputation among private creditors did suffer, but not terribly so. In June 2012, Standard & Poor's upgraded Ecuador's long-term sovereign credit rating to B from B−, citing indications of better growth prospects and government revenues on sustained higher levels of investment. Against this background, Ecuador was able to borrow $137 million from commercial banks in 2013. Furthermore, in May 2013, Ecuador's ambassador to the United States, Nathalie Cely, noted that the country was planning to issue bonds soon: "Yes, we are working on that.... Certainly, we have found a lot of appetite for government bonds.... There are a couple of investment banks that have visited me in Washington to talk about that and to let me know they are looking forward for our bond initiative" (Bases 2013). About a year later, in June 2015, Ecuador successfully returned to the bond market. However, while Ecuador is able to borrow from private markets, it relies less on private creditors than Colombia or Peru.

4.5.3. DAC Loans

DAC loans might be an alternative source of funds for the government, given that Ecuador obtains only limited resources from private creditors and uses only select loans from multilateral institutions. However, consistent with Industry's strong opposition to DAC loans, Ecuador has obtained only a few loans of limited volume from Western governments.

Since 2004, Ecuador has obtained a handful small DAC loans: a single loan from Belgium in 2009 (merely $1 million) and Italy ($13 million in 2015), two loans from Spain ($15 million in 2006 and $30 million in 2014), while Germany provided four loans ($15 million in 2003, $2 million in 2005, $2 million in 2009, and $10 million in 2013). France provided the largest loans, with $120 million in 2013 and $200 million in 2015.

4.5.4. BRIC Loans

In responding to a Corporatist Coalition, the Ecuadorian government has relied primarily from BRICs. Most prominently, it has obtained several loans from China. According to interviewees, Chinese were first approached in 2008, and in 2010 the first loan contract was signed (Interview 78). In 2010, Ecuador borrowed a total of $2.7 billion from China, but signed multiple loan agreements. It borrowed $1.682 billion from the China EXIM bank to finance 85% of the Coco Codo Sinclair project, a remarkably large hydropower dam that will produce 1,500 MW of electricity (Interview 83). Project loans are typically tied loans. As such, the project was awarded to the Chinese company Sinohydro, which began construction shortly after the agreement was signed (Interview 97). The same year, Ecuador also obtained $1.0 billion from the Chinese Development Bank. This loan was not tied to a particular project but paid directly into the budget of the recipient government. The majority of the funds are intended to finance various projects outlined in the *plan nacional de inversión*, but at the discretion of the Ecuadorian government. Interviewees provided information that $200 million of this loan was supposedly earmarked for a specific project (Interview 97). Others noted that the Coco Coda Sinclair project gets part of the budget loan (Interview 84). It might be the case that this "specific project" is the Coco Coda Sinclair venture, but I was unable to confirm this information.

Ecuador obtained additional loans in subsequent years. For example, in 2011 it obtained a total of $2.6 billion. One of the loans signed was a $1.4 billion untied loan from the Chinese Development Bank denominated in US dollars. In addition, it obtained $600 million denominated in renminbi, and tied to a specific project (Interviews 83, 97).

Another loan for $600 million was obtained from the China EXIM bank to fund the construction of the Sopladora electrical project, which is expected to yield 487.8 MW. The contract was awarded to the Chinese consortium China Gezhouba Group-Fopeca (Interview 83). Ecuador made similar arrangements with China in subsequent years. In 2012, it obtained a total of $1.7 billion, and in 2013 loans worth $664 million, from China.[3]

In addition to Chinese loans, Ecuador also borrowed from other BRIC creditors. For example, in 2011, Ecuador borrowed $123 million from the Russian EXIM bank to finance the expansion of the Toachi Pilaton hydropower project, which will yield 252 MW. The Ecuadorian company Constructora de los Andes will construct the project, while the Chinese firm Harbin Electric Machinery will supply the electrical turbines (Interview 97). Similarly, Ecuador borrowed $195 million from Russia in 2013. Ecuador also received loans from Brazil,[4] $268 million in 2010, $90 million in 2012, and $137 million in 2013. To my knowledge, Ecuador did not receive any loans from India.

---

[3] In addition to these explicit loans in the form of project loans or budget loans, Ecuador has obtained implicit loans. As government representatives do not count these transactions as loans, they are not recorded as such in the budget (Interview 79). These transactions involve so-called advance sales of oil, which are the prepayment of future oil exports to China at today's market prices (Interview 83). Ecuador obtained $1 billion in 2009 and another $1 billion in 2011 using these operations.

[4] It is also interesting to examine Ecuador's repayment patterns. While Correa effectively stopped servicing existing debt from traditional Western creditors in 2007, he continued to pay interest and principal on debt owed to BRICs. For instance, in January 2007 the installment due on loans to Brazil for the San Francisco hydropower project were paid on time.

While Ecuador did borrow large amounts from BRICs, Correa did not choose these creditors because he was particularly fond of them. Negotiations for the first Chinese loan intended to fund the Coca Codo Sinclair dam were wrought with difficulties. A year after the negotiations began, Correa rejected China's conditions for the $1.7 billion loan to build the plant. In his weekly report on government activities, Correa said some of the conditions China's EXIM bank required for the loan were "really a threat against our sovereignty" (Hall 2010; La Hora 2009). He noted, "Suddenly negotiating with China is worse than negotiating with the International Monetary Fund. They're asking us for ridiculous guarantees," referring to Beijing's demand that Ecuador's Central Bank should "use its national assets as a guarantee" (Cardenal and Araujo 2013, 148). Correa described this as an "outrage" and considered it "ill-treatment" of the Ecuadorian negotiators, warning that "if Eximbank did not change its loan conditions, . . . Ecuador would rethink its China policy" (*Latin American Herald Tribune* 2009). China's ambassador to Ecuador, Cai Runguo, told the US ambassador that "China was disconcerted by Correa's verbal attack in December 2009 over China's negotiating position for loans to Ecuador, in which Correa alleged that even the IMF had not treated Ecuador as poorly as did China" (US Embassy in Ecuador 2010). In examining the aftermath of these conflicts, Cardenal and Araujo (2013, 149) quote Diego Vega, director of international relations at the National Planning and Development Office: "The key point was that Correa said: 'If China forces those conditions on us, we'll go to Taiwan, as they're prepared to treat us better.' The following day the Chinese ambassador in Ecuador reacted to this news and two days later negotiations started up again." Shortly thereafter, on January 15, 2010, China's ambassador to Ecuador confirmed that "the [People's Republic of China] is moving forward with negotiations with the [government of Ecuador] on financing various commercial projects, but that Ecuadorian President Correa's criticisms of China's tough negotiating position had caused some concern in Beijing" (US Embassy in Ecuador 2010).

Contrary to conventional wisdom, this anecdote illustrates that Correa did not borrow from China because he personally favored this creditor. Instead, Correa was concerned about Chinese conditions just as he was concerned about conditions of other creditors. In other words, Correa himself did not have strong feelings about the source of credit, while the dominant societal coalitions did.

4.5.5. Other Policy Issues

Importantly, the interests of the Corporatist Coalition have not only shaped Ecuador's borrowing portfolio, but other areas of economic policy as well.

For example, Correa used tariffs on multiple occasions to favor domestic producers and consumers (Wolff 2016, 133). In July 2008, the government eliminated tariffs on 282 imported goods, especially capital goods and equipment needed for agricultural and industrial production (Ecuavisa 2008), and in January 2009, Ecuador introduced temporary protective tariffs on 627 import goods that competed with domestic production (Bowen 2014, 108). In addition, the currency export tax was increased twice: from 1% to 2% in 2009 and to 5% in 2011. This is consistent with an industrial policy aimed at protecting domestic markets while enabling domestic companies to upgrade their productive capacities. Citing concerns for citizens, the Correa government also intervened to regulate food prices (rice, corn, milk, and bread) in 2008 and 2009 (Stefanoni 2012, 245).

Another example of the Ecuadorian government implementing policies to protect domestic Industry concerns investor protection treaties. All such treaties that Ecuador had signed before 2008 were renounced that year. Moreover, Correa announced that such agreements were not to be signed again in the future because such treaties "overprotected foreign investment" by granting foreign firms more rights than domestic companies. This argument was illustrated by the arbitration clauses of these treaties allowing foreign companies to sue Ecuadorian public and private actors in foreign courts, while domestic firms did not have this option (Interview 95).

Similarly, North argues that land reform would have helped Correa to achieve his goals of improved social justice and equity. However, he did not pursue such policies because industrialists "are the politically powerful exporters of bananas, shrimp, cut flowers, and broccoli, and they keep dollars flowing into Ecuador's economy. They form the core of the elite whose properties Correa either does not want to touch (because he believes they are efficient producers and exporters) or cannot touch because of their political power" (North 2013, 125). Again, this is consistent with Correa's appeal to an informal coalition between Labor and Industry.

I acknowledge, however, that appeasing both Industry and Labor is not without challenges, and not all decisions have been viewed favorably by both groups. For example, with respect to conflicts about mining projects in Ecuador, Correa has drawn criticism from groups representing workers (Becker 2013; Kuecker 2016; Avcı and Fernández-Salvador 2016; Van Teijlingen and Hogenboom 2016; Velásquez 2017; Conaghan 2017).

There is no question, however, that Correa's government implemented policies not favored by the financial sector. I have argued that Finance did not agree with the government's decision to borrow from BRICs. Similarly, other government policies intended to tame the financial sector and channel its resources to domestic industrialization. In May 2009, the government established a domestic liquidity coefficient, "which required that 45% of all banks' liquid assets had to be held domestically" (Weisbrot, Johnston, and Lefebvre 2013, 3), which was raised to 60% in 2012. Higher reserve requirements are costly for banks, but domestic clients benefit from lower risk of bank runs. In December 2009, new regulations were adopted to promote savings-and-loan cooperatives, which should boost the establishment of small businesses (Acosta 2009, 122). A further reform of financial regulation was explicitly framed as a distributional issue between Labor and Finance. In November 2012, the government approved the Ley Urgente de Redistribución del Gasto Social. This law raised taxes on banks in order to increase social spending for the poor (*América Economía* 2012).

4.6. A Corporatist Coalition in Ecuador

In this chapter, I have shown that Labor and Industry dominate the political landscape in Ecuador. Interviews with representatives of these groups revealed that they both prefer government borrowing from BRICs rather than Western creditors. Following these insights, the qualitative evidence strongly suggests that politicians respond to the demands of this Corporatist Coalition by emphasizing employment (desired by Labor) and industrial policy (demanded by Industry). Politicians can act upon these preferences by influencing borrowing decisions, which are, as I have shown, an explicitly political process. As a result, Ecuador has relied more on BRICs for loans than other creditors. However, it is worth noting that the government did not cut ties to other creditors completely.

The next chapter presents qualitative evidence gathered in Colombia. In contrast to Ecuador, Colombia did not borrow from BRICs but relied primarily on private creditors. Interviews with Colombian stakeholders suggest that demand-side factors help explain this borrowing strategy.

5

Colombia

A Capital Coalition Prefers Private Creditors

Colombia's government borrows primarily from private creditors. Colombia also obtains loans from Western creditors, including international financial institutions (IFIs) and Western governments (DACs). However, it has—to date—never obtained a loan from emerging creditors such as Brazil, Russia, India, and China (BRICs). I conducted fieldwork in Colombia to examine the reasons for this particular composition of Colombia's borrowing portfolio.

If my theory is correct, I expect to find that Colombian politicians chose private creditors over others to satisfy the preferences of a Capital Coalition between Finance and Industry.

This chapter presents the qualitative evidence gathered from interviews with government officials, representatives of societal groups, and creditors. The chapter is organized as follows: First, I examine which societal groups dominate the political landscape, concluding that Finance and Industry form a Capital Coalition. Section 5.2 presents insights gathered from interviews regarding the preferences of societal actors across creditors. I argue that Finance and Industry exhibit a strong preference for private creditors. I subsequently show that Colombia's politicians listen to, and act upon, the preferences of the Capital Coalition. Section 5.5 examines the borrowing decisions resulting from this process. In sum, there is strong evidence that societal coalitions shape Colombia's borrowing portfolio.

5.1. The Coalition: Finance and Industry in Control

Colombian politics are managed by elites for elites. Interviewees describe the political system as dominated by the "oligarchy" of Finance and Industry

(Interview 96). This situation is the result of a historic "pact" between the Liberal Party and the Conservative Party in 1958 that consolidated their power (Dix 1980). As a result, Colombia had a comparatively exclusive political system dominated by the Liberals and Conservatives for most of the 20th century (Interview 105). A civil war between the establishment and left-wing forces led to an increasing concentration of elites and a repression of Labor and popular movements (Interview 95). This reinforced the dominant position of Industry and Finance in the political system.

On the surface, the monopoly of the Liberal and Conservative parties has changed in the past two decades. With the introduction of a new constitution in 1991, small and regional parties were founded. Many of these parties were either incorporated into existing parties (Interview 105; Leongómez 2002) or vanished, as they were based on the aspirations of office-seeking politicians who did not stand a chance against the established parties (Interview 7). Others, however, were successful. For example, in the early 2000s, the Primero Colombia (Colombia First) political movement successfully supported Álvaro Uribe's bid for president in 2002 and 2006. Similarly, his successor, President Juan Manuel Santos, was elected on a ticket of the newly founded Partido Social de Unidad Nacional (Social Party of National Unity). Consequently, the distribution of seats in the Colombian parliament reveals that new parties have replaced the monopoly of the Liberal and Conservative parties.

Yet these changes in the party landscape did not fundamentally change the oligarchic structure of Colombian politics. Colombia still has an exclusive political system in which elites have disproportional influence. The new parties replacing the old establishment also have strong ties to some parts of society—namely Industry and Finance—just as the Liberals and Conservatives used to have strong links to domestic producers and banks (Interview 96). Several interviewees mentioned that business groups remain the primary social forces in Colombia (Interviews 19, 90). They suggested that although the names of political parties had changed, the fundamental political dynamics of elites managing politics for elites remains in place.

One of the reasons for the continued influence of Industry and Finance on Colombian politics is that "there exists already a stock of domestic entrepreneurs who are capable of defending their interests" (Interview 34). In particular, business associations have developed the capacity to lobby over the past decades (Interview 17). The strong ties between Industry and the political parties have endured despite changes in the party landscape. One reason for this dominance of Industry is its diversity. Several interviewees stated that Colombian elites are dispersed geographically, as there are several industrial hubs, Cali, Bogotá, Medellin, and others, which makes it impossible for politicians to marginalize these actors (Interviews 26, 105; Paramio and Hopenhayn 2010). In contrast, the strength of domestic Finance stems from its size. A well-developed financial sector with strong banks has meant that Finance remains an enormously influential actor in both economics and politics.

In contrast, Labor is a marginalized actor in Colombian politics. This applies to both institutionalized representation and informal influence (David and José 2012, 232). With respect to the former, virtually all interviewees agreed that unions are weak and not important (Interview 2, 4, 7). One interviewee noted that issues relevant to Labor, such as trade, are not represented by labor organizations in the Colombian context: "The trade organization in Argentina is Labor, while the trade constituency in Colombia is business" (Interview 3). Similarly, broad societal movements that encompass the majority of workers have been unable to develop in Colombia. Consequently, social movements do not have the opportunity to participate in the political process (Interview 95).

Interviewees cited the legacy of the civil war as the reason for the weak position of Labor in the Colombian political system. During the war, there was no political space for social groups representing workers or other groups such as indigenous movements (Interview 99). One interviewee told me, "If you were a bit left, then you were immediately thought of being part of the FARC" (Interview 91; see also Interview 90).[1] In contrast to Ecuador, social movements in Colombia did not have the opportunity to get a foothold in the political system (Interviews 90, 95, 99). This legacy contributed to the consolidation of Finance and Industry and the strong influence of this coalition on Colombian politicians.

Labor, however, has been marginalized politically. This implies that a Capital Coalition dominates in Colombia.

5.2. The Preferences: Industry and Finance Alarmed by Chinese Competition

The previous section has shown that a Capital Coalition consisting of Finance and Industry dominates Colombia's political arena. Which types of creditors does this coalition prefer? According to my theory, Capital Coalitions strongly favor private creditors because both Industry and Finance generally prefer them. Capital Coalitions also exhibit a weak preference for IFI loans, which are strongly preferred by Finance, while Industry is somewhat ambivalent toward them. In contrast, Finance and Industry differ in their evaluation of BRIC and

---

[1] FARC stands for Fuerzas Armadas Revolucionarias de Colombia, the Revolutionary Armed Forces of Colombia, a Marxist-Leninist revolutionary guerrilla organization and among the most prominent armed groups involved in the war.

DAC loans: While Finance favors DAC loans and dislikes BRICs, the opposite is the case for Industry. For this reason, Capital Coalitions should be indifferent to bilateral loans from either BRIC or DAC governments. The interviews in this section consider whether the theoretical predictions accurately represent actors' preferences across creditors.

5.2.1. BRICs

Colombian Finance strongly dislikes BRIC loans, for three reasons. First, Finance is concerned about increased Chinese activities in the natural resource sector, specifically their macroeconomic consequences. On August 16, 2011, a front-page story in Colombia's largest daily newspaper, *El Tiempo*, reported on President Santos's proposal to contain the negative effects of the "enfermedad Holandesa," the so-called Dutch disease. This "disease" can befall countries that discover new reserves of natural resources, just as Colombia had done earlier that year. Its symptoms include rising inflation (Bunte 2016). Interviewees were extremely concerned with the Dutch disease leading to higher inflation, which would devalue the capital of the financial sector.

Second, Finance is concerned with increased Chinese competition in the area of investment finance. Colombian bankers closely follow the developments in neighboring Ecuador, where Chinese loans have been used to fund investment projects that were previously funded by the domestic financial sector. Finance fears the potential loss of market share in the face of potent external financiers. In short, just as Colombian Industry is concerned about more competition from Chinese imports, "Similar developments can be seen in the banking sector" (Interview 3).

Faced with this threat, interviewees expressed their support for the current regulatory framework of capital flows to Colombia. These rules were introduced after the financial crisis of Brazil in 1999 as well as the Asian Crisis in 1997 (Interviews 6, 8). These capital controls allowed the country to gain a degree of monetary and exchange-rate control (Ocampo and Tovar 2003). They also provided a significant degree of protection to the financial sector, resulting in a relatively captive market. The Colombian central bank requires foreign companies to hold their balance sheets in Colombian pesos. Unlike in Peru, companies are not allowed to hold liquid assets denominated in dollars (Interview 6).

Corporate debt and other capital flows must be converted into local currency to avoid currency mismatch (Interview 24). In addition to these permanent requirements, the central bank has "temporary controls" at their disposal. These additional capital controls can be imposed in times of crisis to avoid the outflow of "hot money." For example, between 2006 and 2008, additional reserve requirements were introduced to address the effects of the global financial crisis (Interview 23). As a result of these rules the domestic financial sector is quite protected. The Colombian financial market, in the words of one interviewee, "is not as free as you think. You cannot bring as much money as you want" (Interview 8). This provides domestic finance with some degree of protection against Chinese competition.

Third, while the capital market regulations technically apply to all investors equally, interviewees nevertheless pointed to the potential for implicit discrimination based on the country of origin (Interview 3). Companies intending to comply with these rules are required to either open a local branch or have some other legal representation within Colombia (Interview 10). Yet Chinese companies face far greater challenges establishing legal representation in Colombia than their Western counterparts. For example, when the Chinese company Huawei first arrived in Colombia in 2001, no local financial institution wanted to work with it. Even Colombian branches of international banks such as Citibank were unwilling to do so, despite Citibank's strong presence in China. Colombian banks frequently refuse to allow Chinese to open accounts, claiming that they do not have any prior experience in Colombia. The lack of a track record, in turn, prevents an assessment of creditworthiness, which is then cited as the official reason why Colombian banks do not typically work with Chinese customers (Interview 35).

In addition, cultural animosities might play a role. In interviews, representatives of the Colombian financial sector expressed a strong antipathy toward Chinese banks and investors. Several interviewees noted that the Chinese use their apartments as their offices. Colombian bankers regard this practice as unprofessional. If a Colombian banker works with a representative of a Chinese bank, colleagues in other banks are likely to harass him. One interviewee recalled being asked, "How can you support these Chinese, these dirty people?" When asking about the reasons for the perceived "dirtiness," interviewees referred to differences in business culture. When Colombians negotiate with Western partners, they receive the comments by their Western counterparts neatly printed on paper to facilitate effortless review. Chinese partners, in contrast, are said to scribble their annotations on the original proposals and are therefore considered "dirty" and unprofessional by Colombian bankers. Another Colombian banker reported snide remarks by colleagues when their oldest daughter was sent to China to study abroad. The parents of the other children in the "best and most expensive private school in Bogotá" were outraged, saying, "Are you crazy? To send your daughters to China?"

In contrast to these negative perceptions of Chinese business culture, representatives of the Colombian financial sector have a different view of Western partners. One interviewee summarized this, saying, "Americans are the maximum level of everything" (Interview 35) in terms of their living style, professional work environment, and clothing.

While Colombian Finance views BRICs in a thoroughly negative light, Industry's perspective is more differentiated. To be sure, industrial interests do have concerns with respect to two issue areas. First, echoing earlier negative experiences with commodity booms (Edwards 1984), Industry shares Finance's concern about the possibility of the Dutch disease. However, while Finance is worried about inflationary effects, domestic Industry is more concerned about the long-term effect of increased Chinese investment on the structure of the Colombian economy (Interview 96). The Dutch disease can lead to a contraction of the domestic tradable sector, such as in manufacturing (Bunte 2016). Thus, increased reliance on natural resource exports could undermine existing manufacturing industries. In other words, the Dutch disease could result in de-industrialization of the economy (Gallagher and Porzecanski 2010; González 2008). Colombian Industry is aware of this threat (Interview 12). While "we will become very rich in terms of exporting raw materials" (Interview 19), the macroeconomic effects of increasing natural resource exports might threaten domestic industry. For example, a former deputy minister for business development noted that "Dutch disease could hurt domestic industry" (Interview 13). As a result, a former deputy minister of the National Planning Department (Departamento Nacional de Planeación) reported increased lobbying activities by the affected businesses (Interview 16) in an attempt to protect domestic industry from negative effects of Chinese investment in natural resources.

Second, while the appreciation of the Colombian currency due to the Dutch disease could threaten Industry's ability to export, import competition by Chinese manufacturers could undermine Industry's position in the domestic market. Thus, multiple interviewees mentioned that Colombian companies resisted opening the domestic market to Chinese goods. This might be explained by the fact that Colombian Industry is somewhat more developed, which implies less complementarity and more risk of displacement by Chinese firms entering their market than in Peru or Ecuador. Colombian industrial establishments in sectors such as the pharmaceutical industry (Interview 1), agriculture (Interviews 4, 26), and manufacturing in general (Interview 11) would be most threatened.

Within manufacturing, interviewees indicated that the textile industry (Interviews 1, 4, 10, 12, 28), car manufacturers (Interviews 3, 4, 26), and the metal-mechanic sector (Interviews 12, 28) expect negative effects from increased Chinese imports. Moreover, these industries are taking steps in the political arena to avoid these negative distributional consequences. Representatives of the Consejo Gremial National (National Business Council) confirmed that these industries are organizing to lobby against a possible free trade agreement between China and Colombia (Interview 10).

Thus, Industry worries about Chinese engagement in the natural resource sector as well as increased imports from China. Yet Industry exhibited positive attitudes toward Chinese investment in other sectors of the economy. For example, the largest business association in Colombia, Asociación Nacional de Empresarios de Colombia (National Association of Manufacturers, ANDI) has created a new office within the organization dedicated to improving relations with China (Interview 12). It works toward attracting Chinese loans and investment, particularly in technology-intensive sectors. It also pursues more immediate goals, such as streamlining the process by which Chinese businesspersons obtain a Colombian work visa.

Interviews suggested that Colombian businesses are not afraid of an "invasion" by Chinese companies. Instead, they want foreign technology and knowledge, as they "recognize that we can learn a lot from foreigners. I would not be concerned at all [about the Chinese]" (Interview 10). However, the presence of an already established manufacturing sector implies that Colombian businesses have an incentive to ensure that Chinese investments benefit domestic industry. In the words of one observer, "Colombians are not sitting there and waiting for investment to happen. . . . Colombia is already too strong to simply give up the crown jewels" (Interview 34). Asking whether there would be any resistance to Chinese investments that might follow Chinese loans provoked open laughter. This is apparently a ridiculous thought (Interview 24). In addition, one businessman told me that he is on the board of an agribusiness company, whose equity is currently held by a Chinese investor, "and nobody cares" (Interview 3). Chinese interviewees confirm this perspective. A representative of the Chinese embassy to Colombia confirmed that it has "not received any complaints from local businesses. The Colombians have a welcoming attitude" (Interview 25).

On balance, interviews with Industry representatives indicate that they have mixed, and on balance slightly positive, attitude toward BRICs, in line with my theoretical expectations.

However, given their strategic cooperation with Finance, the Capital Coalition as a whole does not view BRIC loans in an extremely favorable light.

5.2.2. DACs

Finance favors DAC loans. Historical bonds, particularly with the United States, appear to play a large role. Interviewees recognize that bilateral loans from DACs—particularly the United States—purchase influence among Colombian policymakers. However, since financial sectors in developing countries have closer ties to Western money centers than those in China or India, Finance actually welcomes the influence from DACs. In an interview, a Colombian businessman stated, "With the US, Colombia isn't quite sure what their political agenda is. However, whatever it is, we can live with it." In contrast, a Colombian business lawyer stated, "We simply don't know about China" (Interview 14), while a Colombian professor of international business added, "We see a big monster—we don't know what they [the Chinese] want" (Interview 11).

In contrast, Industry in Colombia was less enthusiastic about DAC loans. Interviewees noted the good-governance requirements that would prohibit the government from implementing industrial policy. For example, Colombian Industry representatives support the government's program to boost productivity in specific sectors (Interviews 12, 13). President Uribe instigated the Productive Transformation Program, and most Industry representatives are glad that President Santos is continuing this program, albeit under a different name (Locomotivas). For this reason, Industry disapproves of DAC loans with conditions that would undermine the government's ability to pursue an industrial policy.

5.2.3. IFIs and Private Creditors

While Finance and Industry exhibit contradictory preferences with respect to BRIC and DAC loans, they agree that the Colombian government should borrow from private creditors and IFIs. Recalling the traumatic experiences of the Latin American debt crisis (Ocampo 1987), Finance exhibits a strong desire to prevent similar events. Interviewees noted two reasons why IMF loans are popular among domestic financial interests. On the one hand, the IMF's macroeconomic conditions are in line with their own preferred policies; on the other hand, the availability of an IMF bailout is reassuring. Furthermore, interviews revealed that Finance prefers private creditors for similar reasons. The government is likely to pursue probusiness policies if it is subjected to the scrutiny of foreign bondholders. Moreover, by purchasing government bonds, the domestic financial sector gives the government a stake in the survival of the banking sector (Grossman and Woll 2014; Culpepper and Reinke 2014). As a result, the government has the incentive to bail out banks in the event of a crisis.

Interviews with representatives of Industry in Colombia did not reveal a strong preference for or against IFIs. In fact, interviewees representing Industry in Colombia hardly ever mentioned IFI loans, perhaps because private creditors are significantly more important.

In line with scholarship (Aguilar et al. 2006), there is a strong emphasis on developing a corporate bond market to increase the financing options available to corporations. Observing the Colombian government successfully placing bonds serves as a signal of a favorable business climate, thereby improving the ability of domestic firms to obtain finance themselves (Elton et al. 2001). Overall, there is widespread conviction among Colombian political elites that strengthening ties with the northern public and private actors is desirable.

5.2.4. Preferences of Labor

The preferences of Finance and Industry align well with the theoretical expectations. Is this also the case for Labor, the actor that is dominated by a Capital Coalition? If my theory is correct, Labor will exhibit positive preferences for BRIC loans. Did the interviews with representatives of Labor in Colombia confirm these expectations?

Interviews revealed that Labor's preferences in Colombia are similar to those in Ecuador or Peru. Specifically, BRIC loans are viewed in a positive light. Because BRIC loans are tied to investment projects, workers expect positive employment effects. Several Colombian interviewees noted that employment opportunities are the main reason Labor is in favor if BRIC loans (Interviews 3, 9). I also asked about the conventional wisdom that Chinese companies tend to import workers and thus do not have positive employment effects. However, interviewees did not view Chinese firms as different from Western companies in this regard. A Colombian representative stated that, in his opinion, "if Siemens [a Western company] would open a plant in Colombia, they would bring their own engineers and consequently there would be no spillovers. In contrast, if China opens a plant, they use it as a production hub for the region. Simply because of their language, they are required to hire more local staff, and thus there will be spillovers" (Interview 29). As in Ecuador, Colombian workers prefer BRIC loans over others.

5.3. The Politicians: Defending Interests of Industry and Finance

Are Colombian politicians responsive to the preferences of Finance and Industry? The qualitative evidence suggests that this is the case. Interviewees noted two channels of influence.

First, Colombian politics is characterized by frequent transitions between political posts and business employment. This "revolving door" facilitates the recurrent exchange of personnel between politics and business. It also implies that politicians obtain significant campaign financing from domestic Industry and Finance (Interview 17). Second, a strong presence of organized business interests ensures that politicians are sensitive to the demands of

Industry. A representative of ANDI emphasized that it is the largest business association in Colombia, as its members produce 40% of Colombian GDP. To ensure that their interests are adequately represented, they maintain 10 offices in different metropolitan areas. An ANDI representative thus noted that "when you call, people listen" (Interview 12). I asked about the activities ANDI undertakes to represent its members. The interviewee listed tasks such as lobbying congress to pass laws, working with the Ministry of Commerce and the Ministry of Foreign Affairs to develop policies, and accompanying the president on trips. "Whenever there is a trip, the president of ANDI goes along. We are not that far away" (Interview 12).

Interviews with politicians confirmed that they mirror the preferences of domestic Industry and Finance. For example, a Colombian senator indicated that he is sensitive to the demands by his constituency that consists primarily of business people. Consequently, "I am running a populist campaign against foreign investors in my district" (Interview 21). Foreign officials also noted the strong influence that domestic interests have over Colombian foreign economic policy (Interview 63). For instance, a Peruvian official involved in negotiations in the context of the free trade agreement with the United States recalled that Peru wanted to negotiate en bloc with the Colombians. This was difficult because Peru was much more willing to liberalize economically than Colombia. The interviewee stated, "The Colombians were quite complicated. They can be difficult. Why? Because Colombia has a strong private sector that pressures the government to be more cautious" (Interview 53).

These findings align well with existing scholarship. For instance, Álvarez (2004, 2005) shows that shifts in policy preferences of Colombian politicians corresponded closely to changes in the dominant business interests over time. Dallanegra Pedraza (2012, 37) argues that Colombia's relationship with Western countries "obeys a logic that has nothing to do with the existing order but with politics and decisions by the ruling elite." Politicians do not pay much attention to Labor. In 1990 Urrutia noted that, "unlike most other major Latin American countries, Colombia has never had a populist president, nor have populist movements obtained majority representation in Congress" (Urrutia 1990, 370). Similarly, Álvaro Uribe—Colombia's president for much of the 2000s—"made no concerted effort to cultivate political support among the masses. [Instead, Uribe is a] politician who appeals primarily to the middle and upper classes" (Dugas 2010, 1117). Thus, there is little influence by groups such as trade unions, ethnic groups, or minorities (Garcia 2011, 179).

5.4. The Process: Negotiating Loan Agreements with Colombia

My theory suggests that politicians can influence borrowing portfolios and that they attempt to influence borrowing decisions in accordance with the preferences of societal interest groups. For this to be possible, politicians must have a role in making borrowing decisions. However, it could be the case that such decisions are made by bureaucrats without any input by politicians. In fact, Dargent (2011) claims that Colombian technocrats are independent from politicians, resulting in economic policies unrelated to citizens' preferences. I disagree.

This section will first describe the sequence of borrowing decisions and illustrate that political actors, not technocrats, dominate the decision-making process. I then show how politics affects the choice of creditors both with budget loans and with project loans.

5.4.1. Sequence and Actors

The Colombian process of signing debt agreements is similar to the Ecuadorian process.[2] The procedure begins with the National Planning Department, in conjunction with the government, identifying the purposes for which external resources should be obtained. This could be either for general budget purposes or to finance a particular project. In the case of the latter, the project must be presented to the Economic and Social Policy Council (El Consejo Nacional de Política Económica y Social, CONPES). This body is Colombia's senior planning council and is composed of the vice president, every minister of the cabinet, the director of the Office of the President of the Republic, the director of national planning, and the director of the Administrative Department of Science, Technology and Innovation. CONPES reviews the viability of the project before the Council for Fiscal Policy (Consejo Superior de Política Fiscal, CONFIS) then determines how the undertakings should be financed. CONFIS is composed of the minister of finance, the director of the Administrative Department of National Planning, the economic adviser to the president, the deputy ministers of finance, the director of the national Treasury, and the director of public credit. Next, the authorization of the Council of Ministers ("El Compes") is required to proceed with the plans. The council needs to approve the project's

---

[2] The information of this section is based on interviews with several governmental officials (Interviews 32, 38), as well as representatives of foreign creditors (Interviews 33, 40).

alignment with the intentions of the national development plan (*plan national de desarrollo*).

Once the approval of the Council of Ministers is obtained, reports of both CONPES and CONFIS are forwarded to the Interparliamentary Public Debt Commission (Comisión Interparlamentaria de Credito Público, CICP). Decree 2681/1993 charges this committee with analyzing the implications of each loan for the sustainability of Colombia's overall debt burden (Interview 32). This commission consists of six members, three members of the House of Representatives and three of the Senate. Due to the political character of this committee, "It is a complex process" (Interview 38).

After the CICP initially approves the government's request for a loan, the Ministry of Finance and Public Credit (Ministerio de Hacienda y Crédito Público, MHCP) is authorized to solicit loan offers. Public officials repeatedly stated, "We have lots of sources of funding" (Interview 38). Once the various creditors have made loan offers, the MHCP takes all offers back to the CICP for a "final opinion." In particular, the committee must ensure that the proposed loan agreement does not increase the Colombian debt burden to an unsustainable level. Thus, "We actually have to present it twice to the committee, first to get approval to negotiate for a loan, and once the negotiations are finished, we need an authorization to actually hire the debt" (Interview 38).

Once the commission has concluded that the loan offer conforms to Colombian law and policy guidelines, it authorizes the MHCP to sign the loan agreement. If the undertaking is a budget loan, the process stops here. If, however, the loan funds a specific project, a bidding process is organized for the construction of the project. Unlike Peru and Ecuador, Colombia separates the processes of obtaining funding for projects and contracting the construction of the project.

In sum, there are multiple opportunities for politics to influence the process of contracting loans in Colombia. This is apparent when considering the membership of the committees whose approval is required. As noted above, both committees consist of high-ranking politicians: CONPES includes the vice president and the government ministers, while CONFIS includes the minister of finance, the economic adviser to the president, and the deputy ministers of finance, among others. In addition, the Council of Ministers' approval is required, which includes every minister of the cabinet.

The influence of politics on the process of contracting loans is most obvious in the case of the CICP. As previously mentioned, the commission is composed not of experts in public finance, but of three members of the House of Representatives and another three from the Senate. The interviewees consistently pointed out that this is an essentially political body. As it has the right to veto loan proposals, its ability to shape the borrowing decisions cannot be overstated.

5.4.2. High Hurdles for Budget Loans

Given the political nature of the actors involved in the decision-making process, it is reasonable to expect that borrowing choices in Colombia are politically motivated. However, how precisely does the borrowing process create bias against BRIC loans? I first examine budget loans, which are obtained not to fund a specific project, but instead are paid directly into the budget of the recipient government and can be spent at the government's discretion.

A Ministry of Finance official, who works in the department responsible for obtaining loans from multilateral organizations and governments, noted that "hiring with governments is very cumbersome. This is because our laws and internal regulations are very specific about how to hire such debt" (Interview 38). The use of a parliamentary commission to approve loans (as opposed to a technocratic committee) allows the rejection of loan proposals for political reasons. As a result, a Colombian senator said that "there is little government-to-government lending because of these rules" (Interview 21).

When asked about the reasons for rejecting Chinese loan offers in particular, an official in the Ministry of Finance and Public Credit commented on the unfavorable conditions of Chinese loans. "The Chinese have offered cheap finance but wanted the guarantee that they would get petroleum exports—which is how the Venezuelan government and African nations have done deals with China. But we do not work this way. Just because the loan is cheap, we do not agree to send them petroleum. So that is the reason why it has not worked" (Interview 38). A different government official in the same ministry said, "We have not been able to finalize anything with the Chinese because it is complex. They are not very transparent with the costs. They have their way of negotiating, but with our very strict process, it does not work for us, because we cannot agree to hire a loan until we know how much it is going to cost us. But they are not very transparent with the costs—they are like, 'We will tell you later once you give us this or that'" (Interview 38).

I triangulated these statements by interviewing creditors. Representatives of the Chinese government in Colombia are very aware of the challenges posed by this process of contracting loans. For instance, the economic and commercial counselor of the Chinese embassy to Colombia noted, "To use loans from a foreign government, there are a series of procedures to go through. For example, congress needs to approve these loans, as they would increase the external debt of Colombia" (Interview 25). Moreover, he stated that "China has not been able to lend to Colombia because the Colombian government has been hesitant" (Interview 25).

It appears, then, that Colombian politicians have the opportunity to veto Chinese loans. When asked about the reasons for rejecting budget loan offers, these statements indicate that government officials focus on the conditions attached to loan proposals, not the lending volume. Further, politicians mirror the preferences of Finance and Industry by preferring private creditors over BRIC loans.

5.4.3. Two Separate Bidding Processes for Project Loans

As I have noted, the Colombian government shuns the Chinese as a source for budget loans. Yet their aversion to Chinese loans is even more explicit with respect to project loans funding a specific undertaking. To be clear, there is no law that specifically bars loans from China but allows loans from Western governments. The discrimination is not officially tied to the identity of the creditor. Nevertheless, Colombian politicians have implemented a series of rules and procedures governing the contracting of project loans that are technically impartial, but informally prevent precisely the types of loans that China typically offers.

Colombian law mandates that all projects financed with external resources go through a sequence of two bidding processes. First, the government secures funding through a competitive bidding process. Once the funding is obtained, a second bidding process awards the contract for the project construction. Due to these processes, Chinese loans are disadvantaged compared to Western creditors in two ways.

First, Chinese loans are often not admissible in the financing stage. Officials from the Ministry of Finance and Public Credit, the Ministry of Commerce, Industry, and Tourism, and the Ministry of Foreign Affairs confirm that tied loans are not permissible under Colombian law (Interviews 18, 32, 39).[3] An official of the Ministry of Finance and Public Credit pointed out that "we have a very bureaucratic process that applies to all debt. For us it is the same process

---

[3] A former Colombian finance minister indicated that Colombia had negative experiences with tied loans in the past. He recalled the case of the Medellín Metro. Local municipalities had borrowed internationally—with the central government guaranteeing these loans—and in return were required to use a foreign company for building the metro. However, after spectacular cost overruns, the municipality was unable to repay the loan and the federal government was required to take on repayment. "The nation did not have [an] interest . . . [in] falling for this trick again" (Interview 43).

to hire with the Citibank as it is to hire with the German government. We have to follow the same procedure" (Interview 38). "We cannot direct a bidding process to a specific country—we cannot discriminate among creditors" (Interview 32). Technically, the process of securing funding for public investment is not biased. However, the Colombian rules do implicitly disadvantage a particular type of loan—namely the type that is primarily offered by the Chinese.

An official in the Ministry of Foreign Affairs recognized that this process clashes with the Chinese understanding of economic cooperation between countries: "[The Chinese] always have the government-to-government process in mind. However, it works differently in China, as essentially all enterprises are state owned. For them, if a government official says that they want you to undertake this project, then it is understood that this project is given to a certain company. However, we always have to go through a bidding process. Thus, they have to enter and compete [with other companies]" (Interview 32). Colombia views economic interactions among sovereigns as market relationships that do not necessarily carry political weight. An official in the Ministry of Commerce, Industry, and Tourism added that China views loans as tools for economic foreign policy, while Colombia understands the process of contracting loans as an arm's-length relationship (Interview 39).

In addition to tied loans not being admissible, the CICP must approve any untied loan. Just as with budget loans, the small committee of elected members of congress must approve the loan used for funding public investment projects. Thus, these politicians have the opportunity to veto Chinese loan offers at this stage, even if China should comply with Colombian rules and offer an untied loan.

In addition to the difficulties of participating in the first bidding process for funding a project, several interviewees stated that the Chinese are also disadvantaged with respect to the second bidding process concerning the project construction.

A foreign company needs to meet certain requirements to win a contract. The most important among these requirements is that the foreign company must have "Colombian experience." To win a contract, the foreign company needs to have a track record in the Colombian economy. In the words of a former Colombian ambassador to China during EXPO 2010 in Shanghai, "Companies are required to show that they have some experience in making business in Colombia as an indication that you are able to do business successfully" (Interview 29). In addition, foreign companies need a Colombian partner to win a contract, as they are not allowed to bid without legal presence in Colombia. Both industry representatives (Interview 12) and government officials confirm this (Interviews 18, 39).

However, obtaining a Colombian partner can be difficult, for both supply and demand reasons. On the supply side, section 5.2 outlines the barely concealed antipathy that Colombian businesses have toward working with Chinese companies. On the demand side, interviewees mentioned that "Chinese companies do not like to set up joint ventures, while the Americans have less trouble with this idea. It is a question of business culture" (Interview 12).

The situation presents a dilemma for Chinese companies. On the one hand, a Chinese company is less likely to obtain a Colombian partner. This makes it impossible to develop a track record in the Colombian economy. Without a track record, the company does not have the opportunity to successfully enter the bidding process for constructing a project. "You only get experience by having won a tender, which you cannot win without experience. It is like a glass wall—the Chinese can see the light at the other side, but they cannot get there. They just bang their heads at the glass wall. It is a dead-flies syndrome" (Interview 29).

One final hurdle remains. Even if China offered an untied loan and a Chinese company obtained a Colombian partner, the Chinese would need to obtain approval from Congress twice: First, when the company presents the project, approval is required by CONPES, Colombia's senior planning council. Second, approval of the CICP is required for the Colombian government to sign the loan (Interview 33). Since elected politicians dominate both committees, the possibility exists that Chinese proposals are vetoed quickly.

Describing this process in detail is necessary to understand why public officials can credibly claim that "if the Chinese want to come and if they meet the legal requirements set out, then they are more than welcomed" (Interview 24). Similarly, a representative of domestic business interests can state—without being inaccurate—that "there is no legal discrimination based on nationality. After fall, this would be illegal, as Colombia is a member of the WTO" (Interview 10).

Yet, de facto discrimination against Chinese loans exists, and it serves the interests of domestic Finance and Industry. Finance benefits from these rules directly, as it is in a strong position to offer financing to the government directly by purchasing sovereign bonds. It also benefits indirectly by providing funding for public investment projects. Industry benefits, as foreign companies willing to bid for public tenders require a Colombian partner.

In both instances, domestic economic interests are favored over the Chinese. In addition, the type of loans primarily offered by the Chinese (but not by Western creditors) is inadmissible, just as the requirement for a Colombian partner is easier to accomplish for Western companies than Chinese firms.

Colombian politicians and observers recognize this bias (Interview 5). By organizing a bidding process with particular rules, the government can effectively exclude Chinese loans and companies in favor of domestic Finance and Industry. One official in the Colombian Foreign Ministry stated

> We are thinking very differently. Business is very different among our culture and the Asian culture. . . . This process is open to any investor, whether domestic or foreign. But we cannot direct a bidding process to a specific country—we cannot discriminate among investors. . . . It has been quite difficult with [the Chinese], as it is another way of doing business. It is understandable that they say, "I am giving you a very cheap financing option; thus I have to be the one to implement it." But we cannot do it, as it would imply . . . direct[ing] the bidding process. (Interview 32)

A different government official added, "Of course, [the Chinese loans] are very interesting, as they are cheap and have long periods of amortization and grace periods—thus they would be good for the debt portfolio. . . . Obviously, free money is interesting, but free money also comes with an agenda—it is all tied, and it is difficult and cumbersome" (Interview 38).

Considering these hurdles, it is not surprising that the Chinese are unlikely to win the bidding process for funding a public investment project, nor the bidding process for constructing the project. A former minister of finance and public credit as well as of mining and energy noted the hesitation of the Chinese to even bother submitting bids on public tenders (Interview 22). An investment manager noted that the Chinese are unhappy. "They don't want to abide by these rules, as the laws do not allow them to present themselves in the best light" (Interview 29). After all, the Chinese offers are competitive only if they can provide financing in conjunction with the implementation, but not separately.

Common wisdom typically suggests that the Chinese seek out countries with "bad" institutional environments for their loans and investments. However, in the Colombian case this perspective is inaccurate. The Chinese would like to lend to and invest in a country with comparatively good institutions. However, the Colombian version of the "rules of the game" is precisely the reason why Chinese loans and investment have not materialized. For this reason, it is important to complement the supply-side approach to explaining loans with a demand-side perspective.

5.5. The Decision: Use Private Creditors and Reject Chinese Loan Offers

5.5.1. BRIC Loans

Given the dominant societal coalition, their preferences, politicians' actions, and the institutional rules, it comes as no surprise that Colombia has not obtained loans from BRICs. In fact, the data available show that Colombia has never borrowed from either Brazil, Russia, India, or China.[4] It was not for a lack of trying, though, as numerous interviewees noted that China made several loan offers to Colombia.

With respect to budget loans, the Chinese Development Bank would have been available for talks. In fact, in 2007 the Chinese Development Bank established a permanent office in the capital of Colombia, Bogotá (Interview 35).[5] In addition, several loan offers were extended to the Colombian government. Public officials told me of loan proposals by the China EXIM bank that were rejected by the government (Interview 18). A public official in the department that coordinates Colombia's external relations with Asian countries stated that "loans with China have *not yet* worked out" (Interview 39), implying that there were talks. Similarly, Chinese officials indicated that loans have not yet been extended because the Colombian government has been hesitant to accept loan offers (Interview 25).

China also offered to finance several public works projects using project loans. An official in the Ministry of Commerce, Industry, and Tourism confirmed that loans were offered, but they were not accepted (Interview 18). For example, in 2005 Colombia wanted to build an alternative to the Panama Canal, a so-called Canal Seco (Dry Canal). The government inquired whether foreign creditors—the Chinese among them—would be interested in financing this project. An official involved in this process told me that while the Chinese were initially thought of highly, they were not selected for the project (Interviews 1, 11). Colombia also rejected a Chinese loan offer for financing a hydropower project, the Acueducto Metropolitano de Bucaramanga. Instead it favored borrowing from a regional multilateral organization, the Andean

---

[4] While Colombia did not obtain bilateral loans from China, it did accept Chinese foreign aid in one instance in 2010. "In September 2010, one month after his inauguration, Santos accepted $1 million in aid from China to be used to acquire Chinese logistical military equipment [though] the deal is insignificant when compared to the more than $7.3 billion Bogotá has received from Washington under Plan Colombia" (Castaneda 2011).

[5] The CDB closed its office in Bogotá in 2014. It is telling that the rumored reason for this development was the lack of business.

Development Corporation (Corporación Andina de Fomento). Even though these negotiations fell through, Colombia still did not use Chinese money but rather borrowed from a private creditor, Bancolombia.

A former employee of Proexport indicated that China was also interested in renovating and updating the airport in Bogotá but lost both financing and project implementation bids to the Colombian consortia Opain (Interview 9). A consultant to foreign banks that want to enter the Colombian market confirmed that the Chinese loan offers had favorable financial conditions, with a 40-year maturity and 2% interest rate (Interview 16). Nevertheless, the government found the conditions attached to the loan requiring the purchase of materials in China as well as the use of Chinese staff unacceptable (Interview 18).

5.5.2. Private Creditors

Instead of borrowing from BRICs, the Colombian government has relied on private creditors. After the debt crises of the 1980s (Ocampo 1987), Colombia has successfully issued bonds since the mid-1990s (Interview 38). Between 2004 and 2015, Colombia has obtained loans from private creditors in every year. About 70% of debt is domestic, while only 30% is external. This is due to a robust domestic debt-issuing program (Interview 38). An adviser to foreign banks told me that domestic banks or pension funds own most of the domestic debt, while foreign banks own most of the external debt (Interview 16). Despite its access to private creditors, the situation is not rosy. Between 2004 and 2015, Colombia's bonds have been rated between BB and BBB, which does not signal strong endorsement. In justifying their ratings, credit rating agencies admit that monetary policy does not cause concern, thanks to a comparatively independent central bank. However, the agencies are concerned about fiscal policy (Interview 6).

Given this situation, a government official admitted that Colombia faces a trade-off. It can either seek "cheap" bilateral loans that are complicated to obtain or "expensive" private loans that are comparatively easy to acquire. "We have to decide whether we want to be children or adults. Being an adult has implications—if you can raise US$2 billion in the international bond markets because you are that good, why are you trying to get very complicated G2G [government-to-government] loans" (Interview 38).

5.5.3. IFIs

Colombia also obtained loans from multilateral institutions. Colombia no longer qualifies for some of the loan programs of the concessional loans from the World Bank (via is concessional lending arm, the International Development

Association) due to its relatively high level of income per capita (Interview 38). However, it borrowed from the nonconcessional lending arm of the World Bank, the IBRD, on seven occasions between 2004 and 2015, with a total lending volume of $10.5 billion. For example, Colombia resorted to IFIs during the financial crisis in the late 2000s (Interview 16).

5.5.4. DAC Loans

Colombia's reliance on sovereign lending from Western creditors is limited (Interview 38). It frequently obtains loans from DACs, but these are typically of small volume. For example, between 2004 and 2015, Colombia obtained one loan from Canada ($300 million) and Sweden ($100 million), three loans from Spain ($18 million, $14 million, and $14 million) and Germany ($12 million, $0.01 million, and $144 million), five loans from Japan (totaling $211 million), and six loans from France (totaling $2.2 billion). By far the most important bilateral creditor, however, is the United States. In the year 2012 alone, it provided loans totaling $2.6 billion. In addition, some state-owned enterprises have obtained loans from the US EXIM bank. For example, ColPetrol has purchased equipment from US companies that are financed with a loan from the US EXIM bank.

The Chinese also wanted to lend to ColPetrol, but the financial conditions were not as attractive, so ColPetrol decided not to hire this loan (Interview 38).

5.5.5. Other Policy Issues

Just as the preferences of the Capital Coalition strongly shape Colombia's borrowing portfolio, the same preferences also affect other policy areas. For example, in contrast to Ecuador and Peru, Colombia has yet to negotiate a free trade agreement with China. Guzmán and Berger (2012, 98) argue that "a free trade agreement between Colombia and China is unlikely in the short term, considering the Colombian position of not recognizing China as a market economy." Colombia, however, did sign free trade agreements with Canada, the United States, and the European Union.

Similarly, Colombia's diplomatic strategy toward China is characterized by a lack of initiative and attention. Specifically, the gap between official rhetoric and substantive action is significant. Following up on its statements indicating closer ties with emerging powers, Colombia opened consulates in Shanghai and Guangzhou. However, according to Ellis (2012), the limited budget allocated to these offices does not correspond to the rhetoric of the Colombian government's supposed interest in increased cooperation with China.

5.6. Colombia's Capital Coalition

Colombia's borrowing portfolio exhibits a strong preference for private creditors and, to a lesser degree, Western lenders. At the same time, several loan offers from BRICs have been rejected. The qualitative evidence in this chapter suggests that these borrowing decisions are not accidental outcomes. Rather, they reflect the interests of the dominant Capital Coalition, as the joint preferences of Industry and Finance strongly favor private creditors. The interviews show that Finance and Industry indeed hold preferences consistent with my theoretical expectations and that politicians are responsive to the interests of these core constituencies. Moreover, the analysis of the process by which Colombia signs loan contracts reveals that politicians have much influence over what type of creditor is used. As a result, the borrowing portfolio mirrors the joint preferences of Industry and Finance.

I have identified Ecuador as an example of a Corporatist Coalition between Labor and Industry and argued that Colombia represents a Capital Coalition of Industry and Finance. In the next chapter, I will argue that Peru can be characterized as a Consumer Coalition aligning Labor and Finance. If my theory is correct, this coalition should also exert its influence on policymakers in Peru, and its borrowing portfolio should correspond to the joint preferences of Finance and Labor. The next chapter examines if this is the case.

6

Peru

A Consumer Coalition Wants Western Creditors

Peru's borrowing portfolio indicates that its government relies more on bilateral loans from Western governments (DACs) than either Ecuador or Colombia. It does not borrow from emerging creditors such as Brazil, Russia, India, and China (BRICs). If my theory is correct, this is the result of Peruvian politicians satisfying the joint preferences of Finance and Labor. A Consumer Coalition between these groups prefers Western creditors—particularly DACs—over other lenders.

This chapter is structured as follows. I first examine whether Finance and Labor are the two dominant societal interest groups in Peru and show that they indeed are. Section 6.2 subsequently examines what creditors Finance and Labor prefer. The interviews indicate that both actors prefer DAC loans, but also have strong preferences for private creditors. Yet these preferences must be translated into policy. Section 6.3 shows that politicians listen to the demands by Finance and Labor, while Section 6.4 traces the process by which politicians shape borrowing decisions. The final section illustrates that Peru indeed relies more on DAC loans than governments that are responding to other coalitions. In sum, the qualitative evidence suggests that distributional consequences and societal coalitions shape Peru's borrowing portfolio.

6.1. The Coalition: Labor and Finance are the Strongest Societal Forces

Peru's societal structure is characterized by polarization. Interviewees repeatedly noted the small elite concentrated in Peru's capital, Lima, that is primarily white (Interview 26). A small middle class, created by the industrialization policies of the 1940s and 1950s, is also concentrated in Lima (Interview 105). The popular sector is comparatively large and influential. The indigenous share of the population is larger than in either Colombia or Ecuador and constitutes the majority of the popular sector (Interview 96).

Despite its size, the political representation of Labor is not straightforward, for historical reasons. In 1985, the center-left Alan García was elected president. His term was characterized by severe economic difficulties. The cumulative total inflation for the duration of his term was more than 2,000,000% with annual inflation rates as much as 7,000% in 1990. The hyperinflation as well as massive increases in foreign debt severely destabilized the Peruvian economy and increased social tensions. García's failed economic policies contributed in part to the rise of the violent rebel movement Sendero Luminoso (Shining Path).

The election of Alberto Fujimori in 1990 was a major turning point. He has been credited with restoring macroeconomic stability by introducing neoliberal reforms, also known as the "Fujishock." These measures included a sudden withdrawal of the state from the economy by eliminating price controls and reducing government subsidies. Moreover, the economy was liberalized, as exchange rate controls were removed and tariffs eliminated. Peru opened up to foreign companies by easing restrictions on investment and liberalizing capital inflows.

At the same time, the government established a $400 million poverty relief fund and quadrupled the minimum wage to address the painful adjustment process for the majority of the population.

By the mid-1990s, the Peruvian economy had returned to impressive growth rates and macroeconomic stability. In 1992, Fujimori carried out a presidential coup with the support of the military to address political deadlock that prevented further reforms. He dissolved the judiciary as well as Congress and assumed full judicial and legislative powers.

It is noteworthy that these drastic measures in the economic, security, and political realms actually improved public opinion of Fujimori in the early 1990s. Interviewees mentioned repeatedly that a large segment of the populace welcomed the changes due to their positive implications for economic growth and physical security. Following the disastrous economic situation in the 1980s, Labor "hailed anything new as the new solution" (Interview 96). As a result, left parties were discredited among Labor, which in turn resulted in the unusual situation of workers supporting neoliberal reforms (Interviews 99, 105). The success of these policies in curbing inflation had a long-lasting effect on Labor's political preferences, just as Germany's current anti-inflationary preferences are commonly explained by the memory of hyperinflation in the 1930s.

The legacy of these developments is visible in the political representation of Labor today. Workers are a dominant political force in the political landscape of Peru. Nevertheless, most workers are not organized in formal employee organizations (Interview 45). Consequently, unions themselves are not a significant political force (Interview 96). Fujimori's policies also resulted in "weak parties generally, none of which are particularly appealing to the popular sector" (Interview 96). At the same time, social movements did not develop because they were repressed by Fujimori (Interview 91). This resulted in a political landscape characterized by politicians that have incentives to appeal to the masses to get elected as independent candidates. For example, Ollanta Humala campaigned successfully for the presidency without a party to speak of. Similarly, only two of 25 regional presidents represent a national political party (*The Economist* 2013).

As a result, Labor's political demands are not expressed through institutionalized channels such as established parties or strong unions. Rather, interviewees noted that the political arena is characterized by independent politicians who run on the platform of their own newly founded party. To win elections, these newly founded platforms need to find a way to get votes and therefore typically appeal to the masses (Interview 67). The result is that Peruvian politics is marked by a quick succession of newly founded but short-lived political parties with populist tendencies. This creates a situation where a strong institutional representation of Labor is nonexistent, and yet Labor has a strong voice in Peru's political landscape.

The radical doses of neoliberal medicine, which resolved Peru's economic crisis in the 1990s, hurt businesses with fixed capital more than those relying on mobile capital (Interview 53). Fujimori's neoliberal policies had severe negative consequences for Industry. By abolishing the system of price controls, small businesses were threatened by dramatic increases in domestic prices for inputs. In addition, liberalizing trade meant stronger competition, which wiped out much of the import-competing domestic production. A strong export-oriented manufacturing sector did not develop under these conditions. For this reason, Peru's exports are dominated by natural resource exports stemming from foreign-owned mining operations. Peru has experienced vibrant growth since 2002 led by raw material exports, but at the expense of manufacturing exports (Wise and Quiliconi 2007, 410). The lack of manufacturing industry and a small stock of entrepreneurs contrasts starkly with the situation in both Colombia and Ecuador, where Industry is well established. One interviewee noted that almost 80% of the labor force works in the informal sector, which creates about 60% of GDP (Interview 45).

Since domestic Industry is not significant economically, it does not have a strong voice in the political arena. A former government official noted that the Peruvian government pays less attention to domestic industry than does the Colombian government because Industry lacks influence. Other observers agreed with the impression that Colombian Industry has more influence over foreign economic policy of their government than the Peruvian counterpart (Interview 63).

Recent economic policy reflects the weakness of domestic industry. A Colombian observer noted that "Peru has been much more neoliberal than Colombia. They opened up totally and believed in the internationalization of the economy. Colombia is one step behind. We believe in free trade, but not that much" (Interview 28). A former Peruvian prime minister added that Colombia is comparatively protectionist (average tariff of 7%–8%), while Peru is not (average tariff of 2%) (Interview 55). The reason for these differences is that no organized action of domestic industry against foreign investors exists (Interview 66). Even though some interviewees noted that there was resistance among the Peruvian textile and pharmaceutics industry, "The resistance was not very strong" (Interview 45). The former Peruvian prime minister acknowledged that the domestic textile industry was not happy about increased clothing imports, particularly from China. "However, the population is in favor of cheap clothing; thus this was no difficulty during free trade negotiations" (Interview 55).

One of the chief negotiators of the free trade agreement between Peru and the United States recounted an anecdote illustrating the situation succinctly. Peru wanted to negotiate en bloc with Colombia, but this was difficult because of different positions. Peru was open to negotiating a free trade agreement jointly with Colombia. In contrast, the Colombian government did not prefer joint negotiations because its strong industrial sector demands caution. This, in turn, is reflective of the fact that the Colombians did not have a crisis in the 1990s. In Colombia, "There was no context to do radical things—like the ones that Fujimori did in the beginning of the 1990s, which hurt the domestic industry a lot" (Interview 53). Another observer added that Colombian manufacturing is afraid of China.

This problem is absent in Peru because no manufacturing sector exists. Therefore, Peru can move more quickly in negotiating free trade agreements with China (Interview 49).

In contrast to Industry, Finance benefited from the neoliberal reforms. Interviewees noted two reasons why owners of mobile capital were able to adjust to the new situation more easily than owners of fixed capital. First, the increased capital mobility allowed Finance to seek profitable investments not only in Peru but also abroad. Second, the reforms provided macroeconomic stability and significantly reduced inflation. This directly benefited Finance, as inflation would have devalued the type of asset financial investors own.

However, just as Industry faced increased competition due to trade liberalization, capital mobility increased competition for Finance. A high-ranking manager of a private Peruvian bank revealed that his bank initially had significant difficulties competing with the multitude of foreign banks that had come to Peru since its financial liberalization. This necessitated a change in the domestic bank's strategy. Instead of competing with foreign banks for funding large, capital-intensive projects, his bank now focuses on serving consumers in the informal sector. He stated that this is a logical decision, as "the margins are bigger and we can avoid the competition of foreign banks because we have more local knowledge" (Interview 66). A representative of a different bank told me that it also changed its strategy, for similar reasons. It too stopped funding large projects, focusing instead on administering accounts for individuals and offering financial services for smaller clients (Interview 44). In short, Peruvian banks have survived the neoliberal reforms by adjusting their business model. This resulted in a division of labor where foreign banks fund large investment projects while domestic banks focus on the local market with small clients. Considering its success, observers judge the financial sector in Peru to be more developed than that in Ecuador or even Colombia (Interview 59). The prominent role of Finance in the domestic economy translates into an influential voice in the political landscape.

In sum, Peru represents a Consumer Coalition with Labor and Finance dominating Industry in the political arena. This corresponds to the assessment by Tanaka and Rojas (2010, 87), who suggest that "the legacy of the structural reforms implemented by Fujimori has generated a 'neo-dualist' situation, where a modern and growing sector that supports moderate policies coexists with a marginalized sector that sympathizes with anti-system rhetoric."

6.2. The Preferences: Preference Congruence Due to Exposure to Hyperinflation

The previous section established that Labor and Finance dominate the political landscape, while Industry is politically marginalized. What are the preferences of the resulting Consumer Coalition? According to my theory, Consumer Coalitions prefer DAC loans more strongly than do other coalitions, as both Finance and Labor have positive preferences with respect to this creditor. However, Finance and Labor disagree on how they view other creditors: while Finance dislikes BRIC loans, it should exhibit positive attitudes toward multilateral loans from IFIs and private creditors. In contrast, Labor prefers BRIC loans and is expected to have negative preferences for IFIs and private creditors. This section examines whether actors' preferences across creditors align with these theoretical assumptions.

6.2.1. BRICs

Labor is in favor of Chinese loans. Because BRIC loans are tied to investment projects, workers expect positive employment effects. Several interviewees noted that employment opportunities are the main reason Labor is in favor of BRIC loans (Interview 45). In addition, studies show that Chinese projects increase wages. Irwin and Gallagher (2013, 220) quote a manager of Chinalco, a Chinese mining company, that "demand is so high for these workers that 'no company can afford to pay little.'" Their calculation shows that Peruvian workers at Chinalco's Shougang mine earn about 2.5 times more than Peru's minimum wage.

However, interviewees also recognized that Chinese companies used to have a bad reputation. In particular, the lack of environmental and labor standards of the iron ore mine Shougang has left a negative impression on workers. This has attracted scholarly attention, but it appears that perceptions and reality differ. Irwin and Gallagher (2013, 207) "find that Shougang Hierro Peru has indeed established a poor labor and environmental record in Peru. However, a counterpart firm from the United States performed worse." Similarly, Sanborn and Chonn (2015, 1) suggest that "Chinese mining firms do not appear to be either the best or worst in the country." In fact, there are "cases where Chinese companies have exceeded local standards and outperformed their peers, including Andes Petroleum in Ecuador, Chinalco in Peru, and Golden Dragon Affiliates in Mexico" (Ray et al. 2015, 3).

My interviews confirm these findings. A representative of Minera Chinalco Peru, a Chinese mining operator, was proud to provide examples of workers receiving breakfast, the introduction of new water treatment plants, and education for truck drivers (Interview 70). In sum, Labor has positive attitudes toward Chinese loans, though perceptions of low labor standards might render them less enthusiastic than Labor in Ecuador.

In contrast, interviews with representatives of the financial sector in Peru revealed a strong resistance to the Chinese. An investment manager of a Peruvian private equity fund noted that "the Chinese are not a good business to have.... We are going to miss the Americans. They may be as corrupt as anyone else, but their values of how to do business are not shared by the Chinese" (Interview 61). As a consequence, Chinese bankers report animosities by actors in the Peruvian financial sector. Recalling experiences of such behavior, a representative of the Industrial and Commercial Bank of China exclaimed, "Other foreign companies are allowed to enter Peru as well, so why shouldn't the Chinese? Further, the other companies are welcomed in China as well, thus it is only fair that the Chinese go to Peru as well. Also, the pie is so big that you have to be able to profit somehow. If you do not profit from doing business with the Chinese, then this is your problem, not mine" (Interview 74).

Yet despite antipathy on part of Peruvian bankers, liberalizing capital flows has allowed foreign competitors to enter the Peruvian market. A representative of the Chinese Development Bank noted that "the Peruvian market is very open. It is easy to bring in capital. The rules do not discriminate between foreigners and domestic firms. Other countries are not as fair" (Interview 75). A different official of the same bank added, "We operate like a normal commercial bank. We consider the market conditions. Thus, we are not different from others" (Interview 73).

The increased competition by foreign banks has made it difficult for the domestic financial sector to provide funding for large investment projects. This is particularly true for the multitude of Chinese projects in Peru (Interview 45). A former prime minister noted that the Chinese "bring the cash themselves—they have no connection to the domestic banking sector" (Interview 55). A representative of the largest domestic bank in Peru noted, "[We] do not even bid on [such projects] because we do not have the resources" (Interview 44). Chinese investors confirmed this. For example, Minera Chinalco Peru obtained funding from the Chinese EXIM bank. The company does not use private equity funds or other private funding sources (Interview 70). As I have noted, this has prompted Peruvian banks to change their strategy away from funding large investment projects to catering to small businesses and individuals.

In some cases, the new focus of Peruvian banks on local small-scale markets has actually allowed a few isolated instances of small-scale cooperation with Chinese banks. For example, a recent project valued at $1 billion was funded with $800 million from a Chinese bank and $200 million by several Peruvian banks, among which were Interbank and the Banco de Credito del Peru. However, a representative of the latter stated, "They don't need our money—they just want local partners" (Interview 44). Similarly, Chinese banks have lent Peruvian banks very small amounts to fund small-scale projects in Peru. Interbank has received $30 million, while the Banco de Credito del Peru has received a similarly small loan. Intrigued, I inquired as to why Chinese banks would fund projects indirectly through Peruvian banks instead of funding projects directly. The private banker responded that, with these small projects, the Chinese "are not competitive. Only if the project has a time horizon of five years or more [do] the Chinese have a chance. The Chinese are simply not cheap enough" (Interview 44). These statements reinforce the impression that Finance found a niche in the local market that allows profits in spite of increased foreign competition.

6.2.2. DACs

While Labor and Finance have conflicting preferences regarding BRICs, they agree that DAC loans are beneficial. For example, interviews revealed that Labor is attracted by Western governments' focus on social issues such as health and education. Given the liberalization of the Peruvian economy, workers appear aware of the need to build human capital to succeed in a market-based economy. In addition, interviewees mentioned that corruption is an important issue to most, which the good-governance requirements attached to DAC loans might help prevent.

Similarly, Finance views bilateral loans from Western governments favorably, but for different reasons. In an interview already quoted, a representative of an investment firm noted that actors from the financial sector prefer Western business partners, as they share the same values (Interview 61). As a result of the strong correlation between DAC loans and investment by Western companies (Bunte 2018a), Finance favors DAC loans. In addition, interviewees had the opinion that the good-governance conditions attached to DAC loans— while not as strong as those attached to IMF loans—nevertheless push their government in the "right" direction.

6.2.3. Private Creditors

My theory assumes that Finance strongly favors private creditors, while Labor does not. I find qualified support for these expectations. As predicted, interviews with Finance revealed strong preferences in favor of private creditors. The positive implications of neoliberal reforms under Fujimori have left a mark on the preferences of Finance. In particular, Finance favors the government issuing bonds over using bilateral creditors.

Finance would benefit from this in several ways. First, it represents the vast majority of domestic bondholders and would benefit from the use of tax revenues to pay interest on bonds. Second, if the sovereign government issues more bonds, the bond market deepens, creating positive spillovers for financial institutions, which would be able to issue corporate bonds. Lastly, and most importantly, if domestic financial interests purchase government bonds, they create a stake by the state in the survival of the banking sector: Should government bond prices fall, local banks take a large hit. To prevent the perception that vulnerable banks may drag sovereigns down, the Peruvian government may be more likely to bail out Finance should an economic crisis occur.

In contrast, Labor is less enthusiastic about private creditors, though its preferences are not as strongly negative as I expected. The historical context helps explain this finding.

The failed left-wing policies of the 1980s resulted in hyperinflation and macroeconomic instability. Labor's collective memory is therefore scarred by experiences of rapidly dwindling real wages and lack of investment due to macroeconomic instability. The depth of the economic crisis of the 1980s and its negative effects on Labor were much stronger in Peru than in Ecuador or Colombia. Because of this, several interviewees noted that the neoliberal project succeeded in part because Labor was in favor of it. Faced with hyperinflation that undermined wages, Labor welcomed any policy that differed from the previous economic policies (Interview 96). Anything new, even if unknown, was better than the unsuccessful attempts of the past. This explains the remarkably positive public opinion toward Fujimori in the early 1990s. It also explains why Labor remains supportive of a promarket approach to economic policy.

This aversion to inflation, which Labor shares with Finance, has implications for the type of creditors that Labor prefers. Since Labor approves of promarket approaches, the most logical creditor is the private market. In my conversations, interviewees still expressed dissatisfaction with bonds. The reason was that only a small fraction of Labor can afford purchasing bonds directly or benefit indirectly through the participation in pension funds. Consequently, interest payments on bonds represent a redistribution of tax revenues from the entire population to white-collar bondholders. Yet Labor's objections to bonds are not as strong as in Ecuador or Peru, as the positive experiences with promarket approaches in the 1990s are still influential.

6.2.4. IFIs

Finance has positive attitudes toward multilateral loans due to the success of the IMF program that Peru implemented in the early 1990s. The conditions attached to IMF loans reduced inflation and increased capital mobility, which benefited Finance.

Labor in Peru, in contrast, exhibited conflicted preferences with respect to IFIs like those we have observed with private creditors. On the one hand, workers recall negative distributional consequences resulting from the structural adjustment reforms implemented in an IMF program in the 1990s. For example, scholars have observed strong protests against the privatization of state-owned enterprises that was required by the IMF (Arce 2008).

However, I expected Labor's preferences to be more negative than they are. Drawing on recent, personal experiences with hyperinflation, workers know that uncontrolled inflation reduces real wages and understand to some degree why the IMF's drastic promarket reforms were necessary. Civil society has subsequently adopted Labor's positions (Arce 2006). In sum, the position of Labor toward multilateral loans is negative, but workers in Peru are less opposed to IMF loans than workers in Ecuador or Colombia.

In sum, Finance and Labor have conflicting preferences with respect to BRIC loans but agree on the virtues of DAC loans. With respect to private creditors, however, Peruvian Labor differs from Labor in Ecuador and Colombia: While workers exhibit negative attitudes toward private and IFI creditors, their preferences are not as strong as initially expected.

6.3. The Politicians: Catering to Labor and Finance

The previous sections show that Finance and Labor jointly prefer DAC loans and weakly prefer private creditors. Do politicians listen to the demands of this Consumer Coalition?

With respect to Finance, interviewees noted that the financial sector has a strong voice in the political arena (Interview 59). Faced with strong foreign competition, domestic financial firms ceased funding large projects and instead focus on offering financial services for individuals, such as personal accounts, consumer loans, and the management of remittances (Interview 44).

As a consequence, Peruvian politicians in search for both campaign contributions and votes can cater to Finance and at the same time claim that their support for Finance benefits Labor. Therefore, Peruvian politicians have a strong incentive to listen to Finance.

Similarly, politicians have an incentive to listen to Labor. Peru's party system is extremely weak, as no traditional left- or right-wing parties are institutionalized (Tanaka 2011). Instead, Peru's political culture is characterized by "the proliferation of candidate-centered movements" (Levitsky and Cameron 2008, 2). Given the absence of institutionalized constituencies, these candidates often attempt to appeal to Labor using populist arguments. An example is President Fujimori's (1990–2000) electoral strategy. According to Cameron (2011, 379), "Fujimori understood that the key to his regime's electoral survival lay in attending to the interests of voters who had in the past voted for the Left ... and whose loyalty could be purchased through concrete and targeted policy measures and spending. At the same time, he kept business and the urban middle classes content with economically orthodox macroeconomic policies." President Toledo (2001–2006) provides a second example. Barr (2003, 1161) argues that "Peru's Alejandro Toledo can be considered a neopopulist leader. Neopopulists seek to develop personalistic ties with the dispossessed, unorganized masses, while also appealing to international economic interests."

This stands in stark contrast to neighboring Colombia, where President Uribe "made no concerted effort to cultivate political support among the masses. [Instead, Uribe is a] politician who appeals primarily to the middle and upper classes" (Dugas 2010, 1117). A third example is Alan García, Peru's president from 2006 to 2011. Cameron (2011, 380) notes that the urban poor voted overwhelmingly for populist García instead of traditional left-wing candidates such as Humala. In sum, considering the absence of established traditional parties and the lack of strong domestic industry, Peruvian political candidates have a strong incentive to appeal to Labor's demands.

This bias toward Labor and Finance—and against Industry—is visible in various policy areas. For example, when deciding between competing bids for public investment projects, a representative of the Government Procurement Supervisory Authority (Organismo Supervisor de las Contrataciones del Estado, OSCE) noted that, conditional on the technical aspects of the bids being satisfactory, politicians exhibit a strong preference for accepting the bid that promises the lowest cost for consumers, irrespective of its impact on domestic industry (Interview 62). More importantly, politicians are concerned that public investment contracts granted to foreign companies do not create sufficient spillovers into the local economy and therefore do not benefit the local population (Interviews 57, 60). To address this concern, Peru requires that at least 75% of the employees for a project be Peruvians, and they have to earn at least 70% of all wages, but does not require any materials to be purchased from Peruvian companies (Interview 75). In contrast, Colombian rules favor domestic industry, as 20% of the services and materials used must be obtained from domestic companies, but the requirements do not mention a specific number of Colombian workers that must be used. These differences illustrate how Colombia's regulations favor domestic Industry, while Peru's rules primarily benefit Labor.

Proinversion, the governmental department that coordinates public investment projects and selects projects, is a more elaborate illustration of politicians catering to Finance and Labor. The selection process is a major political battleground, as politicians seek to win electoral support by securing projects for their constituencies (Interview 67). In this area, Peruvian politicians tend to cater to the interests of Labor and Finance and ignore Industry. This differs from Colombia, where politicians primarily act in the interests of Industry and Finance. For example, one former government official told me that in 2008 and 2009 the Peruvian president issued two decrees to boost the economy during the economic downturn. These highly publicized decrees required the implementation of 12 and 20 investment projects, respectively, within a year. Notwithstanding, only five of these 32 projects were realized. One observer noted that "this was a populist action to show the people that the government is doing something. However, these kinds of projects need more time for preparation" (Interview 53).

This is not an isolated incident. Populist motivations, rather than business considerations, underlie the selection of public investment projects. One indication of this is the relative quality of project preparation in Colombia and Peru. Because Colombia caters to the interests of Industry, the government has an interest in proposing realistic projects that can be implemented and, as a result, benefit Industry. In contrast, Peru's Proinversion appears to announce projects despite a lack of preparation. A former deputy minister of the economy admitted that Peru does not have a priority list of future public investment projects: "There is no plan, and consequently no technical studies regarding the feasibility and viability of potential projects" (Interview 47). Officials of the central bank further indicated that there are two types of project proposals. Some proposals are well prepared and come with feasibility studies, while others lack sufficient documentation (Interviews 57, 60). An official working within Proinversion confirmed this state of affairs (Interview 56).

To explain this behavior, several interviewees pointed to the composition of Proinversion's board. It consists of five ministers who are not technocrats and are unfamiliar with project finance and implementation (Interview 53). It is apparent that technical experts do not have a voice at board meetings. One former participant of these board meetings told me that a minister barked at him: "If you are not a minister, you are just taking notes." He added, "That's why my wife is quite happy that I changed jobs. It is hard to raise my voice when something can happen to you." Another interviewee added, "The meeting is completely informal. There are no rules. There is not even the obligation to present written reports before presenting a project to the board" (Interview 53).

Under these conditions, politicians "have the political incentive to propose projects regardless of their cost-benefit analysis" (Interview 67). Consequently, "Technical decisions were not respected if [the board members] wanted something" (Interview 47). A former public official pointed out that the well-prepared projects, which included a formal presentation along with the necessary legal and technical reports disseminated prior to the meeting, were generally those prepared by Proinversion staff members. In contrast, if ministers proposed projects, they were generally presented in an ad hoc fashion, without prior documents, without technical analysis disseminated beforehand, and without PowerPoint slides—just an oral presentation (Interview 53). In addition, the political cycle reinforces the tendency to produce poorly prepared proposals. Interviewees noted that the politicians' four- or five-year terms do not coincide with the cycle of a typical project, which lasts about seven years from planning to implementation. Thus, if a politician is to use a project as a signal to his constituency, the approval process needs to be shortened. This can most easily be accomplished by disregarding the need for careful legal and technical studies (Interview 67).

To summarize, the high number of project proposals, their poor preparation, and the subsequently low number of projects realized suggest that this process serves populist considerations rather than business interests. Project announcements are political signals to Labor, while the interests of Industry in viable preparation of projects are disregarded.

6.4. The Process: Borrowing Procedures in Peru

The borrowing procedure in Peru starts with a ministry preparing a request for funding.[1] For example, the Finance Ministry might outline the need for a budget loan, while a sectoral ministry might propose financing a particular project with external resources. These proposals are then evaluated by the Ministry of Economics and Finance (Ministerio de Economia y Finanzas, MEF) for viability. If a suggested project is deemed worthwhile, the MEF solicits loan offers.

Once these offers have been obtained, the MEF does not have to coordinate with other ministries or committees but can decide directly which creditor to use. The MEF consequently plays a prominent role, as no other ministry is involved in the process (Interview 69). As one official put it, "Only the MEF negotiates the actual loan" (Interview 65). The MEF then negotiates the financial terms of the agreement, such as the loan amount, grace period, interest rate, and commission. Once the loan agreement has been drawn up, politicians have the final word. The Council of Ministers (Consejo de Ministros) reviews the proposed loan contract and, upon approval, signs the loan (Interview 46).

In contrast to the process in Ecuador and Colombia, the borrowing procedure in Peru involves comparatively few actors. The central role of the Ministry of Economy and Finance in soliciting loan offers and drawing up the contract, however, does not mean that technocrats control the process. First, the minister of economy and finance has a say in the in-house decision on which loan offer to select. Second, and more importantly, every loan must be approved by the Council of Ministers. This implies that an explicitly political body has the right to veto loan offers. In this regard, Peru's Council of Ministers fulfills a function similar to those of Ecuador's Debt Committee and Colombia's Interparliamentary Public Finance Commission (CICP).

---

[1] The information of this section is based on interviews with several government officials (Interviews 65, 72).

However, while the Colombian and Ecuadorian committees are involved throughout the process of contracting loans, the Peruvian political veto player enters only at the end. Because of this late entrance, Dargent (2011) argues that Peruvian technocrats are independent from politicians and have preferences of their own. I disagree, for two reasons. First, just because politicians enter into the decision-making process of borrowing relatively late does not mean that they do not exert influence. In fact, interviewees noted that the opposite is the case: the bureaucratic process has to predict the preferences of the Council of Ministers when deciding which loan offer to pursue. This requires backward induction on part of the Ministry of Economy and Finance. It is therefore not surprising that interviewees noted "preemptive obedience," as the MEF tries to anticipate the loan proposal that the Council of Ministers will prefer. Second, Arce (2010) argues that dominant interest groups are able to advance their preferences in economic policy by promoting the appointment of technocrats in high positions in the MEF. As a result, the borrowing decisions by Peruvian politicians reflect the demands of Labor and Finance, as opposed to Industry.

This is most obvious when comparing the approach to funding public investment in Colombia with that of Peru. Section 5.4 shows that Colombia implicitly discriminates against Chinese loans by requiring separate bidding processes for funding and constructing a project. Tied loans are not allowed, a significant disadvantage to Chinese creditors, which primarily offer tied loans.

In contrast to Colombia, the Chinese are not at a disadvantage in Peru because tied loans are permitted. An interviewee in the Ministry of Foreign Trade noted that project financing and execution are not separate bidding processes (Interview 63). In fact, a company first wins the bid for a project and is only then responsible for securing the necessary funds from either public or private sources (Interview 67). A representative of the Government Procurement Supervisory Authority (OSCE) added that the agency does not care how the project is financed—it is entirely up to the company executing the project. The company only has to show that it has 10% of the required funds available at the beginning of the construction (Interview 62). An official of Proinversion added, "I am just looking for you to invest. It is up to you how you finance the project. It's your business" (Interview 56). Officials are interested only in royalties and in the contractor's adhering to social and environmental standards. Interviews with the Chinese Development Bank confirmed that "Peru doesn't care where the money comes from as long as there is investment in Peru" (Interview 75).

While Chinese loans are not disadvantaged, they are also not preferred. Labor and Finance expose politicians to conflicting demands, as the former prefers Chinese loans but the latter rejects them. This results in inconclusive attitudes among politicians. For example, a former prime minister commented that China's growing engagement in Peru is likely a positive prospect as the

Chinese "are very pragmatic" (Interview 55). Nevertheless, officials were hesitant. A representative of the OSCE noted, "If practices of Chinese state-owned enterprises are not so good, then we need to be careful" (Interview 62). Another interviewee added that this is particularly the case with respect to labor and environmental issues. "We asked them to change their attitudes and behaviors" (Interview 46). In response to rejected bids, Chinese companies have become more professional and are now "sophisticated" (Interview 46). In sum, the Peruvian process of contracting project loans does not discriminate against the Chinese (unlike the Colombian process), but it does not favor Chinese loans (unlike the Ecuadorian process).

6.5. The Result: Preference for Western Loans
6.5.1. BRIC Loans

As noted earlier, Labor views BRIC creditors favorably, while Finance does not. Considering these contradictory preferences within the Consumer Coalition, politicians are rather ambivalent about BRIC loans. This explains the governments' hands-off approach: In comparison to Colombia or Ecuador, the Peruvian government plays a small role in obtaining funding for investment projects. Consequently, direct loans from BRIC creditors are rare, as confirmed by both central bankers and government officials (Interviews 57, 63, 65). Peru obtained no loans from Brazil, Russia, India, or China between 2004 and 2015. An interviewee in the debt department of the Ministry of Economy and Finance confirmed that only small loans from the Chinese Development Bank obtained in the 1990s are still on the books (Interview 65).

Unlike in Ecuador or Colombia, the high degree of capital mobility implies a different role for the Peruvian government in investment projects. As previously noted, the state does not first secure funding from an external creditor to, in turn, pay a foreign contractor to execute a project. When President Pedro Pablo Kuczynski visited China in 2016, he noted that his delegation did not "go to Beijing 'to borrow' but to seek collaboration in infrastructures, commerce, and tourism. 'We are not looking for credits or financial aid, but investment'" (*El Comercio* 2016).

Instead, Peru's liberal approach means that investors themselves obtain funding for a project from external creditors. Companies use institutions such as the China EXIM bank and the Chinese Development Bank directly (Interviews 64, 73). Representatives of the CDB added that the bank's headquarters in China can transfer the resources directly to a Chinese company that is also located in China. In this case, the money never leaves China (Interview 73).

Consequently, Chinese companies do not require the government borrowing to fund the project, nor do the companies themselves need to issue equity to finance their operations (Interviews 44, 45, 55). Examples of this practice are the Toromocho Mining project, where the Chinese company Chinalco obtained $2.5 billion directly from the Chinese EXIM bank (Interviews 55, 70). China MinMetals obtained a $2.5 billion loan from the Chinese EXIM bank for the Galeno copper mine. Similarly, the $1 billion expansion of the Marcona mine owned by Shougang was financed primarily with Chinese loans directly to the company (Interview 44). Infrequent use of BRIC loans corresponds to the theoretical expectations for governments responding to a Consumer Coalition.

6.5.2. IFI Loans

In line with the theoretical expectations, Peru did not rely on IFI loans. Between 2004 and 2015, Peru has obtained only two small loans from the IMF ($185 million in 2004 and $109 million in 2007). Interviewees note that in the past some small loans were obtained from the Inter-American Development Bank (IDB) and the Development Bank of Latin America (Corporación Andina de Fomento) (Interviews 45, 66).

However, the total volume currently on the books amounts to only about US$200 million. Moreover, a Peruvian observer commented that these loans were obtained "less for the money, but more to get the technical cooperation" (Interview 47).

6.5.3. DAC Loans

In contrast, between 2004 and 2015, bilateral loans from Western governments are common (Interview 46). For example, there are loans from the German Investment and Development Corporation (Deutsche Investitions- und Entwicklungsgesellschaft, DEG), Netherlands Development Finance Company (Financierings-Maatschappij voor Ontwikkelingslanden, FMO), the French development financial institution PROPARCO, and the EXIM bank of the United States (Interview 66). Similarly, the Japan International Cooperation Agency funds several small projects (Interview 47). Among these creditors, Germany and Japan provide the largest loan volume, with $565 million and $781 million respectively.

In the creditor country, different government agencies facilitate DAC lending. However, these institutions differ as some provide concessional loans for development purposes, while others follow a more market-based approach.

What is common to the bilateral loans obtained by the Peruvian government is that creditor institutions are typically of the market-based type. For example, PROPARCO is a development financial institution whose majority shareholder is the French government, as the Agence Française de Développement owns 57% of shares. FMO is a bilateral private-sector development bank that is majority owned by the Dutch government. Similarly, the DEG is a federally owned company. All of these institutions lend to developing countries with the intention of facilitating private sector investments.

Obtaining bilateral loans from these organizations is fitting given the neoliberal orientation of both Finance and Labor in Peru. In addition, the conditions of these loans align with this approach to economic development. For example, the two loans totaling US$65 million lent by the EXIM bank of the United States to Peru in 2014 will be used to build two wind power projects. The blades and the 129MW wind turbines will come from Siemens plants in Iowa and Kansas (*renews*, 2014). Similarly, the Canadian government has announced US$53 million to facilitate both a mining-related initiative and improvement of the local education system (*CP24* 2013). This focus of bilateral loans on social expenditure also fits into the neoliberal character of Peruvian reforms. Ever since the Fujishock, economic reforms have focused on privatization and liberalization to make markets more efficient and to better exploit existing comparative advantages. The government needs to ensure that the population has the necessary skills to succeed in a market environment. This explains not only domestic reforms such as the last reform in 2013, which included improved tax incentives for worker training (*The Economist* 2013), but also why the bilateral loans from Western creditors sought out by the Peruvian government often include conditions aimed at improving education.

6.5.4. Private Creditors

The reliance on bilateral loans from Western governments and the simultaneous underutilization of both Chinese loans and multilateral creditors aligns well with the theoretical expectations of borrowing patterns by governments responsive to Consumer Coalitions. However, Peru heavily relies on private creditors. The reliance on market mechanisms to obtain loans is in line with the overall economic strategy of Peru and, in itself, does not contradict the theoretical hypotheses. But Peru relies on bonds to a larger degree than expected. Peru has been successful in placing bonds both internationally and domestically (Interviews 47, 57, 60) that have been denominated in both US dollars and Peruvian soles (Interview 45). Between 2004 and 2015, Peru obtained a total of $13.8 billion from private creditors.

The strategy of recent bond issuances is instructive with respect to its distributional consequences. For example, in 2014 Peru sold 7.41 billion soles (US$2.54 billion) in 10-year bonds, and US$500 million in a reopened dollar-denominated global bond. Finance minister Alonso Segura commented that "more than 80% of the operation was really to manage our debt.... We're continuing to de-dollarize our debt, which is a strategy we have been implementing for some time" (*Reuters* 2014). Peru has reduced its reliance on debt denominated in dollars from 85% in 2004 to 44% 2013, and intended to cut the amount of dollar-denominated debt to 30% by 2017. The government intends to spur domestic securities trading by relying on local currency bonds instead of dollar-denominated bonds (*Bloomberg* 2015). Clearly, a deepening of the domestic securities market would be in the interests of domestic Finance, which can expect positive distributional consequences from these operations.

6.5.5. Other Policy Issues

Politicians' deference to Labor and Finance is not limited to the choice of creditors. Rather, the preferences of the Consumer Coalition also shape trade policy, where politicians side with consumers rather than producers. For example, Peru signed a free trade agreement with China in 2009 (Sanborn and Yong 2013, 7). This agreement was not uncontroversial. In particular, the domestic textile industry was opposed (Gonzalez-Vicente 2012, 108). A former prime minister recalled tensions ahead of the negotiations, but "the population was in favor of cheap clothing. Thus this [resistance] posed no difficulty during the negotiations" (Interview 55). An official in the Ministry of Foreign Trade and Tourism noted that the societal demand for trade protection is less intense in Peru than in Colombia, "because there are simply more people who demand higher tariffs in Colombia than in Peru" (Interview 52). He recognized that demands for protectionism exist as well, such as in the agricultural and poultry sectors. Yet politicians typically decide in favor of Labor, lowering prices for consumers rather than protecting domestic industry.

6.6. A Consumer Coalition in Peru

My theory predicts that governments responsive to the preferences of Finance and Labor will rely more on DAC loans than other governments. The qualitative evidence offered in this chapter provides support for this assertion. Peru's political landscape is dominated by Finance and Labor, while domestic Industry is a comparatively weak actor. Interviews confirm that the preferences of the two coalitional partners are surprisingly congruent. While they disagree about BRIC loans, they both view DAC loans as beneficial and exhibit weakly positive (Labor) and strongly positive (Finance) preferences for private creditors. Qualitative evidence suggests that politicians have the incentive to pay attention to demands by Finance and Industry, and that they have the opportunity to shape borrowing decisions. As a result, Peru relies more on DACs than other governments, while the majority of loans are obtained from private creditors.

In sum, the fieldwork in Peru confirms the insights gained in Ecuador and Colombia: Societal coalitions have preferences across creditors, and politicians are responsive to these preferences, resulting in distinct borrowing portfolios. The question is whether the insights based on qualitative evidence from three countries also apply to other developing nations. The next part of the book offers a quantitative analysis examining whether societal interest groups shape borrowing portfolios in all developing countries.

PART II

QUANTITATIVE EVIDENCE

7

Generalizing the Findings with Statistical Analyses

The qualitative evidence presented in chapters 4, 5, and 6 strongly supports the argument that societal coalitions shape borrowing portfolios. A Corporatist Coalition dominates the political arena in Ecuador, a Capital Coalition in Colombia, and a Consumer Coalition in Peru. The statements and actions by politicians and government officials in all three countries mirror the joint preferences of the two dominant groups. This results in distinct borrowing patterns. In Ecuador, politicians, responding to incentives created by the Corporatist Coalition, favor BRIC loans over Western creditors. Politicians in Colombia, motivated by the Capital Coalition, reject Chinese loan proposals and instead rely on bonds and private banks. Politicians in Peru, responding to a Consumer Coalition, prefer bilateral loans from Western governments and private creditors. Societal coalitions, therefore, have a strong effect on the borrowing decisions of governments.

7.1. The Merits of Fieldwork and Statistical Analysis

Fieldwork evidence has several advantages: interviews with societal actors, creditor representatives, and politicians make it possible to delineate the decision-making process. However, qualitative approaches have two distinct drawbacks.

First, the time and resources required to conduct fieldwork make analyzing more than a handful of cases difficult. In my case, fieldwork produced evidence from only three countries. Considering this small number of cases, my findings may not be generalizable. Furthermore, Ecuador, Colombia, and Peru are all located in South America, and the political economy of African countries, for example, may differ significantly. I must show that borrowing decisions in a large number of countries and over a long period of time follow the empirical regularities that my theory expects.

Second, it is difficult to account for confounding factors. As noted in chapter 3, I intentionally chose countries that share political, cultural, economic, and geographic similarities. The intention was to generate ceteris paribus conditions to rule out possible alternative explanations. For instance, any variation in borrowing portfolios cannot be a result of regime type, as Ecuador, Colombia, and Peru do not differ in this regard: They are all democracies. While this research design has the advantage of being able to control for regime type, it also implies a drawback: my qualitative evidence cannot provide insights into whether societal coalitions also shape borrowing portfolios in nondemocracies. Interest groups may be able to influence dictators, but it is equally possible that they are irrelevant in autocracies. My fieldwork cannot speak to this question, as it did not study an autocratic country. In short, the advantages of the qualitative research design (controlling for differences in regime type) also imply drawbacks (inability to study the phenomenon in question across different regime types).

For this reason, I complement the qualitative analysis with a quantitative investigation. I conduct statistical analyses of 92 developing countries between 2004 and 2015 to test if the type of coalition in a particular country shapes the government's borrowing portfolio.

7.2. Three Challenges for Quantitative Evidence

Conducting statistical analyses requires quantitative information on both the dependent and independent variables. Furthermore, the data must be analyzed using an appropriate methodology to ensure accurate findings. In this context, I face three challenges.

The first challenge relates to the outcome to be explained. To conduct a statistical analysis, I need information on the borrowing portfolio of developing countries. While loan data are available for most creditors, obtaining credible data for emerging lenders is challenging. For example, Chinese lending data are state secrets and not available from the Chinese government. Researchers have pursued various strategies to estimate capital *outflows* from emerging lenders with limited success. In contrast, I analyze all capital *inflows* to recipient countries. Once I collected all inflows to developing countries originating from China, I was able to reverse-engineer Chinese lending data. The resulting data set covers the borrowing activities of 127 developing countries from Western governments (DAC), emerging creditors (Brazil, Russia, India, and China, the

BRICs), international financial institutions (IFIs), and private creditors for the years 2004–2015. Note that these data capture only loans obtained by the recipient government. As noted in chapter 1, loans are not the same as foreign aid, also known as official development assistance (ODA), which also includes grants, in-kind transfers, food aid, and technological assistance. Extremely cheap loans may qualify as ODA, while more expensive loans do not. Because the overall share of loans in total ODA has declined over time, there is little empirical overlap between foreign aid and bilateral loans (Brech and Potrafke 2014, 63).

The second challenge relates to the key independent variable. The analysis requires a quantitative measure capturing which societal coalition dominates a particular developing country. Such data are not easily available, as these coalitions are not directly observable. For instance, Finance and Industry do not have a formal agreement to lobby the government for their preferred choice of creditor. Yet interviews with politicians clearly indicate that they understood whose interests were aligned, and that politicians intended to satisfy two interest groups at once. Measuring the "power" of societal groups (Finance, Industry, and Labor) reliably and "objectively" across a large number of cases is challenging.

Faced with this difficulty, I create three novel measures capturing the relative power of Finance, Industry, and Labor. Using these measures as independent variables in the statistical analysis allows me to estimate which type of coalition dominates the political landscape of a particular country at a specific time.

Lastly, I also face a methodological hurdle. The outcome to be explained—recipient countries' borrowing portfolios—is a compositional variable. It measures the share of lending volume obtained from four types of creditors. This implies that all shares must add up to 100% and, importantly, an increase in one creditor's share must be offset by a relative decrease in the shares of the remaining creditors. It is difficult to account for these characteristics of compositional data with an appropriate estimation method, particularly if individual loan shares from a particular creditor are allowed to equal zero. I address this challenge by extending a fractional logit model to multiple fractions.

7.3. Preview of the Quantitative Evidence

Chapter 8 provides details on the data used for quantitative analysis. It discusses in detail the source and definition of borrowing data and how borrowing portfolios—the dependent variable—are constructed. In addition, it explains how I empirically measure the strength of societal groups across developing countries, which is the key independent variable. In short, I combine two types of information: First, I utilize information on the ability of groups to overcome collective action problems to measure whether interest groups are able to organize politically. Second, even if a group is able to overcome collective action problems, politicians might listen to its demands only if the group is essential in the domestic economy. I combined information on the organization capabilities of groups with that on their economic significance to create a proxy for their political influence.

Chapter 9 utilizes these measures of political strength to examine whether societal coalitions shape borrowing portfolios. I first discuss the difficulties of accurately modeling compositional dependent variables. I then model the determinants of borrowing portfolios. The statistical analysis shows that societal coalitions strongly shape borrowing portfolios across the developing world. Countries dominated by a Corporatist Coalition between Labor and Industry borrow more from BRIC creditors than do governments responding to other coalitions; nations in which a Capital Coalition is the strongest societal force borrow more from private creditors than other countries; governments responding to a Consumer Coalition borrow more from DAC creditors than countries accountable to other types of coalitions.

The effect of societal coalitions is robust to the inclusion of control variables such as existing debt and other economic variables. Furthermore, the analysis shows that societal coalitions shape borrowing portfolios in a variety of institutional environments. For example, societal interest groups are influential in both democracies and autocracies, across different types of electoral systems, and under both left- and right-wing governments. I also test whether the impact of BRIC loans stems primarily from Chinese loans, or if loans from Brazil, Russia, and India also show consistent effects. The findings indicate that the effect is consistent across all four BRICs and that the results are not driven by China alone. The findings point to significant differences in the conditions attached to loans from Western creditors versus those attached to loans from emerging creditors.

Chapter 10 examines the validity of rival explanations. For example, differences in borrowing patterns persist even after accounting for variation in access to creditors. Here I consider borrowing portfolios conditional on income levels, credit rating, and default history. The findings suggest that borrowing portfolios are the result of *both* supply- and demand-side considerations. In addition, the analysis provides strong support for the argument that the governments of developing countries do not choose creditors with specific tasks in mind. For example, countries with similar infrastructure needs use either BRIC or World Bank loans, depending on the societal coalition. Similarly, borrowers with similar social needs, as measured by infant mortality or literacy rates, use different creditors. Furthermore, countries with similar default histories differ in their preferred source of credit depending on the dominant societal coalition. I show that societal coalitions exert significant influence on borrowing decisions even after taking into account differences in loan prices, indicating that the financial terms of loan offers are not as important as the political conditionalities attached to them. The findings are also robust to alternative demand-side explanations, such as borrowing from ideologically aligned creditors (as measured by UN voting patterns) or security alliances.

8

Measuring Borrowing Portfolios and Group Strength

The qualitative evidence in the previous chapters shows that borrowing decisions in Ecuador, Colombia, and Peru are shaped by societal coalitions. Does my argument apply to all developing countries? To examine this question, I complement the qualitative investigation with statistical analyses of data from a large set of developing countries. Statistical analyses require data to explain both the outcome and the key explanatory variable. The present chapter describes the process of obtaining these data.

With respect to the outcome variable, I need data on the portfolio of loans obtained by developing countries. This is challenging, as some creditors are not forthcoming with data on their lending activities. For example, China treats their lending data as state secrets. In section 8.1, I explain how I obtain accurate lending data despite these difficulties. In short, instead of collecting information on capital *outflows* from creditor countries, I collect data on capital *inflows* into debtor countries to reverse engineer Chinese outflows.

Regarding the key explanatory variable, I need data on societal coalitions. Such data are not easily available, as informal coalitions are not directly observable. For instance, I cannot obtain and code contracts between Finance and Industry to lobby the government for their preferred choice of creditor, as such contracts do not exist. Yet interviews with politicians clearly indicated that they understood whose interests were aligned, and their political choices were designed to satisfy two interest groups at once. Section 8.2 describes how I create measures that proxy the political strength of Labor, Industry, and Finance. Here I combine information on their respective ability to overcome collective action problems and their importance to the domestic economy. However, I want to emphasize that the measures of the political strength of Labor, Industry, and Finance are necessarily imperfect, as they attempt to measure a factor that cannot be observed directly. Thus, the measures developed for the independent variables should be understood as *proxies* for the phenomenon in question.

8.1. The Dependent Variable: Borrowing Portfolios

The outcome to be explained is the share of loans obtained by governments from four different creditors: bilateral loans from Western governments (DACs), bilateral loans from emerging creditors Brazil, Russia, India, and China (BRICs), multilateral loans from international financial institutions (IFIs), and private creditors. For this reason, I need information on loans received from each of these types of creditors. Data on loans obtained from IFIs, such as the World Bank and the IMF, are easily available from the institutions themselves. Similarly, there is reliable information on loans obtained from Western governments, while data for private creditors are available from official sources.

However, obtaining reliable data on BRIC loans is a challenge. In particular, data on Chinese loans to developing countries are difficult to obtain as China regards its lending activities as state secrets. Without information on Chinese loans to developing countries, I cannot calculate the borrowing portfolio of recipient governments. In this section, I briefly summarize existing approaches to collecting data on Chinese lending activities. I subsequently introduce my data and discuss its advantages over existing data.

8.1.1. Existing Approaches to Measuring Chinese Lending

Two approaches have been used to address the lack of Chinese lending data. The first strategy involves working with Chinese sources. Occasionally, the Chinese government publishes so-called white papers that provide information on their foreign aid. However, the available statistics suffer from several shortcomings. The white papers offer data only on total aid volume, not which debtor governments received loans, nor do they include information on the loan volume for each recipient. Furthermore, the definitions used by Chinese officials are unclear, making it hard to differentiate between grants, loans, and other types of foreign assistance.

In light of these limitations, scholars have attempted to improve the quality of data provided by Chinese sources. Brautigam (2009) attempts to disaggregate these numbers to obtain information on Chinese loan amounts by geographical region. While an admirable effort, these endeavors do not yield systematic information on the Chinese lending volume to individual recipient countries. Kitano (2014) pursues a different approach, aggregating individual items in the budgets of different Chinese ministries engaged in foreign aid to arrive at estimates of Chinese foreign lending. However, this approach assumes that numbers reported by Chinese ministries are accurate. As this is highly questionable, doubts remain as to the precision of lending data derived from these numbers.

Recognizing these difficulties with data from Chinese sources, AidData—a research organization located at the College of William & Mary—has pursued a second approach. AidData has employed considerable resources to systematically collect newspaper articles on Chinese aid activities. News reports mentioning Chinese aid projects or loan agreements are collected, organized, and triangulated (Strange et al. 2015). These articles are then coded to obtain data suitable for statistical analysis. The resulting data set offers information on Chinese foreign aid activities—both aid projects and loans—disaggregated by recipient country. AidData subsequently incorporates data on aid and lending activities by traditional Western governments, which are obtained from the OECD creditor reporting system, as well as information on aid by multilateral organizations (Tierney et al. 2011). The resulting data set is impressive, as it offers rich information on aid activities in virtually all developing countries.

8.1.2. My Approach to Collecting Reliable Data

I pursue a third approach. Every loan extended by a creditor must have a recipient. For this reason, it should be possible to "look through the books" of developing countries to determine which creditors the governments have used. By systematically exploring their capital inflows, I am able to reverse-engineer information on the lending activities by BRICs. To acquire data on capital inflows to developing countries, I obtained access to an internal databank of the World Bank. As a membership organization, all members of the World Bank are required to report detailed information on their financial positions to the Debtor Reporting System.[1] This includes information on their revenues and expenses. On the revenue side, governments are required to report their sources of

---

[1] Note that the data were obtained from the *internal* databank of the World Bank. Accordingly, the information acquired is of confidential nature, since governments have reported their information on the sources of income on good-faith terms to the World Bank. To quote a World Bank official, "By supporting your work, we are exposing creditors based on debtor's data, which is always a concern to us." I was required to sign waivers prohibiting me from distributing these data myself. However, I was assured that requests for replication data are looked upon favorably. I ask any interested researchers to contact me directly to obtain the reference number of my interactions, which would allow them to obtain the data directly from the World Bank.

income, ranging from taxes and custom duties to transfers of external resources. The latter include loans from external creditors. Identifying and obtaining these data on the borrowing activities of recipient governments allows me to build a comprehensive data set on government-to-government loans. Importantly, I use this method to obtain data on loans from *all* creditors, resulting in comparable data across lenders.

Of the three approaches, the first approach using official data from Chinese sources has the most obvious drawback. The accuracy of the source data is extremely questionable. For this reason, I do not use these data. The second approach pursued by AidData offers fantastic data to study foreign aid. The information collected on individual aid projects, such as schools and hospitals, is unparalleled. However, I study bilateral loans obtained by governments, not individual aid projects. While AidData does offer some information on bilateral lending, my data are superior for the study of government-to-government loans, for three reasons.

First, AidData obtain data for loans by different creditors for separate sources: DAC and IFI data are obtained from the OECD creditor reporting system, Brazilian data from a Brazilian ministry, and Chinese data from coding newspaper articles. AidData itself suggests that these data may not be comparable. Combining them into a single data set is not advisable. Consequently, using these data to analyze the relative importance of creditors may result in biased findings: observed differences may result from different data-generating mechanisms rather than substantive differences. In contrast, my data offer information on multiple creditors obtained with the same data-generating process, which facilitates comparisons across creditors.

Second, scholars have raised questions about the accuracy of information on Chinese loans included in AidData, which are based on coded newspapers. In a rival effort, the China-Africa Research Initiative (CARI) at the School of Advanced International Studies at Johns Hopkins University has also collected media reports of Chinese loans (Brautigam and Hwang 2016). With the help of native Chinese speakers, as well as French, Portuguese, and Arabic speakers, CARI triangulated and cross-checked all reports of loans. Just as with AidData, the result offers disaggregated loan data by country. However, the figures reported by AidData and CARI differ significantly. This may be because newspaper articles about large projects funded by Chinese loans often conflate the value of the foreign investment (i.e., the price of a hydropower dam) with the loan amount provided by the Chinese government, which typically funds only a part of the total project cost. Similarly, newspaper articles may report on initial announcements of investment projects involving Chinese loans, but coverage may be less complete if projects are subsequently modified or fall apart completely. My data are not without difficulties either, as debtor governments may misreport information to the World Bank. However, the Debtor Reporting System features an extensive monitoring system. This system ensures that numbers reported by debtors correspond to the countries' internal databases and are in line with data provided in the past. As a result of the monitoring system, data are likely to be more accurate than information derived from newspaper articles.

The third reason is most important. It concerns the fact that loan data gathered by AidData has systematically missing observations:

- *DAC loans*: AidData omits nonconcessional loans by Western governments. AidData obtains information from the OECD creditor reporting system. However, the data collected by this system are incomplete: in an effort to protect the competitiveness of the respective export credit agencies, DAC creditors agreed not to report nonconcessional loans to the OECD creditor reporting system (see OECD 2016). This implies that AidData systematically lacks data on the most expensive loans provided by Western governments.
- *IFI loans*: AidData reports 62 IMF loans between 1962 and 2011, while the IMF itself reports 179 loans for the same time period (IMF 2017).
- *Chinese loans*: There is no doubt that the creators of AidData are taking many precautions and, to the best of their ability, correct for possible mistakes when coding newspaper articles (Strange et al. 2015). However, reliance on newspaper articles is known to have drawbacks. AidData acknowledges that coding newspaper articles may lead to *underreporting of the number of loans* (Muchapondwa et al. 2016). Aid projects, such as wells, schools, and hospitals, are tangible outcomes that journalists can visit, verify, and report. In contrast, bilateral loans may not be associated with physical objects (such as loans paid directly into the government's budget). Given the differences, loans and aid projects have different chances of being "detected" using a method that relies on newspaper articles. Correspondingly, only 2% of all AidData entries are loans, while 98% are aid projects.
- *Other BRICs*: Lastly, AidData offers data on Chinese loans (by coding newspaper articles) and Brazilian lending (obtained directly from the Brazilian governments). However, as of 2017, the data do not include information on loans from India and Russia.

To be sure, any data set may suffer from missing observations. If these observations are omitted randomly, they do not undermine the validity of inferences drawn from the data. However, in the case of AidData, information on loans is *systematically* missing. Including only concessional DAC loans while ignoring more expensive DAC loans biases the analysis. In contrast, as my information relies on loan *inflows*, it is less susceptible to bias introduced when creditors do not report specific *outflows*.

8.1.3. The Resulting Dependent Variable

I calculate each government's borrowing portfolio once the loan amounts granted by BRIC, DAC, IFI, and private creditors to individual governments are collected. For example, if a country obtains $100 million of new loans in a particular year, $30 million from BRICs, $25 million from DACs, $25 million from IFIs, and $20 million from private creditors, the borrowing portfolio would be 30%, 25%, 25%, and 20% respectively.

The dependent variable, thus, yields a four-category composition {BRIC, DAC, IFI, Private}, which will always sum to 1, or 100%. The variable is available for 127 developing countries between 2004 and 2015.

8.2. The Independent Variable: Societal Coalitions

A quantitative test of my theory requires data on societal coalitions. However, measuring which type of coalition is present in a particular country at a specific time is challenging, as such interest alignments are not directly observable: interest groups typically do not sign contracts that can be coded. Empirical research on coalitions generally focuses on whether interest groups use the coalition strategy at all (Hojnacki 1997; Mahoney 2008; Baumgartner et al. 2009), how much they participate within a given coalition (Hojnacki 1998; Hula 1999), and the size and stability of a given coalition (Holyoke 2011; Nelson and Yackee 2012). However, only few attempts exist at measuring their relative power. To test my theory, data on coalitions among societal interest groups have to satisfy two criteria: First, the measures must capture the *identity* of the respective interest groups. Second, the measures must account for groups' ability to exert influence. In the following, I first review existing techniques to measuring coalitions and examine if they meet these two criteria. I then introduce my approach to estimating the strength of societal groups.

8.2.1. Existing Approaches to Measuring Societal Coalitions

One existing approach focuses on identifying leadership changes where new leaders' primary support is drawn from societal groups different from those that supported their predecessors. Such information is offered by the CHISOLS (Change in Source of Leader Support) data set (Mattes, Leeds, and Matsumura 2016; also see Mattes, Leeds, and Carroll 2014 and Leeds, Mattes, and Vogel 2009 for prior versions of these data). To create these data, the authors "follow the basic rule that whenever a leader with a different party affiliation comes to power, this constitutes a source of leader support change" (Mattes, Leeds, and Carroll 2014, 285). The coding rules differ across democracies and autocracies: in democracies, a change in the "source of leadership support" is observed whenever a leader with a different party affiliation comes to power. Coding changes in the source of leadership support in nondemocracies depends on the type of regime: for example, in monarchies, a change in the source of leadership support is observed only if the new ruler descends from a dynasty different from that of her predecessor. Using these coding rules, Mattes, Leeds, and Matsumura (2016) create a dummy variable that is coded 1 if a new leadership with a different source of leader support than her predecessor enters into office in a given year. The authors have undertaken truly admirable efforts to ensure accurate coding of country-years. As a result, these data have been used in subsequent studies to account for "leadership turnover" (Thomas, Reed, and Wolford 2016; Gray and Kucik 2017). Ryckman and Braithwaite (2018) pursue a similar approach by coding whether the change in leadership came from within the regime or from outside. The variable Outsider is coded 1 if a new leader from outside the previous regime came to power in a given year, and 0 otherwise. The variable Insider is coded as 1 if there was a change from within the existing regime in a given year, and 0 otherwise.

The data created by Mattes, Leeds, and Matsumura (2016) and Ryckman and Braithwaite (2018) represent significant progress that will allow serious advances in studying the process of policymaking. Yet these data do not allow me to test my theory. Both Mattes, Leeds, and Matsumura (2016) and Ryckman and Braithwaite (2018) code instances of changes in societal coalitions, but they do not identify the societal coalitions themselves. My theory, however, engages the *identity* of these social groups, with a focus on how the relative strength of specific groups matters for foreign policy decisions. For this reason, I go beyond data that points out instances of change and instead identify what groups are now influential.

Gray and Kucik (2017) incorporate ideology in their data. They use information on the left-to-right spectrum when coding changes in leadership. However, their core variable of interest is not the leadership's ideology itself, but whether that ideology has varied from one leader to the next. A change from a left-wing to a right-wing leader might indicate a change in underlying societal coalitions, just as might a change from a right-wing to a left-wing leader. For this reason, they create a dichotomous indicator capturing whether the ideology of the chief executive changed in year t relative to $t-1$.

While this approach makes use of information on identity, the resulting data would not allow me to test my theory. First, the variable created by Gray and Kucik focuses on the changes in societal coalitions but does not capture the identity of these coalitions.

Second, I could use the underlying data on whether a left- or a right-wing government is in power directly. However, it is not clear how to map three interest groups (Industry, Finance, and Labor) onto two political dimensions (Left versus Right). While it is possible to argue that left-wing governments probably represent Labor, I would be unable to differentiate between Industry and Finance, as both are likely associated with right-wing governments.

Third, applying a left-to-right spectrum across all countries is difficult because the meanings of "left" and "right" vary across countries (Benoit and Laver 2006).

A third existing approach does not rely on coding changes in leadership to proxy for societal interest group coalitions but focuses on these interest groups directly. To identify networks of interest group coalitions, scholars have used data on amicus curiae, or "friend of the court," briefs. In the United States, such briefs before the Supreme Court may be submitted in support of the petitioner or respondent. Importantly, cosigners coordinate the content and signatories. A large percentage of amicus briefs come from interest groups attempting to affect a case outcome (Collins 2008). Collins (2004) and Wasby (1995) argue that groups may join amicus briefs specifically to build and maintain relationships with similar groups. Thus, these ties between interest groups based on cosigner status provide a measure of purposive, coordinated action. Box-Steffensmeier and Christenson (2014, 2015) use information regarding which groups appear on the same amicus curiae brief to map networks among interest groups. This way, they are able to identify coalitions among specific interest groups. These data have significantly propelled the study of tacit coalitions that shape policy in the United States (Whitford 2003; Lowery 2007; Box-Steffensmeier and Christenson 2015).

This approach to measuring interest group coalitions results in fantastic data. Unfortunately, these data do not allow me to test my theory, as they are available only for a single country, the United States. Data that capture networks of interest groups in a systematic manner do not exist for developing countries. Further, while mapping the network among specific advocacy organizations might facilitate identifying sets of groups interested in the same topics, it is not clear if they provide insights into the relative strength of interest group coalitions. For instance, a large number of cosigners might not necessarily translate into political strength, as larger groups tend to be hampered by more severe collective action problems (Olson 1971).

8.2.2. My Approach to Measuring Political Strength

Without doubt, existing approaches to measuring societal interest groups have produced impressive data. Unfortunately, these data are unsuited *for my purposes*. To test my theory, data on coalitions among societal interest groups have to satisfy two criteria: First, they must capture the *identity* of the respective interest groups; measures merely indicating changes without identifying what groups are now influential are insufficient. Second, they must account for groups' *influence*. Influence has both demand- and supply-side components. With respect to the former, my approach must account for groups' ability to overcome collective action problems, which is a precondition for the ability to exert influence. With respect to the latter, the measures must capture the incentives for politicians to listen to this group. This is closely connected to groups' importance to the domestic economy.

The central idea of my approach involves calculating the political strength of three interest groups (Labor, Industry, and Finance) in a way that satisfies the requirements I have outlined. Subsequently, I can use these measures to simulate the predicted borrowing portfolio under certain circumstances, such as strong Labor and Industry and weak Finance.

I suggest that the political strength of any group can be captured by analyzing the interaction of two components:

$$\text{Group's political strength} = \text{Group's ability to organize} \times \text{Group's importance to the economy} \quad (8.1)$$

The first component refers to the demand side of political strength: The group must be able to organize its members to coordinate any political demands it might make of its government. For a group to lobby effectively, it must overcome any collective action problems and limit the free-riding behavior of individual group members. However, a group's ability to organize does not imply that politicians will listen to that group's demands (Woll 2007). After all, even if a group is well organized, politicians might not deem it important enough to respond to and enact the policies it desires. The second component of the equation accounts for this supply-side aspect of political strength. In sum, a group is politically influential if it possesses both organizational capacities to overcome collective action problems and sufficient importance to the economy to warrant the attention of politicians.

In the following sections, I apply this approach to operationalize the political strength of Labor, Industry, and Finance.

8.2.2.1. Political Strength of Labor

Scholars have used a variety of measures to capture the political strength of Labor. For example, union density might capture the strength of workers in the political arena (Botero et al. 2004; Owen 2013, 2015). Others have combined union density data with additional information, such as the structure of collective bargaining and the number of International Labor Organization conventions ratified (see McGuire 1999; Segura-Ubiergo 2007). However, such efforts face the limitation that little systematic data on union density is available over long periods of time for developing countries. Furthermore, high union density does not necessarily equal power: for example, interviews in Ecuador revealed that Labor is a powerful actor in Ecuadorian politics, yet the labor force is not unionized. Similarly, unionization rates are extremely high in authoritarian China, yet this "unionization by default" does not mean that workers have a strong political voice.

Rudra (2002) developed an alternative approach. Her pathbreaking work introduced a measure to capture the potential political power of workers, based on a combination of their skill levels and the availability of surplus labor: the former proxies the ability of workers to overcome collective action problems, while the latter measures the "replaceability" of individual workers and thus captures their political influence. Subsequent work has made use of this smart way to measure the political power of labor (see Caraway, Rickard, and Anner 2012; Mosley and Uno 2007; Wibbels 2006; Yoon 2009). However, this measure is available for only 53 developing countries and ends in the year 2000. Furthermore, the data have high rates of missing observations for many countries in the sample (Berliner et al. 2015). Due to the small sample, limited temporal coverage, and high rates of missing observations, I cannot use her variable for my analysis.

However, her approach to combining supply- and demand-side factors is convincing.

For this reason, I draw on her work while developing my own measure of Labor's strength. Rudra uses the relative number of high-skilled versus low-skilled workers to capture the degree to which they are able to overcome collective action problems. She reasons that low-skilled workers are difficult to mobilize because they have little education and erratic work hours. In contrast, skilled labor groups are better educated and typically work in stable workplaces. For this reason, skilled labor can more easily organize than low-skilled workers. Corroborating this line of argument, related work shows that—in contrast to high-skilled labor—unskilled workers may not have the political strength to prevent reductions in welfare state policies (Rudra 2002), avoid a shift in the tax burden from capital to Labor (Wibbels and Arce 2003), or bargain effectively with employers (Weeks 1999).

Given this logic, an increase in the number of skilled workers relative to low-skilled workers would help Labor as a whole to overcome its collective-action problems (Rudra 2002, 420). She obtains the number of employees in certain professions—identified by their Standard International Trade Classification (SITC) and International Standard Industrial Classification (ISIC) categories—from the UNIDO Database of Industrial Statistics to create the ratio of high- versus low-skilled workers. Her data end in 2000. Attempts to extend her data were unsuccessful, as changes in the SITC and ISIC codes made it impossible to replicate Rudra's classification of high- and low-skilled professions.

Instead, I pursue a different strategy to obtain information on the relative reliance on skilled versus unskilled labor. A yearly survey conducted by the World Economic Forum (World Economic Forum 2016) includes questions on the economy's use of skilled versus unskilled labor. Data are available for 152 countries. The survey includes the following question: "What is the competitive advantage of your country's companies in international markets based upon?" The scale of the responses ranges from 1 to 7. Lower numbers indicate that an economy relies on low-cost labor or natural resources, while higher values signify the creation of unique products and processes that use high-skilled labor. The average score for each country can therefore serve as a measure of relative reliance on low- versus high-skilled workers. Following the argument by Rudra, this should capture the degree to which Labor is able to overcome collective action problems.

However, even if workers are able to overcome collective action problems, politicians might not listen to their demands. The second component of calculating Labor's political strength consequently captures the forcefulness with which workers can make demands.

Rudra (2002, 419) argues that workers' influence is conditional on the size of the surplus labor pool. If a large reservoir of surplus labor exists, workers are more easily replaceable. As a consequence, firms do not depend on particular workers. For this reason, the size of the surplus labor pool determines the degree to which politicians are receptive to the demands by workers.

While I follow Rudra's logic, I operationalize surplus labor differently for both data-related and conceptual reasons. Rudra calculates surplus labor as "(working age population minus students enrolled in secondary education minus students enrolled in 'post-secondary' education) minus (labor force / the working age population)" (Rudra 2002, 422). However, I was unable to obtain reliable data on students enrolled in secondary and postsecondary education for a significant number of country-years. For this reason, I use a simpler definition for which reliable data exist: the unemployment rate as a percentage of the total labor force obtained from the World Bank (2017). This captures the degree to which a country is characterized by the presence of surplus labor.

Following equation 8.1, I calculate the political strength of Labor (PSL) as

$$\text{Political Strength of Labor (PSL)} = \text{Average skill level of workers} \times \left(\frac{1}{\text{Unemployment rate}} \right) \quad (8.2)$$

I subsequently normalize the variable so that the measure varies between 0 and 1. This measure captures the nature of Labor's influence. It increases as the prevalence of high-skilled workers increases relative to low-skill workers, and as surplus labor is reduced. This results in a measure of Labor's political strength that is comparable across developing countries.

The resulting measure is available for 115 developing countries for the period of 2005–2015.

Figure 8.1 illustrates the average PSL score for the countries. It also displays the minimum and maximum values to illustrate the variability over time. The figure shows that the political strength of Labor varies across countries, and, in some cases, across time.

Examining individual countries more closely reveals that this measure quite accurately captures Labor's strength across countries. For instance, Malaysia scores highly on PSL. This is no surprise considering that important industries such as electronics and automotive require a large pool of skilled workers. While workers are not organized in unions, they exert much influence, as evidenced by the introduction of minimum wage laws (Gooch 2012). Their influence is also reflected in the policies addressing financial crises (Pepinsky 2008). The PSL of Sri Lanka is also high, but for different reasons. Saxena (2014) argues that multifiber arrangements from the 1970s to 2005 played a pivotal role in upgrading Sri Lanka's economy. These agreements set quota limits for imports to industrialized economies and therefore provided firms in Japan and Korea with incentives to move to Sri Lanka, which had excess quota. As a consequence of the upgrading, the demand and subsequent supply of skilled labor increased.

Other countries exhibit low scores on PSL. The political influence of workers in the Dominican Republic is low, as the workforce consists primarily of low-skilled workers in low-value-added export industries such as sugar, coffee, and tobacco, as well as clothing, footwear, and leather products. As a result, Johnson (2013) estimates that labor's contribution to growth is only about 0.7% to 0.9%. Considering these figures, Labor's lack of political influence is not surprising. South Africa also scores low on PSL. Magruder (2012, 140) argues that the "majority black population was prohibited from entrepreneurship during Apartheid.

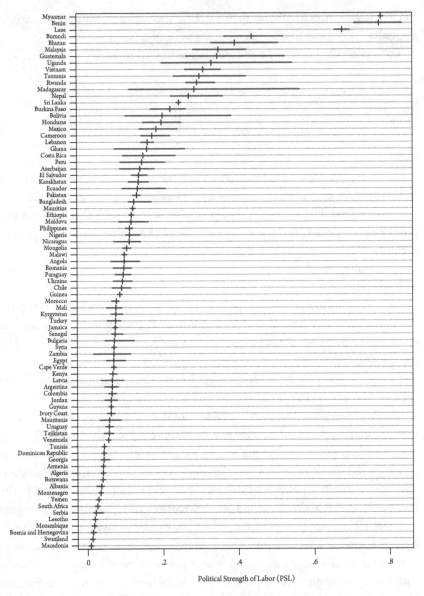

Figure 8.1 Political strength of Labor. Note: The graph displays the average score between 2005 and 2015 along with the minimum and maximum values to illustrate the variability over time. For better visualization, the graph excludes two outliers, Cambodia and Thailand.

While these laws are no longer in place, their effects on skill sets . . . may have a lingering impact." In addition, unemployment in South Africa is extremely high. In sum, these examples illustrate that PSL captures the political strength of Labor in a competent manner.

8.2.2.2. Political Strength of Industry

Scholars have used different ways to measure the political strength of Industry. One prominent approach utilizes the size of the industrial sector as a proxy for the influence of Industry.

Examples include the share of GDP produced by industries and the number of industrial companies (Schneiberg and Bartley 2001). Such indicators are meant to capture the structural power of Industry (Hall 1986; Bell 2012). However, this approach ignores the organizational difficulties: Even a large industrial sector may not have much political power if its actors are unable to overcome collective action problems. For this reason, Akard (1992) observed that business is powerful only if it is able to unify and organize. Similarly, Jacobs (1988) argues that increases in the asset concentration ratio (percentage of total assets held by the hundred largest firms) correspond to an increase in business power, as they allow larger firms to cooperate more easily. In addition, focusing on the industrial sector's size ignores context. Industry's power might be amplified if it is able to credibly threaten relocation to another country. Scholars have argued that such exit options have strengthened the influence of business in social policymaking (Farnsworth 2004) and corporate governance rules (Wilks 2013).

A second approach to measuring Industry's power focuses on the monetary resources available for political action. In the context of the United States, considerable research effort has gone into understanding so-called political action committees (PACs) (Bowles, Gordon, and Weisskopf 1989; Boies 1989; Wright 1985). PACs pool campaign contributions from individuals and organizations to fund political campaigns or lobbying efforts. Scholars have used the ratio of corporate PACs to total PACs (Quinn and Shapiro 1991; Williams and Collins 1997) and the ratio of financial contributions by corporate PACs to the total volume contributed to all PACs (Vogel 1983) to measure business influence.

However, some have criticized this indicator, as not all corporations have PACs (Wilson 1990). Furthermore, others lament that most studies treat business PACs as homogenous even though PACs funded by industries in different sectors might pursue mutually exclusive objectives (Masters and Keim 1985). Most importantly, however, this measure exists only for the United States, while data for developing countries are not available.

I operationalize the political strength of Industry (PSI) as the interaction between the group's ability to organize politically and the incentives of politicians to listen to the demands of domestic Industry. Industry's ability to overcome collective action problems is related to the types of products a country's industrial sector typically produces. For example, if Industry's competitive advantage is producing goods primarily with low-cost labor or natural resources, there are two reasons to expect little cooperation among companies. First, firms using simple technologies and labor-intensive (as opposed to knowledge-intensive) production processes are less likely to develop an interdependent network of linkages between firms. Second, considering the lack of unique characteristics of these products, it is likely that companies compete on price, not quality. Both characteristics should limit their ability to overcome collective action problems. In contrast, Industry's organizational capacities are likely higher if its companies produce sophisticated and unique products. To create unique products, firms typically use high-tech fabrication techniques and knowledge-intensive processes. As a result, they are typically positioned at the end of a value-added production chain. An economy in which many firms use such sophisticated production processes is likely to have many backward and forward linkages. They require reliable inputs of high quality, and thus are likely to cooperate closely with other firms in the value chain. As a consequence of these networks, firms are able to overcome collective action problems and barriers to effectively organize their political demands.[2] It is also easier to overcome collective action problems when there is little direct competition among firms producing unique goods.

I measure the organizational capacity of Industry across countries with data from the previously mentioned survey conducted by the World Economic Forum (World Economic Forum 2016). The survey includes the following question: "In your country, how sophisticated are production processes? [1 = not at all: production uses labor-intensive processes or old technology; 7 = highly: production uses sophisticated and knowledge-intensive processes]." Following the logic I have outlined, the average score on this question captures the degree to which an interfirm network based on backward and forward linkages has developed, and by extension, the organizational capacity of Industry.

Yet even if an industrial sector is able to overcome collective action problems, politicians may not have the incentive to listen to its demands. For this reason, measuring the political strength of Industry must account for the sector's importance to the domestic economy.

The degree to which a country's economy depends on domestic versus imported inputs is likely to capture Industry's importance. Politicians are likely to pay attention to the demands of Industry if economic activities rely

---

[2] Observers might wonder how agriculture fits into this approach, which is powerful in some developing countries. In response, consider that landowners are unlikely to be influential if the agricultural sector is characterized by subsistence farming or by farms primarily using manual labor. In contrast, landowners may be powerful if the sector has achieved some degree of modernization. Thus, it is likely that the power of agricultural sectors is correlated with their use of machinery and the existence of supply chains linking this sector to other industries (machinery, fertilizer, food processing, etc.). If this is correct, my measure of their political strength may accurately capture these dynamics.

primarily on domestically made inputs. In contrast, politicians are more likely to ignore Industry's demands if economic actors utilize foreign inputs instead of those from local suppliers. The utilization of domestic suppliers also has a second-order effect. If domestic inputs dominate the supply chain, the economy is more likely to consist of an interconnected web of firms. As a result, even small interruptions in the supply chain may have disastrous consequences, giving politicians an incentive to listen to the demands of Industry. In contrast, if domestic firms are not interdependent, politicians will probably dismiss demands by individual firms as isolated incidents without repercussions for the entire economy. To operationalize these considerations, I use the ratio of domestic to foreign inputs calculated with data from the World Bank Enterprise Survey (World Bank 2016). According to the preceding argument, politicians in developing countries should have more incentive to listen to Industry if economic actors use primarily domestic, rather than foreign, inputs for their activities.

I subsequently rewrite equation 8.1 to obtain a measure of the political strength of Industry (PSI). It consists of the interaction between the group's ability to organize politically—as measured by the sophistication of the production process—and the incentives of politicians to listen to the demands of domestic Industry:

$$\text{Political Strength of Industry (PSI)} = \text{Sophistication of the production processes} \times \left(\frac{\text{Economy's reliance on domestic inputs}}{\text{Economy's reliance on foreign inputs}} \right) \quad (8.3)$$

I subsequently normalize the resulting numerical data so that the variable varies between 0 and 1. PSI captures the political strength of Industry in an intuitive manner. The measure increases as the prevalence of low-tech production processes decreases relative to the use of high-tech, knowledge-intensive techniques. Similarly, the political strength of Industry increases as economic actors use more domestic rather than foreign, inputs.

PSI is available for 95 countries for the period of 2005–2015. Figure 8.2 displays countries' average PSI scores along with their minimum and maximum values. The figure illustrates that the political strength of Industry varies across countries, and in some cases also across time.

A precursory look at the distribution of values across countries suggests that this measure can serve as an appropriate proxy for the political strength of Industry. Sri Lanka has a high PSI, which corresponds to qualitative accounts of business influence, particularly of the textile and garment industries. Their ability to organize stems from the long tradition of successful business

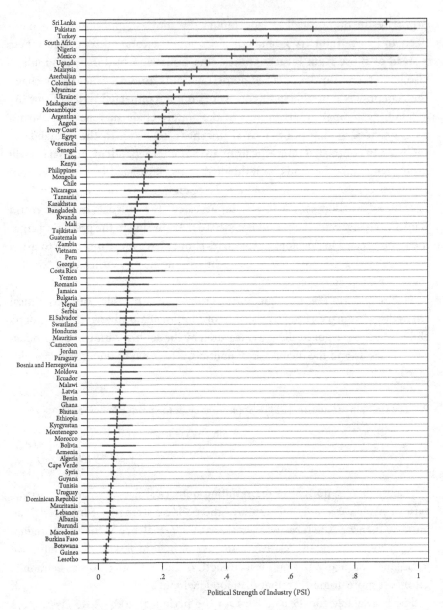

Figure 8.2 Political strength of Industry. Note: The graph displays the average score between 2005 and 2015 along with the minimum and maximum values to illustrate the variability over time. For better visualization, the graph excludes three outliers, Panama, Indonesia, and Thailand.

associations that systematically coordinate the economic and political activities of the largest manufacturing firms (Moore and Hamalai 1993). Politicians have an incentive to listen to this industry, as it "accounts for the largest exports and employment in the recent past" (Kelegama 2009, 582). In sum, both factors result in strong political influence: Moore and Hamalai (1993, 1904) note the "acceptance by the [Sri Lankan] government of business associations as representatives of legitimate interests. They have been increasingly involved in formal and informal consultations with government agencies at various levels, and are becoming an accepted voice." Pakistan also features a high PSI score, which corresponds to qualitative accounts. For instance, 71% of Pakistani companies state that they believe they have political influence on government decisions (Desbordes and Vauday 2007, 423). This agrees with evidence by Saeed, Belghitar, and Clark (2014), who also find that Pakistani firms have significant links to politicians.

Similar correspondence between qualitative accounts and PSI scores exists for countries at the bottom of the distribution. On the demand side, Lesotho is an example of Industry's limited organizational ability. Maliehe (2017) shows that indigenous entrepreneurs do not lack adequate entrepreneurial spirit and business acumen, but Lesotho's business associations are unable to effectively organize their interests against the influence of European companies. On the supply side, there are many examples of politicians who have little incentive to listen to Industry because it is of limited importance to the local economy. Amuedo-Dorantes and Pozo (2006, 940) show that domestic industry in the Dominican Republic is weak and blame a high level of remittances. Despite their potentially important role as a source of capital for business investments, apparently, these monetary inflows seem to promote consumption of imported goods rather than boost entrepreneurship. Schrank (2008) adds that, with few exceptions, import-competing industrialists in the capital of Santo Domingo have resisted calls for technological change, and landlords have been unwilling to diversity into manufacturing. Both developments have led to a comparatively weak industrial sector with little influence.

Guinea's economic activities are concentrated in the aluminum industry, which is dominated by foreign firms. Knierzinger (2014, 23) observes that "due to the high capital intensity and the low spin-off effects of the aluminum industry, the actual number of workers in these towns only constitutes a small fraction of the entire population. CBG, the largest operator, only prepares its bauxite for export from Kamsar to a wide range of ports in Europe and the U.S. and only involves a few Guinean companies through backward linkages. The two procurement agencies of CBG are located in Brussels and Pittsburgh and rarely order products from Guinea or other African countries." The lack of spillover effects into the local economy precludes opportunities for domestic firms to gain political influence, as reflected by a low PSI score. In sum, these examples illustrate that PSI is a reasonable measure of the political influence of Industry.

8.2.2.3. Political Strength of Finance

Several approaches have been used to measure the political influence of Finance. The first strategy involves using the size of the financial sector to proxy for its political power. Young (2017, 450) attempts to "measure the structural prominence of the financial industry through information about its changing sectoral composition over time. What we need specifically is a measure of the financial industry's importance relative to that of other industries." However, this approach conflates the sector's size with its political influence. As noted previously, collective action problems may actually be more severe in larger vis-à-vis smaller sectors.

A second approach focuses on an economy's reliance on the financial sector. Here scholars make use of the "increased dependence of non-financial corporations on earnings through financial channels rather than traditional earnings via sales" (Alvarez 2015, 451). Scholars have thus measured the participation of nonfinancial corporations in capital markets and financial services (Crotty 2016; Froud et al. 2006). Krippner (2005), Lin and Tomaskovic-Devey (2013), and Dünhaupt (2016) measure this as the ratio of financial receipts— which include interest, dividends, and capital gains— to business receipts, the revenue generated from the selling of goods and services. The argument suggests that increasing reliance on the financial sector grants Finance more political power, as the threat of moving its business elsewhere has larger consequences (Sennholz-Weinhardt 2014). Yet this approach implicitly assumes that Finance is able to overcome its collective action problems, which may not always be the case (Tsingou 2015; Kalaitzake 2017). Woll (2016) emphasizes the distinction between politically organized and politically disorganized national financial sectors to explain the variation in bailout schemes in Germany, France, Denmark, and Ireland after the financial crises in 2008. She argues that variations in the costs of different national bailout schemes depended crucially on the willingness or capacity of the banking sector to act collectively (see also Woll 2014a, 2014b). A further difficulty with this approach is that such data exist only for OECD economies, whereas data for developing countries are not available.

A third approach centers on the idea of financialization. Tomaskovic-Devey and Lin (2011) argue that financialization is a system of income redistribution in which actors in the financial industry use the government to extract "rents" from others. More specifically, financialization describes the process by which the financial industry uses its influence with politicians and regulators to extract rents and engage in upward redistribution from consumers to wealthy investors and firm managers (Lin and Tomaskovic-Devey 2013).

The volume of rents transferred from nonfinancial sectors to the financial sector reflects the increasing political power of Finance (Duménil and Lévy 2002; Epstein and Jayadev 2005; Greider 1998). As a result of this argument, scholars have attempted to calculate the rentier income. Some have used interest, dividends, and capital gains received by the owners of financial assets in relation to total income from the nonfinancial business sector (Jayadev and Epstein 2007; Stockhammer 2004; Duenhaupt 2012), while others use the percentage of total economic output (GDP) derived from the finance, insurance, and real estate sector as a percentage of the operating surplus of all other sectors (Witko 2014; Van Arnum and Naples 2013; Flaherty 2015). This approach, however, suffers from two shortcomings.

First, it estimates the result of Finance exercising power, not the power itself. Following Young (2017, 444), it is important to differentiate the causes of political influence from the hypothesized effects. Second, these data are not available for the vast majority of developing countries.

Instead, I adapt the logic illustrated in equation 8.1 to operationalize the political strength of Finance. I combine a measure of the group's ability to politically organize and the incentives of politicians to listen to the domestic financial sector. In developing countries, stock markets are generally underdeveloped. For this reason, commercial banks are the most common financial actors. However, the structure of the banking sector varies across developing countries: in some countries, banking activities are concentrated in a handful of companies, while other countries have a multitude of equally sized banks. Following Olson (1971), banks in a concentrated commercial banking sector find it easier to coordinate their actions and overcome collective action problems. This argument follows Jacobs (1988), who observed that firms have a greater incentive to cooperate in working for tax decreases in countries with a high, rather than low, degree of concentration of the country's asset base. In this sense, asset concentration is one indication of class political organization and class power (Quinn and Shapiro 1991, 854). To measure bank concentration, I use the ratio of the three largest banks' assets to total banking sector assets, obtained from Beck, Demirgüç-Kunt, and Levine (2010).

However, banks might not be able to organize to the extent that they have political influence if Finance is a relatively minor sector of the domestic economy. In this case, politicians might not have an incentive to listen to the demands of Finance, despite its ability to organize. For this reason, I account for the amount of credit provided by Finance to the domestic economy. After all, politicians are more likely to pay attention to the demands of Finance if it is a major provider of credit to the domestic economy. I operationalize this idea using the domestic credit provided by the financial sector (as a percentage of GDP) provided by World Bank (2017).

Substituting these measures into equation 8.1 results in a measure of the political power of Finance (PSF). It consists of the interaction between the group's ability to organize politically—as measured by bank concentration—and the importance of the financial sector to the domestic economy, which proxies for the incentives of politicians to listen to Finance.

$$\text{Political Strength of Finance (PSF)} = \text{Bank Concentration} \times \text{Domestic credit provided by Finance} \quad (8.4)$$

I normalize the resulting numbers to ensure that the measure varies between 0 and 1. As a result, PSF increases as banks' organizational capacities increase, which is the case if they are active lenders and thus develop interbank networks. Similarly, the political strength of Finance increases as the credit provided by the financial sector to the domestic economy increases.

PSF is available for 128 countries from 2004 through 2015. Figure 8.3 visualizes countries' average PSF score, along with the maximum and minimum values. The figure illustrates that PSF scores vary both across countries and across time.

Inspecting PSF values more closely reveals that this measure appears to capture variation quite accurately. South Africa exhibits a high PSF score. The reason lies in the dominant position of domestic banks. South Africa features four banks (Nedbank, ABSA, Standard Bank, and First Rand) that provide vast amounts of capital to the private sector and thus are extremely important to the domestic economy (Mlambo and Ncube 2011). In addition, qualitative accounts confirm that South Africa's financial sector gained political influence since the 1990s (Bassett 2008). Malaysia also features a high PSF score, and appropriately so: Rethel (2010) documents an increasing financialization of the Malaysian political economy. Rethel argues that "the expansion of capital markets has significantly affected the dynamics of contemporary Malaysian capitalism. . . . [Focus has] shifted from a concern with distribution and the economic empowerment of the Malay political majority towards the pursuit of wholesale economic growth and a finance-friendly stable macroeconomic environment" (2010, 503). Moreover, the importance of the capital sector not only increased economically, but also developed significant influence on politics (Johnson and Mitton 2003). Chile's financial sector is also influential but for different reasons. Gourevitch and Shinn (2005) note the effect of pension reforms implemented by the authoritarian Pinochet government. As a result, Chile's private pension system is an important source of capital for the financial

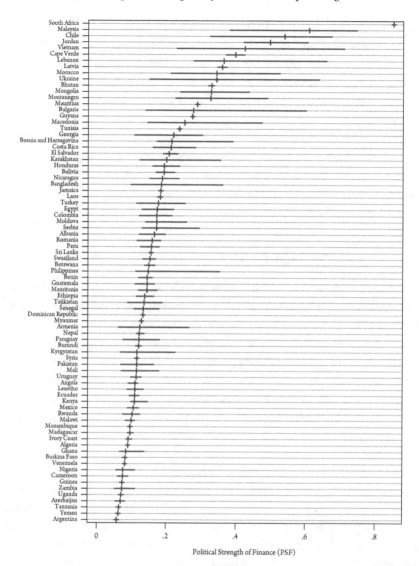

Figure 8.3 Political strength of Finance. Note: The figure presents the average score between 2005 and 2015 along with the minimum and maximum values. The political strength of Finance varies across countries and time.

sector. The large amount of resources available and a liberal regulatory environment have resulted in the expansion of Chile's financial sector in size and political influence.

In contrast, Uganda, Tanzania, and Cambodia exhibit low PSF scores. In Uganda, scholars note that citizens have limited access to finance (Johnson and Nino-Zarazua 2011; Okurut, Schoombee, and van der Berg 2005). Similarly, weak institutions and the lack of capital prevent the development of a strong financial sector in Tanzania (Odhiambo 2005). Hill and Menon (2013, 62) note that in Cambodia, the "destruction of economic and financial institutions after the 1970s, economic mismanagement in the 1980s, and the large inflows of U.S. dollars... in the early 1990s" explain the underdeveloped financial system. In sum, these examples illustrate that PSF is a sensible measure of Finance's political strength.

However, before moving on, I want to emphasize that the measures of the political strength of Labor, Industry, and Finance are necessarily imperfect. They attempt to measure a factor—political influence of specific societal groups—that cannot be observed directly. For this reason, the measures developed should be understood as proxies for the phenomenon in question.

8.2.3. Translating Group Strength into Coalitions

My theory suggests that politicians will respond to the two strongest actors in their country. After all, they can maximize their political benefits by satisfying the two most important groups simultaneously. The measures PSL, PSI, and PSF represent the political strength of Labor, Industry, and Finance, respectively. I will use these measures in chapter 9 to estimate whether societal coalitions predict borrowing decisions. In this process, I will assume that a Corporatist Coalition is present when PSL and PSI are high and PSF is low, a Capital Coalition when PSF and PSI are high and PSL is low, and a Consumer Coalition when PSL and PSF are high and PSI is low.

I examine the validity of this approach with the help of UN general assembly votes. Voeten, Strezhnev, and Bailey (2013) measure the frequency with which countries vote in line with the United States and China. If my theory is correct, voting records by governments responding to Corporatist Coalitions should, on average, align with those of China more than those of the United States. The opposite should be the case for Capital and Consumer Coalitions, which prefer Western private, multilateral, and bilateral lenders.

The data confirm these expectations. On average, countries cast the same vote as the United State in 18% of cases. However, significant heterogeneity emerges once we differentiate among coalitions. Corporatist Coalitions vote with the United States only 13% of the time, while Capital and Consumer Coalitions 20% and 19% of the time, respectively. Conversely, on average, all developing countries vote with China in 78% of cases. Yet differentiating among coalitions again results in heterogeneous patterns. Corporatist Coalitions agree with China in 84% of votes, while Capital and Consumer Coalitions vote with China in only 77% of all cases.

8.3. Review and Next Steps

The objective of this book is to explain how governments decide between competing loan offers. I argue that politicians respond to the dominant societal coalition when making these decisions. Chapters 4, 5, and 6 present qualitative evidence supporting this argument in the context of Ecuador, Colombia, and Peru. However, it is important to determine whether the argument holds for a larger set of developing countries.

For this reason, I conduct a statistical analysis of borrowing behaviors. However, such an analysis requires data on the outcome to be explained (the borrowing portfolios of developing countries) as well as the key explanatory variable (the type of coalition present in each country). This chapter describes the process of obtaining these data. In the following chapter, I will use these variables to test whether different societal coalitions accurately predict the borrowing decisions of governments.

9

Governments' Borrowing Decisions across the Developing World

Politicians have incentives to borrow from the type of creditor preferred by the dominant political coalition. In the preceding chapters, I have argued that if Labor and Industry are the strongest societal actors—a Corporatist Coalition—politicians will favor borrowing from emerging creditors such as Brazil, Russia, India, and China (BRICs) over other lenders.

This is not to say that such a government will never obtain multilateral loans from international financial institutions (IFIs), bilateral loans from Western governments (DACs), or private creditors. However, compared with governments responding to other political coalitions, a government responding to a Corporatist Coalition will tend to rely on BRICs. My theory suggests three hypotheses:

H1: Corporatist Coalition
Governments of countries in which Labor and Industry dominate tend to borrow from BRICs more than other creditors.

H2: Capital Coalition
Governments of countries in which Finance and Industry dominate tend to borrow from private creditors more than other creditors.

H3: Consumer Coalition
Governments of countries in which Labor and Industry dominate tend to borrow from DACs more than other creditors.

The qualitative evidence presented in chapters 4, 5, and 6 provides evidence in support of these hypotheses: The Ecuadorian government favors borrowing from BRICs to appease a Corporatist Coalition between Labor and Industry. Colombia obtains loans primarily from the private market or IFIs, as this is in the interest of the dominant Capital Coalition between Finance and Industry.

Peru borrows from DACs to meet the preferences of a Consumer Coalition between Labor and Finance.

In short, the societal coalitions in Ecuador, Colombia, and Peru shape the borrowing decisions of their respective governments. However, does this argument apply to countries outside of Latin America? This chapter presents a statistical analysis of quantitative data to determine if societal coalitions explain borrowing portfolios in developing countries around the world. I first discuss the challenges of compositional data. As borrowing portfolios must add up to 100%, increased borrowing from one creditor must be offset by reducing the share of loans from other creditors. Section 9.1 presents a methodological approach that accounts for such interdependencies. Section 9.2 offers the main findings. These findings are robust to accounting for economic conditions (Section 9.3) and political context (Section 9.4). Section 9.5 offers additional robustness tests such as analyzing Chinese loans separately from lending by Brazil, Russia, and India.

9.1. Methodological Approach

9.1.1. Data and Sample

The statistical analysis aims to explain why the borrowing portfolios of developing countries differ. The outcome to be explained is the share of credit obtained from one of four types of creditors. For example, if a country obtains $100 million in new loans in a particular year, of which $30 million is from BRICs, $25 million from DACs, $25 million from IFIs, and $20 million from private creditors, the borrowing portfolio is 30%, 25%, 25%, and 20%, respectively. The analysis needs to explain a four-category composition, {BRIC, DAC, IFI, Private}, which will always sum to 1, or 100%. These data are available for 127 developing countries between 2004 and 2015. Section 8.1 offers details on the source and characteristics of these data.

My theory suggests that the strength of three societal groups in the recipient country is key to explaining the variation in borrowing portfolios. Testing this claim requires a measure of the political strength of interest groups. Section 8.2 describes how I create measures to proxy the political strength of Labor, Industry, and Finance. In short, I combine data on the organizational capacity of the respective interest group (i.e., the demand side) with information on the incentives of politicians to listen to this particular group (that is, the supply side). This results in three variables: the political strength of Labor (PSL), the political strength of Industry (PSI), and the political strength of Finance (PSF).

I capture the presence of different coalitions by examining the configuration of interest group strength. For example, if Labor and Industry are strong (high PSL and PSI) while Finance is weak (low PSF), a Corporatist Coalition is dominating the political arena. In contrast, a Capital Coalition exists if Finance and Industry are strong (high PSF and PSI) while Labor is weak (low PSL). Lastly, strong Finance and Labor (high PSF and PSL) combined with weak Industry (low PSI) characterizes a Consumer Coalition.

The measure of political strength for Labor is available for 115 countries. While this sample does not include the full universe of developing countries, it compares favorably to the sample used by Rudra (2002, 425), whose measure for Labor strength is available for 53 developing countries. PSI can be calculated for 95 countries, while PSF is available for 128 countries. However, only 92 countries are common to PSL, PSI, and PSF, with a temporal coverage between 2005 and 2015. Even though I have data on the loan portfolio of 127 countries between 2004 and 2013, the statistical analyses need to be restricted to this smaller subsample.

9.1.2. The Particularities of Compositional Data

Political economists have long been interested in explaining political and economic phenomena that are compositional in nature. Examples include the share of government spending on different parts of the budget or the share of respondents choosing one of several possible political candidates. In my case, the dependent variable is a debtor's borrowing portfolio: the share of loans obtained from one of four creditor types. However, analyzing compositional data represents a challenge. In the words of Adolph (2013a, 105), compositional data "are ubiquitous in political science and the social sciences generally, but they are often modeled incorrectly."[1]

One reason is the specific characteristics of compositional dependent variables. Adopting the notation of Katz and King (1999), let V_{ij} denote the share of loans obtained by country i ($i = 1, \ldots, n$) from creditor j ($j = 1, 2, 3, 4$). In this case, a compositional variable has four defining characteristics. First, each component of the composition must have a value between 0 and 1.

$$0 < V_{ij} < 1, \text{ for all } i \text{ and } j. \tag{9.1}$$

---

[1] A related literature explores compositional *independent* variables. Here much work has focused on the problem of interpreting the marginal effect of compositional independent variables on a dependent variable: without applying what Adolph calls the "ration-preserving counterfactual," the independent effect of the components of the compositional variable cannot be identified.

Second, for each country, the components must sum to 1:

$$\sum_{j=1}^{4} V_{ij} = 1, \text{ for all } i \qquad (9.2)$$

As a result of equations 9.1 and 9.2, any change in a single component must be bounded by −1 and 1:

$$-1 < \delta V_{ij} < 1, \text{ for all } i \text{ and } j. \qquad (9.3)$$

And that all changes among component parts must sum to 0:

$$\sum_{j=1}^{4} \delta V_{ij} = 0, \text{ for all } i \qquad (9.4)$$

These characteristics of the dependent variable prevent the application of traditional regression models. For example, one might use the share of a single creditor (i.e., fraction of borrowing from BRICs) as the dependent variable and regress each on a set of independent variables (separately, or via seemingly unrelated regression). In this case, the results would violate constraints 9.1 and 9.2 and produce impossible predictions: This approach allows that borrowers obtain more than a total of 100% from creditors, or borrow negative amounts from individual creditors.

Similarly, Katz and King (1999) note that using a logistic function to transform V_{ij} to an unbounded scale (separately for each creditor j) and subsequently use ordinary least squares (OLS) will not work either: while the predicted values will satisfy constraint 9.1, they will violate constraint 9.2. Conversely, estimating $J - 1$ regressions and competing the predictions for the left-out creditor by subtracting $J - 1$ predictions from 1 satisfies constraint 9.2 but not constraint 9.1.

Lastly, and most importantly, constraint 9.2 introduces negative correlations with at least one component part (Aitchison 1982). After all, if the share of loans obtained from one creditor increases, the shares of at least one other creditor must decrease to offset the increase. In other words, the shares of the four creditors are not independent. However, OLS assumes independence, resulting in models that produce impossible fitted values and predictions. A good model of compositional data must, at a minimum, jointly estimate the components of V and respect the unit constraint.

9.1.3. Existing Approaches to Modeling Compositional Dependent Variables

Aitchison (1982) was the first to develop a viable solution to these problems. A compositional data set consists of an $N \times J$ matrix, W, with ith row denoted ω_i. If we were to analyze these data using OLS, the model would assume that the columns of W are independent.

Aitchison's central insight is that the logarithms of the ratios of compositional data are independent and unbounded, and thus can be jointly modeled with a multivariate distribution such as the multivariate normal. Transforming the data involves selecting one creditor as the reference category, for example, $J = DAC$, of the compositional variable. Note that the choice of which of the J categories is set as the baseline does not alter the resulting statistical inferences. Subsequently, the value of the dependent variable for all other categories, $y_i \forall j \neq DAC$, is divided by the value of the baseline category, y_j, and taking the natural log of each resulting ratio. In other words, this calculates the natural log of each creditor's share of the borrowing portfolio, relative to that of a reference creditor, resulting in a $N \times J - 1$ matrix Y. While the columns of Y are assumed to be independently distributed, the new matrix retains all the ratio information in W. Aitchison then assumes that Y is distributed multivariate normal with mean vector μ_i and variance matrix Σ. This setup allows modeling μ_i as a linear function of explanatory variables x, and estimating the model using standard maximum likelihood techniques. The results can then be transformed back to the unit-sum-restricted composition space to arrive at the quantities of interest: the predicted loan shares by creditor.

Aitchison's innovations have been widely used in political science research. For example, Katz and King (1999) and Tomz, Tucker, and Wittenberg (2002) use variants of this model to estimate vote shares in multiparty elections. Philips, Rutherford, and Whitten (2015) expand on this work by modeling how vote shares of multiple parties evolve over time. In a different context, Breunig and Busemeyer (2012) analyze how electoral institutions shape government decisions to allocate public spending across areas such as pensions, public investment, and labor market policies. Brehm, Gates, and Gomez (1993) study the factors affecting time-budgets in bureaucratic agencies. Winters and Martinez (2015) apply this method to examine the proportion of different types of foreign aid (i.e., project, programmatic, and technical assistance). Dietrich (2013) uses compositional data analysis to study the fraction of foreign aid provided directly to recipient governments versus via nonstate actors.

However, Aitchison's approach has an Achilles heel: It cannot be used if any of the elements of W are zero. As the log of zero is undefined, log-ratio methods cannot accommodate observations in which one or more shares equal zero. In the case of multiparty elections, for example, such instances occur when a party does not run in a specific district. Unfortunately, as shown in figure 1.2, governments frequently borrow from one, two, or even three creditors, but borrowing from all four creditors simultaneously is uncommon. For this reason, I cannot use the approach proposed by Aitchison (1982).

To avoid this problem of observations with one or more shares that equal zero, scholars have proposed different approaches (see Adolph 2013b): first, it is possible to replace zeros with some small value and perturb other components accordingly. For example, Winters and Martinez (2015, 522) substitute the smallest observed value for a given log-ratio for these zero values. However, this procedure risks creating outliers, particularly if the number of shares equal to zero is greater than 1. A second approach could involve imputing a nonzero value using covariates. For example, Katz and King (1999) do not use the actual vote share as their dependent variable. Instead, they calculate the effective vote share that a party would have received, effectively imputing vote shares for parties that did not run in specific districts. However, this approach is sensitive to the assumptions used to impute data. Third, scholars could estimate separate models for each pattern of nonzero observations. Tomz, Tucker, and Wittenberg (2002) estimate separate models for each pattern of contestation. This involves 2^J separate analyses, where J is the number of parties. For example, in the three-party case, the possible combinations of contestation include $\{1, 2, 3\}, \{1, 2\}, \{1, 3\}, \{2, 3\}, \{1\}, \{2\}, \{3\}$, and $\{\}$. It is not clear, however, how to interpret the effect of campaign spending on vote shares if, for example, divergent estimates emerge from the individual analyses.

9.1.4. Alternative Approaches Capable of Accommodating Zeros

Clearly, none of the approaches I have discussed are satisfying. However, recent advances have produced two types of models that allow for simultaneously analyzing zero and nonzero shares.

The first approach involves estimating a two-stage model, where the first stage generates zeros. This is similar to familiar hurdle or zero-inflated models that use covariates to separate zero from nonzero components (Adolph 2013b). These models are appropriate for data generated by two distinct processes. For example, the proportion of time spent taking care of children will have a reasonably smooth distribution well away from zero except for a spike at zero for those persons without children. In this case, zeros (childless persons do not spend time with children) and nonzeros (parents spend varying degrees of time with children) differ significantly, which two-stage models take into consideration.

However, this approach is inappropriate for my data. As the qualitative evidence indicates, a single political entity makes borrowing decisions.

Moreover, when a government decides on sovereign loans, all creditors are considered jointly. For this reason, it is inappropriate to assume that the choice not to borrow from, say, DACs reflect a different decision-making process than the choice to borrow from BRICs. In other words, in my data, zeros are no different from nonzeros: a government may have nothing in principle against borrowing from DACs, but doing so has such a low priority that the government has not borrowed from them.

I fit a fractional multinomial logit model, as it does not have these difficulties. It allows for analyzing zero and nonzero shares jointly. Moreover, this model assumes a single process by which both zero and nonzero observations are generated. Just as the multinomial logit extends binary logit models, fractional multinomial logit models extend fractional logit estimations. Fractional logit models were designed specifically to handle proportions of exactly zero or one, and when zero and nonzero observations stem from the same data-generating process (Papke and Wooldridge 1996). It models the relationship between mean proportions and explanatory variables. The log-likelihood function for single fractional models is of the form

$$\ln L = \sum_{j=1}^{N} y_i \ln\left\{\frac{exp(x_j'\beta)}{1+exp(x_j'\beta)}\right\} + (1-y_i)\ln\left\{1 - \frac{exp(x_j'\beta)}{1+exp(x_j'\beta)}\right\} \quad (9.5)$$

Subsequent work has extended these models of single fractions (bounded between 0 and 1) to allow estimating multiple fractions simultaneously where all fractions add up to 1 (Buis 2017; see also Mullahy 2014). As previously noted, this extension to multiple proportions corresponds to the more traditional multinomial logit model. Multinomial logit models estimate the effects of explanatory variables x on a single dependent variable consisting of multiple categories. However, a different way of representing the same information is to conceptualize the dependent variable with a set of dummy variables, $y_0, \ldots, y_J$, where these variables contain only the values 0 and 1. The predicted probabilities of choosing one category in relation to x are estimates with

$$\hat{y}_{0i} = \frac{1}{1+\sum_{k=1}^{J} exp(x_i\beta_k)}$$
$$\hat{y}_{1i} = \frac{exp(x_i\beta_1)}{1+\sum_{k=1}^{J} exp(x_i\beta_k)} \quad (9.6)$$
$$\vdots$$
$$\hat{y}_{Ji} = \frac{exp(x_i\beta_J)}{1+\sum_{k=1}^{J} exp(x_i\beta_k)}$$

The log-likelihood function is a function of the predicted values:

$$\ln(L_i) = y_{0i}\ln(\hat{y}_{0i}) + y_{1i}\ln(\hat{y}_{1i}) + \cdots + y_{Ji}\ln(\hat{y}_{Ji}) \qquad (9.7)$$

With a multinomial logit model, the ys are just 0 or 1, so in that case their function is to pick, for each country i, which $\hat{y}$ should enter the log-likelihood function. Put differently, multinomial logit models maximize the following:

$$\ln(L_i) = \begin{cases} \ln(\hat{y}_{0i}) & \text{if } y_{0i} = 1 \\ \ln(\hat{y}_{1i}) & \text{if } y_{1i} = 1 \\ \vdots \\ \ln(\hat{y}_{Ji}) & \text{if } y_{Ji} = 1 \end{cases} \qquad (9.8)$$

In contrast to the multinomial logit model, the ys in the fractional multinomial logit model contain the proportions (not 0s and 1s). For this reason, maximizing equation 9.8 will not work. Instead, the fractional multinomial logit maximizes equation 9.7, which can accommodate ys containing proportions including proportions equal to zero. These models have been used to study the participation rates of employees in firms' 401(k) retirement plans (Papke and Wooldridge 1996) and to evaluate an education policy by studying the pass rates for an exam administered to a cross section of students (Papke and Wooldridge 2008).

I utilize a fractional multinomial logit model for $J-1$ equations, utilizing DAC creditors as the base category. Each equation includes the three key independent variables, political strength of Labor (PSL), political strength of Industry (PSI), and political strength of Finance (PSF).

In addition, I cluster the errors on debtors. This implies that the observations are independent across debtors, but not necessarily within debtors, and thus accounts for time dependence of repeated observations on countries.

I also utilize a range of control variables and include them in all $J-1$ equations. Adolph (2013b, 256) notes, "There is little if any theoretical justification for excluding any covariates from any of the equations." After all, if the existing level of debt affects the share of BRIC loans, it should also affect the share of IFI loans, as the individual proportions are negatively correlated. In my case with four creditors, adding an extra variable to the model entails estimating three additional parameters. This imposes a severe degrees-of-freedom penalty.

As a result, I follow Adolph (2013b) and start with a simple baseline specification and then show the robustness of this baseline model to serially added controls.

9.1.5. Interpretation of Compositional Data Models

As with most nonlinear models, tables of estimated parameters obscure both the quantity of interest and the uncertainty around these quantities. Although the signs of the estimated model indicate the direction of effects, the parameters are difficult to interpret. The best approach with nonlinear models is to calculate expected values of the outcome variable and show how that expected value depends on the covariates.

For this reason, I present the findings by calculating the expected borrowing portfolio.

Specifically, I calculate the expected loan share obtained from each of the four creditor types (BRIC, DAC, IFI, and private), conditional on the type of coalition (Corporatist, Capital, and Consumer). As this involves twelve separate estimates—three coalitions with borrowing shares from four creditors each—I present the results visually to facilitate comparisons across coalitions and creditors.

9.2. Findings

I examine the average borrowing portfolio of developing countries before analyzing how societal coalitions affect borrowing decisions. Figure 9.1 presents the sample averages before taking into account any heterogeneity across countries. On average, countries obtain 37% of new loans from private creditors.

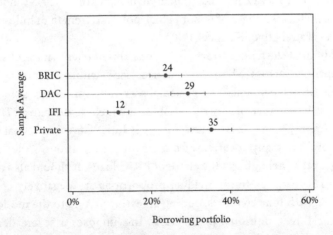

Figure 9.1 Average borrowing portfolio. Note: Average borrowing portfolio as predicted by the baseline model without differentiating between different societal coalitions. On average, countries borrow 24% from BRICs, 29% from DACs, 12% from IFIs, and 35% from private creditors.

Bilateral creditors jointly provide 52% of loans, with Western governments supplying 29%, while BRICs contribute 23%. International financial institutions provide the smallest share, with 11% of new loans.

However, the political landscape differs across countries. I argue that politicians respond to the preferences of societal coalition dominating their country, and that the borrowing portfolio of a country should reflect that coalition's preferences. Note that I do not suggest that a government should *only* borrow from the coalition's preferred creditor and borrow *nothing* from any other creditor; rather, I hypothesize that the relative use of creditors differs.

To account for societal interest groups, I include measures estimating the political strength of Labor, Finance, and Industry introduced in chapter 8. I then estimate predicted borrowing portfolios for each coalition using different configurations of groups' relative strength. For example, when simulating the borrowing portfolio of a Corporatist Coalition, I assume that the strength of both Labor and Industry is in the 90th percentile of their respective distribution, while the strength of Finance is in the 10th percentile. Figure 9.2 displays the expected borrowing portfolio across the three types of coalitions. The borrowing portfolios differ significantly: Corporatist Coalitions prefer borrowing from BRICs, while avoiding IFIs if possible; Capital Coalitions strongly rely on loans

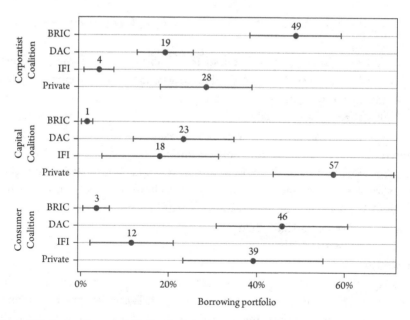

Figure 9.2 Borrowing portfolios by coalition. Note: If societal coalitions matter for borrowing decisions, we would expect borrowing portfolios to differ across coalitions. Specifically, my theory predicts that Corporatist Coalitions will use BRIC creditors most, Capital Coalitions private creditors, and Consumer Coalitions private and DAC loans. The results provide support for these expectations.

from private creditors, while disregarding BRIC loans; Consumer Coalitions prefer DAC creditors. The findings suggest that societal coalitions do shape borrowing decisions, resulting in significant differences in borrowing portfolios across coalitions.

These findings are consistent with my hypotheses. The average borrowing portfolio obtains about 23% of its loans from BRICs; however, differentiating among coalitions reveals that this average conceals significant heterogeneity across coalitions, with Corporatist Coalitions obtaining 48% of their portfolio from BRICs, while Capital and Consumer Coalitions do not often use BRICs. The average loan share obtained from private creditors—35%—similarly conceals significant heterogeneity across coalitions: With 57%, Capital Coalitions obtain a significantly larger share of loans from private creditors than Corporatist Coalitions, who only obtain 28% of their loans from this creditor. Similarly, the average borrowing portfolio obtains 28% of its loans from DACs, but again this masks significant heterogeneity: Consumer Coalitions obtain 46% of their loans from Western governments, while Corporatist Coalitions receive only 19% of their loans from these lenders. In sum, the expected differences in loan shares obtained from four types of creditors align closely with the expectations formulated in table 2.3.

9.3. Accounting for Economic Conditions

I verify the robustness of the effect of societal coalitions on borrowing portfolios. Specifically, I use several control variables to account for other factors that could also affect borrowing decisions. Existing work shows that a range of economic variables affects sovereign debt.

Including all variables at once is not possible, as each additional variable enters the model in three equations, resulting in significant reduction in the degrees of freedom. For this reason, I follow Adolph (2013b, 260) and include the variables sequentially. I vary the values of each control variable from the 10th to the 90th percentile of their respective distributions to observe how the expected borrowing portfolio changes.

First, the existing debt of countries might affect the composition of the borrowing portfolio.

Large debt burden might imply higher risk of default, thereby reducing opportunities to borrow from presumably risk-adverse private creditors (Krugman 1988). For the same reason, the probability of borrowing from IFIs might increase (Koeda 2008). Figure 9.3 depicts borrowing portfolios for each coalition across the range of external debt as a percentage of GDP. The findings highlight two observations: the share of loans obtained from IFIs does increase

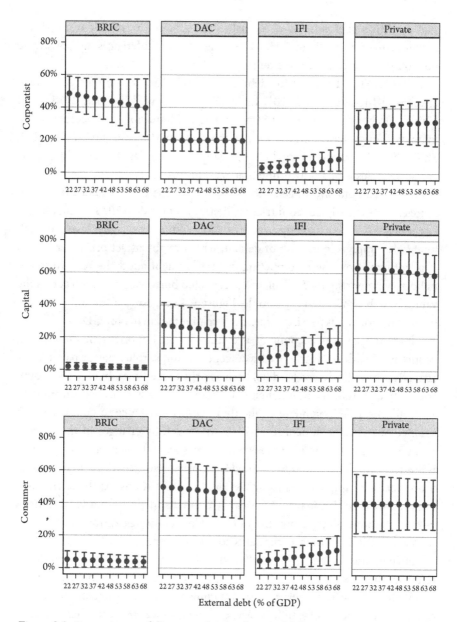

Figure 9.3 Borrowing portfolios across levels of external debt. Note: If societal coalitions matter even after accounting for existing debt, we would expect differences across coalitions to exist irrespective of the level of debt. The graph shows that this is the case.

slightly with higher external debt, just as the share of borrowing from private creditors decreases slightly. However, the overall differences in borrowing portfolios across coalitions are remarkably stable.

In a next step, I control for debtor GDP. Scholars have argued that Brazil (Burges 2014; Magnoni 2010), India (Fuchs and Vadlamannati 2013), and China (Dreher and Fuchs 2016) use foreign aid and loans to access foreign markets, though some find evidence to the contrary (Semrau and Thiele 2017). Similarly, DAC creditors might target larger economies. Lending by export credit agencies—quasi-governmental institutions that exist in most OECD countries (Auboin and Engemann 2014)—have the explicit mandate to promote exports to recipient countries (Felbermayr and Yalcin 2013). Accordingly, larger markets are particularly attractive. At the same time, higher levels of GDP might also imply a lower risk of default, which might attract private creditors. It is not clear how these competing dynamics might affect the relative shares of borrowing portfolios. I calculate the expected borrowing portfolio across the values of debtor GDP in my sample. Figure 9.4 suggest that the differences in borrowing portfolios persist, across both coalitions and debtor GDP.

Third, the current account of a country is an important measure of an economy's health. Countries with a current account surplus may be particularly attractive for risk-adverse lenders, such as private creditors. In contrast, countries with a current account deficit may increase their share of loans from IFIs. After all, the IMF's mandate explicitly includes assistance to countries with balance-of-payment difficulties, which are driven by changes in the current account. Figure 9.5 shows that such dynamics exist, though their magnitude is limited. The share of loans obtained from private sources does increase with more positive capital accounts across the three coalitions. At the same time, the proportion of IFI loans increases for Capital and Consumer Coalitions as current accounts deteriorate. In contrast, Corporatist Coalitions see a slight increase in BRIC lending as capital accounts worsen.

As a next step, I investigate the effect of trade in more detail. Specifically, I differentiate between trade with DACs and trade with BRICs. Countries might choose to borrow from their preferred trading partner to further strengthen economic interdependence. In this case, we would expect that the effects of trade with DACs and BRICs diverge across coalitions. However, Figures 9.6 and 9.7 indicate the differences in borrowing portfolios change little after taking into account trade: while the tendency of Corporatist Coalitions to borrow from BRICs is somewhat reduced by trade with DACs, a similar tendency is visible with increasing trade with BRICs, suggesting that borrowing by Corporatist Coalitions is shaped more by the amount of trade a country does than by the identity of its trading partners.

Modeling Governments' Borrowing Decisions

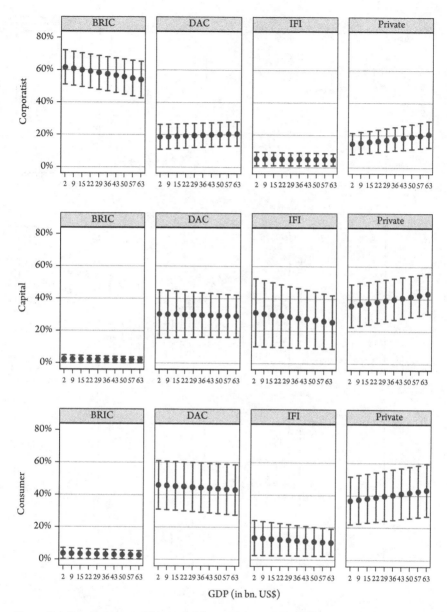

Figure 9.4 Borrowing portfolios and debtor GDP. Note: If my argument is correct, we would expect that societal coalitions result in significant differences in borrowing portfolios across coalitions even after controlling for debtor GDP. The findings provide support for this expectation.

Fifth, scholars have argued that BRICs such as China (Carmody 2013; Economy and Levi 2014; Caceres and Ear 2013; Andrews-Speed and Dannreuther 2011) and India (Beri 2008; Mawdsley 2010) use loans to obtain access to natural resources. In several cases, China has allowed borrowers to

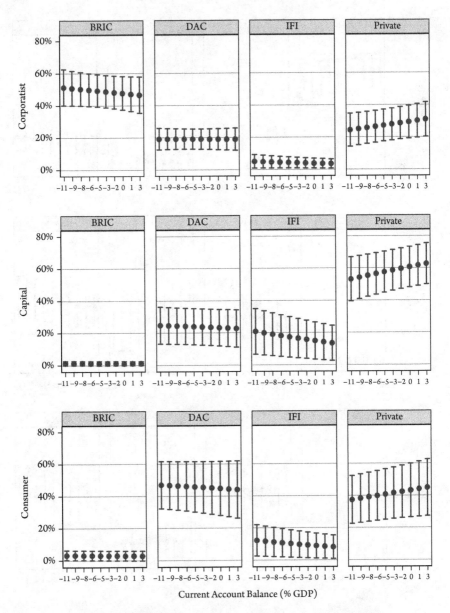

Figure 9.5 Borrowing portfolios and debtor current account. Note: If societal coalitions shape borrowing decisions even after accounting for a country's economic situation, we would expect differences across coalitions to exist irrespective of the current account balance. The graph shows that this is the case.

repay loans in the form of oil exports (Brautigam 2011; Taylor 2006). For this reason, I analyze how borrowers' fuel exports shape the relative share of loans obtained from BRICs versus other creditors. Figure 9.8 indicates that the relative loan shares are stable across coalitions after accounting for fuel exports.

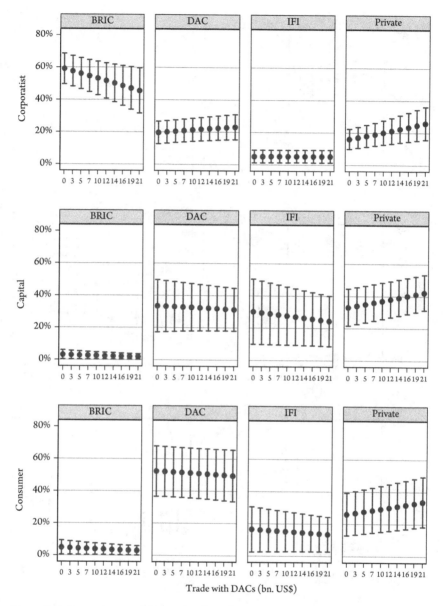

Figure 9.6 Borrowing portfolios and trade with DACs. Note: The graph shows that differences across coalitions are robust to changes in trade with DACs. This suggests that societal coalitions shape borrowing decisions even after controlling for trade with DACs.

In sum, the results of these tests are reassuring: control variables such as existing debt levels, current account deficits, and debtor GDP shape borrowing portfolios in expected ways. However, even after controlling for these economic factors, fundamental differences in borrowing portfolios exist across coalitions.

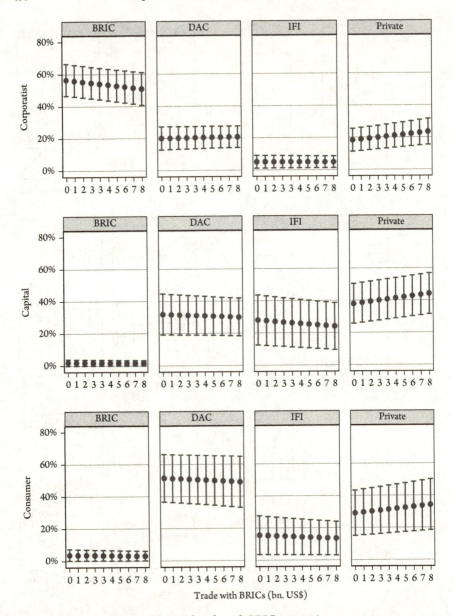

Figure 9.7 Borrowing portfolios and trade with BRICs. Note: If my argument is correct, we would expect clear differences in borrowing portfolios across coalitions, irrespective of the level of trade with BRICs. The graph supports this expectation.

9.4. Accounting for Political Context

In addition to economic factors, politics may shape borrowing decisions. In particular, institutions can shape the process by which societal interest groups can influence government policy (see Moe 2005; Bunte and Vinson

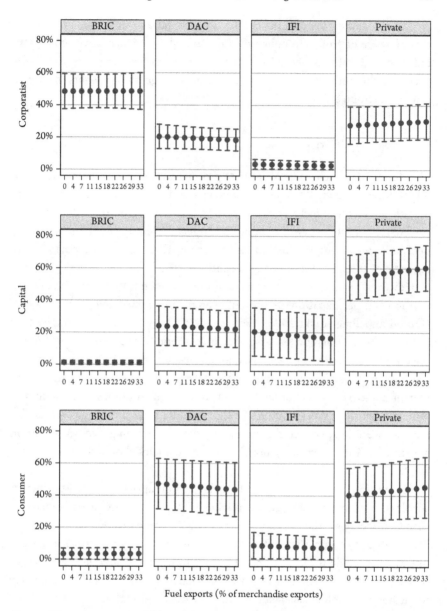

Figure 9.8 Borrowing portfolios and natural resources. Note: My theory suggests that societal coalitions influence borrowing decisions, even after controlling for the presence of natural resources. The graph provides support for this assertion, as differences in borrowing portfolios exist across coalitions regardless of a country's volume of fuel exports.

2016). This occurs from two related, but separate, angles. On the one hand, institutions can affect the access of societal groups to politicians, thereby shaping the demands that reach political decision-makers. On the other hand, institutions also affect the incentives politicians have to listen to societal demands.

Taken together, institutions can be understood as mechanisms that shape the influence of groups in policymaking. The following analyses examine how different political and institutional characteristics may shape the relative influence of Labor, Industry, and Finance, and how strongly these weights shape borrowing portfolios.

9.4.1. Democracy versus Autocracy

The degree to which societal interest groups can affect borrowing decisions might differ significantly across democracies and autocracies. For instance, autocratic leaders may feel less need to listen to interest groups. In this case, the preferences of interest groups would be largely inconsequential for borrowing decisions. According to this line of argument, then, borrowing portfolios of autocracies should not differ across coalitions.

However, recent scholarship provides much evidence that elements of competition and participation are present even in autocracies (Svolik 2009, 2013; Gandhi and Przeworski 2006; Vanhanen 2000). While not dependent on a full electorate, autocratic leaders nevertheless require sufficient support of the selectorate to remain in power (Bueno de Mesquita et al. 2005). For instance, the foreign policy behavior of autocracies might not differ significantly from that of democracies, as autocrats need to respond to domestic audiences to remain in power (Weeks 2008, 2012; Weiss 2013). If this suggestion is correct, we would expect interest groups to shape borrowing decisions even in autocracies. Thus, borrowing portfolios of autocracies should differ across societal coalitions.

In addition, regime type might matter for creditors as well. Specifically, scholars noted that private creditors might be more willing to lend to democracies than to autocracies. Schultz and Weingast (2003) argue that the diffusion of political authority to a parliament constrains leaders: while autocratic leaders can unilaterally decide to default on debt obligations, democratic leaders need to bargain with a representative assembly on such issues. As these issues are likely to include stakeholders against default, the parliament may act as a veto player. As a result, Schultz and Weingast (2003) and Beaulieu, Cox, and Saiegh (2012) argue that democracies are less likely to default, which in turn improves their ability to obtain loans from private creditors.[2] If supply-side considerations

---

[2] Note, however, that DiGiuseppe and Shea (2016) disagree. They argue that access to credit is more important to autocrats than democratic leaders, as the availability of resources directly affects their chances of survival in office. As a result, autocratic leaders should be particularly hesitant to default.

overpower any influence by societal coalitions, borrowing from private creditors should be identical across all coalitions.

Figure 9.9 illustrates the borrowing portfolios of democracies and autocracies across the three possible coalitions. It appears that borrowing portfolios differ across coalitions, but do not vary significantly with regime types. While there are slight differences, none are statistically significant. Consistent with existing evidence, the findings point to the presence of a "democratic advantage," as democracies borrow slightly more from private creditors than do autocracies. However, borrowing portfolios differ significantly across coalitions independently of regime type: Corporatist Coalitions in both democracies and autocracies borrow more from BRICs than do Capital or Consumer Coalitions, irrespective of regime type.

9.4.2. Proportional Representation versus Majoritarian Electoral System

Regime type is not the only institutional characteristic that differs across countries. Political scientists have also examined the process by which preferences are aggregated. For instance, Saiegh (2009), Kohlscheen (2010), and Van Rijckeghem and Weder (2008) examine the effect of electoral systems on default risk. I follow Saiegh and differentiate between majoritarian and proportional representation systems. The former is more confrontational, as it typically dominated by only two large parties. In contrast, proportional representation systems, characterized by multiple parties represented in parliament, result in a more "consensual" way of governance. As a result, minority opinions are more easily dismissed in majoritarian than proportional representation systems. In the case of Saiegh (2009, 236), this implies that "the probability of debt repudiation should be lower under a multiparty coalition than in a single-party government" because "multiparty coalition governments can provide guarantees for those with a stake in debt repayment because, regardless of their electoral size, coalition partners can potentially 'make or break' governments."

With respect to borrowing portfolios, this points to an interesting possibility: In a proportional representation system, societal actors excluded from a particular coalition may be able to moderate the borrowing preferences of the dominating coalition. For example, we might expect that a Corporatist Coalition can implement its preference for BRIC loans without much resistance in the context of majoritarian electoral systems. In contrast, in proportional representation systems, the group excluded from the Corporatist Coalition, Finance, may have more sway: Finance may not be able to completely dissuade policymakers from obtaining BRIC loans, but it may be able to soften these preferences. As a

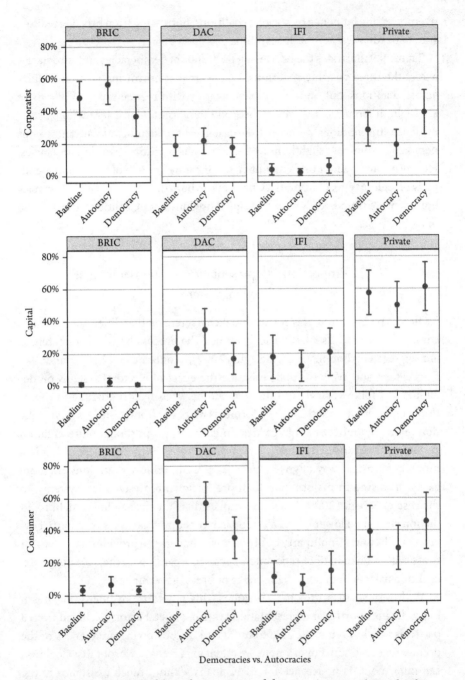

Figure 9.9 Borrowing portfolios of autocracies and democracies. Note: If societal coalitions shape borrowing decisions irrespective of regime type, we would expect distinct patterns in the use of different creditors across coalitions in both democracies and autocracies. Moreover, we would expect these systematic differences across coalitions to be similar in democracies and autocracies. The results indicate that societal coalitions affect borrowing decisions across different regime types.

result, we should observe that the share of BRIC loans obtained by Corporatist Coalitions is higher with majoritarian than with proportional representation systems.

Figure 9.10 suggests that there is evidence in support of these considerations.

Corporatist Coalitions do indeed borrow a higher share from BRICs and a lower share from private creditors in the context of majoritarian rather than proportional representation systems. However, these differences are not statistically significant. Overall, the coalition-specific patterns in borrowing portfolios exist in different electoral systems.

9.4.3. Left- versus Right-Wing Governments

The ideological orientation of the executive may shape the degree to which the lobbying efforts of societal actors are successful. Following Bearce (2003, 397), societal actors may have less access to policymakers if their political preferences do not align with the party identity of the government. For instance, one might assume that Labor has better access to the executive if a left-wing government is in power, while it might lack the necessary political back-channels with right-wing governments. Conversely, the ideological orientation of Finance and Industry might be more closely aligned with right-wing governments, while their voices are less likely to be heard if a left-wing executive is in power.

If these assumptions are accurate, they might shape borrowing portfolios. If a Corporatist Coalition between Labor and Industry dominates the political landscape, it is reasonable to expect that Labor's aversion to private creditors is more likely to be reflected under a left-wing government, resulting in a higher share of BRIC loans than under a right-wing government. In contrast, Industry's preference for private creditors might result in a higher proportion of private loans under right-wing than left-wing governments.

I use data on the chief executive party orientation by Cruz, Keefer, and Scartascini (2016) to account for left- and right-wing governments. Figure 9.11 differentiates the borrowing portfolios across coalitions depending on the ideology of the executive. The findings provide some evidence in favor of these considerations. For example, a Corporatist Coalition borrows slightly more from BRIC creditors and slightly less from private creditors if a left-wing government is in power. Conversely, it borrows less from BRICs and more from private creditors if a right-wing government is in power. This aligns with the relative preferences of the constituent groups—Labor and Industry—of this coalition. However, while the point estimates differ, these differences are not statistically significant. Importantly, however, the differences across coalitions still exist: A right-wing government responding to a Corporatist Coalition still borrows more

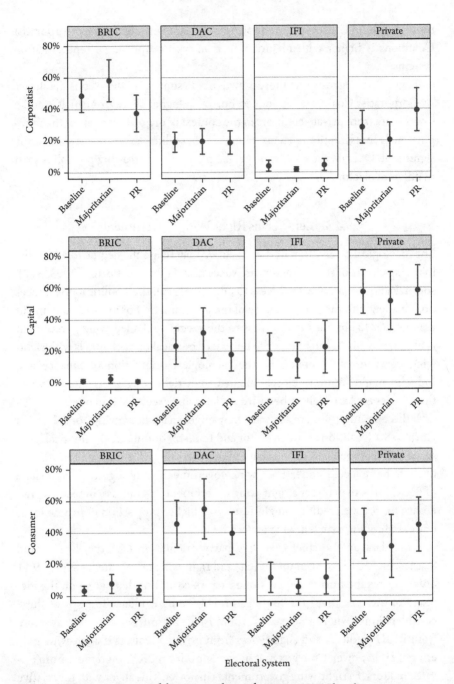

Figure 9.10 Borrowing portfolios across electoral systems. Note: If my theory is correct, we would expect differences across electoral systems to be minor, while differences across coalitions would remain significant. The graph indicates that borrowing portfolios do not differ significantly across proportional representation and majoritarian electoral systems, but do differ across coalitions. This suggests that societal coalitions shape borrowing portfolios in a variety of institutional settings.

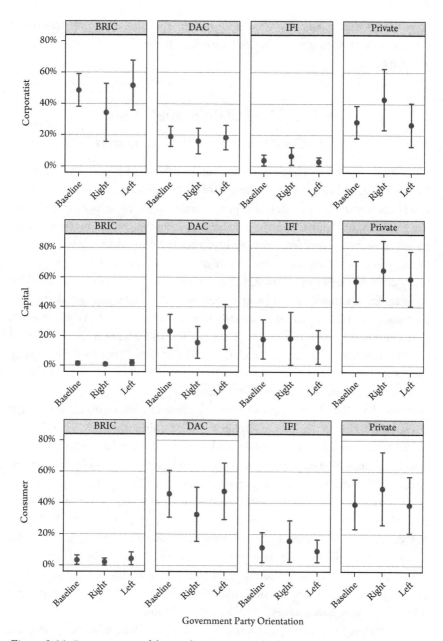

Figure 9.11 Borrowing portfolios and government ideology. Note: My theory expects coalitions to differ in their relative use of creditors, even after accounting for the ideology of the government. These findings show strong differences across societal coalitions, but only minor differences across left- or right-wing governments. This suggests that societal coalitions shape borrowing decisions irrespective of government ideology.

from BRICs than a left-wing Capital Coalition. Thus, the diverging patterns of borrowing portfolios across coalitions are robust to the ideology of the executive party in office.

9.5. Additional Robustness Tests

9.5.1. China versus Brazil, Russia, and India

Throughout this book, I have compared total lending by BRICs—that is, Brazil, Russia, India, and China jointly—to that of other types of creditors. I justify this aggregation with reference to the types of strings attached to loans from Brazil, Russia, India, and China: each of these creditors requires the borrowed resources be spent on companies from the creditor country; they share a preference for funding large infrastructure projects; and none imposes strong economic or political conditions. For this reason, the distributional consequences of Brazilian, Russian, Indian, and Chinese loans should be very similar. Consequently, I expect societal coalitions to react similarly to each of these creditors: Corporatist Coalitions will borrow from each of the BRICs, while Consumer and Capital Coalitions will avoid loans from each of the BRICs. This implies that I can group these four creditors together.

However, figure 1.1 shows that China provides significantly higher loan volumes than Brazil, Russia, and India. Against this background, one might question whether my argument applies to China only, rather than to all BRICs. In the context of the "One belt, one road" initiative, China has embarked on an ambitious project to expand its influence across the globe. In contrast, Brazil, Russia, and India have refrained from framing their foreign lending activities in these grand terms. The domestic politics in the recipient countries may thus be less about distributional consequences than about the question of whether the country should participate or resist the Chinese expansionist agenda. Corporatist Coalitions may still prefer loans from China while Capital and Consumer Coalitions may shun them; however, we would not necessarily expect large differences across coalitions with respect to loans from comparatively insignificant creditors such as Brazil, Russia, and India.

I investigate this claim by differentiating between Chinese lending and loans offered by Brazil, India, and Russia. Figure 9.12 illustrates the proportion of borrowing portfolios across coalitions. The findings illustrate that China does indeed provide the bulk of financing obtained from BRICs. However, the figure also shows marked differences across coalitions with respect to loans from Brazil, Russia, and India: Corporatist Coalitions obtain a significant share of their borrowing portfolio from these countries, while Capital and Consumer Coalitions do not. The findings suggest that coalitions view Brazil, Russia, and

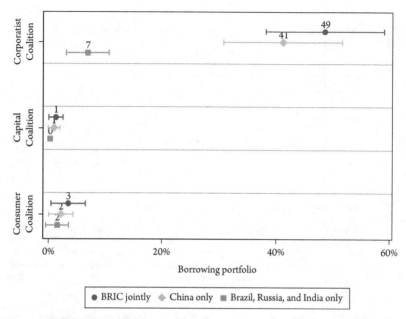

Figure 9.12 Comparing China to Brazil, Russia, and India. Note: If my theory is correct in grouping these four creditors together, we would expect societal coalitions to respond to Brazil, Russia, and India no differently than to China. The graph shows that this is the case: Corporatist Coalitions prefer Chinese as well as Brazilian, Indian, and Russian loans, while this is not the case for Capital and Consumer Coalitions. This lends credibility to the decision to group BRICs together.

India the same way they view China, lending credibility to the decision to group the BRICs together.

9.5.2. Combining DACs and IFIs

The analysis so far has differentiated between government-to-government loans from Western countries (DACs) and loans obtained from multilateral organizations (IFIs). This modeling decision was motivated by the differences in conditions attached to loans from these creditors: IFIs often attach macroeconomic conditions, such as balancing budgets, reducing inflation, and subjecting recipients to rigorous monitoring. In contrast, DAC loans may not only target different sectors (education, health) but also involve some explicitly political objectives, such as good governance, control of corruption, and even human rights.

However, one might take a different approach and argue that DACs and IFIs should be grouped together into a broader category of "Western lenders." DACs and IFIs might not differ much, for several reasons. First, Western governments might shape IFI lending from within. Scholar such as Stone (2004, 2008) and

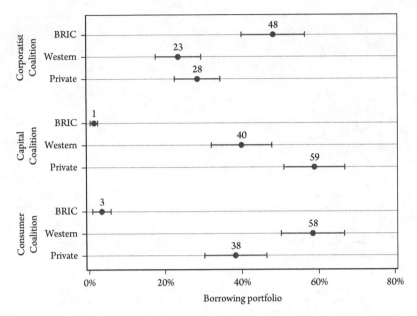

Figure 9.13 Comparing all Western to non-Western creditors. Note: The graph illustrates that the borrowing portfolios of Corporatist Coalitions differ significantly, even if all Western creditors (i.e., DACs and IFIs) are combined.

Copelovitch (2010), among others, have shown that important DACs dominate decision-making processes within IFIs: There is reason to believe that decisions about loan volumes provided by IFIs and the degree of conditionality attached to these loans are shaped by the interests of important Western governments. Second, Western governments may also explicitly coordinate their lending activities with IFIs (Moschella 2016; Hodson 2017). For example, faced with the euro crisis, the heads of state of European countries declared themselves ready "to contribute to coordinated bilateral loans" as part of "a package involving substantial International Monetary Fund financing and a majority of European financing."[3] In sum, loans from DACs and loans from IFIs may be sufficiently coordinated to consider them a single type of lender. The question is whether combining DAC and IFI creditors negates the differences in borrowing portfolios across coalitions.

Figure 9.13 illustrates that such concerns are unfounded. Even after combining DACs with IFI lenders and re-estimating the predicted shares, differences exist: Corporatist Coalitions still obtain a significantly higher share of loans from BRICs than from Western creditors, while the opposite is true for

---

[3] Statement by the heads of state and government of the Euro area, March 25, 2010.

capital and Consumer Coalitions. Moreover, differences in the use of private and Western creditors across Capital and Consumer Coalitions become even more pronounced.

9.6. Conclusion

This chapter presents the findings of a statistical analysis examining the borrowing portfolios of 92 developing countries between 2005–2015. My theory predicts that societal coalitions shape borrowing decisions. Specifically, I expect Corporatist Coalitions to prefer borrowing from BRICs while avoiding IFIs, Capital Coalitions to rely primarily on private creditors, and Consumer Coalitions to use DAC and IFI loans.

The results provide strong support for my theory: borrowing portfolios differ significantly across coalitions consistent with the theoretical expectations. These distinctions are robust to various controls, such as the amount of existing debt, debtor current accounts and GDP, the level of trade with DACs and BRICs, and the presence of natural resources.

Similarly, the borrowing portfolios of coalitions are distinct, even after accounting for differences between democracies and autocracies, proportional representation and majoritarian electoral systems, and right- versus left-wing governments. The findings are also robust to varying conceptualization of creditor groups.

In sum, the quantitative analysis confirms the insights of the qualitative evidence presented in chapters 4, 5, and 6: societal interests are significant predictors of borrowing decisions.

Nevertheless, a range of alternative explanations might also be at work. The following chapter analyzes their merit.

10

Evaluating Alternative Explanations

The previous chapters have shown that borrowing portfolios of countries differ: Some rely heavily on emerging creditors such as Brazil, Russia, India, and China (BRICs), others obtain the majority of loans from Western governments (DACs) or multilateral institutions (IFIs), and yet others borrow primarily from private creditors.

Existing explanations for this variation focus chiefly on the supply side. According to this approach, creditors—and creditors alone—determine the loan volume obtained by a developing country. There is no doubt that creditors and their motivations play an important role in loan negotiations. Creditors may have concerns about the creditworthiness of potential borrowers, they may be worried about the economic fundamentals of debtors, and they may have political motivations. My work does not negate the importance of supply-side considerations. After all, the outcome of any voluntary transaction—such as a loan agreement—should reflect the intersection of supply- and demand-side considerations. Instead, my work complements this supply-side approach with a demand-side perspective.

The motivation for developing a demand-side explanation was the observation that developing countries are not passive recipients: borrowers have preferences as well, and they have the political will to act upon them (Vreeland 2003a; Nooruddin and Simmons 2006). To explain these preferences, I rely on insights from the existing scholarship on trade: the pivotal work by Rogowski (1989) shows that trade flows affect some domestic groups positively and others negatively. I extend this logic of distributional consequences to sovereign borrowing: The strings attached to loans differ across creditors. For this reason, some groups benefit from a particular loan, while others do not. Coalitional dynamics in the recipient country then explain governments' borrowing choices.

To reiterate, my intention is not to dispute the importance of supply-side factors but to complement this approach with a demand-side perspective. However, it is worthwhile to examine the relative importance of both approaches: after all, they may differ across creditors.

In addition, my demand-side explanation focuses on distributional consequences and societal coalitions. However, alternative demand-side explanations are conceivable, and their relative merit needs to be examined. This chapter evaluates various alternative explanations.

10.1. Debtors Have No Choice and Only Creditors Decide

An important supply-side explanation focuses on the willingness of creditors to lend. This explanation focuses on creditors' incentive to provide loans, which may differ across potential recipients. As a result, prospective borrowers may not have access to their preferred creditor. In this case, the observed variation in borrowing portfolios will not reflect a conscious choice by recipient governments but instead will reflect the decisions of creditors.

For instance, some governments may prefer private creditors. If they are able access private capital markets, governments will obtain private finance. However, if private creditors are unwilling to provide loans, these countries may be forced to borrow from less preferred, alternative sources of loans. For example, these countries might perceive BRICs as the lender of last resort. Some interviewees supported this view (Interviews 79, 86, 96). A private banker argued that "the Chinese were the only option left" after Ecuador had defaulted on private creditors and rejected the IMF for ideological reasons (Interview 87). For this reason, the Chinese "are lending to desperate markets" (Interview 92).

It is possible, and indeed likely, that some governments may have access to more creditors or receive more favorable financial conditions than others. If demand factors are important in explaining borrowing portfolios, we should observe variation in the borrowing decisions of countries with a similar set of options.

To examine this claim, I distinguish loan portfolios across debtors that should have comparable access to creditors. Following the World Bank, I classify developing countries as low, lower-middle, or upper-middle income. It is reasonable to assume that loan choices become more advantageous as a country's income increases. If *only* supply-side considerations explain sovereign lending, we would expect borrowing portfolios of countries with the same income classification to be extremely similar. If supply-side considerations overpower demand-side factors, we would not expect differences across coalitions within the same income classification; rather, we would expect drastic differences across income levels. In contrast, should *only* demand-side factors matter, we would expect borrowing portfolios to differ only across coalitions, but not across income classifications.

I expect borrowing portfolios to be guided by both supply- and demand-side considerations.

However, the relative influence of supply versus demand considerations might vary across creditors in predictable ways. Private creditors are guided by economic considerations, such as the desire to make a profit. In contrast, lending by government creditors (BRICs and DACs) as well as multilateral organizations (IFIs) might be guided by political considerations as well. For this reason, private creditors are likely more risk-adverse than public creditors.

Consequently, we would expect supply side factors to be most visible with private creditors (stark differences across income groups, but not coalitions), while demand-side factors would be most visible with sovereign creditors (stark differences across coalitions, but not income groups).

Figure 10.1 shows that both supply and demand factors are at play. Consider BRIC loans: consistent with supply-side expectations, lower-income countries obtain a larger share of new loans from BRIC creditors than countries with higher incomes; however, consistent with my demand-side explanation, Corporatist Coalitions still obtain more BRIC loans than either Capital or Consumer Coalitions, irrespective of their level of income.

Distinct borrowing profiles exist across coalitions even after accounting for differences in loan choices.

As expected, supply-side factors exert a stronger influence on the share of loans obtained from private creditors. While the relative use of private creditors across coalitions still follows expectations (Corporatist Coalitions borrow less from private creditors than Capital and Consumer Coalitions), these differences are not remarkable, while notable differences across income groups exist.

Differentiating developing countries by their income is obviously only one proxy for differences in loan options available to prospective borrowers. It is likely, for instance, that countries with superior credit ratings have better access to creditors. Figure 10.2 illustrates borrowing portfolios of countries differentiated by credit rating and across coalitions.

As before, the estimated borrowing portfolios show that both supply- and demand-side factors are at play, though their relative importance differs across creditors. For private lenders, supply-side considerations dominate, as the differences in the share of loans obtained from private creditors does not vary much across coalitions; it does, however, vary across credit ratings. In contrast, demand-side considerations dominate for emerging lenders. For instance, the share of loans obtained from BRIC creditors differs significantly across coalitions.

Obviously, this is just one way in which to test the relative importance of supply- and demand-side explanations. The preceding findings suggest that borrowing portfolios are the result of an interaction between demand- and

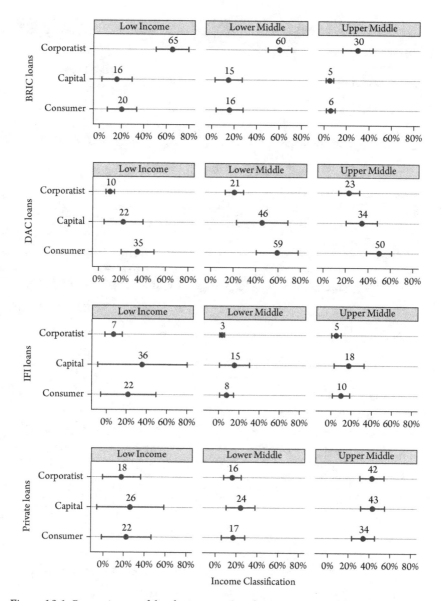

Figure 10.1 Borrowing portfolios by income classification. Note: Supply-side approaches predict differences across income classifications, while my demand-side approach expects differences across coalitions. The graph illustrates that supply- and demand-side factors jointly explain borrowing portfolios but that their relative importance differs across creditors: for BRIC loans, strong differences exist across coalitions for BRIC loans, pointing to the importance of societal coalitions. In contrast, for private loans, differences across income levels are more pronounced than differences across coalitions. This suggests that the use of private loans is shaped by supply-side factors.

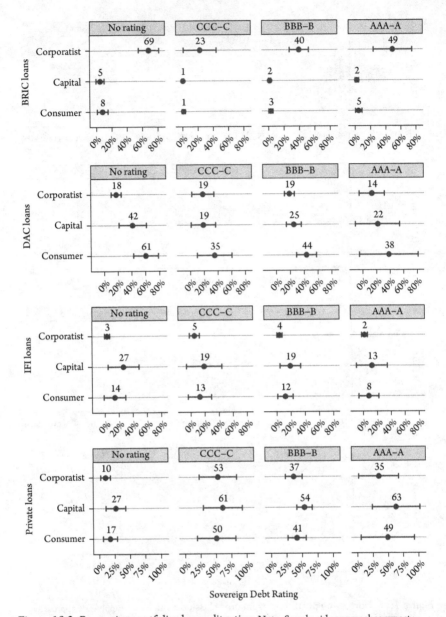

Figure 10.2 Borrowing portfolios by credit rating. Note: Supply-side approaches expect differences across credit ratings, while my demand-side approach predicts differences across coalitions. The findings suggest that supply- and demand-side factors jointly explain borrowing portfolios. Again, their relative importance differs across creditors: for BRIC loans, strong differences exist across coalitions, suggesting that societal coalitions explain the use of this creditor. In contrast, the private loans differ more across credit ratings than coalitions. This points to the importance of supply-side factors for this creditor.

supply-side factors. Moreover, the relative importance of these factors differs across creditors: demand-side considerations appear to dominate supply-side concerns with respect to public creditors, while supply-side factors appear to be more important than demand-side factors in explaining the share of loans obtained from private creditors.

A further test of the relative influence of supply and demand factors utilizes the exogenous variation in the London Interbank Offering Rate (LIBOR). LIBOR is a benchmark interest rate, which is why LIBOR rates correlate closely with interest rates demanded by private bondholders. At the same time, however, it is unlikely that changes in societal coalitions in developing countries affect LIBOR. We can thus conceptualize a sudden increase in LIBOR as an exogenous shock on the price of private loans for sovereign debtors. We can leverage this information to gain insights into the interplay of supply- and demand-side factors: should the supply-side effects overpower demand-side considerations, we would expect all debtors—irrespective of their coalition—to reduce the proportion of private loans if private creditors become more expensive; we should even observe that the share of private loans converges across coalitions. In contrast, if demand-side factors are at play as well, differences in the utilization of private creditors should persist, irrespective of the price of private loans.

Figure 10.3 illustrates the change in the proportion borrowed from private creditors across the three creditors as private loans become more expensive (as measured by an increase in LIBOR). We see a limited effect: the share obtained by Corporatist, Capital, and Consumer Coalitions responds only marginally to increases in loan prices. More importantly, however, the relative utilization of private creditors remains distinct: Corporatist Coalitions rely less on private creditors than Capital or Consumer Coalitions, irrespective of cost. This evidence strengthens the conclusion that demand-side considerations play a significant role.

Multiple anecdotes corroborate the insights gained from the preceding statistical analyses. Specifically, several examples illustrate how countries with similar access to lenders decide to use different creditors. In 2013, for instance, Indonesia and the Philippines had many factors in common, besides their geographical proximity (they are neighboring island archipelagos). Both countries had the same credit rating in 2013 (BBB−), similar levels of economic development (GDP per capita of $2,048 and $2,574, respectively), and the same Polity IV democracy score of 8 (on a scale from −10 to 10). That year, Indonesia sold $1.5 billion of dollar-denominated bonds at an interest rate of 6.125% and a maturity of 5.5 years. The government hired Standard Chartered, Citigroup, and Deutsche Bank to arrange the sale. Indonesia allocated 15% of the notes to local investors, 25% to the rest of Asia, 24% to the United States, 16% to Europe, and 20% to Islamic and Middle Eastern funds.

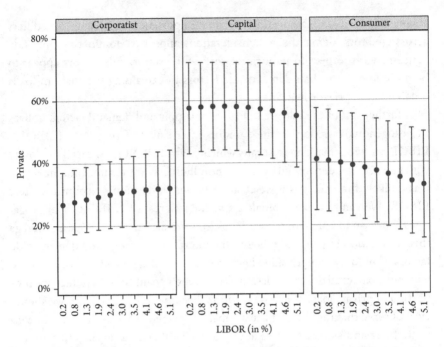

Figure 10.3 LIBOR and private loans. Note: Should supply-side effects have more explanatory power than demand-side considerations, we would expect all types of coalitions to reduce the proportion of private loans if private creditors become more expensive. This figure, however, illustrates that differences in borrowing from private creditors persist across coalitions as private loans become more expensive. This suggests that demand-side considerations play a role in explaining borrowing portfolios, irrespective of loan price.

In contrast, the Philippines pursued a different approach: national treasurer Rosalia de Leon stated that the government was currently not sure what type of creditor to use to cover the budget gap equal to 2% of GDP under next year's expenditure plan. De Leon said that the borrowing program could include issuing bonds, but that possibility "does not mean we will proceed. Just like this year, we also had it in the financing plan but eventually we decided not to issue offshore.... [Issuing bonds] is always one of our funding options" (*Malaysian Insider* 2013). Finance secretary Cesar Purisima added that the Philippines planned to borrow $2.2 billion from foreign lenders in 2014 but had not yet decided on the sources. While issuing bonds is an option "some of [the borrowed resources] would be in the form of official development assistance (ODA) loans" (Dela Penña 2013).

Later that year, the Philippine government announced that it had decided not to borrow from foreign private creditors that year (Remo 2013).

Uganda and Rwanda are two similar countries that also made different borrowing choices. In 2013, these neighboring countries in East Africa had similar credit ratings (B+ and B, respectively), comparable levels of economic development (GDP per capita of $424 and $473), and similarly unfavorable democracy scores (−1 and −, respectively).

Yet while Rwanda attracted more than $3 billion of orders for its $400 million 10-year bond sale at an interest rate of 6.875%, the Ugandan government announced that it had decided not to issue bonds in international financial markets. In communicating this decision, the Ugandan Ministry of Finance, Planning and Economic Development noted, "Sovereign bonds are expensive, and [the ministry] is concerned that public debt could rise to unsustainable levels during currency depreciation, increasing bond yields" (Prizzon, Greenhill, and Mustapha 2017). Thus, despite access to a similar set of creditors, Uganda and Rwanda chose to borrow from different lenders.

My fieldwork in Ecuador, Colombia, and Peru also indicates that it is necessary to complement the supply-side explanation with a demand-side perspective. For example, in Ecuador, several interviewees pointed out that it was Ecuador's decision to obtain Chinese loans rather than borrow from the IMF. An interviewee in the office of the undersecretary for public investment indicated that Ecuador received loan offers from the IMF at the same time it considered borrowing from China but decided against it (Interview 94). A representative of the Coordinating Ministry of Economic Policy added, "The IMF demands that the money is spent on the financial sector. However, Ecuador wants to spend it on social development. Essentially, Ecuador wants to do a different type of capitalism" (Interview 78). According to an employee in office of the undersecretary of public credit within the Finance Ministry, it was Ecuador that closed the door to the IMF and Western creditors, and only because of Ecuador's actions do the Chinese appear to be the "only option" (Interview 83).

Even in Ecuador, a country likely to be credit rationed due to past defaults, public debt officers noted that they typically receive several competing credit offers from multilateral, bilateral, and private creditors (Interview 10). This narrative is corroborated by facts: while Ecuador did reject IMF loans and did obtain several large loans from China and Brazil, it also borrowed from private capital markets. For example, in 2013 under President Correa, Ecuador obtained $185.62 million from private creditors. Obviously, this amount is dwarfed by the $996.42 million Ecuador obtained from BRICs in the same year. However, this mix of funding sources (76% from BRICs, 14% private creditors, 10% DACs) is precisely what we would expect from a Corporatist Coalition.

Colombian officials also stated that they have access to multiple types of creditors. A representative of the Ministry for Trade and Public Finance noted, "We have a lot of sources of funding so that we don't depend on [government-to-government loans]. Of course, they are very interesting as they are cheap and have long periods of amortization and grace periods. Thus they would be good for the debt portfolio, but we can get resources elsewhere." While the

Colombian government is not generally opposed to bilateral loans—the interviewee mentioned loans from Korea, France, and Spain—they are not utilized often (Interview 38).

In addition, a Colombian official in the Ministry of Commerce, Industry and Tourism confirmed that China offered loans, but that they were not accepted (Interview 18). A public official in the department that coordinates Colombia's external relations with Asian countries stated that "loans with China have *not yet* worked out" (Interview 39), despite their favorable financial conditions with 40-year maturities and 2% interest rate (Interview 16). For example, in 2005 a Chinese loan was offered to build the Canal Seco (Dry Canal), but it was not accepted. Colombia also rejected a Chinese loan offer to finance a hydropower project, the Acueducto Metropolitano de Bucaramanga (Interviews 1, 11). China was also interested in funding the modernization of the Bogotá airport (Interview 9).

In each instance, the Chinese loan proposal was not selected. When asked why they had been rejected, one interviewee noted that "[their loans] are cheap, but there are a lot of conditions . . . so that is why it has not worked out" (Interview 38).

In Peru, debt officers noted that if the Ministry of Economics and Finance solicits loan offers, it typically receives multiple proposals from multilateral institutions, bilateral creditors (in particular, the German Kf W Bankengruppe, Japan International Cooperation Agency, and the Agence Française de developpement), and private creditors (Interviews 65, 72). Two representatives of the Economic Studies Department of Peru's Central Bank indicated that Peru could obtain loans from China but chooses other creditors instead (Interviews 57, 60).

In sum, the qualitative evidence is consistent with the statistical analyses: while supply-side considerations are important, they need to be complemented with a demand-side perspective.

Developing countries have choices. Even if we acknowledge that some have better choices than others, analyzing countries with similar alternatives reveals significant variation in their borrowing decisions.

10.2. Political Recognition of Taiwan

A second alternative supply-side explanation concerns Chinese lending and recipients' political recognition of Taiwan. The relationship between China and Taiwan is fraught with challenges: the government of mainland China considers the island of Taiwan to be part of its territory, while the Taiwanese government insists on its autonomy. This conflict has resulted in a battle for diplomatic recognition whereby China and Taiwan each attempt to convince third-party governments to cease recognizing the other as a legitimate government. Periodically, therefore, newspapers report that developing countries have switched allegiances: for example, Panama recently established ties with China and ended its political recognition of Taiwan (Horton and Myers 2017). Observers have suggested that China follows a simple rule: countries recognizing Taiwan do not receive loans from China (Atkinson 2010; Van Fossen 2007; Rich 2009).

However, such exclusion criteria are not apparent in the raw data. In fact, the underlying data render the idea that China does not lend to countries recognizing Taiwan a popular myth: in the period from 2000 to 2015, 31 countries recognized Taiwan politically. Of these countries, 13 countries received loans from China *in years in which they recognized Taiwan*. During this period, several countries even received multiple loans from China: in Latin America, Belize received eight, Honduras six, and El Salvador three Chinese loans; in Africa, Swaziland acquired three loans, while Burkina Faso secured two loans. These data suggest that political recognition of Taiwan does not preclude Chinese loans. These observations correspond to the findings of the statistical analysis. Figure 10.4 suggests that borrowing portfolios do not differ between countries that recognize Taiwan and those that do not. The explanation, however, may be simple: instead of applying exclusion criteria, China may use loans to incentivize countries currently recognizing Taiwan to switch their allegiance. After all, "Countries deploy economic links in the hopes that economic interdependence itself will, over time, change the target's foreign policy behavior" (Kahler and Kastner 2006, 525).

10.3. Loan Price

Besides alternative explanations that emphasize supply-side considerations, alternative demand-side explanations are conceivable as well. Specifically, while this book proposes an explanation based on distributional consequences and societal coalition, there might be other demand-side explanations that merit analysis. For example, politicians might base borrowing decisions merely on the price of different creditors, rather than on societal interests. Presumably, price-conscious politicians would prefer cheaper loans. This implies that borrowing portfolios do not differ significantly across societal coalitions; instead, borrowing portfolios should change significantly with changes in the price of loans.

I utilize information on the grant element that measures the degree of generosity implicit in a loan: a loan with a high interest rate, short maturity, and brief grace period has a low grant element, while a loan with low interest rate,

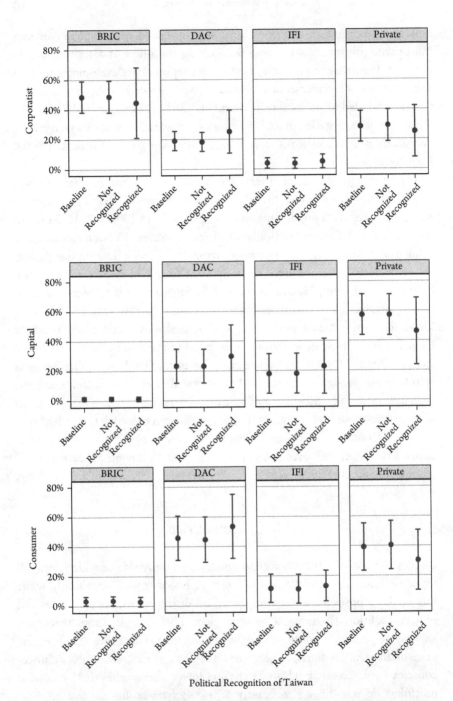

Figure 10.4 Borrowing portfolios and political recognition of Taiwan. Note: One supply-side argument suggests that countries recognizing Taiwan do not receive loans from China. If that is true, we would expect the use of BRIC loans to differ significantly across countries that do recognize Taiwan versus those that do not, while differences across coalitions should be minor. However, the graph illustrates that countries recognizing Taiwan are just as likely to receive loans from BRICs as those that do not, but differences across coalitions persist.

long maturity, and extensive grace period has a high grant element. Figure 10.5 illustrates how borrowing portfolios respond to changes in loan price.[1] The first row shows how the proportion of loans obtained from BRIC creditors changes as BRIC loans become more expensive (i.e., lower grant element). The findings indicate that borrowing from BRICs is not responsive to changes in price; moreover, the stark differences across coalitions persist even after controlling for BRIC loan prices. Similarly, DAC and IFI loan shares are fairly robust to changes in prices. In contrast, increasing the price of private loans significantly reduces the share obtained from private creditors. However, the relative differences of utilizing this creditor persist across coalitions: at any given price, Capital and Consumer Coalitions borrow more from private creditors than do Corporatist Coalitions.

Observers might also point out that some loans are so inexpensive that OECD rules allow governments to consider such lending as foreign aid. Specifically, loans with a grant element larger than 25% can be added to a donor's ODA statistics. Foreign aid flows—including concessional loans—might have different determinants than nonconcessional loans. The concerns of societal interest groups about distinct distributional consequences of specific creditors may matter less to politicians if creditors offer concessional loans. If this reasoning is accurate, differences across coalitions should disappear when we analyze only concessional loans.

Consequently, I re-estimate the analysis with the smaller subset of concessional loans only. Figure 10.6 compares the borrowing portfolios of the baseline model with those of concessional loans. We can see some changes. Capital and Consumer Coalitions reduce their exposure to private sources once concessional loans are available from sovereign creditors. However, the fundamental differences across coalitions still exist: when offered concessional loans from BRICs, DACs, and IFIs, Corporatist Coalitions still choose BRIC loans, while Capital and Consumer Coalitions do not.

10.4. Specific Creditors for Specific Purposes

Besides societal coalitions and loan price, a third demand-side explanation suggests that politicians select creditors based on their respective expertise. For example, BRICs and the World Bank are known for their expertise in funding

---

[1] Note that each row shows how the proportion of *that* creditor changes in response to changes in the price of *that* creditor, but does not show how these changes affect the shares obtained from other creditors. Thus, the estimates shown for each coalition do not add up to 100%.

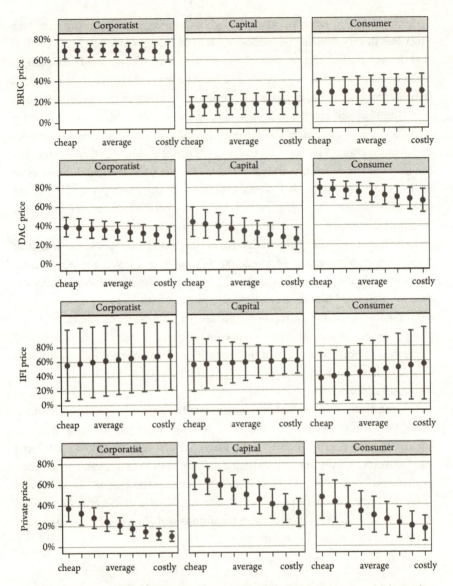

Figure 10.5 Borrowing portfolios and loan prices. Note: Debtor governments might simply choose the cheapest loan option and disregard societal preferences. In this case, borrowing portfolios should differ depending on the price of loans, but we would not expect differences across coalitions. However, the graph shows that differences across coalitions persist, even after accounting for the price of loans. A note regarding the interpretation of the figure: Loan prices vary by one standard deviation below and above the mean grant element for each creditor. Each row shows how the proportion of *that* creditor changes in response to changes in the price of *that* creditor, but does not show how these changes affect the shares obtained from other creditors. Thus, the estimates shown for each coalition do not add up to 100%.

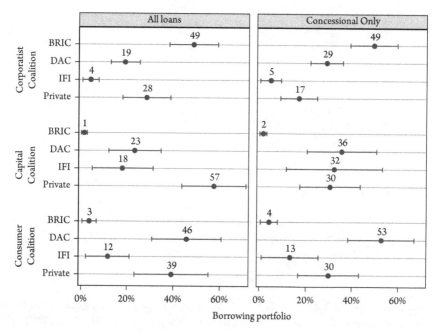

Figure 10.6 Comparing concessional loans to all loans. Note: Concessional loans can count toward creditors' official development aid (ODA). Thus, these inexpensive loans might have distinct determinants. In particular, the preferences of societal coalitions might not apply. However, the graph shows that even when analyzing only inexpensive loans, different coalitions utilize different creditors.

large infrastructure projects; DAC creditors are thought to specialize in lending for social purposes such as health; and IMF loans are often associated with crisis lending. Depending on debtors' needs—infrastructure, health projects, or dealing with an economic crisis—governments may want to match the purpose of the loan with the appropriate creditor.

Examine the case of lending for infrastructure projects. A government interested in funding a hydroelectric power dam might naturally select loans from BRICs or the World Bank while disregarding other creditors. This line of argument yields an interesting empirical implication: if the expertise of the creditors trumps the possible influences of societal coalitions, the utilization of World Bank and BRIC loans will not differ across coalitions.

However, this does not appear to be the case. Figure 10.7 disaggregates the baseline model to compare the use of BRIC and World Bank loans across coalitions. One might expect Corporatist Coalitions utilizing BRIC loans to be equally likely to use World Bank credit, and if Capital Coalitions use World Bank loans, they might also use BRIC loans. However, this is not the case: differences across coalitions do persist, even when we compare lenders that focus on infrastructure projects.

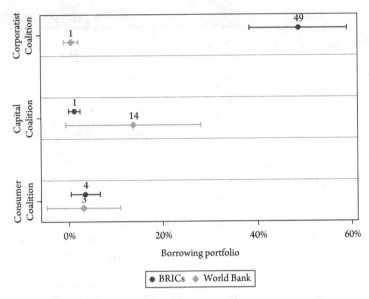

Figure 10.7 World Bank versus BRICs. Note: It is possible that debtors use specific creditors for specific purposes. If this were the case, we would expect that the use of World Bank and BRIC loans does not differ across coalitions, as both specialize in funding infrastructure. However, the results indicate that Corporatist Coalitions prefer BRIC loans, while Capital Coalitions favor IFIs.

Yet this analysis may be inaccurate because countries governed by Corporatist Coalitions might have systematically different infrastructure needs from those countries with capital and Consumer Coalitions. To examine this possibility, I use data on countries' estimated infrastructure investment gap (Global Infrastructure Hub 2017). These data calculate the difference between actual investment expenditure and the projected infrastructure investment needed to achieve the Millennium Development Goals. If governments prefer borrowing from creditors with expertise in infrastructure, we would expect them to use this type of creditor more frequently if their infrastructure investment needs were significant irrespective of societal coalitions. Figure 10.8 suggests, however, that differences across coalitions persist both in levels and in trends: Corporatist Coalitions borrow more from BRICs, and the share obtained from this creditor rises as their need for infrastructure projects increases. In contrast, Capital and Consumer Coalitions borrow significantly lower levels from BRICs, and their propensity to use this creditor is barely affected by infrastructure requirements. The situation is reversed with respect to World Bank loans, though the differences are not as prominent. In sum, data suggest that countries with similar infrastructure needs borrow from different creditors depending on their societal coalition.

I extend the analysis to DAC creditors. Western governments are said to have a preference for, and expertise in, funding projects conducive to social

Evaluating Alternative Explanations 223

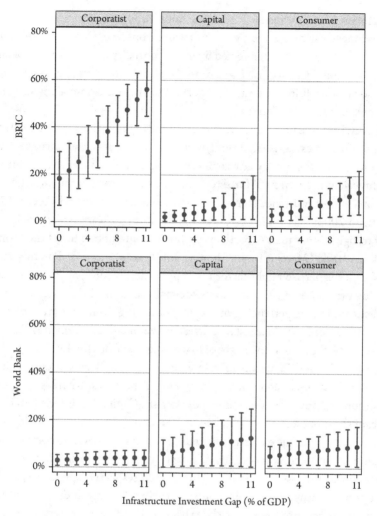

Figure 10.8 World Bank versus BRICs by infrastructure needs. Note: The graph displays the use of World Bank and BRIC loans across coalitions as a function of the estimated infrastructure investment gap. Both creditors specialize in funding infrastructure, yet we see different utilization across coalitions, even as infrastructure needs increase. The results confirm that Corporatist Coalitions prefer BRIC loans, while Capital Coalitions favor IFIs, even if both creditors offer funding for the same type of projects.

development, such as health and education projects. If borrowers select creditors based on their need for human development projects, we would expect that countries with high social needs will prefer DAC loans, irrespective of societal coalitions. For this reason, I examine borrowing patterns conditional on infant mortality to capture the need for health projects, and conditional on primary school enrollment to account for the need for education projects. We would expect that the share of DAC loans would be particularly high in countries with high infant mortality and low primary school enrollment. Figure 10.9 shows that this is indeed the case, but only in Capital and Consumer Coalitions. In contrast, the use of DAC loans is unaffected by infant mortality or primary school enrollment in Capital Coalitions. These differences in both levels and trends suggest that societal coalitions are more important to the decision-making calculus of borrowers than humanitarian needs.

Lastly, I analyze borrowing from multilateral organizations. These institutions have significant expertise in dealing with economic crises, and borrowers might want to access their policy advice in such situations. For instance, governments might welcome an external force to implement necessary, but painful, domestic reforms against resistance from their constituencies (Smith and Vreeland 2005; Vreeland 2003b). Furthermore, a government might want policy advice from IFIs to signal other market participants that it is attempting to get the economy back on track (Marchesi and Thomas 1999; Gould 2003). For this reason, IFIs' crises expertise might factor more prominently into politicians' decision-making process than pressures from societal coalitions. In this case, we would expect countries experiencing or recently emerging from debt crisis to turn to the IMF for immediate assistance irrespective of societal demands. However, figure 10.10 shows that the share of loans obtained from the IMF differs across coalitions: Capital Coalitions obtain a comparatively large share of their loan portfolio from multilateral institutions after debt crises, whereas Corporatist Coalitions do not. Even years after a debt crisis, Capital Coalitions obtain a significant share of their loans from IFIs.

Without doubt, the expertise of creditors differs. However, in deciding which creditor to use, debtors apparently do not closely match the expertise of the creditor with the purpose of the funds. Due to their respective specialties, creditors are not necessarily functionally equivalent. However, my findings point to the fungibility of resources once they have been received by borrowers: for example, a developing country might want to spend $100 million for large infrastructure projects and $50 million for microprojects in the education sector. Assume that the country obtains a DAC loan of $20 million under the condition that the resources are spent in the education sector. However, even if the funds are tied to the education sector, this does not imply that the country's education budget rises to $70 million. Knowing the loan will arrive shortly, the government can reduce the budget for education to $30 million and reallocate the "saved" resource to the infrastructure budget.

The infrastructure budget would then amount to $120 million while the education budget supplemented with the external loan would stand at $50 million. Ultimately, the DAC loan intended for education has allowed the government to increase its spending on infrastructure.

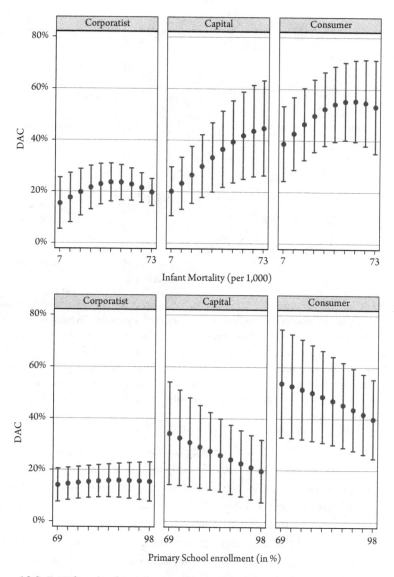

Figure 10.9 DAC loans and recipient need. Note: DAC loans offer generous funding for health and education projects. If debtors use specific creditors for specific purposes, we would expect that DAC loans increase with higher infant mortality and lower primary school enrollment irrespective of societal coalitions. However, the findings indicate that the utilization of DAC loans as a function of humanitarian needs depends on the type of societal coalitions.

This example illustrates that even if loans are tied to a particular project, governments have flexibility in allocating funds. As a consequence, we would not necessarily expect to observe a close correlation between a country's needs and the creditors' expertise.

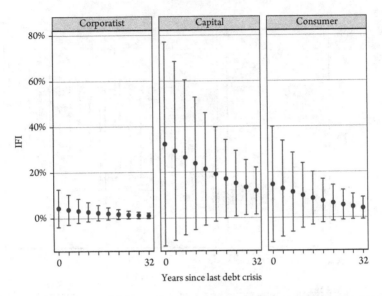

Figure 10.10 IFI loans and debt crises. Note: As a lender of last resort, IFIs provide crises loans. If debtors use specific creditors for specific purposes, we would expect countries facing debt crises to use IFI loans irrespective of their societal coalition. The figure displays the use of IFI loans conditional on the time since the last debt crisis. The findings suggest that the use of IFIs differs across societal coalitions even after accounting for debt crises. As predicted by the argument, Capital Coalitions are significantly more likely to use IFI loans, even years after a debt crisis. However, note the imprecise estimates due to low number of observations as the analysis is restricted to the subsample of countries that experienced default.

As noted in chapter 1, evidence suggests that fungibility is an empirical reality (Jones 2005; Pettersson 2007; Feyzioglu, Swaroop, and Zhu 1998). Even with respect to IMF loans, whose conditions are among the most stringent and specific, scholars suggest that the IMF cannot adequately ensure that recipient governments use the funds for their intended purpose (Dreher 2009, 246). For example, Rodrik (1996, 26) shows that governments use IMF loans to repay private creditors, and that the IMF cannot veto such reallocation of resources. Epstein and Gang (2009, 17) remark that "for many years, at least since the introduction of structural adjustment aid in the 1980s, aid policy has assumed near 100% fungibility." In sum, "Targeting assistance to specific projects is essentially a futile exercise" (Svensson 2000, 72). Instead, creditors and donors "should take it for granted that their financing is fungible because that is reality" (Dollar and Pritchett 1998, 91).

10.5. Ideological Alignment

Political factors might also shape the choices politicians make among creditors. For example, politicians in developing countries might prefer borrowing from creditors with similar ideological orientation. Such considerations might underpin Ecuador's decision to borrow from China, while Colombia continues to rely on loans from traditional lenders.

The increased likelihood of loans from like-minded partners might be due to the ideological alignment itself, as creditors and debtors might ramp financial cooperation to further common goals. It is also possible, however, that ideological alignment itself operates indirectly: establishing sustainable working relations while negotiating other international issues might spill over into bilateral lending and facilitate loan agreements. If either of these mechanisms is operating, we would expect countries with similar ideological beliefs to tend to sign loan agreements.

I test for this possibility by utilizing voting patterns in the United Nations (Voeten, Strezhnev, and Bailey 2013). Specifically, the frequency with which debtor nations vote with either the United States or China is a reasonable proxy for shared ideological beliefs. Note that this is an imperfect measure: it is not clear whether similar ideology might cause bilateral loans, or if loan agreements reflect shared beliefs, or if both shared beliefs and loans are the result of the underlying societal coalition. However, for the present purpose, establishing the association between loans and ideology suffices.

We would expect the strongest correlation between ideology and loans when comparing countries aligned with the United States but not China, and vice versa. For this reason, I compare countries exhibiting an above- and below-median frequency of voting with the United States or China. Figure 10.11 illustrates how the degree of agreement with the United States and China is associated with bilateral loans. Countries aligned with the United States but not China tend to borrow less from bilateral creditors—BRICs in the case of Corporatist Coalitions, DACs in the case of Capital and Consumer Coalitions—and more from the private market. However, these differences are not statistically significant.[2] It appears that coalitions have distinct borrowing portfolios, even after accounting for possible ideological alignments with creditors.

10.6. Conclusion

My argument suggests that societal coalitions shape borrowing portfolios. However, a number of plausible alternative explanations exist that could also explain variation in borrowing decisions. This chapter examined the relative merit of these alternative explanations.

---

[2] Note that these findings are in line with models comparing borrowing patterns of left- and right-wing governments. Figure 9.11 suggests that borrowing portfolios do not differ significantly between left- and right-wing governments.

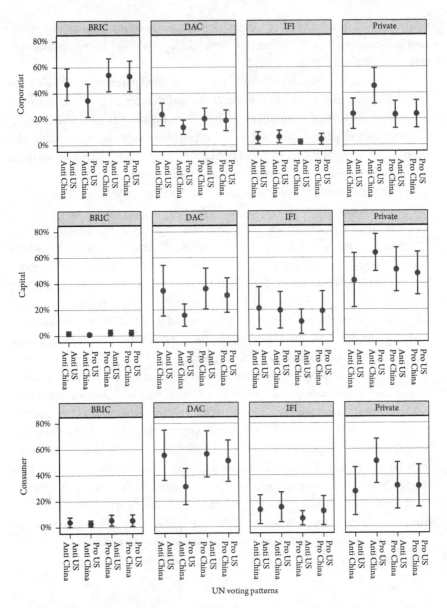

Figure 10.11 UN voting and borrowing portfolios. Note: Debtors might borrow from creditors that share their ideological disposition. If that is the case, we would expect differences in borrowing portfolios across ideological alignments but no variation across societal coalitions. The graph displays borrowing portfolios of countries depending on their voting patterns with or against either the United States or China. It appears that ideological alignment with the United States or China does not significantly affect borrowing decisions, while differences across coalitions persist.

For example, it is possible that differences in borrowing portfolios is not a result of debtors' choices, but rather reflects variation in creditors' willingness to provide loans. Thus, it would be the supply side (creditors), not the demand side (debtors), that shapes borrowing portfolios. These approaches must not be mutually exclusive; in fact, they should not be: the outcome of any voluntary economic transaction *should* reflect the intersection of supply- and demand-side considerations. I show that the share of loans obtained from various creditors is shaped by both supply and demand factors. Importantly, the relative importance of these factors differs across creditors: demand-side considerations appear to dominate supply-side concerns with respect to public creditors, while supply-side factors appear to be more important than demand-side factors in explaining the share of loans obtained from private creditors.

Second, I examined the robustness of my demand-side theory—by distributional consequences and societal coalitions—to alternative demand-side explanations. For instance, in deciding among loan offers, politicians might consider the relative costs of loans and choose the cheapest option. If this were the case, we would expect borrowing portfolios not to differ across societal coalitions, but only across loan prices. However, the evidence suggests that this is not the case. Alternatively, politicians might choose creditors depending on the type of project, matching the respective creditors' expertise to the purpose of the loan. However, I have shown that borrowing portfolios differ across societal coalitions, even if countries face similar infrastructure needs, humanitarian emergencies, or economic crises. Furthermore, political considerations such as ideological alignment might influence the decisions of politicians. However, the analyses suggest that borrowing portfolios vary across societal coalitions, even after accounting for ideological similarities or military alliances.

In sum, the effect of interest groups on the choice of creditors is robust to a variety of alternative explanations. The empirical evidence shows that societal coalitions are key to explaining the variation in borrowing portfolios across developing countries.

11

Why Greater Choice Matters for Developing Countries

Borrowing portfolios of developing countries differ significantly. Why do some governments prefer to borrow from BRICs (Brazil, Russia, India, and China), while others rely on private creditors, and yet others obtain loans from Western governments (DACs)? I argue that a demand-side perspective must complement explanations focusing on the behavior of creditors: Developing countries are not merely passive recipients, but instead can choose among the creditors available to them. My demand-side theory argues that the distributional consequences differ across creditors. This explains why different societal interest groups have diverging preferences with respect to which loan their government should obtain. Politicians then respond to the preferences of the dominant societal interest groups and borrow from the creditor these groups prefer. Since interest group coalitions differ across countries, so do borrowing portfolios.

The qualitative and quantitative evidence offered in this book provides strong support for this theory. But what are the implications of these findings? After a brief summary of the findings, this chapter will explore several possible implications. First, the rise of new creditors—Brazil, Russia, India, and China—represents a challenge to the existing international financial architecture. Section 11.2 analyzes the increased competition among creditors and examines how my theory provides insights into the likely evolution of the relationship between emerging and traditional creditors. Section 11.3 explores the implications of increased competition among creditors for developing countries. Specifically, does this change imply increased autonomy from creditors? If this new situation does provide recipient countries with more freedom to implement policies of their own volition, what types of policies will they choose? I subsequently explore my theory's implications for economic development, as well as the ramifications for democracy in developing countries.

11.1. Summary of Findings

The borrowing decisions of governments differ. Ecuador rejected multilateral and Western bilateral loan offers and instead borrowed from Brazil and China. In contrast, Colombia used multilateral and private creditors but rejected Chinese loan offers. As a consequence, the borrowing portfolios of these countries vary. What explains this variation across countries?

Undoubtedly, the behavior of creditors plays a role: If a lender is unwilling to provide a loan, the lack of access will prevent a government from borrowing. However, a comparison of the borrowing portfolios of countries with similar access to creditors reveals significant variation: given the same set of loan offers, governments choose different creditors, suggesting that the supply-side perspective focused on creditors' decisions must be complemented with a demand-side perspective examining borrowers' actions. This book presents a theory explaining how borrowers choose their creditors.

My starting point is the insight that the distributional consequences of loans vary across creditors. Two creditors offering the same loan amount may attach different strings to the loan. IMF loans require governments limit inflation and cut spending to balance the budget. In contrast, BRIC loans are typically attached to specific investment projects. These differences in the characteristics of the loan imply distinct economic consequences.

Some societal groups might benefit from one set of consequences but not another. I argue that there are three key groupings in societies, each linked to the economic activity from which individuals in the groups derive the bulk of their income, and which are for the purposes of analysis internally homogenous. The factor that distinguishes these groups is the kind of assets that they own. The first group is made up of financial market actors, who own intangible assets. The second group is composed of producers in industry, who own tangible, fixed assets. And the third group is workers, who do not own assets.

My theory connects choices among types of creditors to distributional outcomes in a plausible way. For instance, IMF conditions benefit Finance because lower inflation preserves the value of its capital, but IMF-imposed spending cuts often hurt Labor. In contrast, BRIC loans benefit Labor by funding investment projects that provide employment opportunities. Yet BRIC loans mean that Finance will face competition from a powerful external actor funding domestic investment. Thus, Finance prefers IMF loans but dislikes BRIC loans, while the opposite is the case for Labor. By connecting the interests of three major societal groups—Finance, Industry, and Labor—to the characteristics of four types of loans—multilateral loans, bilateral loans from Western governments, bilateral loans from BRICs, and loans from the private sector—I derive which group benefits from what creditor.

When the distributional consequences of a choice are sizable—some groups will win and some will lose—and the members of different groups understand how the policy affects their economic interest, the policymaking process becomes a battleground between competing interests and their affiliates in the government. I argue that the three societal interest groups can form three varieties of societal coalitions: (1) a Capital Coalition in which Finance and Industry are powerful; (2) a Corporatist Coalition in which Labor and Industry are strong; (3) and a Consumer Coalition in which Finance and Labor are politically influential. Each coalition will prefer its government to choose a particular creditor.

Because of the distinct distributional effects of different types of loans for these societal groups, the underlying political coalitions that sustain ruling governments lead survival-seeking policymakers to select particular creditors. Specifically, if politicians respond to a Capital Coalition, they tend to borrow from private creditors more than other governments. In contrast, politicians have the tendency to use BRIC loans more frequently if they face a Corporatist Coalition. Lastly, when confronted with a Consumer Coalition, the government increasingly relies on DAC creditors.

I test this approach using qualitative studies of borrowing decisions made by three South American countries, each of which maps onto the societal coalition types described in the theory. Colombia is the archetypal Capital Coalition, Ecuador represents decision-making when the Corporatist Coalition dominates, and the case of Peru tests the drivers of borrowing choices when the Consumer Coalition is powerful. I use elite interviews—and lots of them, 112 to be precise—to reconstruct the political histories of these countries' borrowing choices from the early 2000s to recent years. I present the insights from interviews with domestic politicians (prime ministers, finance ministers, senators, and public debt officials), societal interest groups (domestic banks, business associations, labor representatives), and creditor representatives (multilateral, Western, and BRIC lenders). The evidence suggests a strong association between coalition type and debt composition in these countries, as predicted by the theory. In addition, the case studies provide illustrations, drawn from the interviews, of the political calculations informing the decisions of the key players during the borrowing process.

I complement the qualitative evidence with a statistical analysis to show that my argument can be generalized to all developing countries. I first collect data on borrowing decisions—a challenging task given the paucity of data on Chinese loans, in particular—to create a measure of governments' borrowing portfolios. I then create proxies measuring the strength of Finance, Industry, and Labor in developing countries. With these data, I show that the configuration of societal interest groups can predict the variation in borrowing portfolios.

In summary, both qualitative and quantitative evidence show that societal coalitions can explain governments' borrowing decisions.

11.2. Increased Competition among Creditors

11.2.1. Competition and Multilateral Lending Institutions

The rise of emerging lenders has resulted in increased competition among creditors. This is particularly visible with respect to multilateral lending institutions. Since 2010, BRICs have established several multilateral institutions that directly compete with established international financial institutions (IFIs). For example, Brazil, Russia, India, and China—plus South Africa—have established the New Development Bank (NDB) with an initial subscribed capital of $50 billion, with the respective governments each contributing $10 billion. The stated purpose of the NDB is to provide funding to infrastructure projects. Emerging creditors feel that traditional lenders failed to deliver on their commitments by prioritizing funding for education, healthcare, and women's rights instead of infrastructure investment (Khanna 2014, 48). With the establishment of the NDB, emerging creditors aim to address this—in their view—incorrect approach. Compared with the World Bank, the NDB provides loans more rapidly and operates through more representative and democratic forms of governance and decision-making (Dixon 2015).

Besides establishing a competitor to the World Bank, BRICs have also created an equivalent to the IMF (Griffith-Jones 2014, 2). In 2014, the BRICs announced the creation of the Contingent Reserve Arrangement (CRA), which was subsequently ratified in 2015. The BRICs pledged to fund the CRA with $100 billion, of which China will contribute $41 billion, while India, Russia, and Brazil provide $18 billion each.[1] Its purpose is to provide emergency assistance to member countries should they experience short-term liquidity problems (Dixon 2015). The maximum amount states can request from the CRA is $20.5 billion (China) or $36 billion (the other member states). The CRA thus represents an alternative to the IMF as a lender of last resort.[2]

---

[1] The remaining $5 billion are provided by South Africa.

[2] In this context, Chiang Mai Initiative Mutilateralisation (CMIM) is an additional way in which emerging markets have begun to coordinate short-term liquidity assistance. The CMIM represents a network of large-scale currency swaps between the central banks of China, South Korea, Japan, and 10 members of the Association of Southeast Asian Nations (ASEAN). It was launched in 2010 and can draw on a foreign exchange reserves pool worth $240 billion.

Importantly, these new multilateral creditor organizations share an important feature that differentiates them from traditional IFIs: just like bilateral BRIC loans, the loans by the NDB and the CRA will be provided without macroeconomic conditionalities (Cooper 2017, 281). This reflects the reluctance of members to submit to conditionalities imposed by Western governments. For example, during the global financial crisis of 2008, Indonesia and South Korea both experienced liquidity crises (Sussangkarn 2010). Neither the Indonesian nor the South Korean government was prepared to apply to the IMF for assistance because of the conditions attached to IMF loans (Dixon 2015). Indeed, in South Korea, the strength of popular feeling against the macroeconomic conditions was such that the government could not survive an approach to the IMF (Sussangkarn 2010). Unconditional loans by the newly established multilateral institutions represent a credible alternative.

Could the establishment of these new institutions act as a catalyst for reform of the IMF, World Bank, and broader international financial architecture? After all, some of the institutions might represent new norms of international financial cooperation. Specifically, all members of the CRA and NDB have an equal vote (with no provision for a veto). Furthermore, individual countries are only able increase their contribution when the majority of the others agree. Both features limit the extent to which one member can dominate the institution (Dixon 2015). This principle of equality stands in stark contrast to the World Bank and IMF, which are dominated by the United States.

It remains to be seen if these rival multilateral organizations will have an immediate impact on established organizations such as the IMF and the World Bank. Two issues might impede significant consequences in the short term. First, while China did not block the establishment of the NDB, its initial ambivalent reaction to India's proposal slowed the process of negotiation and institutional creation. Throughout the protracted negotiations, Chinese commentators questioned whether the principle of equality undercut institutional performance (Cooper 2017, 276). Furthermore, members differ significantly in their assessment of the NDB's mission. For India, the NDB is of great interest as another source of finance for its massive needs for infrastructure development. In contrast, China is motivated by the need to open new markets for its engineering and construction companies and the availability of an enormous current account surplus (Chin 2014). For this reason, China pushed to open up the client base beyond the BRICs; while India—looking to meet needs at home—wanted a more concentrated focus (Cooper 2017). This heterogeneity will limit the scope of the NDB.

Second, so far, these new multilateral organizations have limited monetary might. The proposed financial capacities of the new institutions are modest compared to the IMF's $750 billion liquidity, the World Bank's lending capacity of $200 billion, and the Asian Development Bank's $165 billion (Dixon 2015). Furthermore, the prospects of increasing the available resources are slim. Chin (2014, 371) notes that "if the BRICS follow an approach similar to the World Bank's, the NDB will need to borrow from global capital markets by issuing bonds. However, the cost of borrowing will likely be higher for the [NDB] than for the World Bank." World Bank bonds are AAA-rated, as they are guaranteed by the institution's 187 member states. In contrast, only five economies are acting as guarantors for the NDB. Thus, the cost of funding for the NDB is likely to be less favorable.

11.2.2. Competition among Bilateral Creditors

In contrast to the changes among multilateral creditors, however, the increased competition among bilateral creditors is likely to have significant implications in the short term. This book shows that loans from BRICs and DACs are in direct competition with each other. For example, the US Embassy in Moscow reported on several new loans the Russian government provided to Latin American countries (Bunte and Kinne 2018). It commented, "Although [Russian] officials adhere to the line that Russia's interest in Latin America is simply a normal expansion of ties, and not intended as a challenge to the U.S., Moscow is clearly intent on extending its influence, if not ideologically, at least politically and economically, in the region" (US Embassy in Russia 2008). Similarly, the American embassy in Tajikistan reported that "Tajikistan took advantage of China's 'very special offer' of up to $900 million in low-interest loans. . . . China's credits have raised Tajik expectations when dealing with the United States and other international institutions and could cause Tajikistan to look more and more to Beijing for assistance and investment. The United States cannot compete with China in terms of lending or investment. Even forgiving the $17 million in debt (a repeated Tajik request to the United States) would pale in comparison" (US Embassy in Tajikistan 2006).

Faced with the tremendous competition from bilateral BRIC loans, what options do traditional creditors have? They might attempt to convince BRIC lenders to change their loan conditions and adopt those of Western creditors. Precedents exist: In the 1960s, Germany and Japan were emerging creditors whose loan characteristics initially differed from those of the United States and its allies. Over time, however, these then-new creditors conformed their lending conditions to those of more established lenders. In the context of the Development Assistance Committee, Western governments agreed on a set of rules that codified their norms and moral expectations. For example, loans tied to a specific investment project were prohibited. However, similar developments are unlikely today. Germany and Japan were less important for the world economy in the 1960s than China is today. Furthermore, both were more dependent on US military cooperation during the Cold War than the BRICs are in today's multipolar world. Furthermore, the BRICs' self-interested approach to development assistance almost guarantees that they would have no interest in harmonizing with other creditors. As the BRICs have had no role in authoring current standards, attempts to impose these rules on their lending would invariably be seen as an attempt to stifle domestic growth in BRIC economies.

If the prospects of changing BRIC loan characteristics are slim, a second policy option for Western creditors would be to make their own lending conditions more attractive. For example, Western creditors "may be forced to offer loans with fewer conditions to 'stay in the business' and attract recipients who are faced with an increasing number of options in how to finance their development programs" (Hernandez 2017). There is evidence that Western export credit agencies are adjusting their lending in response to Chinese competition (Bunte, Gertz, and Zeitz 2018). The European Union is re-evaluating its use of conditionality, partly because of the realization that change cannot be imposed from the outside. The coordinator for Africa-China relations at the European Commission noted that "China's focus on a mutual interest-based, commercially driven and politically high-level partnership with Africa has concentrated minds in Europe on how the old donor-recipient partnership could be transformed into a modern partnership" (Wissenbach 2009, 667). Similarly, Hernandez (2017) finds that World Bank delivers loans with significantly fewer conditions to recipient countries that are assisted by China. Yet despite the prospect of a lower *number* of conditions, it is unlikely that Western creditors will change the *content* of its conditionalities. Given the structure of economic interests and public opinion within industrialized countries, IMF loans will continue to emphasize macroeconomic stability, and DAC loans will continue to stress good-governance criteria. As these are the defining characteristics of Western loans, their distributional consequences will remain distinct from those of BRIC creditors.

Given that the character of conditions attached to BRIC and Western loans is likely to remain distinct, my theory suggests that the clientele of the respective creditors will change. Specifically, I expect increasing separation where specific types of borrowers are matched to specific creditors, resulting in distinct set of clients that share important characteristics.

A Capital Coalition prefers IMF loans precisely because they require the government implement a set of structural adjustment reforms that are likely to result in a more favorable business environment for Finance and Industry. Thus, this subset of countries—those dominated by a Capital Coalition—will continue to demand these types of loans. Conversely, Corporatist Coalitions will demand BRIC loans precisely because their loan characteristics differ from those of Western creditors.

Thus, my theory suggests that the IMF and the World Bank will remain relevant actors in the future, but their clientele will change. The IMF may rest assured that its services and loans will continue to be demanded in the future, albeit only by a subset of countries.

This might have positive, if unintentional, consequences, as the IMF might have less difficulty implementing its programs in the remaining recipient countries. After all, the IMF's remaining "customers"—countries characterized by a Capital or Consumer Coalition—will be characterized by a strong domestic financial sector whose interests are well aligned with those of the IMF. Thus, the share of "good performers" in the portfolio of IMF clients is likely to increase.

Similarly, BRICs will face significant opposition in some developing countries, but will be warmly welcomed in others. Zambia and Angola may represent such divisions: In Zambia, anti-Chinese sentiment has become an increasingly important issue in domestic politics. In the 2006 presidential election, the opposition candidate, Michael Sata, ran on the platform explicitly rejecting the exploitation of Zambia's resources by China: "We have to be careful because if we leave them unchecked, we will regret it. China is sucking from us. We are becoming poorer because they are getting our wealth" (Chimangeni 2007). In contrast, an Angolan politician noted that "our relations with China not only allowed us to obtain large loans, but most importantly it forced the West to treat us with more respect and in a less patronizing way. For that we are grateful" (*Diplomatic Courier* 2011). Such divisions between developing countries are likely to deepen.

11.3. Expanded Room to Maneuver for Developing Countries

Prior to the rise of the BRICs as an alternative, developing countries could borrow only from a cartel of Western creditors. Lacking an outside option, it was the IMF, the US government, or private banks that decided if a country received loans. At that time, governments of developing countries were passive recipients, eager to gobble up loans from whichever creditor happened to be willing to lend. Under these circumstances, creditor countries acquired a degree of power over the recipient through granting loans (Waltz 1979).

However, this changed with the emergence of BRICs as creditors. The resulting competition among creditors has important implications for recipient countries: if they can choose among different creditors, developing countries become less dependent on a single lender.

The emergence of the BRICs as an alternative source of finance undermines the monopoly of Western creditors. As a result, recipient countries might have more autonomy in choosing their own policies. Several interviewees mentioned that the availability of non-Western creditors enhanced developing countries' sovereignty (Interviews 89, 100). Interviewees welcomed the existence of an "outside option."

The power to choose among competing loan offers implies that recipient governments can better withstand a creditor's desire to influence domestic policies. I am agnostic as to whether this reduced influence of Western creditors on developing countries is a "good" or a "bad" development. I simply recognize that more room to maneuver implies a higher degree of sovereignty for developing countries.

Angola provides an example of increased room to maneuver. After the civil war in 2002, the IMF together with the World Bank offered financing and assistance for the reconstruction. However, attached to these loans were requirements to liberalize domestic markets and improve transparency. The ruling elite was reluctant to sign such a deal but was desperately in need of funds (Taylor 2006, 947). In this situation, the Chinese EXIM bank offered a $2 billion loan with an interest rate of 1.5% over the LIBOR, repayable over 17 years with a five-year grace period. The credit was agreed in 2003 and disbursement began in 2004 (Hernandez 2017). Importantly, this loan had no conditionalities regarding corruption or transparency attached (Taylor 2006, 947).

Western media and aid organizations denounced China for helping Angola to avoid pressure to clean up corruption. The country director for CARE commented, "This big Chinese loan gives a lot more flexibility for Angola not to comply with the conditions for other deals. It allows the government to escape transparency" (IRIN 2005). In contrast, the Angolan government stated that Western creditors imposed "conditions on developing countries that are nearly always unbearable and sometimes even politically unacceptable," while the Chinese loan imposed no "humiliating conditions" on Angola (Taylor 2006, 948). The US Embassy in Angola noted that "Angola's officials have made it clear that while they welcome a strong working relationship with the IMF, they do not need the IMF to carry out domestic economic policy. China's bilateral credit line to Angola without doubt has increased Angola's range of options and bargaining power vis-a-vis international organizations such as the IMF" (US Embassy in Angola 2006).

Problems with corruption and the lack of transparency undoubtedly exist in Angola. However, it is also true that the Chinese loan helped restore three rail lines essential to Angola's mineral exports, construct a new airport, and build low-income housing (Taylor 2006, 949). As Deborah Brautigam points out,

"There is still enormous corruption, but roads, clinics, and schools are being built" (Brautigam 2009, 274).

If increased competition among creditors offers developing countries more room to maneuver, how will government use this freedom? I argue that analyzing the type of societal coalition can provide insights into the likely types of policies that the recipient country will pursue. In the remainder of this section, I explore the insights of my theory by exploring the prospects for economic development as well as democracy.

11.3.1. Implications for Economic Development

When discussing possible models for economic development, two paradigms dominate the discussions among policymakers: one side argues for exploiting existing comparative advantages of developing countries more efficiently, while the other suggests a focus on creating new comparative advantages.

The first approach corresponds to a neoliberal understanding of economic development (Williamson 2000, 2003). It aims at enabling citizens to become productive members in free markets. The goal is to exploit existing comparative advantages as efficiently as possible by improving the skills and abilities of individuals. Western creditors are committed to this liberal paradigm. The conditions attached to IMF loans require governments to liberalize their economy by removing restrictions that might hold back economic actors.

Similarly, bilateral Western loans emphasize good governance and the rule of law. In addition, by emphasizing education and health, Western creditors intend to enable citizens to maximize their opportunities in free markets.

In contrast, the second approach draws inspiration from the experience of the East Asian Tigers (Wade 1990; Amsden 1992; Chang 2002). These countries industrialized rapidly during the latter half of the twentieth century. Ironically, they accomplished this precisely by disregarding the prescriptions of the Washington Consensus. Instead of exploiting existing comparative advantages, countries like South Korea and Taiwan focused on creating new comparative advantages. Massive state intervention guided the upgrading of their economies to move into positions higher up the value-added production chain. Instead of producing rice (their initial comparative advantage), they now produce computers (a new comparative advantage). BRIC loans tend to support this type of development (Bunte et al. 2018). For example, Chinese loans funding hydroelectric power dams in Ecuador will make that country a net electricity exporter instead of relying on imports of electricity.

My work shows that developing countries have some say in choosing a creditor. By extension, the availability of BRIC loans offers governments more autonomy regarding the path to economic development they want to pursue. For this reason, societal coalitions might shape a government's strategy for development. It is reasonable to expect that a government responsive to a Corporatist Coalition will attempt to create new comparative advantages instead of exploiting existing endowments. In contrast, governments catering to a Capital or even Consumer Coalition might be more likely to trust the benefits of free markets to help them make use of their current comparative advantages. Thus, the type of creditor might predict the type of development model they want to pursue.

Anecdotal evidence suggests that this is the case. The democratically elected president of Senegal, Abdoulaye Wade, published an op-ed in the *Financial Times* (Wade 2008) In it, he praises China's pragmatic approach to his country,

> The Chinese model for stimulating rapid economic development has much to teach Africa. With direct aid, credit lines and reasonable contracts, China has helped African nations build infrastructure projects in record time—bridges, roads, schools, hospitals, dams, legislative buildings, stadiums and airports. In many African nations, including Senegal, improvements in infrastructure have played important roles in stimulating economic growth.... It is a telling sign of the postcolonial mindset that some donor organizations in the West dismiss the agreements between Chinese banks and African states that produce these vital improvements—as though Africa was naïve enough to just offload its precious natural resources at bargain prices to obtain a commitment for another stadium or state house.... I have found that a contract that would take five years to discuss, negotiate and sign with the World Bank, takes three months when we have dealt with Chinese authorities. I am a firm believer in good governance and the rule of law. But when bureaucracy and senseless red tape impede our ability to act—and when poverty persists while international functionaries drag their feet—African leaders have an obligation to opt for swifter solutions.

In sum, my theory might not only provide insights into which type of creditor a government chooses, but also help predict the model of development it pursues.

11.3.2. Ramifications for Democracy

The emergence of BRIC creditors might have not only economic, but also political implications. For example, critics argue that these loans might undermine democracy in recipient countries. BRICs do not have moral reservations against lending to dictators and autocracies, while Western creditors are supposedly more hesitant to lend to them. Naim (2017) criticizes China for providing unconditional loans to dictators, which he argues undermine Western attempts to promote democracy. These loans might provide autocratic leaders with resources that allow them to remain in office longer than otherwise possible, thwarting transitions to democracy. This might be an unintended side effect.

However, some argue that it is a deliberate strategy by Russia and China in an effort to extinguish or dampen democratization around the world (Silitski 2010; Ambrosio 2009; Bader, Grävingholt, and Kästner 2010; Coyne and Ryan 2009).

In addition to providing loans to autocrats, BRIC loans might also undermine democratic structures in existing democracies. For example, at the G8 meeting in Heiligendamm in 2007, German finance minister Peer Steinbrück stated that BRIC loans undermine the promotion of "good governance" by Western creditors (Wenping 2007). Former president of the World Bank Paul Wolfowitz claimed that international financial institutions are "losing projects in Asia and Africa to Chinese banks because [the Chinese] don't bother about social or human rights conditions" (Beattie and Callan 2006). The head of the US-China Economic and Security Review Commission testified before Congress that China is offering "a wealth of assistance in building African infrastructure without concern about whether the benefits are accruing to the African people or only corrupt leaders" (US Congress 2005). The promotion of China's alternative authoritarian development model, they argue, contributes to "a world that is more corrupt, chaotic, and authoritarian" (Naim 2017, 95).

However, these claims are mostly supported by anecdotal evidence. In contrast, systematic analyses examining the effect of BRIC loans on democratic institutions and good-governance norms are more hesitant in their judgments. For example, Bader (2014) finds that Chinese money transfers have no effect on the survival of autocratic leaders. Similarly, Bunte (2018b) finds no evidence that BRIC lenders undermine debt sustainability by targeting their loans at recipients of debt relief by Western creditors. Instead, Kleine-Ahlbrandt and Small (2014) argue that economic self-interest is currently compelling China to overhaul its policies toward autocratic governments. Given the growing stock of investments in autocratic countries, China needs to devise a more sophisticated approach to protecting its assets and its citizens abroad. China might recognize that providing uncritical and unconditional support to unpopular, and in some cases fragile, regimes might not be the most effective strategy.

What are the implications of my theory regarding the prospects for democracy in developing countries that borrowed from BRICs? While still speculative,

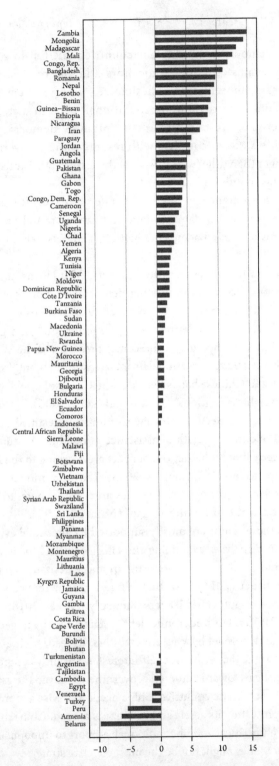

Figure 11.1 Change in Polity score after first major BRIC loan. Note: Difference in average Polity score in the five years before and the five years after a country obtained its first BRIC loan of at least US$10 million between 1990 and 2015. The figure shows that—more often than not—countries have become more (not less) democratic after receiving a BRIC loan.

my argument provides for an interesting prediction. I note that BRIC loans are typically tied to specific investment projects that promise the creation of additional jobs. Similarly, I show that contractors are often paid above-market prices for their services. Both elements suggest that workers' financial situations are likely to improve with Chinese loans, while Western loans do not promise direct monetary benefits to Labor. If BRIC loans benefit primarily the poorer segments of society, they may contribute to a reduction in inequality. According to the research on the relationship between inequality and democracy by Boix (2003) and Acemoglu and Robinson (2006), reducing inequality increases the likelihood of democratic transitions.

If this chain of arguments is accurate, then it implies that Chinese loans might have an indirect prodemocratic effect.

Obviously, detailed empirical analysis is required to test these competing hypotheses on the effect Chinese loans have on democracy. However, preliminary analysis of the relationship between BRIC loans and democracy scores appears to support an optimistic view. A first look at empirical evidence compares the quality of democratic institutions in countries before and after they received a BRIC loan of significant size. For each recipient country between 1990 and 2015, I calculate the average Polity score in the five years prior to receiving the BRIC loan larger than $10 million and compare it with the average Polity score of the five years following the acquisition of this loan. The difference in these scores is displayed in figure 11.1. I want to emphasize that these descriptive statistics represent a preliminary analysis and are only the first step toward understanding the effect of BRIC loans on democracy. Nevertheless, based on these data, the fear that Chinese loans will undermine democracy in developing countries might be premature.

In sum, this book has shown that developing countries are not passive actors helplessly exposed to the whim of globalization. Instead, I show that their citizens have preferences and that their governments act upon them. To the best of their abilities, they attempt to manage the effects of international financial flows. In the area of sovereign debt, the emergence of the BRICs as new creditors may have given developing countries more room to maneuver. It will be an exciting area for future research to explore how governments will use this newfound policy space.

REFERENCES

Aberbach, Joel D. and Bert A. Rockman. 2002. "Conducting and Coding Elite Interviews." *PS: Political Science and Politics* 35(4): 673–676.

Acemoglu, Daron and James A. Robinson. 2006. *Economic Origins of Dictatorship and Democracy*. Cambridge: Cambridge University Press.

Acosta, Alberto. 2009. *Análisis de Coyuntura: Una lectura de los principales componentes económicos, políticos y sociales durante el año 2009*. Quito: FLACSO.

Adolph, Christopher. 2013a. "Agents, Institutions, and the Political Economy of Performance." In *Bankers, Bureaucrats, and Central Bank Politics: The Myth of Neutrality*. Cambridge: Cambridge University Press, pp. 1–26.

Adolph, Christopher. 2013b. "The Politics of Central Banker Appointment." In *Bankers, Bureaucrats, and Central Bank Politics: The Myth of Neutrality*. Cambridge: Cambridge University Press, pp. 240–279.

Africa News. 2015. "Africa Debt Rising." January 22.

Aguilar, Camila, Mauricio Cardenas, Marcela Melendez, and Natalia Salazar. 2006. "The Development of Latin-American Bond Markets: The Case of Colombia." FEDESARROLLO Working Paper.

Ahlquist, John S., Amanda B. Clayton, and Margaret Levi. 2014. "Provoking Preferences: Unionization, Trade Policy, and the ILWU Puzzle." *International Organization* 68(1): 33–75.

Aitchison, J. 1982. "The Statistical Analysis of Compositional Data." *Journal of the Royal Statistical Society, Series B* 44(2): 139–177.

Akard, Patrick J. 1992. "Corporate Mobilization and Political Power: The Transformation of U.S. Economic Policy in the 1970s." *American Sociological Review* 57(5): 597.

Al Shebil, Saleh, Abdul A. Rasheed, and Hussam Al-Shammari. 2011. "Coping with Boycotts: An Analysis and Framework." *Journal of Management Organization* 17(3): 383–397.

Alden, Chris. 2005. "China in Africa." *Survival* 47(3): 147–164.

Alden, Chris. 2007. *China in Africa: Partner, Competitor or Hegemon?* New York: Zed Books.

Almeida, Paul D. 2007. "Defensive Mobilization: Popular Movements against Economic Adjustment Policies in Latin America." *Latin American Perspectives* 34(3): 123–139.

Alvarez, Ignacio. 2015. "Financialization, Non-financial Corporations and Income Inequality: The Case of France." *Socio-Economic Review* 13(3): 449–475.

Álvarez, Jairo Estrada. 2004. *Construcción del modelo neoliberal en Colombia, 1970–2004*. Bogotá: Ediciones Aurora.

Álvarez, Jairo Estrada. 2005. "Élites intelectuales y producción de política económica en Colombia." In *Intelectuales, tecnócratas y reformas neoliberales en América Latina*, edited by Jairo Estrada Álvarez. Bogotá: Universidad Nacional de Colombia, pp. 259–320.

Alvaro, Mercedes. 2014. "Ecuador's Banks Face Tougher Regulations." *Wall Street Journal*, January 24.

Ambrosio, Thomas. 2009. *Authoritarian Backlash: Russian Resistance to Democratization in the Former Soviet Union*. New York: Routledge.

América Economía. 2012. "Ecuador: La compleja relación entre Correa y la banca." *América Economía*, November 4, 1–6.

Amsden, A. H. 1992. *Asia's Next Giant: South Korea and Late Industrialization*. Oxford: Oxford University Press.

Amuedo-Dorantes, Catalina and Susan Pozo. 2006. "Remittance Receipt and Business Ownership in the Dominican Republic." *World Economy* 29(7): 939–956.

Andrews-Speed, Philip and Roland Dannreuther. 2011. *China, Oil and Global Politics*. New York: Routledge.

Arce, Moises. 2006. "The Societal Consequences of Market Reform in Peru." *Latin American Politics & Society* 48(1): 27–54.

Arce, Moises. 2008. "The Repoliticization of Collective Action after Neoliberalism in Peru." *Latin American Politics & Society* 50(3): 37–62.

Arce, Moises. 2010. *Market Reform in Society: Post-crisis Politics and Economic Change in Authoritarian Peru*. University Park: Penn State University Press.

Atkinson, Joel. 2010. "China-Taiwan Diplomatic Competition and the Pacific Islands." *Pacific Review* 23(4): 407–427.

Auboin, Marc and Martina Engemann. 2014. "Testing the Trade Credit and Trade Link: Evidence from Data on Export Credit Insurance." *Review of World Economics* 150(4): 715–743.

Avcı, Duygu and Consuelo Fernández-Salvador. 2016. "Territorial Dynamics and Local Resistance: Two Mining Conflicts in Ecuador Compared." *Extractive Industries and Society* 3(4): 912–921.

Bader, Julia. 2014. "China, Autocratic Patron? An Empirical Investigation of China as a Factor in Autocratic Survival." *International Studies Quarterly* 59(1): 23–33.

Bader, Julia, Jörn Grävingholt and Antje Kästner. 2010. "Would Autocracies Promote Autocracy? A Political Economy Perspective on Regime-Type Export in Regional Neighbourhoods." *Contemporary Politics* 16(1): 81–100.

Bailey, Michael, Anton Strezhnev, and Erik Voeten. 2017. "Estimating Dynamic State Preferences from United Nations Voting Data." *Journal of Conflict Resolution* 61(2): 430–456.

Balakrishnan, Kogila. 2008. "Defence Industrialisation in Malaysia: Development Challenges and the Revolution in Military Affairs." *Security Challenges* 4(4): 135–155.

Ballard-Rosa, Cameron, Layna Mosley, and Rachel L. Wellhausen. 2016. "The Political Economy of Sovereign Debt Issues." Debt Management Workshop Paper, November 1.

Barr, Robert R. 2003. "The Persistence of Neopopulism in Peru? From Fujimori to Toledo." *Third World Quarterly* 24(6): 1161–1178.

Barro, Robert J. and Jong-Wha Lee. 2005. "IMF Programs: Who Is Chosen and What Are the Effects?" *Journal of Monetary Economics* 52(7): 1245–1269.

Bases, Daniel. 2013. "Exclusive: Ecuador Plans Return to International Bond Market." Reuters.com, May 29.

Bassett, Carolyn. 2008. "South Africa: Revisiting Capital's 'Formative Action.'" *Review of African Political Economy* 35(116): 185–202.

Baumgartner, Frank R., Jeffrey M. Berry, Marie Hojnacki, Beth L. Leech, and David C. Kimball. 2009. *Lobbying and Policy Change: Who Wins, Who Loses, and Why*. Chicago: University of Chicago Press.

Bearce, David H. 2003. "Societal Preferences, Partisan Agents, and Monetary Policy Outcomes." *International Organization* 57(2): 373–410.

Beattie, Alan and Eoin Callan. 2006. "China Loans Create 'New Wave of Africa Debt.'" *Financial Times*, December 7.

Beaulieu, Emily, Gary W. Cox, and Sebastiaán M. Saiegh. 2012. "Sovereign Debt and Regime Type: Reconsidering the Democratic Advantage." *International Organization* 66(4): 709–738.

Beck, Thorsten, Asli Demirgüç-Kunt, and Ross Levine. 2010. "Financial Institutions and Markets across Countries and over Time: The Updated Financial Development and Structure Database." *World Bank Economic Review* 24(1): 77–92.

Becker, Marc. 2013. "The Stormy Relations between Rafael Correa and Social Movements in Ecuador." *Latin American Perspectives* 40(3): 43–62.

Bell, Stephen. 2012. "The Power of Ideas: The Ideational Shaping of the Structural Power of Business." *International Studies Quarterly* 56(4): 661–673.

Benoit, Kenneth and Michael Laver. 2006. *Party Policy in Modern Democracies*. Abingdon, UK: Routledge.

Beri, Ruchita. 2008. "India's Role in Keeping Peace in Africa." *Strategic Analysis* 32(2): 197–221.

Berliner, Daniel, Anne Greenleaf, Milli Lake, and Jennifer Noveck. 2015. "Building Capacity, Building Rights? State Capacity and Labor Rights in Developing Countries." *World Development* 72(C): 127–139.

Bermeo, Sarah Blodgett. 2011. "Foreign Aid and Regime Change: A Role for Donor Intent." *World Development* 39(11): 2021–2031.

Bernanke, Ben. 2015. "Monetary Policy and Inequality." *Brookings Blog*, June 1.

Berry, Jeffrey M. 2002. "Validity and Reliability Issues in Elite Interviewing." *PS: Political Science and Politics* 35(4): 679–682.

Berthélemy, Jean-Claude. 2006. "Bilateral Donors' Interest vs. Recipients' Development Motives in Aid Allocation: Do All Donors Behave the Same?" *Review of Development Economics* 10(2): 179–194.

Biglaiser, Glen, Hoon Lee, and Joseph L. Staats. 2015. "The Effects of the IMF on Expropriation of Foreign Firms." *Review of International Organizations* 11(1): 1–23.

Bloomberg. 2015. "Peru Returns to Global Bond Market for First Time since 2012." *Bloomberg*, October 30.

Boies, John L. 1989. "Money, Business, and the State: Material Interests, Fortune 500 Corporations, and the Size of Political Action Committees." *American Sociological Review* 54(5): 821.

Boix, Charles. 2003. *Democracy and Redistribution*. Cambridge: Cambridge University Press.

Botero, Juan C., Simeon Djankov, Rafael La Porta, Florencino Lopez-de-Silanes, and Andrei Shleifer. 2004. "The Regulation of Labor." *Quarterly Journal of Economics* 119(4): 1339–1382.

Bowen, James. 2014. "The Right and Nonparty Forms of Representation and Participation." In *The Resilience of the Latin American Right*, edited by Juan Pablo Luna and Cristóbal Rovira Kaltwasser. Baltimore: Johns Hopkins University Press, pp. 94–116.

Bowles, Samuel, David M. Gordon, and Thomas E. Weisskopf. 1989. "Business Ascendancy and Economic Impasse: A Structural Retrospective on Conservative Economics, 1979–87." *Journal of Economic Perspectives* 3(1): 107–134.

Box-Steffensmeier, Janet M. and Dino P. Christenson. 2014. "The Evolution and Formation of Amicus Curiae Networks." *Social Networks* 36: 82–96.

Box-Steffensmeier, Janet M. and Dino P. Christenson. 2015. "Comparing Membership Interest Group Networks across Space and Time, Size, Issue and Industry." *Network Science* 3(1): 78–97.

Brautigam, Deborah. 2009. *The Dragon's Gift: The Real Story of China in Africa*. New York: Oxford University Press.

Brautigam, Deborah. 2011. "Aid 'with Chinese Characteristics': Chinese Foreign Aid and Development Finance Meet the OECD-DAC Aid Regime." *Journal of International Development* 23(5): 752–764.

Brautigam, Deborah and Jyhjong Hwang. 2016. "China-Africa Loan Database Research Guidebook." November 1.

Brautigam, Deborah and Tang Xiaoyang. 2011. "African Shenzhen: China's Special Economic Zones in Africa." *Journal of Modern African Studies* 49(1): 27–54.

Brech, Viktor and Niklas Potrafke. 2014. "Donor Ideology and Types of Foreign Aid." *Journal of Comparative Economics* 42(1): 61–75.

Brehm, John, Scott Gates, and Brad Gomez. 1993. "Donut Shops and Speed Traps: Evaluating Models of Supervision on Police Behavior." In *Politics, Policy, and Organizations Frontiers in the Scientific Study of Bureaucracy*, edited by George A. Krause. Ann Arbor: University of Michigan Press, pp. 133–159.

Breunig, Christian and Marius R. Busemeyer. 2012. "Fiscal Austerity and the Trade-Off between Public Investment and Social Spending." *Journal of European Public Policy* 19(6): 921–938.

Brooks, Sarah M., Raphael Cunha, and Layna Mosley. 2014. "Categories, Creditworthiness, and Contagion: How Investors' Shortcuts Affect Sovereign Debt Markets." *International Studies Quarterly* 59(3): 587–601.

Browne, William P. 1990. "Organized Interests and Their Issue Niches: A Search for Pluralism in a Policy Domain." *Journal of Politics* 52(2): 477–509.

Broz, J. Lawrence. 2008. "Congressional Voting on Funding the International Financial Institutions." *Review of International Organizations* 3: 351–374.

Broz, J. Lawrence. 2011. "The United States Congress and IMF Financing, 1944–2009." *Review of International Organizations* 6(3-4): 341–368.

Buchanan, Paul G. 2008. "Preauthoritarian Institutions and Postauthoritarian Outcomes: Labor Politics in Chile and Uruguay." *Latin American Politics & Society* 50(1): 59–89.

Bueno de Mesquita, Bruce and Alastair Smith. 2007. "Foreign Aid and Policy Concessions." *Journal of Conflict Resolution* 51(2): 251–284.

Bueno de Mesquita, Bruce and Alastair Smith. 2010. "Leader Survival, Revolutions, and the Nature of Government Finance." *American Journal of Political Science* 54(4): 936–950.

Bueno de Mesquita, Bruce and Alastair Smith. 2012. "Domestic Explanations of International Relations." *Annual Review of Political Science* 15(1): 161–181.

Bueno de Mesquita, Bruce, Alastair Smith, Randolph M. Siverson, and James D. Morrow. 2005. *The Logic of Political Survival*. Cambridge, MA: MIT Press.

Buis, Maarten L. 2017. "Fitting a Fractional Multinomial Logit Model by Quasi-Maximum Likelihood." *maartenbuis.nlsoftware*, July 17.

Bunte, Jonas B. 2016. "Wage Bargaining, Inequality, and the Dutch Disease." *International Studies Quarterly* 60(4): 677–692.

Bunte, Jonas B. 2018a. "Are Bilateral Loans 'Door-Openers' for Subsequent Foreign Direct Investment?" Paper presented at the Annual Meeting of the European Political Science Association, Vienna, Austria, June 23, 2018.

Bunte, Jonas B. 2018b. "Sovereign Lending after Debt Relief." *Review of International Political Economy* 25(3): 317–339.

Bunte, Jonas B., Harsh Desai, Kanio Gbala, Bradley Parks, and Daniel Runfola. 2018. "Natural Resource Sector FDI, Government Policy, and Economic Growth: Quasi-Experimental Evidence from Liberia." *World Development* 107: 151–162.

Bunte, Jonas B., Geoffrey Gertz, and Alexandra Zeitz. 2018. "Competition and Cooperation in the Export Credit Regime." Paper presented at the annual meeting of the American Political Science Association, Boston, MA, August 31, 2018.

Bunte, Jonas B. and Alisha A. Kim. 2017. "Citizens' Preferences and the Portfolio of Public Goods: Evidence from Nigeria." *World Development* 92: 28–39.

Bunte, Jonas B. and Brandon J. Kinne. 2018. "The Politics of Government-to-Government Loans: Interests, Information, and Network Effects." Paper presented at the Texas Triangle Conference, Dallas, TX, January 28, 2017.

Bunte, Jonas B. and Laura Thaut Vinson. 2016. "Local Power-Sharing Institutions and Interreligious Violence in Nigeria." *Journal of Peace Research* 53(1): 49–65.

Burges, Sean. 2014. "Brazil's International Development Co-operation: Old and New Motivations." *Development Policy Review* 32(3): 355–374.

Burgoon, Brian A. and Michael J. Hiscox. 2004. "The Mysterious Case of Female Protectionism: Gender Bias in Attitudes toward International Trade." Paper presented at the Annual Meeting of the American Political Science Association.

Busch, Mark L. and Eric Reinhardt. 1999. "Industrial Location and Protection: The Political and Economic Geography of US Nontariff Barriers." *American Journal of Political Science* 43(4): 1028–1050.

Busch, Mark L. and Eric Reinhardt. 2000. "Geography, International Trade, and Political Mobilization in US Industries." *American Journal of Political Science* 44(4): 703–719.

Caceres, Sigfrido Burgos and Sophal Ear. 2013. *The Hungry Dragon: How China's Resource Quest Is Reshaping the World*. Abingdon, UK: Routledge.

Cameron, Maxwell A. 2011. "Peru—the Left Turn That Wasn't." In *The Resurgence of the Latin American Left*, edited by Steven Levitsky and Kenneth M. Roberts. Baltimore: Johns Hopkins University Press, pp. 375–398.

Caraway, Teri L., Stephanie J. Rickard, and Mark S. Anner. 2012. "International Negotiations and Domestic Politics: The Case of IMF Labor Market Conditionality." *International Organization* 66(1): 27–61.

Cardenal, Juan Pablo and Heriberto Araujo. 2013. "The Foundations of the Chinese World." In *China's Silent Army*, translated by Catherine Mansfield. New York: Crown Publishers, pp. 136–163.

Carmody, Padraig. 2013. *The New Scramble for Africa*. Cambridge: Polity Press.

Castaneda, Sebastian. 2011. "Colombia's Santos Moves to Diversify Foreign Policy." *World Politics Review*, April 1.

Chang, Ha-Joon. 1993. "The Political Economy of Industrial Policy in Korea." *Cambridge Journal of Economics* 17(2): 131.

Chang, Ha-Joon. 2002. *Kicking Away the Ladder: Development Strategy in Historical Perspective*. London: Anthem.

Chase, Jacquelyn. 2002. *The Spaces of Neoliberalism: Land, Place and Family in Latin America*. Bloomfield, CT: Kumarian Press.

Chimangeni, Isabel. 2007. "Is China Sneaking In Deals through the Back Door?" IPE Inter Press Service, March 27.

Chin, Gregory T. 2014. "The BRICS-Led Development Bank: Purpose and Politics beyond the G20." *Global Policy* 5(3): 366–373.

Cho, Hye Jee. 2013. "Impact of IMF Programs on Perceived Creditworthiness of Emerging Market Countries: Is There a "Nixon-Goes-to-China" Effect?" *International Studies Quarterly* 58(2): 308–321.

Choudhury, Nusrat. 2005. "The Economic Impact of Anti-Americanism." June 2.

Chwieroth, Jeffrey M. 2010. "How Do Crises Lead to Change? Liberalizing Capital Controls in the Early Years of New Order Indonesia." *World Politics* 62(3): 496–527.

Chwieroth, Jeffrey M. 2015. "Professional Ties That Bind: How Normative Orientations Shape IMF Conditionality." *Review of International Political Economy* 22(4): 757–787.

Claeys, Gregory, Zsolt M. Darvas, Alvaro Leandro, and Thomas Walsh. 2015. "The Effects of Ultra-loose Monetary Policies on Inequality." *Bruegel Policy Contribution* 15(9): 1–23.

Clegg, Liam. 2014. "Social Spending Targets in IMF Concessional Lending: US Domestic Politics and the Institutional Foundations of Rapid Operational Change." *Review of International Political Economy* 21(3): 735–763.

CNBC. 2017. "China bails out Pakistan with over $1bn loans." *CNBC*, April 25.

Collier, Paul and David Dollar. 2002. *Globalization, Growth, and Poverty: Building an Inclusive World Economy*. New York: Oxford University Press.

Collins, Paul M., Jr. 2004. "Friends of the Court: Examining the Influence of Amicus Curiae Participation in U.S. Supreme Court Litigation." *Law & Society Review* 38(4): 807–832.

Collins, Paul M., Jr. 2008. *Friends of the Supreme Court: Interest Groups and Judicial Decision Making*. New York: Oxford University Press.

Conaghan, Catherine M. 2008. "Ecuador: Correa's Plebiscitary Presidency." *Journal of Democracy* 19(2): 46–60.

Conaghan, Catherine M. 2013. "Ecuador: Rafael Correa and the Citizens' Revolution." In *The Resurgence of the Latin American Left*, edited by Steven Levitsky and Kenneth M. Roberts. Baltimore: Johns Hopkins University Press, pp. 260–282.

Conaghan, Catherine M. 2017. "Contra-associational Strategy in a Hybrid Regime: Ecuador, 2007–2015." *Bulletin of Latin American Research* 36(4): 509–525.

Conway, Patrick. 1994. "IMF Lending Programs: Participation and Impact." *Journal of Development Economics* 45(2): 365–391.

Cooper, Andrew F. 2017. "The BRICS' New Development Bank: Shifting from Material Leverage to Innovative Capacity." *Global Policy* 8(3): 275–284.

Copelovitch, Mark S. 2010. *The International Monetary Fund in the Global Economy: Banks, Bonds, and Bailouts*. Cambridge: Cambridge University Press.

Coyne, Christopher J. and Matt E. Ryan. 2009. "With Friends Like These, Who Needs Enemies? Aiding the World's Worst Dictators." *Independent Review* 14(1): 26–44.

CP24. 2013. "Harper Test-Drives New Approach to Aid in Peru." *CP24*, May 22.

Crotty, James. 2016. "The Neoliberal Paradox: The Impact of Destructive Product Market Competition and Impatient Finance on Nonfinancial Corporations in the Neoliberal Era." *Review of Radical Political Economics* 35(3): 271–279.

Cruz, Cesi, Philip Keefer, and Carlos G. Scartascini. 2016. *DPI2015—Database of Political Institutions: Codebook*. Washington, DC: Inter-American Development Bank.

Crystal, Jonathan. 2003. "What Do Producers Want? On the Origins of Societal Policy Preferences." *European Journal of International Relations* 9(3): 407–439.

Culpepper, Pepper D. and Raphael Reinke. 2014. "Structural Power and Bank Bailouts in the United Kingdom and the United States." *Politics & Society* 42(4): 427–454.

Curtis, Amber, Joseph Jupille, and David Leblang. 2015. "Iceland on the Rocks: Self-Interest and the Politics of Sovereign Debt Resettlement." *International Organization* 68(3): 721–740.

Dallanegra Pedraza, Luis. 2012. "Claves de la política exterior de Colombia." *Latinoamérica: Revista de Estudios Latinoamericanos* 54: 37–73.

Dargent, Eduardo. 2011. "Agents or Actors? Assessing the Autonomy of Economic Technocrats in Colombia and Peru." *Comparative Politics* 43(3): 313–332.

David, Galeano and Héctor José. 2012. "Colombia's Foreign Policy: A Stalled Institution in the History." *Revista de Economía del Caribe* 9: 201–235.

Dela Peña, Zinnia B. 2013. "Philippines to Rely More on Foreign Borrowings." *Philippine Star*, December 27.

Delaney, Kevin J. 2007. "Methodological Dilemmas and Opportunities in Interviewing Organizational Elites." *Sociology Compass* 1(1): 208–221.

Desbordes, Rodolphe and Julien Vauday. 2007. "The Political Influence of Foreign Firms in Developing Countries." *Economics & Politics* 19(3): 421–451.

Devarajan, Shantayanan, Andrew Sunil Rajkumar, and Vinaya Swaroop. 2007. "What Does Aid to Africa Finance?" In *Theory and Practice of Foreign Aid*, edited by Sajal Lahiri. New York: Elsevier, pp. 333–355.

Dietrich, Simone. 2013. "Bypass or Engage? Explaining Donor Delivery Tactics in Foreign Aid Allocation." *International Studies Quarterly* 57(4): 698–712.

DiGiuseppe, Matthew and Patrick E. Shea. 2015. "Sovereign Credit and the Fate of Leaders: Reassessing the 'Democratic Advantage.'" *International Studies Quarterly* 59(3): 557–570.

DiGiuseppe, Matthew and Patrick E. Shea. 2016. "Borrowed Time: Sovereign Finance, Regime Type, and Leader Survival." *Economics & Politics* 28(3): 342–367.

Diplomatic Courier. 2011. "China's Waning Influence in Angola." *Diplomatic Courier*, August 26.

Dix, Robert H. 1980. "Consociational Democracy: The Case of Colombia." *Comparative Politics* 12(3): 303–321.

Dixit, Avinash and John Londregan. 2000. "Political Power and the Credibility of Government Debt." *Journal of Economic Theory* 94(1): 80–105.

Dixon, Chris. 2015. "The New BRICS Bank: Challenging the International Financial Order?" Global Policy Institute Policy Paper No. 28.

Dollar, David R. and Victoria Levin. 2006. "The Increasing Selectivity of Foreign Aid, 1984–2003." *World Development* 34(12): 2034–2046.

Dollar, David R. and Lant Pritchett. 1998. *Assessing Aid: What Works, What Doesn't, and Why.* New York: Oxford University Press.

Drazen, Allan. 2005. "Conditionality and Ownership in IMF Lending: A Political Economy Approach." In *Globalization and the Nation State*, edited by Gustav Ranis, James Raymond Vreeland, and Stephen Kosack. Abingdon, UK: Taylor & Francis, pp. 36–67.

Dreher, Axel. 2006. "IMF and Economic Growth: The Effects of Programs, Loans, and Compliance with Conditionality." *World Development* 34(5): 769–788.

Dreher, Axel. 2009. "IMF Conditionality: Theory and Evidence." *Public Choice* 141(2): 233–267.

Dreher, Axel and Andreas Fuchs. 2016. "Rogue Aid? An Empirical Analysis of China's Aid Allocation." *Canadian Journal of Economics / Revue canadienne d'économique* 48(3): 988–1023.

Duenhaupt, Petra. 2012. "Financialization and the Rentier Income Share—Evidence from the USA and Germany." *International Review of Applied Economics* 26(4): 465–487.

Dugas, John C. 2010. "The Emergence of Neopopulism in Colombia? The Case of Alvaro Uribe." *Third World Quarterly* 24(6): 1117–1136.

Duke, Steven. 2011. "China's Global Reach: Lending More Than the World Bank." *BBC News*, December 9.

Duménil, Gérard and Dominique Lévy. 2002. "Neoliberalism: The Crime and the Beneficiary." *Review* 25(4): 393–400.

Dünhaupt, Petra. 2016. "Determinants of Labour's Income Share in the Era of Financialisation." *Cambridge Journal of Economics* 41(1): 283–306.

Dyer, Geoff, Jamil Anderlini, and Henny Sender. 2011. "China's Lending Hits New Heights." *Financial Times*, January 17.

Economy, Elizabeth and Michael Levi. 2014. *By All Means Necessary: How China's Resource Quest Is Changing the World.* New York: Oxford University Press.

Ecuavisa. 2008. "282 productos de importación fueron gravados con arancel cero por la COMEXI en su sesión de este jueves." *Ecuavisa.com*, July 17.

Edwards, Sebastian. 1984. "Coffee, Money and Inflation in Colombia." *World Development* 12(11–12): 1107–1117.

Eichengreen, Barry, Ricardo Hausmann, and Ugo Panizza. 2004. "The Pain of Original Sin." In *Other People's Money: Debt Denomination and Financial Instability in Emerging Market Economics*, edited by Ricardo Hausmann and Barry Eichengreen. Chicago: University of Chicago Press, pp. 1–49.

El Comercio. 2016. "PPK en China: 'No estamos buscando créditos o ayuda financiera.'" *El Comercio*, September 13.

Ellis, Robert Evan. 2012. "Las relaciones China-Colombia en el contexto de la relación estratégica entre Colombia y los Estados Unidos." In *China en América Latina*, edited by Benjamin Creutzfeldt. Bogotá: Universidad Externado de Colombia, pp. 295–325.

Elton, Edwin J., Martin J. Gruber, Deepak Agrawal and Christopher Mann. 2001. "Explaining the Rate Spread on Corporate Bonds." *Journal of Finance* 56(1): 247–277.

Epstein, Gerald and Arjun Jayadev. 2005. "The Rise of Rentier Incomes in OECD Countries: Financialization, Central Bank Policy and Labor Solidarity." In *Financialization and the World Economy*, edited by Gerald A. Epstein. Northhampton, MA: Edward Elgar, pp. 46–74.

Epstein, Gil S. and Ira N. Gang. 2009. "Good Governance and Good Aid Allocation." *Journal of Development Economics* 89(1): 12–18.

Farnsworth, Kevin. 2004. *Corporate Power and Social Policy in a Global Economy: British Welfare under the Influence.* Cambridge: Policy Press.

Felbermayr, Gabriel J. and Erdal Yalcin. 2013. "Export Credit Guarantees and Export Performance: An Empirical Analysis for Germany." *World Economy* 36(8): 967–999.

Ferraz, Claudio and Frederico Finan. 2011. "Electoral Accountability and Corruption: Evidence from the Audits of Local Governments." *American Economic Review* 101(4): 1274–1311.

Feyzioglu, Tarhan, Vinaya Swaroop, and Min Zhu. 1998. "A Panel Data Analysis of the Fungibility of Foreign Aid." *World Bank Economic Review* 12(1): 29–58.

Financial Times. 2017. "China bails out Pakistan with $1.2bn loans." *Financial Times*, April 25.

Findley, Michael G., Adam S. Harris, Helen V. Milner, and Daniel L. Nielson. 2017. "Who Controls Foreign Aid? Elite versus Public Perceptions of Donor Influence in Aid-Dependent Uganda." *International Organization* 71(4): 633–663.

Findley, Michael G., Helen V. Milner, and Daniel L. Nielson. 2017. "The Choice among Aid Donors: The Effects of Multilateral vs. Bilateral Aid on Recipient Behavioral Support." *Review of International Organizations* 12(2): 307–334.

Flaherty, Eoin. 2015. "Top Incomes under Finance-Driven Capitalism, 1990–2010: Power Resources and Regulatory Orders." *Socio-Economic Review* 13(3): 417–447.

Fordham, Benjamin O. 1998. *Building the Cold War Consensus: The Political Economy of US National Security Policy, 1949–51*. Ann Arbor: University of Michigan Press.

Fordham, Benjamin O. and Katja B. Kleinberg. 2012. "How Can Economic Interests Influence Support for Free Trade?" *International Organization* 66(2): 311–328.

Frieden, Jeffry. 1989. "Winners and Losers in the Latin American Debt Crisis: The Political Implications." In *Debt and Democracy in Latin America*, edited by Barbara Stallings and Robert R. Kaufman. Boulder, CO: Westview, pp. 23–38.

Frieden, Jeffry. 1991. *Debt, Development, and Democracy: Modern Political Economy and Latin America, 1965-1985*. Princeton, NJ: Princeton University Press.

Froud, Julie, Sukhdev Johal, Adam Leaver, Karel Williams, et al. 2006. *Financialization and Strategy: Narrative and Numbers*. Abingdon, UK: Routledge.

Fuchs, Andreas and Krishna Chaitanya Vadlamannati. 2013. "The Needy Donor: An Empirical Analysis of India's Aid Motives." *World Development* 44(C): 110–128.

Gallagher, Kevin P. and Roberto Porzecanski. 2010. *The Dragon in the Room: China and the Future of Latin American Industrialization*. Stanford, CA: Stanford University Press.

Gamso, Jonas. 2015. "A Case of Diversified Dependency." *Latin American Perspectives* 43(1): 109–123.

Gandhi, Jennifer and Adam Przeworski. 2006. "Cooperation, Cooptation, and Rebellion under Dictatorships." *Economics & Politics* 18(1): 1–26.

Garcia, Pio. 2011. "Colombia transpacífica: Opciones de política y liderazgo regional." In *Colombia: Una política exterior en transición*, edited by Diego Cardona. Bogotá: Fundación Friderich Ebert en Colombia, pp. 179–199.

Garuda, Gopal. 2000. "The Distributional Effects of IMF Programs: A Cross-Country Analysis." *World Development* 28(6): 1031–1051.

Gerlach, Allen. 2003. *Indians, Oil, and Politics: A Recent History of Ecuador*. Lanham, MD: Rowman & Littlefield.

Global Infrastructure Hub. 2017. "Global Infrastructure Outlook." *Oxford Economics*, July 1.

Goldsmith, Benjamin E., Yusaku Horiuchi, and Terence Wood. 2014. "Doing Well by Doing Good: The Impact of Foreign Aid on Foreign Public Opinion." *Quarterly Journal of Political Science* 9(1): 87–114.

Goldstein, Judith. 1988. "Ideas, Institutions, and American Trade Policy." *International Organization* 42(1): 179–217.

Goldstein, Judith and Robert O. Keohane. 1993. "Ideas and Foreign Policy: An Analytical Introduction." In *Ideas and Foreign Policy: Beliefs, Institutions, and Rational Choice*, edited by Judith Goldstein and Robert O. Keohane. Ithaca, NY: Cornell University Press, pp. 3–30.

Goldstein, Judith, Yotam Margalit, and D. Rivers. 2008. "Producer, Consumer, Family Member: The Relationship between Trade Attitudes and Family Status." Paper prepared for the Conference on Domestic Preferences and Foreign Economic Policy, Princeton University.

Gonzaález, Francisco. 2008. "Latin America in the Economic Equation—Winners and Losers: What Can Losers Do? In *China's Expansion into the Western Hemisphere: Implications for Latin America and the United States*, edited by Riordan Roett and Guadalupe Paz. Washington, DC: Brookings Institute Press, pp. 148–169.

Gonzalez-Vicente, Ruben. 2012. "The Political Economy of Sino-Peruvian Relations: A New Dependency?" *Journal of Current Chinese Affairs* 41(1): 97–131.

Gooch, Liz. 2012. "Malaysia Enacts Minimum Wage." *New York Times*, May 1.

Gould, Erica R. 2003. "Money Talks: Supplementary Financiers and International Monetary Fund Conditionality." *International Organization* 57(3): 551–586.

Gourevitch, Peter A. and James Shinn. 2005. *Political Power and Corporate Control: The New Global Politics of Corporate Governance*. Princeton, NJ: Princeton University Press.

Grassi, Davide. 2014. "Democracy and Social Welfare in Uruguay and Paraguay." *Latin American Politics & Society* 56(1): 120–143.

Gray, Julia and Jeffrey Kucik. 2017. "Leadership Turnover and the Durability of International Trade Commitments." *Comparative Political Studies* 50(14): 1941–1972.

Greider, William. 1998. *One World, Ready or Not: The Manic Logic of Global Capitalism*. New York: Simon and Schuster.

Griffith-Jones, Stephany. 2014. "A BRICS Development Bank: A Dream Coming True?" UNCTAD Discussion Paper No. 215.

Grossman, Emiliano and Cornelia Woll. 2014. "Saving the Banks: The Political Economy of Bailouts." *Comparative Political Studies* 47(4): 574–600.

Grossman, Gene M. and Elhanan Helpman. 1994. "Protection for Sale." *American Economic Review* 84(4): 833–850.

Guisinger, Alexandra. 2016. "Information, Gender, and Differences in Individual Preferences for Trade." *Journal of Women, Politics & Policy* 37(4): 538–561.

Guzmán, Sandra Borda and María Paz Berger. 2012. "Relaciones bilaterales China y Colombia: 1990–2010." *Colombia Internacional* 75: 83–129.

Hafner-Burton, Emilie M., Stephen Haggard, David A. Lake, and David G. Victor. 2017. "The Behavioral Revolution and International Relations." *International Organization* 71(S1): 1–31.

Haggard, Stephen and Robert R. Kaufman. 1992. *The Politics of Economic Adjustment: International Constraints, Distributive Conflicts, and the State*. Princeton, NJ: Princeton University Press.

Hall, Peter A. 1986. *Governing the Economy: The Politics of State Intervention in Britain and France*. New York: Oxford University Press.

Hall, Peter A. and David Soskice. 2001. "An Introduction to Varieties of Capitalism." In *Varieties of Capitalism*, edited by Peter A. Hall and David Soskice. New York: Oxford University Press.

Hall, Simon. 2010. "China's Exim Bank to Finance Ecuador Project." *Wall Street Journal*, June 3.

Harding, Robin and David Stasavage. 2013. "What Democracy Does (and Doesn't Do) for Basic Services: School Fees, School Inputs, and African Elections." *Journal of Politics* 76(1): 229–245.

Heaney, Michael T. 2006. "Brokering Health Policy: Coalitions, Parties, and Interest Group Influence." *Journal of Health Politics, Policy and Law* 31(5): 887–944.

Heaney, Michael T. and Geoffrey M. Lorenz. 2013. "Coalition Portfolios and Interest Group Influence over the Policy Process." *Interest Groups & Advocacy* 2(3): 251–277.

Hernandez, Diego. 2017. "Are 'New' Donors Challenging World Bank Conditionality?" *World Development* 96: 529–549.

Hey, Jeanne A. K. and Thomas Klak. 1999. "From Protectionism towards Neoliberalism: Ecuador across Four Administrations (1981–1996)." *Studies in Comparative International Development* 34(3): 66–97.

Hill, Hal and Jayant Menon. 2013. "Cambodia: Rapid Growth with Weak Institutions." *Asian Economic Policy Review* 8(1): 46–65.

Hiscox, Michael J. 2002. *International Trade and Political Conflict: Commerce, Coalitions, and Mobility*. Princeton, NJ: Princeton University Press.

Hiscox, Michael J. 2006. "Through a Glass and Darkly: Attitudes toward International Trade and the Curious Effects of Issue Framing." *International Organization* 60(3): 755–780.

Hodson, Dermot. 2017. "The IMF as a De Facto Institution of the EU: A Multiple Supervisor Approach." *Review of International Political Economy* 22(3): 570–598.

Hojnacki, Marie. 1997. "Interest Groups' Decisions to Join Alliances or Work Alone." *American Journal of Political Science* 41(1): 61–87.

Hojnacki, Marie. 1998. "Organized Interests' Advocacy Behavior in Alliances." *Political Research Quarterly* 51(2): 437–459.

Hojnacki, Marie, David C. Kimball, Frank R. Baumgartner, Jeffrey M. Berry and Beth L. Leech. 2012. "Studying Organizational Advocacy and Influence: Reexamining Interest Group Research." *Annual Review of Political Science* 15(1): 379–399.

Holyoke, Thomas T. 2009. "Interest Group Competition and Coalition Formation." *American Journal of Political Science* 53(2): 360–375.

Holyoke, Thomas T. 2011. *Competitive interests: Competition and Compromise in American Interest Group Politics*. Washington, DC: Georgetown University Press.

Horton, Chris and Steven Lee Myers. 2017. "Panama Establishes Ties with China, Further Isolating Taiwan." *New York Times*, June 13.

Huit, Ralph K. and Robert L. Peabody. 1969. *Congress: Two Decades of Analysis*. New York: Harper and Row.

Hula, Kevin W. 1999. *Lobbying Together: Interest Group Coalitions in Legislative Politics*. Washington, DC: Georgetown University Press.

IMF (International Monetary Fund). 2017. *IMF Monitoring of Fund Arrangements (MONA)*. Washington, DC: International Monetary Fund.

IRIN (Integrated Regional Information Networks). 2005. "Angola: Oil-Backed Loan Will Finance Recovery Projects." UN Integrated Regional Information Networks, February 21.

Irwin, Amos and Kevin P. Gallagher. 2013. "Chinese Mining in Latin America." *Journal of Environment & Development* 22(2): 207–234.

Iversen, Torben and David Soskice. 2001. "An Asset Theory of Social Policy Preferences." *American Political Science Review* 95(4): 875–893.

Jacobs, Alan M. 2008. "How Do Ideas Matter? Mental Models and Attention in German Pension Politics." 42(2): 252–279.

Jacobs, David. 1988. "Corporate Economic Power and the State: A Longitudinal Assessment of Two Explanations." *American Journal of Sociology* 93(4): 852–881.

Jameson, Kenneth P. 2008. "The Indigenous Movement and the Economic Trajectory of Ecuador." University of Utah Department of Economics Working Paper No. 08(5).

Jameson, Kenneth P. 2010. "The Indigenous Movement in Ecuador." *Latin American Perspectives* 38(1): 63–73.

Jayadev, Arjun and Gerald Epstein. 2007. "The Correlates of Rentier Returns in OECD Countries." PERI Working Paper No. 123.

Jensen, Nathan M. and René Lindstädt. 2013. "Globalization with Whom: Context-Dependent Foreign Direct Investment Preferences." Working paper.

Johnson, Christian A. 2013. "Potential Output and Output Gap in Central America, Panama and Dominican Republic." International Monetary Fund Working Paper No. 13(145).

Johnson, Omotunde and Joanne Salop. 1980. "Distributional Aspects of Stabilization Programs in Developing Countries." *Staff Papers—International Monetary Fund* 27(1): 1–23.

Johnson, Simon and Todd Mitton. 2003. "Cronyism and Capital Controls: Evidence from Malaysia." *Journal of Financial Economics* 67(2): 351–382.

Johnson, Susan and Max Nino-Zarazua. 2011. "Financial Access and Exclusion in Kenya and Uganda." *Journal of Development Studies* 47(3): 475–496.

Jones, Kelly. 2005. "Moving Money: Aid Fungibility in Africa." *SAIS Review* 25(2): 167–180.

Kahler, Miles and Scott L. Kastner. 2006. "Strategic Uses of Economic Interdependence: Engagement Policies on the Korean Peninsula and across the Taiwan Strait." *Journal of Peace Research* 43(5): 523–541.

Kalaitzake, Manolis. 2017. "The Political Power of Finance: The Institute of International Finance in the Greek Debt Crisis." *Politics & Society* 45(3): 389–413.

Kaplan, Stephen B. 2013. *Globalization and Austerity Politics in Latin America.* New York: Cambridge University Press.

Kattel, Rainer and Veiko Lember. 2010. "Public Procurement as an Industrial Policy Tool: An Option for Developing Countries?" *Journal of Public Procurement* 10(3): 368–404.

Katz, Jonathan N. and Gary King. 1999. "Statistical Model for Multiparty Electoral Data." *American Political Science Review* 93(1): 15–33.

Kaufman, Robert R. 1988. *The Politics of Debt in Argentina, Brazil, and Mexico: Economic Stabilization in the 1980s.* Berkeley: Institute of International Studies, University of California, Berkeley.

Kay, Cristóbal. 2002. "Why East Asia Overtook Latin America: Agrarian Reform, Industrialisation and Development." *Third World Quarterly* 23(6): 1073–1102.

Kelegama, Saman. 2009. "Ready-Made Garment Exports from Sri Lanka." *Journal of Contemporary Asia* 39(4): 579–596.

Kentikelenis, Alexander E., Thomas H. Stubbs, and Lawrence P. King. 2016. "IMF Conditionality and Development Policy Space, 1985–2014." *Review of International Political Economy* 23(4): 543–582.

Khanna, Parag. 2014. "New BRICS Bank a Building Block of Alternative World Order." *New Perspectives Quarterly* 31(4): 46–48.

Kim, Alisha A. and Jonas B. Bunte. 2018. "Demand for Different Types of Public Goods: Evidence from Nigeria." *Review of Social Economy* 76(2): 151–162.

Kim, Yong Kyun. 2013. "Inequality and Sovereign Default under Democracy." *European Journal of Economic and Political Studies* 6(1): 5–40.

Kinne, Brandon J. and Jonas B. Bunte. 2018. "Guns or Money? Defense Cooperation and Bilateral Lending as Coevolving Networks." *British Journal of Political Science*, forthcoming.

Kitano, Naohiro. 2014. "China's Foreign Aid at a Transitional Stage." *Asian Economic Policy Review* 9(2): 301–317.

Kleine-Ahlbrandt, Stephanie and Andrew Small. 2014. "China's New Dictatorship Diplomacy: Is Beijing Parting with Pariahs?" *Foreign Affairs* 87(1): 38–56.

Klimovich, Kristina and Clive S. Thomas. 2014. "Power Groups, Interests and Interest Groups in Consolidated and Transitional Democracies: Comparing Uruguay and Costa Rica with Paraguay and Haiti." *Journal of Public Affairs* 14(183-211): 183–211.

Knierzinger, Johannes. 2014. "The Socio-Political Implications of Bauxite Mining in Guinea: A Commodity Chain Perspective." *Extractive Industries and Society* 1(1): 20–27.

Koeda, Junko. 2008. "A Debt Overhang Model for Low-Income Countries." *IMF Staff Papers* 55(4): 654–678.

Kohlscheen, Emanuel. 2010. "Sovereign Risk: Constitutions Rule." *Oxford Economic Papers* 62(1): 62–85.

Korpi, Walter and Gøsta Esping-Andersen. 1984. "Social Policy as Class Politics in Post-war Capitalism: Scandinavia, Austria and Germany." In *Order and Conflict in Contemporary Capitalism*, edited by John H. Goldthorpe. New York: Oxford University Press, pp. 179–208.

Krippner, Greta R. 2005. "The Financialization of the American Economy." *Socio-Economic Review* 3(2): 173–208.

Kroszner, Randall S. and Philip E. Strahan. 1999. "What Drives Deregulation? Economics and Politics of the Relaxation of Bank Branching Restrictions." *Quarterly Journal of Economics* 114(4): 1437–1467.

Krugman, Paul. 1988. "Financing vs. Forgiving a Debt Overhang." *Journal of Development Economics* 29: 253–268.

Kuecker, Glen David. 2016. "Fighting for the Forests." *Latin American Perspectives* 34(2): 94–107.

La Hora. 2009. "Presidente de Ecuador dice que negociar con China es peor que con el FMI." *La Hora*, December 5.

Laffey, Mark and Jutta Weldes. 1997. "Beyond Belief: Ideas and Symbolic Technologies in the Study of International Relations." *European Journal of International Relations* 3(2): 193.

Lake, David A. 2009. "Open Economy Politics: A Critical Review." *Review of International Organizations* 4(3): 219–244.

Larrea, Carlos and Liisa L. North. 1997. "Ecuador: Adjustment Policy Impacts on Truncated Development and Democratisation." *Third World Quarterly* 18(5): 913–934.

Latin American Herald Tribune. 2009. "Ecuador Feels 'Ill-Treated' in Loan Talks with China." *Latin American Herald Tribune*, December 2.

Leeds, Brett Ashley, Michaela Mattes, and Jeremy S. Vogel. 2009. "Interests, Institutions, and the Reliability of International Commitments." *American Journal of Political Science* 53(2): 461–476.

Leith-Ross, Frederick. 1968. *Money Talks—Fifty Years of International Finance: The Autobiography of Sir Frederick Leith-Ross*. London: Hutchinson.

Leongomez, Eduardo Pizarro. 2002. *La atomización partidista en Colombia: El fenómeno de las micro-empresas electorales*. Bogotá: Grupo Editorial Norma.

Levitsky, Steven and Maxwell A. Cameron. 2008. "Democracy without Parties? Political Parties and Regime Change in Fujimori's Peru." *Latin American Politics & Society* 45(3): 1–33.

Li, Xiaojun and Ka Zeng. 2017. "Individual Preferences for FDI in Developing Countries: Experimental Evidence from China." *Journal of Experimental Political Science* 109(3): 1–11.

Lin, Ken-Hou and Donald Tomaskovic-Devey. 2013. "Financialization and U.S. Income Inequality, 1970–2008." *American Journal of Sociology* 118(5): 1284–1329.

Lowery, David. 2007. "Why Do Organized Interests Lobby? A Multi-goal, Multi-context Theory of Lobbying." *Polity* 39(1): 29–54.

Lu, Xiaobo, Kenneth F. Scheve, and Matthew Jon Slaughter. 2012. "Inequity Aversion and the International Distribution of Trade Protection." *American Journal of Political Science* 56(3): 638–654.

Lucero, Jose Antonio. 2001. "Crisis and Contention in Ecuador." *Journal of Democracy* 12(2): 59–73.

Lupia, Arthur. 1994. "Shortcuts versus Encyclopedias: Information and Voting Behavior in California Insurance Reform Elections." *American Political Science Review* 88(1): 63–76.

Magnoni, Silvia. 2010. "Brazil and Its African 'Neighbours': The Old Aid System for New Global Ambitions." Development Working Paper Series No. 10(2): 1–17.

Magruder, Jeremy R. 2012. "High Unemployment yet Few Small Firms: The Role of Centralized Bargaining in South Africa." *American Economic Journal: Applied Economics* 4(3): 138–166.

Mahoney, Christine. 2008. *Brussels versus the beltway: Advocacy in the United States and the European Union*. Washington, DC: Georgetown University Press.

Mahoney, Christine and Frank R. Baumgartner. 2015. "Partners in Advocacy: Lobbyists and Government Officials in Washington." *Journal of Politics* 77(1): 202–215.

Maizels, Alfred and Machiko K. Nissanke. 1984. "Motivations for Aid to Developing Countries." *World Development* 12(9): 879–900.

Malaysian Insider. 2013. "Philippines Says May Not Tap Global Debt Market in 2014." *Malaysian Insider*, December 19.

Maliehe, Sean. 2017. "The Rise and Fall of African Indigenous Entrepreneurs' Economic Solidarity in Lesotho, 1966–1975." *African Economic History* 45(1): 110–137.

Mansell, Wade and Karen Openshaw. 2009. "Suturing the Open Veins of Ecuador: Debt, Default and Democracy." *Law and Development Review* 2(1): 148–191.

Mansfield, Edward D. and Diana C. Mutz. 2009. "Support for Free Trade: Self-Interest, Sociotropic Politics, and Out-Group Anxiety." *International Organization* 63(3): 425–457.

Marchesi, Silvia and Jonathan P. Thomas. 1999. "IMF Conditionality as a Screening Device." *Economic Journal* 109(454): 111–125.

Mares, Isabela. 2003. *The Politics of Social Risk: Business and Welfare State Development*. New York: Cambridge University Press.

Martens, Bertin, Uwe Mummert, Peter Murrell, Paul Seabright, and Elinor Ostrom. 2002. *The Institutional Economics of Foreign Aid*. New York: Cambridge University Press.

Masters, Marick F. and Gerald D. Keim. 1985. "Determinants of PAC Participation among Large Corporations." *Journal of Politics* 47(4): 1158–1173.

Mattes, Michaela, Brett Ashley Leeds, and Royce Carroll. 2014. "Leadership Turnover and Foreign Policy Change: Societal Interests, Domestic Institutions, and Voting in the United Nations." *International Studies Quarterly* 59(2): 280–290.

Mattes, Michaela, Brett Ashley Leeds, and Naoko Matsumura. 2016. "Measuring Change in Source of Leader Support." *Journal of Peace Research* 53(2): 259–267.

Mattlin, Mikael and Matti Nojonen. 2014. "Conditionality and Path Dependence in Chinese Lending." *Journal of Contemporary China* 24(94): 701–720.

Mawdsley, Emma. 2010. "Non-DAC Donors and the Changing Landscape of Foreign Aid: The (In)significance of India's Development Cooperation with Kenya." *Journal of Eastern African Studies* 4(2): 361–379.

Maxfield, Sylvia. 1990. *Governing Capital: International Finance and Mexican Politics*. Ithaca, NY: Cornell University Press.

Mayer, David. 2001. "The Long-Term Impact of Health on Economic Growth in Latin America." *World Development* 29(6): 1025–1033.

McCarthy, Julie. 2006. "Ecuador Campaign Spiced by Anti-U.S. Rhetoric." National Public Radio, October 15.

McFarland, Andrew S. 1993. *Cooperative Pluralism: The National Coal Policy Experiment*. Lawrence: University Press of Kansas.

McGuire, James W. 1999. "Labor Union Strength and Human Development in East Asia and Latin America." *Studies in Comparative International Development* 33(4): 3–34.

McNamara, Kathleen R. 1999. "Consensus and Constraint: Ideas and Capital Mobility in European Monetary Integration." *Journal of Common Market Studies* 37(3): 455–476.

Meléndez, Carlos. 2007. "Análisis comparado de las agrupaciones políticas de los países andinos." In *La política por dentro: Cambios y continuidades en las organizaciones políticas de los países andinos*, edited by Rafael Roncagliolo and Carlos Meléndez. Lima: Asociación Civil de Transparencia, pp. 41–74.

Milner, Helen V. 2006. "Why Multilateralism? Foreign Aid and Domestic Principal-Agent Problems." In *Delegation and Agency in International Organizations*, edited by Darren G. Hawkins, David A. Lake, Daniel L. Nielson, and Michael J. Tierney. New York: Cambridge University Press, pp. 107–139.

Milner, Helen V., Daniel L. Nielson, and Michael G. Findley. 2016. "Citizen Preferences and Public Goods: Comparing Preferences for Foreign Aid and Government Programs in Uganda." *Review of International Organizations* 11(2): 219–245.

Milner, Helen V. and Dustin H. Tingley. 2010. "The Political Economy of U.S. Foreign Aid: American Legislators and the Domestic Politics of Aid." *Economics & Politics* 22(2): 200–232.

Milner, Helen V. and Dustin H. Tingley. 2011. "Who Supports Global Economic Engagement? The Sources of Preferences in American Foreign Economic Policy." *International Organization* 65(1): 37–68.

Milner, Helen V. and Dustin H. Tingley. 2013. "Public Opinion and Foreign Aid: A Review Essay." *International Interactions* 39(3): 389–401.

Mlambo, Kupukile and Mthuli Ncube. 2011. "Competition and Efficiency in the Banking Sector in South Africa." *African Development Review* 23(1): 4–15.

Moe, Terry M. 2005. "Power and Political Institutions." *Perspectives on Politics* 3(2): 215–233.

Mohan, Giles. 2013. "Beyond the Enclave: Towards a Critical Political Economy of China and Africa." *Development and Change* 44(6): 1255–1272.

Montecino, Juan Antonio and Gerald Epstein. 2015. "Did Quantitative Easing Increase Income Inequality?" New Economic Thinking Working Paper No. 28.

Moore, Mick and Ladi Hamalai. 1993. "Economic Liberalization, Political Pluralism and Business Associations in Developing Countries." *World Development* 21(12): 1895–1912.

Moravcsik, Andrew. 1997. "Taking Preferences Seriously: A Liberal Theory of International Politics." *International Organization* 51(4): 513–553.

Morrison, James Ashley. 2016. "Shocking Intellectual Austerity: The Role of Ideas in the Demise of the Gold Standard in Britain." *International Organization* 70(1): 175–207.

Morsy, Ahmed. 2014. "The Military Crowds Out Civilian Business in Egypt." Carnegie Endowment for International Peace, June 24.

Moschella, Manuela. 2016. "Negotiating Greece: Layering, insulation, and the Design of Adjustment Programs in the Eurozone." *Review of International Political Economy* 23(5): 799–824.

Mosley, Layna and Saika Uno. 2007. "Racing to the Bottom or Climbing to the Top? Economic Globalization and Collective Labor Rights." *Comparative Political Studies* 40(8): 923.

Muchapondwa, Edwin, Daniel Nielson, Bradley Parks, Austin M. Strange, and Michael J. Tierney. 2016. "'Ground-Truthing' Chinese Development Finance in Africa: Field Evidence from South Africa and Uganda." *Journal of Development Studies* 52(6): 780–796.

Mukherjee, Bumba and David Andrew Singer. 2010. "International Institutions and Domestic Compensation: The IMF and the Politics of Capital Account Liberalization." *American Journal of Political Science* 54(1): 45–60.

Mullahy, John. 2014. "Multivariate Fractional Regression Estimation of Econometric Share Models." *Journal of Econometric Methods* 4(1): 1–31.

Mwase, Nkunde and Yongzheng Yang. 2012. "BRICs' Philosophies for Development Financing and Their Implications for LICs." IMF Working Paper No. 12(74).

Naim, Moises. 2017. "Rogue Aid." *Foreign Policy* 159: 95–96.

Naoi, Megumi and Ikuo Kume. 2011. "Explaining Mass Support for Agricultural Protectionism: Evidence from a Survey Experiment during the Global Recession." *International Organization* 65(4): 771–795.

Naoi, Megumi and Ikuo Kume. 2015. "Workers or Consumers? A Survey Experiment on the Duality of Citizens' Interests in the Politics of Trade." *Comparative Political Studies* 48(10): 1293–1317.

Narizny, Kevin. 2003. "Both Guns and Butter, or Neither: Class Interests in the Political Economy of Rearmament." *American Political Science Review* 97(2): 203–220.

Narizny, Kevin. 2007. *The Political Economy of Grand Strategy*. Ithaca, NY: Cornell University Press.

Nelson, David and Susan Webb Yackee. 2012. "Lobbying Coalitions and Government Policy Change: An Analysis of Federal Agency Rulemaking." *Journal of Politics* 74(2): 339–353.

Nelson, Joan M. 1990. *Economic Crisis and Policy Choice: The Politics of Adjustment in the Third World*. Princeton, NJ: Princeton University Press.

Nelson, Stephen C. and David A. Steinberg. 2018. "Default Positions: What Shapes Public Attitudes about International Debt Disputes?" *International Studies Quarterly*, forthcoming.

Neumayer, Eric. 2003. "The Determinants of Aid Allocation by Regional Multilateral Development Banks and United Nations Agencies." *International Studies Quarterly* 47(1): 101–122.

Neumayer, Eric. 2006. "Self-Interest, Foreign Need, and Good Governance: Are Bilateral Investment Treaty Programs Similar to Aid Allocation?" *Foreign Policy Analysis* 2(3): 245–268.

Nooruddin, Irfan and Joel W. Simmons. 2006. "The Politics of Hard Choices: IMF Programs and Government Spending." *International Organization* 60(4): 1001–1033.

North, Liisa L. 2013. "New Left Regimes in the Andes? Ecuador in Comparative Perspective." *Studies in Political Economy* 91(1): 113–136.

Nour, Samia. 2011. "Assessment of Effectiveness of Chinese Aid in Financing Development in Sudan." UNU-MERIT Working Paper No. 2011(5).

Nunnenkamp, Peter and Rainer Thiele. 2006. "Targeting Aid to the Needy and Deserving: Nothing but Promises?" *World Economy* 29(9): 1177–1201.

Oberdabernig, Doris A. 2013. "Revisiting the Effects of IMF Programs on Poverty and Inequality." *World Development* 46(C): 113–142.

Ocampo, Jose Antonio. 1987. "Colombia and the Latin American Debt Crisis." FEDESARROLLO Working Paper, December 13.

Ocampo, Jose Antonio and Camilo E. Tovar. 2003. "Colombia's Experience with Reserve Requirements on Capital Inflows." *CEPAL Review* 81: 7–32.

Odhiambo, Nicholas M. 2005. "Financial Development and Economic Growth in Tanzania: A Dynamic Causality Test." *African Finance Journal* 7(1): 1–17.

OECD (Organization for Economic Cooperation and Development). 2016. "Agreement on Officially Supported Export Credits." TAD/PG(2016)1.

Okurut, Francis Nathan, Andrie Schoombee, and Servaas van der Berg. 2005. "Credit Demand and Credit Rationing in the Informal Financial Sector in Uganda." *South African Journal of Economics* 73(3): 482–497.

Olken, Benjamin A. and Rohini Pande. 2012. "Corruption in Developing Countries." *Annual Review of Economics* 4(1): 479–509.

Olson, Mancur. 1971. "A Theory of Groups and Organizations." In *Logic of Collective Action: Public Goods and the Theory of Groups*. Cambridge, MA: Harvard University Press, pp. 5–53.

Ostrander, Susan A. 1993. "Surely You're Not in This Just to Be Helpful." *Journal of Contemporary Ethnography* 22(1): 7–27.

Owen, Erica. 2013. "Unionization and Restrictions on Foreign Direct Investment." *International Interactions* 39(5): 723–747.

Owen, Erica. 2015. "The Political Power of Organized Labor and the Politics of Foreign Direct Investment in Developed Democracies." *Comparative Political Studies* 48(13): 1746–1780.

Pachano, Simon. 2007. "La trama de Penélope: Procesos políticos e instituciones en el Ecuador." Quito: FLACSO.

Pachano, Simon. 2009. "Calidad de la democracia e instituciones politicas en Bolivia, Ecuador y Peru." PhD dissertation, Universidad de Salamanca.

Pagano, Marco and Paolo F. Volpin. 2001. "The Political Economy of Finance." *Oxford Review of Economic Policy* 17(4): 502–519.

Pagano, Marco and Paolo F. Volpin. 2005a. "Managers, Workers, and Corporate Control." *Journal of Finance* 60(2): 841–868.

Pagano, Marco and Paolo F. Volpin. 2005b. "The Political Economy of Corporate Governance." *American Economic Review* 95(4): 1005–1030.

Pagliari, Stefano and Kevin L. Young. 2013. "Leveraged Interests: Financial Industry Power and the Role of Private Sector Coalitions." *Review of International Political Economy* 21(3): 575–610.

Pandya, Sonal S. 2010. "Labor Markets and the Demand for Foreign Direct Investment." *International Organization* 64(3): 389–409.

Pandya, Sonal S. 2014. "Democratization and Foreign Direct Investment Liberalization, 1970–2000." *International Studies Quarterly* 58(3): 475–488.

Papi, Luca, Andrea F. Presbitero, and Alberto Zazzaro. 2015. "IMF Lending and Banking Crises." *IMF Economic Review* 63(3): 644–691.

Papke, Leslie E. and Jeffrey M. Wooldridge. 1996. "Econometric Methods for Fractional Response Variables with an Application to 401(k) Plan Participation Rates." *Journal of Applied Econometrics* 11(6): 619–632.

Papke, Leslie E. and Jeffrey M. Wooldridge. 2008. "Panel Data Methods for Fractional Response Variables with an Application to Test Pass Rates." *Journal of Econometrics* 145(1–2): 121–133.

Paramio, Ludolfo and Martín Hopenhayn. 2010. *Clases medias y gobernabilidad en América Latina*. Madrid: Fundación Pablo Iglesias.

Pastor, Manuel. 1987. "The Effects of IMF Programs in the Third World: Debate and Evidence from Latin America." *World Development* 15(2): 249–262.

Peabody, Robert L., Susan Webb Hammond, Jean Torcom, Lynne P. Brown, Carolyn Thompson, and Robin Kolodny. 1990. "Interviewing Political Elites." *PS: Political Science and Politics* 23(3): 451–455.

Pepinsky, Thomas B. 2008. "Capital Mobility and Coalitional Politics: Authoritarian Regimes and Economic Adjustment in Southeast Asia." *World Politics* 60(3): 438–474.

Pettersson, Jan. 2007. "Foreign Sectoral Aid Fungibility, Growth and Poverty Reduction." *Journal of International Development* 19(8): 1074–1098.

Philips, Andrew Q., Amanda Rutherford, and G. D. Whitten. 2015. "Dynamic Pie: A Strategy for Modeling Trade-offs in Compositional Variables over Time." *American Journal of Political Science* 60(1): 1–16.

Pinto, Pablo M. 2013. *Partisan Investment in the Global Economy: Why FDI Loves the Left and the Left Loves FDI.* New York: Cambridge University Press.

Pinto, Pablo M. and Santiago M. Pinto. 2008. "The Politics of Investment Partisanship and the Sectoral Allocation of Foreign Direct Investment." *Economics & Politics* 20(2): 216–254.

Pinto, Pablo M. and Stephen Weymouth. 2016. "Partisan Cycles in Offshore Outsourcing: Evidence from U.S. Imports." *Economics & Politics* 28(3): 233–261.

Pontusson, Jonas. 2005. *Inequality and Prosperity: Social Europe vs. Liberal America.* Ithaca, NY: Cornell University Press.

Popkin, Samuel L. 1994. *The Reasoning Voter: Communication and Persuasion in Presidential Campaigns.* Chicago: University of Chicago Press.

Porzecanski, Arturo C. 2010. "When Bad Things Happen to Good Sovereign Debt Contracts: The Case of Ecuador." *Law & Contemporary Problems* 73(4): 251–271.

Presbitero, Andrea F. and Alberto Zazzaro. 2012. "IMF Lending in Times of Crisis: Political Influences and Crisis Prevention." *World Development* 40(10): 1944–1969.

Prizzon, Annalisa, Romilly Greenhill, and Shakira Mustapha. 2017. "An 'Age of Choice' for External Development Finance? Evidence from Country Case Studies." *Development Policy Review* 35(S1): 29–45.

Przeworski, Adam and James Raymond Vreeland. 2000. "The Effect of IMF Programs on Economic Growth." *Journal of Development Economics* 62(2): 385–421.

Przeworski, Adam and Michael Wallerstein. 1988. "Structural Dependence of the State on Capital." *American Political Science Review* 82(1): 11–29.

Quinn, Dennis P. and Carla Inclan. 1997. "The Origins of Financial Openness: A Study of Current and Capital Account Liberalization." *American Journal of Political Science* 41(3): 771.

Quinn, Dennis P. and Robert Y. Shapiro. 1991. "Business Political Power: The Case of Taxation." *American Political Science Review* 85(3): 851.

Ramcharan, Rodney. 2003. "Reputation, Debt, and Policy Conditionality." IMF Working Papers No. 03(192).

Ray, Rebecca, Kevin Gallagher, Andres Lopez, and Cynthia Sanborn. 2015. *China in Latin America: Lessons for South-South Cooperation and Sustainable Development.* Final report of the Working Group on Development and Environment in the Americas Global Economic Governance Initiative, Boston University.

Remo, Michelle V. 2013. "Government Must Keep Peso above 40 to $1—Official Says Weak Currency a Boon to Economy." *Business Inquirer*, July 8.

Renews. 2014. "US Loans $65m to Peru Projects." *Renews*, August 25.

Rethel, Lena. 2010. "Financialisation and the Malaysian Political Economy." *Globalizations* 7(4): 489–506.

Reuters. 2014. "Peru Says Most of $3 Bln in Bonds Sold to Manage Existing Debt." Reuters, October 31.

Rho, Sungmin and Michael Tomz. 2017. "Why Don't Trade Preferences Reflect Economic Self-Interest?" *International Organization* 71(S1): S85–S108.

Rich, Timothy S. 2009. "Status for Sale: Taiwan and the Competition for Diplomatic Recognition." *Issues & Studies* 45(3): 159–188.

Richards, David. 1996. "Elite Interviewing: Approaches and Pitfalls." *Politics* 16(3): 199–204.

Rickard, Stephanie J. 2014. "Compensating the Losers: An Examination of Congressional Votes on Trade Adjustment Assistance." *International Interactions* 41(1): 46–60.

Rodrik, Dani. 1996. "Why Is There Multilateral Lending?" NBER Working Paper No. 5160.

Rodrik, Dani. 2004. "Industrial Policy for the Twenty-First Century." London: Centre for Economic Policy Research.

Rogowski, Ronald. 1989. *Commerce and Coalitions: How Trade Affects Domestic Political Arrangements.* Princeton, NJ: Princeton University Press.

Rogowski, Ronald and Mark Andreas Kayser. 2002. "Majoritarian Electoral Systems and Consumer Power: Price-Level Evidence from the OECD Countries." *American Journal of Political Science* 46(3): 526–539.

Rounds, Zander and Hongxiang Huang. 2017. "We Are Not So Different: a Comparative Study of Employment Relations at Chinese and American Firms in Kenya." China Africa Working Paper 17(10).

Rudra, Nita. 2002. "Globalization and the Decline of the Welfare State in Less-Developed Countries." *International Organization* 56(2): 411–445.

Ryckman, Kirssa Cline and Jessica Maves Braithwaite. 2018. "Changing Horses in Midstream: Leadership Changes and the Civil War Peace Process." *Conflict Management and Peace Science*, forthcoming.

Sabet, Shahrzad. 2016. *"Feelings First: Non-material Factors as Moderators of Economic Self-Interest Effects on Trade Preferences."* Working paper, April 2.

Saeed, Abubakr, Yacine Belghitar, and Ephraim Clark. 2014. "Political Connections and Leverage: Firm-Level Evidence from Pakistan." *Managerial and Decision Economics* 36(6): 364–383.

Saiegh, Sebastián M. 2009. "Coalition Governments and Sovereign Debt Crises." *Economics & Politics* 21(2): 232–254.

Sanborn, Cynthia and Victoria Chonn. 2015. "Chinese Investment in Peru's Mining Industry: Blessing or Curse?" BU Working Paper 15(8).

Sanborn, Cynthia and Alexis Yong. 2013. "Peru's Economic Boom and the Asian Connection." Universidad del Pacifico Discussion Paper 13(5).

Sanderson, Henry and Michael Forsythe. 2012. *China's Superbank: Debt, Oil and Influence—How China Development Bank Is Rewriting the Rules of Finance*. Singapore: John Wiley & Sons.

Sato, Jin, Hiroaki Shiga, Takaaki Kobayashi, and Hisahiro Kondoh. 2011. "'Emerging Donors' from a Recipient Perspective: An Institutional Analysis of Foreign Aid in Cambodia." *World Development* 39(12): 2091–2104.

Sautman, Barry and Yan Hairong. 2015. "Localizing Chinese Enterprises in Africa: From Myths to Policies." HKUST IEMS Working Paper 15(5).

Saxena, Sanchita Banerjee. 2014. *Made in Bangladesh, Cambodia, and Sri Lanka: The Labor behind the Global Garments and Textiles Industries*. Amherst, NY: Cambria Press.

Scheve, Kenneth F. and Matthew Jon Slaughter. 2001. *Globalization and the Perceptions of American Workers*. New York: Columbia University Press.

Schlozman, Kay Lehman and John T. Tierney. 1986. *Organized Interests and American Democracy*. New York: Harper & Row.

Schmidt, Vivien A. 2009. "Putting the Political Back into Political Economy by Bringing the State Back in Yet Again." *World Politics* 61(3): 516–546.

Schneiberg, Marc and Tim Bartley. 2001. "Regulating American Industries: Markets, Politics, and the Institutional Determinants of Fire Insurance Regulation." *American Journal of Sociology* 107(1): 101–146.

Schrank, Andrew. 2008. "Export Processing Zones in the Dominican Republic: Schools or Stopgaps?" *World Development* 36(8): 1381–1397.

Schultz, Kenneth A. and Barry R. Weingast. 2003. "The Democratic Advantage: Institutional Foundations of Financial Power in International Competition." *International Organization* 57(1): 3–42.

Segura-Ubiergo, Alex. 2007. *The Political Economy of the Welfare State in Latin America: Globalization, Democracy, and Development*. New York: Cambridge University Press.

Self, Robert. 2006. *Britain, America and the War Debt Controversy: The Economic Diplomacy of an Unspecial Relationship, 1917–45*. Abingdon, UK: Routledge.

Semrau, Finn Ole and Rainer Thiele. 2017. "Brazil's Development Cooperation: Following in China's and India's Footsteps?" *Journal of International Development* 29(3): 287–307.

Sennholz-Weinhardt, Barbara. 2014. "Regulatory Competition as a Social Fact: Constructing and Contesting the Threat of Hedge Fund Managers Relocation from Britain." *Review of International Political Economy* 21(6): 1240–1274.

Shea, Patrick E. 2016. "Borrowing Trouble: Sovereign Credit, Military Regimes, and Conflict." *International Interactions* 42(3): 401–428.

Shea, Patrick E. and Matthew DiGiuseppe. 2015. "The Politics of Debt Restructuring: Institutions, Preferences and Creditor Losses." Working paper, November 30.

Shen, Xiaofang. 2015. "Private Chinese Investment in Africa: Myths and Realities." *Development Policy Review* 33(1): 83–106.

Shepsle, Kenneth A. 1979. "Institutional Arrangements and Equilibrium in Multidimensional Voting Models." *American Journal of Political Science* 23(1): 27–59.

Siddiqa, A. 2007. *Military Inc: Inside Pakistan's Military Economy*. New York: Oxford University Press.

Sikkink, Kathryn. 1991. *Ideas and Institutions: Developmentalism in Brazil and Argentina*. Ithaca, NY: Cornell University Press.

Silitski, Vitali. 2010. "'Survival of the Fittest:' Domestic and International Dimensions of the Authoritarian Reaction in the Former Soviet Union Following the Colored Revolutions." *Communist and Post-Communist Studies* 43(4): 339–350.

Sinclair, Barbara and David Brady. 1987. "Studying members of the United States Congress." In *Research Methods for Elite Studies*, edited by George Moyser and Margaret Wagstaffe. London: Allen & Unwin, pp. 48–71.

Sippel, Maike and Kasten Neuhoff. 2009. "A History of Conditionality: Lessons for International Cooperation on Climate Policy." *Climate Policy* 9(5): 481–494.

Skocpol, Theda, Dietrich Rueschemeyer, and Peter B. Evans, eds. 1985. *Bringing the State Back In*. New York: Cambridge University Press.

Smith, Alastair and James Raymond Vreeland. 2005. "The Survival of Political Leaders and IMF Programs." Abingdon, UK: Taylor & Francis, pp. 263–289.

Solingen, Etel. 2009. *Nuclear Logics: Contrasting Paths in East Asia and the Middle East*. Princeton, NJ: Princeton University Press.

Stacey, Kiran, Farhan Bokhari, and Henny Sender. 2017. "China Bails Out Pakistan with Over $1bn in Loans." *CNBC*, April 25.

Stasavage, David. 2003. *Public Debt and the Birth of the Democratic State*. New York: Cambridge University Press.

Stasavage, David. 2011. *States of Credit: Size, Power, and the Development of European Polities*. Princeton, NJ: Princeton University Press.

Stefanoni, Pablo. 2012. "Comparación del futuro de la democracia entre Venezuela, Bolivia y Ecuador." In *Democracias en trans-formation ¿Qué hay de Nuevo en los nuevos Estados andinos?*, edited by Anja Dargatz and Moira Zuazo. La Paz: Friedrich Ebert Stiftung, pp. 205–250.

Stockhammer, Engelbert. 2004. "Financialisation and the Slowdown of Accumulation." *Cambridge Journal of Economics* 28(5): 719–741.

Stone, Randall W. 2004. "The Political Economy of IMF Lending in Africa." *American Political Science Review* 98(4): 577–591.

Stone, Randall W. 2008. "The Scope of IMF Conditionality." *International Organization* 62(4): 589–620.

Strange, Austin M., Axel Dreher, Andreas Fuchs, Bradley Parks, and Michael J. Tierney. 2015. "Tracking Underreported Financial Flows: China's Development Finance and the Aid–Conflict Nexus Revisited." *Journal of Conflict Resolution* 61(5): 935–963.

Sun, Irene Yuan, Kartik Jayaram and Omid Kassiri. 2017. "Dance of the Lions and Dragons." McKinsey report.

Sussangkarn, Chalongphob. 2010. "The Chiang Mai Initiative Multilateralisation: Origin, Development and Outlook." ADBI Working Paper Series No. 230.

Svensson, Jakob. 2000. "When Is Foreign Aid Policy Credible? AID Dependence and Conditionality." *Journal of Development Economics* 61(1): 61–84.

Svolik, Milan W. 2009. "Power Sharing and Leadership Dynamics in Authoritarian Regimes." *American Journal of Political Science* 53(2): 477–494.

Svolik, Milan W. 2013. "Introduction: The Anatomy of Dictatorship." In *The Politics of Authoritarian Rule*. New York: Cambridge University Press, pp. 1–41.

Swaroop, Vinaya, Shikha Jha, and Andrew Sunil Rajkumar. 2000. "Fiscal Effects of Foreign Aid in a Federal System of Governance." *Journal of Public Economics* 77(3): 307–330.

Swenson, Peter A. 2002. *Capitalists against Markets: The Making of Labor Markets and Welfare States in the United States and Sweden.* New York: Oxford University Press.

Tanaka, Martín. 2011. "A Vote for Moderate Change." *Journal of Democracy* 22(4): 75–83.

Tanaka, Martín and Sofia Vera Rojas. 2010. "Neodualism in a Democracy without Party System: Democracy in Peru." *Revista de Ciencia Política* 30(1): 87–114.

Tang, Xiaoyang. 2010. "Bulldozer or Locomotive? The Impact of Chinese Enterprises on the Local Employment in Angola and the DRC." *Journal of Asian and African Studies* 45(3): 350–368.

Taylor, Ian. 2006. "China's Oil Diplomacy in Africa." *International Affairs* 82(5): 937–959.

Taylor, Steven J. and Robert Bogdan. 1998. *Introduction to Qualitative Research Methods: A Guidebook and Resource.* New York: John Wiley & Sons.

Thacker, Strom C. 1999. "The High Politics of IMF Lending." *World Politics* 52(1): 38–75.

The Economist. 2013. "Hold On Tight." *The Economist,* February 3.

The Economist. 2014. "The BRICS Bank: An Acronym with Capital." *The Economist,* July 19.

The Economist. 2015. "China and the world: Yuan for All." *The Economist,* January 31.

The Namibian. 2013. "Namibians Must Build Partnerships with Chinese." *The Namibian,* November 4.

Thomas, Jakana L., William Reed, and Scott Wolford. 2016. "The Rebels' Credibility Dilemma." *International Organization* 70(3): 477–511.

Tierney, Michael J., Daniel L. Nielson, Darren G. Hawkins, J. Timmons Roberts, Michael G. Findley, Ryan M. Powers, Bradley Parks, Sven E. Wilson, and Robert L. Hicks. 2011. "More Dollars Than Sense: Refining Our Knowledge of Development Finance Using AidData." *World Development* 39(11): 1891–1906.

Tomaskovic-Devey, Donald and Ken-Hou Lin. 2011. "Income Dynamics, Economic Rents, and the Financialization of the U.S. Economy." *American Sociological Review* 76(4): 538–559.

Tomz, Michael. 2004. "Interests and Information: The Domestic Politics of International Debt." Photocopy.

Tomz, Michael. 2007. *Reputation and International Cooperation: Sovereign Debt across Three Centuries.* Princeton, NJ: Princeton University Press.

Tomz, Michael, Joshua A. Tucker and Jason Wittenberg. 2002. "An Easy and Accurate Regression Model for Multiparty Electoral Data." *Political Analysis* 10(1): 66–83.

Tsingou, Eleni. 2015. "Club Governance and the Making of Global Financial Rules." *Review of International Political Economy* 22(2): 225–256.

Tsoutsoplides, Constantine. 2008. "The Determinants of the Geographical Allocation of EC Aid to the Developing Countries." *Applied Economics* 23(4): 647–658.

Urrutia, Miguel. 1990. "On the Absence of Economic Populism in Colombia." In *The Macroeconomics of Populism in Latin America,* edited by Rudiger Dornbusch and Sebastian Edwards. Chicago: University of Chicago Press, pp. 369–391.

US Congress. 2005. "*China's Influence in Africa: Hearing before the Subcommittee on Africa, Global Human Rights, and International Operations*." US House of Representatives, Committee on International Relations. pp. 1–79.

US Embassy in Angola. 2006. "Angola: A Reality Check on the Chinese Credit Line." May 3.

US Embassy in Ecuador. 2005a. "Minister of Finance on Fiscal Policy: Ambassador's Courtesy Call." May 6.

US Embassy in Ecuador. 2005b. "GoE Considering Chavez Loan." July 14.

US Embassy in Ecuador. 2005c. "Palacio: I Need Your Help." August 23.

US Embassy in Ecuador. 2007. "New Ministry of Finance: Lower Debt's Political Profile." August 31.

US Embassy in Ecuador. 2009. "Foreign Minister on Rebuilding Bilateral Relations and Law Enforcement Cooperation, with an IDB Side Note." February 27.

US Embassy in Ecuador. 2010. "China Cautiously Seeks to Expand Commercial Interests in Ecuador." January 26.

US Embassy in Russia. 2008. "Medvedev Bolsters Russia's Latin American Outreach." December 5.
US Embassy in Tajikistan. 2006. "Chinese Making Big Footprint On Tajikistan's Infrastructure." September 5.
Valdivia, Gabriela. 2008. "Governing Relations between People and Things: Citizenship, Territory, and the Political Economy of Petroleum in Ecuador." *Political Geography* 27(4): 456–477.
Van Arnum, Bradford M. and Michele I. Naples. 2013. "Financialization and Income Inequality in the United States, 1967–2010." *American Journal of Economics and Sociology* 72(5): 1158–1182.
Van Fossen, Anthony. 2007. "The Struggle for Recognition: Diplomatic Competition between China and Taiwan in Oceania." *Journal of Chinese Political Science* 12(2): 125–146.
Van Rijckeghem, Caroline and Beatrice Weder. 2008. "Political Institutions and Debt Crises." *Public Choice* 138(3–4): 387–408.
Van Teijlingen, Karolien and Barbara Hogenboom. 2016. "Debating Alternative Development at the Mining Frontier: Buen Vivirand the Conflict around El Mirador Mine in Ecuador." *Journal of Developing Societies* 32(4): 382–420.
Vanhanen, Tatu. 2000. "A New Dataset for Measuring Democracy, 1810–1998." *Journal of Peace Research* 37(2): 251–265.
Velásquez, Teresa A. 2017. "Tracing the Political Life of Kimsacocha: Conflicts over Water and Mining in Ecuador's Southern Andes." *Latin American Perspectives* 11(3): 1–16.
Vogel, David. 1983. "The Power of Business in America: A Re-appraisal." *British Journal of Political Science* 13(1): 19.
Vogel, Steven K. 1999. "When Interests Are Not Preferences: The Cautionary Tale of Japanese Consumers." *Comparative Politics* 31(2): 187.
Vreeland, James Raymond. 2002. "The Effect of IMF Programs on Labor." *World Development* 30(1): 121–139.
Vreeland, James Raymond. 2003a. *The IMF and Economic Development*. New York: Cambridge University Press.
Vreeland, James Raymond. 2003b. "Why Do Governments and the IMF Enter into Agreements? Statistically Selected Cases." *International Political Science Review* 24(3): 321–343.
Vreeland, James Raymond. 2007. *The International Monetary Fund: Politics of Conditional Lending*. Abingdon, UK: Taylor & Francis.
Wade, Abdoulaye. 2008. "Time for the West to Practise What It Preaches." *Financial Times*, January 23.
Wade, Robert. 1990. *Governing the Market: Economic Theory and the Role of Government in East Asian Industrialization*. Princeton, NJ: Princeton University Press.
Waltz, Kenneth Neal. 1979. *Theory of International Politics*. Reading, MA: Addison-Wesley.
Warmerdam, Ward and Meine Pieter van Dijk. 2013. "Chinese State-Owned Enterprise Investments in Uganda: Findings from a Recent Survey of Chinese Firms in Kampala." *Journal of Chinese Political Science* 18(3): 281–301.
Wasby, Stephen L. 1995. *Race Relations Litigation in an Age of Complexity*. Charlottesville: University of Virginia Press.
Weeks, Jessica L. 2008. "Autocratic Audience Costs: Regime Type and Signaling Resolve." *International Organization* 62(1): 35–64.
Weeks, Jessica L. 2012. "Strongmen and Straw Men: Authoritarian Regimes and the Initiation of International Conflict." *American Political Science Review* 106(2): 326–347.
Weeks, John. 1999. "Wages, Employment and Workers' Rights in Latin America, 1970–98." *International Labour Review* 138(2): 151–169.
Weisbrot, Mark, Jake Johnston, and Stephan Lefebvre. 2013. *Ecuador's New Deal: Reforming and Regulating the Financial Sector*. Washington, DC: Center for Economic and Policy Research.
Weiss, Jessica Chen. 2013. "Authoritarian Signaling, Mass Audiences, and Nationalist Protest in China." *International Organization* 67(1): 1–35.
Welch, Catherine, Rebecca Marschan-Piekkari, Heli Penttinen, and Marja Tahvanainen. 2002. "Interviewing Elites in International Organizations: A Balancing Act for the Researcher." *International Business Review* 11(5): 611–628.

Wellhausen, Rachel L. 2015. "Bondholders vs. Direct Investors? Competing Responses to Expropriation." *International Studies Quarterly* 59(1): 750–764.

Wenping, He. 2007. "China's Loans to Africa Won't Cause Debt Crisis." *China Daily*, June 6.

Whitford, Andrew B. 2003. "The Structures of Interest Coalitions: Evidence from Environmental Litigation." *Business and Politics* 5(1): 45–64.

Wibbels, Erik. 2006. "Dependency Revisited: International Markets, Business Cycles, and Social Spending in the Developing World." *International Organization* 60(2): 433–468.

Wibbels, Erik and Moises Arce. 2003. "Globalization, Taxation, and Burden-Shifting in Latin America." *International Organization* 57(1): 111–136.

Wilks, Stephen. 2013. *The Political Power of the Business Corporation*. Cheltenham, UK: Edward Elgar.

Williams, John T. and Brian K. Collins. 1997. "The Political Economy of Corporate Taxation." *American Journal of Political Science* 41(1): 208.

Williamson, John. 2000. "What Should the World Bank Think about the Washington Consensus?" *World Bank Research Observer* 15(2): 251–264.

Williamson, John. 2003. "The Washington Consensus and Beyond." *Economic and Political Weekly* 38(15): 1475–1481.

Wilson, Graham K. 1990. "Corporate Political Strategies." *British Journal of Political Science* 20(2): 281.

Winters, Jeffrey A. 1996. *Power in Motion: Capital Mobility and the Indonesian State*. Ithaca, NY: Cornell University Press.

Winters, Jeffrey A. 2007. "Power and the Control of Capital." *World Politics* 46(3): 419–452.

Winters, Matthew S. and Gina Martinez. 2015. "The Role of Governance in Determining Foreign Aid Flow Composition." *World Development* 66(C): 516–531.

Wise, Carol and Cintia Quiliconi. 2007. "China's Surge in Latin American Markets: Policy Challenges and Responses." *Politics & Policy* 35(3): 410–438.

Wissenbach, Uwe. 2009. "The EU's Response to China's Africa Safari: Can Triangular Co-operation Match Needs?" *European Journal of Development Research* 21(4): 662–674.

Witko, Christopher. 2014. "The Politics of Financialization in the United States, 1949–2005." *British Journal of Political Science* 46(2): 349–370.

Wolff, Jonas. 2016. "Business Power and the Politics of Postneoliberalism: Relations between Governments and Economic Elites in Bolivia and Ecuador." *Latin American Politics & Society* 58(2): 124–147.

Woll, Cornelia. 2007. "Leading the Dance? Power and Political Resources of Business Lobbyists." *Journal of Public Policy* 27(1): 57–78.

Woll, Cornelia. 2008. *Firm Interests: How Governments Shape Business Lobbying on Global Trade*. Ithaca, NY: Cornell University Press.

Woll, Cornelia. 2014a. "Bank Rescue Schemes in Continental Europe: The Power of Collective Inaction." *Government and Opposition* 49(3): 426–451.

Woll, Cornelia. 2014b. *The Power of Inaction: Bank Bailouts in Comparison*. Ithaca, NY: Cornell University Press.

Woll, Cornelia. 2015. "Firm Interests in Uncertain Times: Business Lobbying in Multilateral Service Liberalization." In *Constructing the Political Economy*, edited by Rawi Abdelal, Mark Blyth, and Craig Parsons. Ithaca, NY: Cornell University Press, pp. 135–154.

Woll, Cornelia. 2016. "Politics in the Interest of Capital." *Politics & Society* 44(3): 373–391.

Woo-Cumings, Meredith. 1999. "Introduction: Chalmers Johnson and the Politics of Nationalism and Development." In *The Developmental State*, edited by Meredith Woo-Cumings. Ithaca, NY: Cornell University Press, pp. 1–31.

World Bank. 2012. "Chinese FDI in Ethiopia—a World Bank Survey." Survey report.

World Bank. 2016. "World Bank Enterprise Survey 2016."

World Bank. 2017. "World Development Indicators 2017."

World Economic Forum. 2016. "The Global Competitiveness Report 2016–2017."

Wright, John R. 1985. "PACs, Contributions, and Roll Calls: An Organizational Perspective." *American Political Science Review* 79(2): 400–414.

Xinhua. 2015. "Talented Workforce Key to Success of Chinese Businesses in Kenya: study." *Xinhua,* January 16.

Yang, Chang and Menghan An. 2017. "Can China Help Lift African Women Out of Poverty?" China Africa Project, September 24.

Yashar, Deborah J. 2005. *Contesting Citizenship in Latin America: The Rise of Indigenous Movements and the Postliberal Challenge.* New York: Cambridge University Press.

Yoon, Jungkeun. 2009. "Globalization and the Welfare State in Developing Countries." *Business and Politics* 11(2): 1–31.

Young, Kevin. 2017. "Not by Structure Alone: Power, Prominence, and Agency in American Finance." *Business and Politics* 17(3): 443–472.

Zettelmeyer, Jeromin and Federico Sturzenegger. 2007. "Ecuador". In *Debt Defaults and Lessons from a Decade of Crises.* Cambridge, MA: MIT Press, pp. 147–165.

Interviews

Interview 1. Colombia. Personal interview, August 11, 2011.
Interview 2, Colombia. Personal interview, August 12, 2011.
Interview 3. Colombia. Personal interview, August 16, 2011.
Interview 4. Colombia. Personal interview, August 16, 2011.
Interview 5. Colombia. Personal interview, August 16, 2011.
Interview 6. Colombia. Personal interview, August 17, 2011.
Interview 7. Colombia. Personal interview, August 18, 2011.
Interview 8. Colombia. Personal interview, August 19, 2011.
Interview 9. Colombia. Personal interview, August 19, 2011.
Interview 10. Colombia. Personal interview, August 19, 2011.
Interview 11. Colombia. Personal interview, August 22, 2011.
Interview 12. Colombia. Personal interview, August 23, 2011.
Interview 13. Colombia. Personal interview, August 23, 2011.
Interview 14. Colombia. Personal interview, August 23, 2011.
Interview 16. Colombia. Personal interview, August 24, 2011.
Interview 17. Colombia. Personal interview, August 24, 2011.
Interview 18. Colombia. Personal interview, August 25, 2011.
Interview 19. Colombia. Personal interview, August 25, 2011.
Interview 21. Colombia. Personal interview, August 25, 2011.
Interview 22. Colombia. Personal interview, August 25, 2011.
Interview 23. Colombia. Personal interview, August 26, 2011.
Interview 24. Colombia. Personal interview, August 26, 2011.
Interview 25. Colombia. Personal interview, August 26, 2011.
Interview 26. Colombia. Personal interview, August 27, 2011.
Interview 28. Colombia. Personal interview, August 29, 2011.
Interview 29. Colombia. Personal interview, August 29, 2011.
Interview 32. Colombia. Personal interview, August 30, 2011.
Interview 33. Colombia. Personal interview, August 30, 2011.
Interview 34. Colombia. Personal interview, August 31, 2011.
Interview 35. Colombia. Personal interview, August 31, 2011.
Interview 36. Colombia. Personal interview, September 1, 2011.
Interview 38. Colombia. Personal interview, September 1, 2011.
Interview 39. Colombia. Personal interview, September 1, 2011.
Interview 40. Colombia. Personal interview, September 2, 2011.
Interview 43. Colombia. Email interview, July 29, 2011.
Interview 44. Peru. Personal interview, September 12, 2011.
Interview 45. Peru. Personal interview, September 12, 2011.
Interview 46. Peru. Personal interview, September 12, 2011.

Interview 47. Peru. Personal interview, September 13, 2011.
Interview 49. Peru. Personal interview, September 14, 2011.
Interview 52. Peru. Personal interview, September 14, 2011.
Interview 53. Peru. Personal interview, September 20, 2011.
Interview 55. Peru. Personal interview, September 21, 2011.
Interview 56. Peru. Personal interview, September 22, 2011.
Interview 57. Peru. Personal interview, September 23, 2011.
Interview 60. Peru. Personal interview, September 23, 2011.
Interview 61. Peru. Personal interview, September 23, 2011.
Interview 62. Peru. Personal interview, September 23, 2011.
Interview 63. Peru. Personal interview, September 23, 2011.
Interview 64. Peru. Personal interview, September 26, 2011.
Interview 65. Peru. Personal interview, September 26, 2011.
Interview 66. Peru. Personal interview, September 26, 2011.
Interview 67. Peru. Personal interview, September 27, 2011.
Interview 69. Peru. Personal interview, September 27, 2011.
Interview 70. Peru. Personal interview, September 28, 2011.
Interview 72. Peru. Personal interview, September 28, 2011.
Interview 73. Peru. Personal interview, September 28, 2011.
Interview 74. Peru. Personal interview, September 28, 2011.
Interview 75. Peru. Personal interview, September 28, 2011.
Interview 77. Ecuador. Personal interview, October 4, 2011.
Interview 78. Ecuador. Personal interview, October 5, 2011.
Interview 79. Ecuador. Personal interview, October 5, 2011.
Interview 82. Ecuador. Personal interview, October 6, 2011.
Interview 83. Ecuador. Personal interview, October 6, 2011.
Interview 84. Ecuador. Personal interview, October 10, 2011.
Interview 85. Ecuador. Personal interview, October 12, 2011.
Interview 86. Ecuador. Personal interview, October 13, 2011.
Interview 87. Ecuador. Personal interview, October 13, 2011.
Interview 89. Ecuador. Personal interview, October 14, 2011.
Interview 90. Ecuador. Personal interview, October 14, 2011.
Interview 91. Ecuador. Personal interview, October 15, 2011.
Interview 92. Ecuador. Personal interview, October 17, 2011.
Interview 93. Ecuador. Personal interview, October 17, 2011.
Interview 94. Ecuador. Personal interview, October 18, 2011.
Interview 95. Ecuador. Personal interview, October 19, 2011.
Interview 96. Ecuador. Personal interview, October 19, 2011.
Interview 97. Ecuador. Personal interview, October 20, 2011.
Interview 98. Ecuador. Personal interview, October 20, 2011.
Interview 99. Ecuador. Personal interview, October 20, 2011.
Interview 100. Ecuador. Personal interview, October 21, 2011.
Interview 101. Ecuador. Personal interview, October 21, 2011.
Interview 102. Ecuador. Personal interview, October 21, 2011.
Interview 103. Ecuador. Personal interview, October 26, 2011.
Interview 104. Ecuador. Personal interview, October 26, 2011.
Interview 105. Ecuador. Personal interview, October 27, 2011.

INDEX

Note: Page numbers followed by *f* and *t* indicate figures and tables respectively.

Agence Française de Développement, 144–45
Aitchison, John, 183–84
Alden, Chris, 7, 44
Andean Development Corporation
    [Corporacion Andina de Fomento
    (CAF)], 92, 125–26
Angola, 2, 46, 58t, 237, 238
Arce, Moises, 137, 142, 165–66
Argentina, 51, 69, 110
Asian Development Bank (ADB), 234–35
Australia, 37–38
Austria, 37–38

Bangladesh, 1
Belgium, 37–38, 103
Belize, 10, 217
Benin, 9
Bhutan, 2
bilateral loans. *See* Brazil, Russia, India, and
    China (BRICs); Development Assistance
    Committee (DAC)
Bolivia, 1
Brautigam, Deborah, 7, 42, 44, 157–58,
    159–60, 238–39
Brazil
    analyzing Brazil, Russia, and India separately
        from China, 28, 79, 204
    establishment of New Development Bank, 233
    financial crisis in 1999, 111
    grouping with Russia, India, and China,
        18–19, 41–42
    lending to access natural resources, 192
    lending volume, 1–2, 3–4, 152–53, 157,
        159, 160

loan repayment to, 5
loans to Ecuador, 96–97, 104
loans to Peru, 143
preferences regarding loans from, 41
BRICs
    analyzing Brazil, Russia, and India separately
        from China, 28, 79, 204
    data about lending by, 158–60
    heterogeneity, 41–42
    implications for western creditors, 2–3
    loans by, 41–42, 103–5, 125, 143–44
    preferences regarding loans from, 41–47,
        86–87, 111–14, 134–35
    See also Brazil, Russia, India, and China
        (BRICs)
BRICS Development Bank. *See* New
    Development Bank
Brooks, Sarah, 49
Bucaram, Abdalá, 96
Bueno de Mesquita, Bruce, 38–39, 53, 198
Bunte, Jonas, 7, 38–39, 42–43, 47, 52, 111, 113,
    136, 235, 236, 239, 241
Burkina Faso, 217

Cambodia, 24–25, 177–78
Canada, 37–38, 127
Cape Verde, 9
case studies
    motivation for, 69–73
    selection criteria, 73–76
Chang, Ha-Joon, 38–39, 40, 93, 239
Chavez, Hugo, 96–97
Chiang Mai Initiative Mutilateralisation
    (CMIM), 233

269

INDEX

Chile, 63, 85, 176–77
China
  analyzing Brazil, Russia, and India separately from China, 28, 79, 204, 205f
  Chinese labor in developing countries, 44–46, 58t, 134
  Colombia rejects loan offers from, 5–6, 125, 215–16
  data sources for loans from, 22, 28, 152–53, 157–60
  differences in conditions, 18, 236
  establishment of New Development Bank, 233–34
  fieldwork concerning Chinese loans, 76, 79
  grouping with Brazil, Russia, and India, 18–19, 41–42
  ideological alignment with, 226–27
  implications for democracy, 240–43
  implications for western creditors, 3, 26, 235, 238, 240
  lending volume, 1–2
  loans tied to investment, 42, 43–44, 87, 103–4, 116, 120, 122–23, 134, 142–43
  loans to access natural resources, 114, 192, 237
  loans to Angola, 238
  loans to Ecuador, 4–5, 87, 96–97, 103–4, 105
  loans to Pakistan, 16–17
  loans to Peru, 143–44, 216
  loans to Tajikistan, 235
  preferences regarding loans from, 39, 41, 89, 93, 94, 99, 105, 112–13, 114–15, 237
  recognition of Taiwan, 28–29, 216–17
  UN voting agreement with, 178, 226–27, 228f
China Development Bank, 16–17, 21, 42, 76, 79, 103–4, 125, 135, 142, 143
China EXIM bank
  loans from, 42, 103–4, 135, 143–44, 238
  resistance against, 5–6, 105, 125
China Gezhouba Group-Fopeca, 104
ChinalCo, 134, 135, 144
Chinese lending data
  AidData, 158, 159–60
  China-Africa Research Initiative (CARI), 159–60
  OECD creditor reporting system, 158, 159
  white papers, 157
  World Bank Debtor Reporting System (DRS), 158–59
Colombia
  access to creditors, 215–16
  alignment with the United States, 226–27
  Bogota, 85, 109–10, 125–26, 215–16
  borrowing portfolio of, 125–27
  capital coalition in, 84–85, 92, 108–10
  capital controls, 111–12
  fieldwork in, 20–21, 72–74, 77, 152
  finance in, 108–9, 111–12, 114–15, 117, 132–33, 143
  government
    Consejo Gremial National [National Business Council], 113
    Council for Fiscal Policy [Consejo Superior de Politica Fiscal (CONFIS)], 118–19
    Council of Ministers ("El Compes"), 118–19
    Economic and Social Policy Council [El Consejo Nacional de Politica Economica y Social (CONPES)], 118–19, 123
    Inter-parliamentary Public Debt Commission [Comision Interparlamentaria de Credito Publico (CICP)], 119, 122–23, 142
    Locomotivas Program, 40, 115
    Ministry of Finance and Public Credit [Ministerio de Hacienda y Credito Publico (MHCP)], 119
    National Planning Department [Departamento Nacional de Planeacion (DNP)], 113, 118–19
    Productive Transformation Program, 40, 115
  industry in, 108–10, 113–14, 115, 117, 131, 132
  labor in, 110, 116, 137
  legacy of the civil war, 110
  loans tied to investment projects, 121–22, 124, 139, 140
  oligarchy in, 108–9
  organizations
    Asociacion Nacional de Empresarios de Colombia (ANDI), 114, 116–17
    Colombia Conservative Party, 108–9
    Colombian Liberal Party, 108–9
    Pardito Social de Unidad Nacional [Social Party of National Unity], 109
    Primero Colombia [Colombia First], 109
    Revolucionarias de Colombia, the Revolutionary Armed Forces of Colombia (FARC), 110
  political system, 83
  politicians in, 116–17, 138–39
  preferences
    regarding BRIC loans, 41–47, 111–14
    regarding DAC loans, 39, 40, 114–15
    regarding IFI loans, 34–37, 115
    regarding Private loans, 47–51, 115
  process of loan negotiations in, 118–24
  projects
    Bancolombia, 125–26
    Canal Seco [Dry Canal], 5–6, 125, 215–16
    Citibank in, 112, 121–22
    ColPetrol, 5–6, 127
    Requirement for Colombian partner, 122–23
  rejecting Chinese loan offers, 5–6, 125
  social movements in, 109, 138–39
  trade policy of, 127, 146

INDEX

comparative advantages
   creating new, 239–40
   exploit existing, 145, 239, 240
compositional data
   Aitchison method, 184
   borrowing portfolios, 157, 161
   fractional multinomial logit, 186–87
   interdependency, 24–25
   negative correlation, 183
   seemingly unrelated regression, 183
   simultaneous estimation, 24–25, 185
Conaghan, Catherine M, 94, 95–96, 106
Contingent Reserve Arrangement (CRA), 233
Copelovitch, Mark, 7–8, 24–25, 35, 38, 52, 205–6
Correa, Rafael, 4–5, 80, 84–85, 90–91, 92, 94, 101, 106, 215
   decision to default, 101–3
   following or creating public opinion? 95–97
   personal opinion of Chinese loans, 105
corruption, 24–25, 38–39, 80, 88, 238
Costa Rica, 9
credit ratings, 8–9, 103, 126, 210, 213–14
credit rationing. *See* private creditors, access to
creditors
   access to, 209–16
   changing clientele, 236
   expertise, 219–26
   See also Brazil; China; Development Assistance Committee (DACs); India; International Monetary Fund (IMF); Private creditors; Russia; World Bank
crisis
   banking crisis, 19, 35, 48, 115, 136
   currency crisis, 16–17
   debt crisis, 32–33, 50–51, 224
Czech Republic, 37–38

debt
   debt swap, 5, 102–3
   default, 4, 50–51, 82–83, 90, 100–3, 198–99
   haircut, 50–51
   legitimacy, 4, 91, 101, 102–3
   relief, 97, 241
   repayment, 4, 9, 35, 36–37, 50–51, 52–53, 92, 101–2, 104, 199
   rescheduled, 101
   risk premium, 48
   rollover, 88
   service, 51, 90, 100, 101
   sustainability, 8–9, 119, 215, 241
democracy, 198–99, 240–43
Democratic Advantage Theory, 8–9, 199
Denmark, 37–38, 59–60
Development Assistance Committee (DAC)
   competition with BRICs, 235–37
   conditions, 38–39
   data on loans by, 159–60
   expertise, 6, 14, 37–38, 222–24
   heterogeneity, 41–42
   loans by, 37–39, 103, 127, 144–45
   motivation for loans, 192, 219
   preferences regarding loans from, 39–41, 58t, 87–89, 114–15, 136
Djibouti, 10
Dominican Republic, 167–68, 173
Durán-Ballén, Sixto, 96–97

East Asian development model, 38–39, 40, 239
Ecuador
   access to creditors, 98, 209, 215
   advance sales of oil, 104
   Anti-Americanism in, 96, 97, 226–27
   anti-neoliberal protests, 95–96
   arbitration clause [clausula arbitraje], 98–99, 106
   borrowing portfolio of, 75–76, 82–83, 99–105
   corporatist coalition in, 83–85
   Correa following public opinion, 95–97
   Correa's opinion of Chinese loans, 105
   default on loans, 4–5, 82–83, 100–3
   fieldwork in, 20–21, 72, 74, 151
   finance in, 20, 39, 72–73, 85, 88–90, 94–95, 132–33
   government
      Comision para la Auditoria Integral del Credito Publico [Commission to Audit the Entirety of Public Debt (CAIC)], 4, 101
      Debt Committee [Comite del Deuda], 98–99, 141
      National Institute of Procurement [Instituto Nacional de Contratacion Pública (INCOP)], 93
      National Secretariat for Planning and Development [Secretaria Nacional de Planificacion y Desarrollo (SENPLADES)], 93, 98–99
      Public Debt Office [Subsecretario de Credito Publico], 98–99
   Guayaquil, 83, 85
   industry in, 43–44, 83, 87, 93–94, 106, 131
   investor protection in, 106
   labor in, 36, 83, 86, 88, 92, 106, 116, 137–38
   loans
      from Brazil, 5, 96–97, 104
      from China, 4, 96–97, 103–4
      from IMF, 100, 215
      from Private creditors, 100, 103, 215
      from Russia, 5, 104
      tied to investment projects, 42, 93, 103–4

Ecuador (cont.)
    Organizations
        Democratic Left [Izquierda Democratica], 83–84
        Democratic People's Movement [Movimiento Popular Democratico], 83–84
        Grupo Nacional contra la Deuda, 97
        January 21 Patriotic Society Party [Partido Sociedad Patriotica 21 de Enero], 84
        Jubileo 2000, 94–95, 97, 100
        Pachakutik Plurinational Unity Movement [Movimiento de Unidad Plurinacional Pachakutik -- Nuevo Pais], 84
        Partido Renovador Institucional de Accion Nacional, 4
        Popular Democracy (PD), 96–97
        Proud and Sovereign Fatherland Alliance [Alianza Patria Altiva y Soberana (Alianza PAIS)], 4, 84–85, 97
        Republican Unity Party, 96–97
    pativideos, 88, 91
    persons
        Abadi, Carlos, 88
        Cely, Nathalie, 103
        Dayan, Alan, 88
        Guzman, Jorge, 100
        Noboa, Gustavo, 96–97
        Ortiz, Fausto, 100
        Patino, Ricardo, 88, 91
        Rodas, Armando, 88, 91
        Runguo, Cai, 105
        Vega, Diego, 105
    politicians in, 85, 91, 92, 94–95, 99
    preferences
        regarding BRIC loans, 41–47, 86–87, 88–89
        regarding DAC loans, 37–41, 87–88, 89
        regarding IFI loans, 34–37, 86, 89–90
        regarding Private loans, 47–51, 88, 90
    process of loan negotiations in, 98–99, 119
    projects
        Coca Codo Sinclair, 42, 103–4, 239
        San Francisco hydropower project, 5, 104
        Sopladora Electrical project, 104
        Toachi Pilaton hydropower project, 104
    Quito, 83, 85, 96, 101
    social movements in, 84–85, 90–91, 110
    trade policy of, 106
Edwards, Sebastian, 113
Egypt, 32
El Salvador, 217
elections
    in Ecuador, 4–5, 84, 96, 102–3
    in Pakistan, 16–17
    in Peru, 130, 131, 138–40
    in Zambia, 237
electoral system, 184, 199–201

Eritrea, 9
Ethiopia, 44, 46, 47–48, 58t

fieldwork. *See* interviews
finance
    crowding out of, 42–43, 57–59, 88–89
    distributional consequences of BRIC loans for, 42–43, 88–89, 111–12, 134–35
    distributional consequences of DAC loans for, 39–40, 89, 114–15, 136
    distributional consequences of IFI loans for, 35, 89–90, 115, 137
    distributional consequences of Private loans for, 48–49, 90, 115, 136
    intangible assets, 31
    material interests of, 31
    political strength of, 85, 108–9, 132, 174–78
    stock market, 85, 175
Finland, 37–38
fooling someone. *See* practical joke
foreign aid
    difference loans vs. foreign aid, 2, 152–53, 160, 219
    distributional consequences of, 70–71
    from China, 125, 157–59
    fungibility, 16, 226
    lobbying for, 52–53
Foreign Direct Investment (FDI), 49, 71
France, 8–9, 37–38, 103, 127, 215–16
Frieden, Jeffry, 25, 32–33, 52, 53
Fujimori, Alberto, 75, 81, 130–31, 132, 133, 136, 137, 138–39

Gabon, 47–48
Gallagher, Kevin P., 7, 113, 134
García, Alan, 130, 138–39
Germany, 8–9, 37–38, 103, 127, 130, 144, 235–36
Ghana, 9, 47–48
Gourevitch, Peter A, 31, 55, 57, 59, 60, 63
government-to-government loans. *See* bilateral loans
Greece, 37–38
Guinea, 173
Gutiérrez, Lucio, 53, 84

Honduras, 217
Huawei Technologies, 112
Humala, Ollanta, 130–31, 138–39

Iceland, 37–38
India
    AidData information on loans from, 160

analyzing Brazil, Russia, and India separately from China, 28, 79, 204
establishment of New Development Bank, 233, 234
establishment of the Contingent Reserve Arrangement (CRA), 233
grouping with Brazil, Russia, and China, 18–19, 41–42
lending volume, 1–2, 3–4
loans to access natural resources, 192
preferences regarding loans from, 39, 41
Indonesia, 8, 57, 60–61, 213, 234
Industrial and Commercial Bank of China, 16–17, 134–35
industry
    crowding out of, 43–44, 87
    distributional consequences of BRIC loans for, 43, 86–87, 113–14
    distributional consequences of DAC loans for, 40, 87–88, 115
    distributional consequences of IFI loans for, 35–36, 86, 115
    distributional consequences of Private loans for, 49, 88, 115
    fixed assets, 31–32
    industrial policy, 40, 87–88, 93–94, 106, 115
    manufacturing, 31–32, 36, 40, 47, 113, 114, 131–32
    material interests of, 31–32
    military as an industrial actor, 32
    political strength of, 83–85, 108–9, 131–32, 169–73
    subcontracting, 20, 43–44, 80, 87, 93
infant mortality, 14, 222–24
Inter-American Development Bank (IDB), 144
interest groups. *See* finance; industry; labor
International Financial Institutions. *See* International Monetary Fund (IMF); World Bank
International Labour Organization (ILO), 165
International Monetary Fund (IMF), 34–35
    conditions, 13–14, 16, 18, 19, 33, 34, 35, 93, 226, 238
    data on loans from, 160
    demand for, 89–90, 105, 115, 137, 192
    distributional consequences, 32–33, 35, 36, 80, 86, 231–32, 239
    expertise, 6–7, 13, 192, 224
    implications for the IMF, 233–37
    lender of last resort, 209, 215
    loans from the, 1, 100, 144
    resistance against, 4, 16–17, 19, 33, 35, 80, 86, 90–91, 92, 95–96, 105, 137, 238
interviews
    elite vs. non-elite, 77–78
    institutional affiliations, 77
    interview partners, 76
    interview questions, 78–79
    interview technique, 79–80
    recruitment process, 76
Ireland, 37–38
Italy, 37–38, 103
Ivory Coast, 47–48

Jamaica, 10
Japan, 8, 37–38, 60, 70, 127, 144, 167, 233, 235–36

Kenya, 46, 47–48, 58*t*
Korea, Republic of, 8, 37–38, 40, 41, 57, 93, 96–97, 167, 215–16, 234, 239
Kreditanstalt für Wiederaufbau (KfW), 216
Kuczynski, Pedro Pablo, 143

labor
    distributional consequences of BRIC loans for, 44–47, 86–87, 116, 134
    distributional consequences of DAC loans for, 40–41, 87–88, 116, 136
    distributional consequences of IFI loans for, 36–37, 86, 137
    distributional consequences of Private loans for, 49–51, 88, 136–37
    employment of Chinese workers, 44–47*t*
    material interests of, 32–33
    political strength of, 83–85, 110, 129–31, 165–67
Lake, David A, 69, 72
Laos, 47–48
Lesotho, 9, 47, 173
Li Group, 46
Liberia, 47
loans
    budget loans, 120–21, 125
    concessional loans, 42, 126–27, 144–45, 219, 221*f*
    conditionality, 30, 34, 38, 70, 205–6, 234, 236, 238
    difference loans vs. foreign aid, 2
    distributional consequences, 17–19, 31, 37, 41–42, 50*t*, 58*t*, 93, 113, 137, 204, 208, 217–19
    distributional consequences of loans vs. foreign direct investment, 49
    grace period, 2, 141, 217–19, 238
    grant element, 217–19, 220*f*
    interest rate, 2, 8, 47–48, 89–90, 101, 125–26, 141, 213–16, 217–19, 238
    loan offers, 4–6, 19–20, 24–25, 27, 52, 79, 98, 119, 120, 125, 141, 216, 229
    maturity, 2, 8, 47–48, 101, 125–26, 213, 217–19
    nonconcessional loans, 126–27, 160–61
    project loans, 121–24, 125, 142

loans (cont.)
    tied loans, 14–15, 19, 39, 42–43, 48, 80, 87, 88–89, 103–4, 116, 121–22, 124, 134, 142, 224, 235–36
London Inter-Bank Offered Rate (LIBOR), 213, 238
Luxembourg, 37–38

Mahuad, Jamil, 96
Malaysia, 32, 60–61, 167, 176–77
Maldives, 1
Manufacturers Association of Nigeria, 47
market exclusion. *See* credit rationing
Mauritius, 9
Measuring coalitions, 161–78
    CHISOLS (Change in Source of Leader Support) dataset, 161–62
    group's importance to the economy, 164
    overcoming collective action problems, 164
Mexico, 134
Milner, Helen V, 38, 52, 53, 70–71
Mongolia, 9
Mosley, Layna, 47–48, 49, 165
Mozambique, 47–48
multilateral loans. *See* International Financial Institutions; International Monetary Fund (IMF); World Bank

Namibia, 46, 58t
natural resources, 193–94
    Copper, 86, 144
    Dutch Disease, 111, 113
    Iron ore, 134
    Oil, 83, 88–89, 96–97, 100, 104, 193–94
Netherlands, 37–38, 144
New Development Bank (NDB), 233–34
New Zealand, 37–38
Nigeria, 46, 47–48, 58t
Noboa, Álvaro, 4
Norway, 37–38

Ocampo, Jose Antonio, 111, 115, 126
Official Development Assistance. *See* foreign aid
Olson, Mancur, 163, 175
Open Economy Politics, 69–73
Organization for Economic Cooperation and Development (OECD), 37–38, 219
    Arrangement on Officially Supported Export Credits, 160
    OECD creditor reporting system, 158, 159, 160

Pachano, Simon, 83, 85
Pakistan, 16–17, 32, 171–73
Palacio, Alfredo, 96–97

Panama, 216–17
Pepinsky, Thomas B, 31, 57, 60–61, 167
Peru
    access to creditors, 216
    borrowing portfolio of, 143–46
    consumer coalition in, 75, 81, 129–33
    fieldwork in, 20–21, 72–73, 74, 79, 151–52
    finance in, 39, 94–95, 132, 134–35, 136, 137
    Fujishock, 81, 130, 145
    government
        Council of Ministers [Consejo de Ministros], 141–42
        Government Procurement Supervisory Authority [Organismo Supervisor de las Contrataciones del Estado (OSCE)], 139, 142
        Ministry of Economics and Finance [Ministerio de Economia y Finanzas (MEF)], 141–42
        Proinversion, 139–40, 142
    hyperinflation, 130, 137
    industry in, 84–85, 113, 117, 129–30, 131–32
    labor in, 116, 130–31, 134, 136–37
    Lima, 85, 129–30
    loans
        from BRICs, 143, 216
        from DAC creditors, 144–45
        from private creditors, 145–46
        from the IMF, 144
        tied to investment projects, 142–44
    organizations
        Candidate-centered movements, 130–31, 138–39
        Sendero Luminoso [Shining Path], 130
    politicians in, 138–41, 142
    preferences
        regarding BRIC loans, 41–47, 134–35
        regarding DAC loans, 37–41, 136
        regarding IFI loans, 34–37, 137–38
        regarding Private loans, 47–51, 136–37
    process of loan negotiations in, 141–42
    projects
        Banco de Credito del Peru, 135
        China MinMetals, 144
        Galeno copper mine, 144
        German Investment and Development Corporation [Deutsche Investitions- und Entwicklungsgesellschaft (DEG)], 144
        Netherlands Development Finance Company [Financierings-Maatschappij voor Ontwikkelingslanden (FMO)], 144
        PROPARCO, 144
        Shougang mine, 134, 144
        Toromocho Mining, 144
    Segura, Alonso, 146
    social movements in, 138–39
    trade policy of, 117, 127, 146

Philippines, 8, 213–14
Pinochet, Augusto, 63, 176–77
Poland, 37–38
politicians
  ideology, 162, 201, 203f, 226–27
  politicians using public opinion surveys, 52–53, 80, 95–97, 130, 137
  politicians versus technocrats, 98–99, 118–24, 141–42
  preferences of their own, 52–53
  regime type (Autocracy vs. Democracy), 198–99
  responding to lobbying, 53–54, 90–94, 116–17, 138–41
Portugal, 37–38
Porzecanski, Roberto, 7, 82–83, 102, 113
poverty, 3, 240
practical joke. See fooling someone
primary school enrollment, 14, 222–24
private creditors
  access to, 8–11, 209–10
  bonds, 4, 8, 47–49, 50, 88, 90, 96–97, 100–3, 126, 137, 145, 213–15, 234–35
  characteristics, 47–48
  commercial banks, 47–48
  loans to Colombia, 126
  loans to Ecuador, 100–3
  loans to Peru, 145–46
  preferences regarding loans from, 47–51, 88, 115, 136–37
Przeworski, Adam, 35, 56–57, 198
Putin, Vladimir, 3

Quinn, Dennis P., 47, 49, 169, 175

Rodrik, Dani, 16, 38–39, 226
Rogowski, Ronald, 25, 31, 56–57, 208
room to Maneuver. See sovereignty
Rudra, Nita, 165–66, 182
Russia
  AidData information on loans from, 160
  analyzing Brazil, Russia, and India separately from China, 28, 79, 204
  establishment of New Development Bank, 233, 234
  establishment of the Contingent Reserve Arrangement (CRA), 233
  grouping with Brazil, India, and China, 18–19, 41–42
  implications for Democracy, 241
  implications for western creditors, 3, 235
  lending volume, 1–2, 3–4
  loans to access natural resources, 192
  loans to Ecuador, 5, 104
  preferences regarding loans from, 39, 41

Russian EXIM bank, 104
Rwanda, 8–9, 47–48, 214–15

Saiegh, Sebastián M., 7, 8, 198–99
Sanborn, Cynthia, 134, 146
Santos, Juan Manuel, 40, 109, 111, 115, 125
Scheve, Kenneth F, 70, 71
Schultz, Kenneth A, 7–8, 198–99
selectorate theory, 198
Senegal, 47–48, 240
Siemens, 116, 145
Sikkink, Kathryn, 69–70
Sinohydro, 43–44, 58t, 87, 103–4
Slovakia, 37–38
Slovenia, 37–38
societal coalitions
  Capital Coalition, 56–57, 108–10
  Consumer Coalition, 61–63, 129–33
  Corporatist Coalition, 59–61, 83–85
  informal coalitions, 53–55, 156–57
South Africa, 47–48, 167–68, 176–77, 233
South Korea. See Korea, Republic of
sovereignty, 97, 105, 238
Spain, 37–38, 103, 127, 215–16
Sri Lanka, 167, 171–73
Stasavage, David, 40–41, 50
Steinbrück, Peer, 241
Stone, Randall W., 7–8, 34, 38, 205–6
Sudan, 42
Suharto, 57
supply- versus demand side explanations, 6–11, 209–16
Swaziland, 217
Sweden, 37–38, 127
Switzerland, 37–38

Taiwan, 28–29, 40, 105, 216–17, 239
Tajikistan, 235
Tanaka, Martín, 133, 138–39
Tanzania, 10, 13, 17, 47–48, 177–78
taxes, 34, 50, 63–64, 87–88, 106, 145, 165–66
Taylor, Ian, 193–94, 238
Toledo, Alejandro, 138–39
Tomz, Michael, 7, 24–25, 36–37, 51, 69, 70–71, 184–85
trade
  coalitions regarding trade policy, 59–60, 110
  distributional consequences, 52, 56–57, 69–70, 113, 132, 146, 208
  free trade agreements (FTAs), 113, 117, 127, 132, 146
  liberalization, 34, 131
  trade with BRICs and DACs, 192
Tunisia, 9

Uganda, 8–9, 11, 44, 53, 58t, 177–78, 214–15
United Kingdom, 37–38
United Nations (UN), 227
United States Agency for International Development (USAID), 37–38
United States EXIM Bank, 127, 144, 145, 160, 192, 236
United States of America, 37–38, 40–41, 49, 51, 53, 93–94, 114–15, 134, 144
    data on group strength for the, 163, 169
    implications of BRIC loans for, 3, 26, 234, 235
    loans from, 127, 145
    trade with, 127, 132
    UN voting with, 178, 227
Uribe, Alvaro, 40, 109, 115, 117, 138–39
Uruguay, 13, 17, 60–61

Venezuela, 96–97, 120
Vietnam, 2, 9, 47–48
Vreeland, James R., 11–14, 24–25, 32–33, 34–36, 208, 224

Wade, Abdoulaye, 240
Washington Consensus, 3, 34, 95–96, 239
western bilateral creditors. *See* Development Assistance Committee (DAC)
Winters, Matthew, 32, 184–85
Wise, Carol, 131
Wolfowitz, Paul, 241
Woll, Cornelia, 69, 115, 164, 174
workers. *See* labor
World Bank, 13, 21, 24–25, 27, 34–35, 44, 97
    conditions, 96–97, 126–27, 238, 240
    data from the, 157, 158–59, 166–67, 170–71, 175–76, 209
    expertise in infrastructure, 154–55, 219–22
    implications for, 233, 234, 236, 241
    International Bank for Reconstruction and Development (IBRD), 76, 126–27
    International Development Association (IDA), 76, 126–27
    preferences regarding, 34–37
World Trade Organization (WTO), 123

Zambia, 1, 47–48, 237